D1030356

Democratic Chile

Democratic

CHILE

The Politics and Policies
of a Historic Coalition,
1990–2010

edited by
Kirsten Sehnbruch
Peter M. Siavelis

LYNNE
RIENNER
PUBLISHERS

BOULDER
LONDON

Published in the United States of America in 2014 by
Lynne Rienner Publishers, Inc.
1800 30th Street, Boulder, Colorado 80301
www.rienner.com

and in the United Kingdom by
Lynne Rienner Publishers, Inc.
3 Henrietta Street, Covent Garden, London WC2E 8LU

Library of Congress Cataloging-in-Publication Data
Democratic Chile : the politics and policies of a historic coalition,
1990–2010 / edited by Kirsten Sehnbruch and Peter M. Siavelis.
    pages cm
 Includes bibliographical references and index.
 ISBN 978-1-58826-873-0 (hc : alk. paper)
 1. Democratization—Chile—History. 2. Democracy—Chile—History.
3. Chile—History—1988– 4. Chile—Economic conditions—1988–
5. Chile—Social conditions. I. Sehnbruch, Kirsten. II. Siavelis, Peter.
 JL2681.D467 2013
 320.98309'049—dc23

                                                    2013014722

British Cataloguing in Publication Data
A Cataloguing in Publication record for this book
is available from the British Library.

Printed and bound in the United States of America

The paper used in this publication meets the requirements
of the American National Standard for Permanence of
Paper for Printed Library Materials Z39.48-1992.

5 4 3 2 1

Contents

Foreword

Alan Angell

In this foreword I consider two issues of relevance to the theme of the book: first, the starting point of the return to democracy in Chile in 1990 and, second, the extent to which policies of the governments since then follow, or differ from, those of the Augusto Pinochet dictatorship (1973–1990).

It is often assumed that the incoming democratic government in 1990 had such a favorable inheritance from the Pinochet government that it enjoyed a comfortable start. In fact, the new government faced a host of difficult economic, political, and social challenges.

Not least were the difficulties on the economic front. Undoubtedly there were reforms during the Pinochet period that were of benefit to the macroeconomy—for example, in trade promotion, improving national and international competitiveness, and, at least in the years following the crisis of 1982–1983, promoting a market economy. Yet Pinochet's government left office in 1990 with the economy in a far from healthy condition. The short-term legacy was growing macroeconomic disequilibrium. In a burst of populist expenditure targeted at the plebiscite of 1988 (organized to decide if Pinochet would continue in office for another eight years) and the general elections of 1989, real demand rose by an unsustainable 22 percent in the period 1988–1989; inflation for the period September 1989 through January 1990 on an annualized basis rose to 31.5 percent; and though exports rose by 20 percent in the same period, imports rose by an alarming 46 percent (Ffrench-Davis and Muñoz 1990; Ffrench-Davis 1991).

Economic growth from 1988 to 1989, therefore, rested on precarious foundations. It was based on using underutilized capacity, but investment to increase capacity had been inadequate. The growth of new investment in the economy was only 15.4 percent per year in the 1981–1989 period compared with 20.2 percent per year from 1961 to 1971. The Pinochet government cut social expenditure, contributing to an already serious poverty problem, which in 1987 affected 45.1 percent of the population (of which 17.4 percent lived in extreme poverty). In addition, the adverse effects of the Gulf War on international prices (high oil prices always create economic difficulties for a country so dependent on imports as Chile) made macroeconomic management very difficult for the new government and called for immediate stabilization measures (Boylan 1996).[1]

Moreover, the Pinochet government had tied up state funds to deprive the Patricio Aylwin government of freedom of action. An estimated US$2 billion in the Copper Stabilization Fund, on which the Aylwin government was counting as a cushion against likely future falls in copper prices, had already been spent by the Pinochet government to repay the bad debts accumulated in the Central Bank when it bailed out the financial sector from the collapse of 1982–1983.

The constitutional and political system also imposed real constraints on the capacity of the government to formulate and implement progressive policies. The constitution of 1980 established areas of authoritarian control over democratic processes. The military, in the original version that was later modified, was given a tutelary role over the political system. Congress lacked powers to perform an adequate regulatory and monitoring role over the executive. There were nine designated senators in the Senate, four of whom were nominated directly by the military. The constitution safeguards private property rights against the state and gives the courts extra powers to ensure that the free market economy remains intact. The courts, largely staffed by Pinochet appointees, steadfastly refused to support efforts to bring human rights abusers to justice. The constitution is difficult to reform—only in 2005, after fifteen years of trying, was there agreement to abolish the designated senators, increase congressional investigatory powers, and increase the authority of the president over military appointments. During the first eight years after the return to democracy, the Right enjoyed a veto power over legislation through a combination of Pinochetista-designated senators and an electoral system that benefited the Right (and also the Concertación, though to a lesser extent).[2] Of equal benefit to the Right were the provisions of the constitution that required more than a simple majority for the approval of many laws in congress. Reform of the constitution required the votes of three-fifths of the senators and deputies; economic reforms required an absolute majority, not just a majority of those present in congress; and organic laws, for example, concerning the armed forces or institutions of the state, required a four-sevenths majority. The constitutional reforms under Ricardo Lagos may have removed the designated senators, but not those voting provisions that gave a continuing veto to the Right over progressive reforms (Sierra and Mac-Lure 2012).[3] However, there were differences among the members on the Right, and at least some sectors of Renovación Nacional lent their support on occasion—notably with the major tax reform of 1990, which allowed the government to increase social spending.[4]

Pinochet intended that, when the constitution came into force in the 1990s, he would be president until 1997. But in a plebiscite held in October 1988, Pinochet lost with only 43 percent of the vote in favor and 55 percent against, and he had to call for a presidential election to be held in December 1989. Nevertheless, the 43 percent of the vote that he obtained in 1988 was testimony to the extent of support that he still enjoyed, even if part of that vote is discounted because of the fear of opposing the military regime. That support—translated into the number of votes for the Right—provided a solid base for the Right to oppose the government and block progressive reforms.

Pinochet's strategy after the October plebiscite defeat was to safeguard his own position by insisting on his constitutional right to remain as commander in chief of the army, no matter who won the elections in 1989. His aim was a military free of civil interference in internal matters such as promotions, while the military continued to enjoy a privileged budgetary position for equipment, salaries, and pensions. The military budget could not be reduced below its 1989 level in real terms, and the obligatory 10 percent share of copper sales from the state corporation CODELCO assured a considerable sum for arms purchases (Lahera and Ortúzar 1998).[5] Pinochet also sought to make impossible any trials of members of the armed forces for human rights abuses. A great deal of time was spent by the Aylwin administration—not always with success—in trying to curb the activities of Pinochet and his supporters.

Constitutional amendments in 1989 removed some of the objectionable parts of the constitution. But the outgoing government also passed laws to restrict future governments—the *leyes de amarre* (literally, the binding laws)—intended to limit the discretionary power of the incoming government (Angell and Pollack 1990). One law granted tenure in the public sector, so that the incoming government had few posts at its discretion. Another law prohibited the incoming congress from investigating the activities of the Pinochet government. Members of the Supreme Court were offered handsome payments to retire to make way for equally conservative but considerably younger judges.

So the Aylwin government took office with a constitution it largely rejected, an electoral system that was not of its choice, an armed forces over which it had relatively little formal control, a judiciary that had been an unquestioning loyal ally of the outgoing government, an entrepreneurial class confident in its ability to mobilize the political Right if necessary, and a hostile media. Meanwhile, its own supporters expected a great deal, including the restitution of many social and economic rights. The new government was a coalition of forces that united only in the late 1980s. Previously the major parties—the Christian Democrats, the Socialists (several varieties), and the Communists—had been engaged in recriminations over responsibility for the coup and how to confront the Pinochet regime. These parties had never collaborated before—indeed, they had been hostile to each other from the 1960s onward.

It is important to stress that the economic difficulties, an unfavorable constitution, the untried political coalition, and a Right with veto power all demanded of the new government considerable tactical skill and vision to combine positive policy outcomes with strengthening of democratic practices. Far from an easy ride, it is clear that the government faced major challenges.

How well the democratic governments since 1990 created a stable and institutionalized political system and promoted economic growth and social welfare are the topics of the chapters in this book. As with all governments, the record is mixed; but the reelection of Concertación governments in four successive presidential elections and electoral majorities in numerous congressional and municipal elections show at least that Chileans were satisfied enough not to want a change of government until 2010.

There are three lines of criticism of democratic government in Chile after 1990. One variety denigrates the achievements of the Concertación governments, or claims that what achievements there were directly resulted from the Pinochet legacy (Allamand 2007). Another argues that the Concertación essentially followed the Pinochet model—and not just because of limitations on its ability to act, but because it was ideologically committed to central elements of the economic and social policies of the dictatorship. The third line of criticism is more convincing and points to the weaknesses of the system—summed up in the notion of incomplete democracy—that cannot solely be attributed to the Pinochet legacy. I will look at the three sorts of criticism in turn.

President Sebastián Piñera, in an article published in *El Mercurio* shortly after his 2010 election, delivered this devastating assessment:

> Social inequality continues here without changing, almost like a law of nature. Our low quality of education very often rather than correcting inequity simply perpetuates it, and it continues generation after generation. We have a health system incapable of providing proper, prompt and effective health care for all Chileans. Thousands of Chilean workers suffer from insecure and precarious conditions of employment. We see before us mountains of injustices, of unfulfilled dreams and promises.[6]

This statement is remarkable in several ways. If the failures were so immense, it is difficult to understand how the Concertación candidate in the second round of the presidential elections in 2010 obtained a vote not far short of a majority (48.39 percent). There is no acknowledgment in Piñera's statement of the economic and social achievements of the Concertación governments that produced record levels of growth with low inflation over a long period and saw substantial if incomplete social improvements. Chile had by far the best economic performance in Latin America over the twenty years of democratic government (including skillful management of the international economic crisis of 2008–2009) and performs well on international indicators of human development.[7]

Neither is there acknowledgment of the negative role played by the parties of the Right in blocking social reform. Modest attempts at labor reform, for example, were systematically vetoed by the Right in congress. There is an implicit promise here—made more explicit in the campaign promises of Piñera—that he would make major advances in these areas. Yet he must have realized that in a short four-year presidency, lacking a majority in congress and with a Right that was far from united, reform would be slow and complicated (as it was for the Concertación and indeed as Piñera was soon to find out for himself when in office). Finally, there is the paradox that such language might be expected from the radical Left but hardly from a politician of the Right.

Piñera's statement may be dismissed as the typical rhetoric of a politician seeking to make points. But the fact that such views were widely shared on the Right—and notably in the major party of the Right, the Independent Democratic Union (UDI)—helps to account for the deeply entrenched polarization of Chilean politics. It is true that compromise between the two parties grew easier as the years progressed, but certainly at the outset and for a decade afterward the divisions between government and opposition were deep enough to make seeking compromise a difficult and delicate operation.

The second strand of criticism, more common in academic circles, views the Concertación governments as a continuation of the economic and social policies of the Pinochet period. It is a frequent assumption in the literature on this period that the Concertación essentially followed the neoliberal economic model of the Pinochet regime, and that the Pinochet model was a uniformly dogmatic policy (Borzutzky and Weeks 2010; Winn 2004).[8]

It is true that both the Pinochet period and that of the Concertación had in common a move away from the statist economic model of the Frei and Allende governments (1964–1973) to one based on the market economy. And it is also true that certain policy innovations of the Pinochet era, such as opening the economy to international trade and encouraging entrepreneurship, were maintained. However, we might distinguish between those areas in which there was marked continuity between Pinochet and democracy such as trade policy, other areas where there have been significant changes but not major departures such as macroeconomic policy, and areas where there have been substantial changes such as social policies that have increasingly emphasized universal coverage.[9]

Oscar Muñoz, in his excellent account of the Concertación's economic model, points to the confusion that exists between the analytical concept of the model and the normative one—the model is not a description of reality. He states that "the debate in Chile over the 'economic model' suffers from many ambiguities and lack of precision because there has been a failure to specify what is essential and what is contingent."[10]

He further distinguishes between what he calls Pinochet's first—or Chicago—model and the later Washington consensus model. The Pinochet model shifted significantly after the crisis of 1982–1983 to greater involvement of the state, so it is more accurate to think of two models of the dictatorial period. Moreover, was economic policy under Pinochet the strict neoliberal model that is often depicted? Several of the privatizations of the Pinochet regime, especially in the early years, transferred public monopolies to private ones without an adequate regulatory framework—a model of crony capitalism rather than of neoliberalism. If the Pinochet model was strictly neoliberal then how is this compatible with the largest state enterprise in the country—CODELCO—remaining in the state sector?[11] The Pinochet government showed a disregard for fiscal rectitude by indulging in populist expenditures in 1988–1989 to try to influence the outcome of the plebiscite and the election, leaving an inflation rate running at 30 percent. One could also argue that the "binding laws" passed at the end of the Pinochet regime offended neoliberal principles by restricting the action of the incoming government (for example, by securing tenure for government employees appointed by the Pinochet government).

It is also worth emphasizing that the growth record of the Pinochet government over seventeen years was mediocre and had immense social costs; whereas the growth record of the Concertación was impressive—well above the regional average—and saw major social improvements brought about by active government policies. It is true that the international policy context for a considerable part of the Pinochet period was very unfavorable, but even taking that into consideration the relative success of the Concertación governments can hardly be explained solely by a favorable international context. Compare, for example, the way the dictatorship managed the international crisis of 1982–1983 (when the gross domestic product fell almost as much as it did during the depression of the 1930s) with the successful way the Bachelet government managed the international crisis of 2008–2009.

Muñoz argues that there is a distinct model for the Concertación period based on democratic governability and the ability to plan for the long term, economic policies that regulate the market in the interests of long-term developmental goals, and a social vision based on public policies targeted at the poorest sectors of society. (Targeting was admittedly initiated in the Pinochet regime but was limited compared to that of the democratic governments.) In Muñoz's view this Concertación model has little to do with the two models of the Pinochet regime. In essence one could see the Concertación period as an incipient social democratic model reaching its high point in the pension reform of the Bachelet government, which made pensions universal and payments more generous, extended health care reform with the creation of the Plan Auge, created a universal program for day care centers, and extended preschool education. But this is only to argue that aspects of policies resembled those of social democracy and not that the overall system in Chile can be regarded as social democracy.

In an article by Manuel Antonio Garretón and Roberto Garretón, the authors advance the notion of "incomplete democracy" to describe Chile under the Concertación (Garretón and Garretón 2010). The authors are well aware that an obvious objection to the notion is that all democracies are incomplete, but they highlight the legacy of what they call the authoritarian enclaves inherited from the Pinochet government. They criticize the antidemocratic nature of the electoral system imposed by the Pinochet government and modified later only in marginal ways. This system creates an institutional structure that discourages popular participation and restricts power to a narrow circle of political elites. Garretón and Garretón (2010) also emphasize the lack of civil rights for minorities and the severe nature of inequalities, not just in income but also in power. They point to a sharp discrepancy between an impressive economic performance, including the reduction of poverty, and an incomplete democratic political system.

It might be observed that all electoral systems produce greater or lesser distortions, that political participation is low and declining in many countries, that respect for minority rights is by no means universal, and that growing inequality characterizes much of the developed and developing world (the exception here is Brazil). But it is right to point out that Chile is unique in that after more than twenty years of democracy the country is still governed by a military-imposed constitution that for all the reforms, both formal and by convention, limits and restricts democracy.

While accepting that the issues raised by Garretón and Garretón (2010) represent the unfinished reform agenda in Chile, what remains impressive is the number of advances the Concertación made in the face of such restraints. This positive assessment is broadly supported by a recent poll. In a survey conducted by the research and polling agency CERC in 2011, the respondents were asked for their opinion on the twenty years of Concertación governments (CERC 2011). Thirty-six percent of the respondents rated it very good or good, 49 percent rated it as regular, and only 9 percent rated it as bad. For a government that dealt with difficult issues of human rights, created the basis for a democratic and legitimate political system, pursued progressive social policies, faced the effects of two severe international economic crises, suffered at the end from divisions between and within the political parties, and faced well-financed and powerful forces on the Right, the overall record of the Concertación seems to me to be an impressive achievement.

But what worked well in the past fell apart in the days approaching the elections of 2009 and 2010. There are contingent factors that explain the narrow defeat of the Concertación, such as a poor campaign conducted by an uninspiring candidate and divisions inside the coalition and inside the parties of the coalition. Yet, the decline of the Concertación is more fundamental. We need to assess what effects the economic policies of the Concertación governments had on the political system. If it is far from accurate to label those policies simply as neoliberal, they were nevertheless based upon the free market, and in this system the all-powerful political actor was the minister of finance. Politics was seen through the prism of the Finance Ministry, which had a broad influence on policies throughout the political system. If income distribution remained extremely unequal in Chile, then it had a great deal to do with the fact that a privileged position was given to the business sector—even by the two socialist presidents. While the administration of the tax system was exemplary in Chile, the structure of taxation gave privileged treatment to the rich and allowed them to evade high rates of taxation. These factors help to explain the erosion of faith in politics and in parties among the wider public. If government becomes technocratic administration, what role is there for political parties, what role is there for public participation? One can exaggerate the extent of electoral abstention in Chile, but the abstention of so many young people is an alarming symptom of indifference toward the formal political system. Social protest in Chile is based on unsatisfied demands from many groups who feel excluded from the successes of the system— and the opposition parties in the Piñera government were not seen as vehicles for translating that protest into political action. There is much talk about renovation in the political parties, but little evidence so far of it happening.[12]

In essence, the model of the Concertación did not change—but Chilean society did. The protests that broke out in 2006 and intensified in 2011 and 2012 showed a society impatient with the restricted political system and demanding changes of a radical nature. One need not take the argument too far—this does not look like a challenge to the survival of Chilean democracy, but it does look like a demand for fundamental change (which must involve a change in the electoral system). The Concertación period, by many criteria, was a resounding success. But it created a society that found the prevailing institutional system inadequate for the demands that came from that success. And at least as I write this, it does not look as if the Piñera government is able to offer an acceptable alternative.

It is important that we have a book like this one that provides an overall evaluation of the successes and limitations of the twenty years of democracy in Chile. Whether one evaluates those years positively or negatively it is a remarkable story, and one told with intelligence, balance, and insight in the chapters of this outstanding book.

Notes

I am grateful for the comments of Diego Sánchez, Sofia Donoso, Oscar Muñoz, Rosemary Thorp, Carlos Huneeus, and Samuel Valenzuela. I am also grateful to Stanford University Press for allowing me to use part of my chapter in Scott Mainwaring and Timothy Scully, *Democratic Governance in Latin America* (2010) for the first section of this foreword.

1. Which the government used as a reason for implementing a major tax increase—one of the very few measures supported by enough of the opposition to enable it to pass in congress.

2. After the first eight-year term of the designated senators, the majority of the new ones were appointed by the democratic government.

3. I am grateful to Carlos Huneeus for bringing my attention to this excellent United Nations Development Programme (UNDP) publication on the issue (Sierra and MacClure 2012).

4. One of the major architects of the reform was Sebastián Piñera, elected in 2010 as the first right-wing president since the return to democracy.

5. Expenditure on the military during the Pinochet regime by one calculation was the highest in Latin America (outside Cuba) as a percentage of gross domestic product and continued to be so during the democratic governments—though in Chile the police was included in the military budget, as were the generous military pensions paid by the only part of the pension system that remained in state hands. Figures of military expenditures are difficult to calculate because many items appear in the budgets of other ministries—military hospitals under the Health Ministry and subsidies for defense industries under economic development.

6. *El Mercurio*, October 17, 2010; my translation.

7. The UNDP Human Development report using aggregate data to compose an index of human development ranks Chile at 0.783 in 2010, which makes it the forty-fifth country out of 169 and the best ranking overall in Latin America—one place above Argentina and six places above Uruguay. The score for 1990 was 0.675. Gross domestic product per capita (purchasing power parity) for 2008 was US$14,780.

8. Yet the individual chapters in this book, once this assertion is put aside, are generally excellent accounts of the topic under discussion. Similarly the chapters in Winn (2004) are much more nuanced than the title would suggest.

9. My thanks to Diego Sánchez for this point. An example of the differences in policies between the military government and democracy can be seen in the example of the policy toward fishing of the Chilean *loco* (a sea-snail much in demand in Japan). Under Pinochet, fishing was unrestricted and by 1989 the fisheries were closed and stocks were exhausted; when the democratic government reopened the

fisheries, priority was given to local small cooperatives with limits on catches. Since then the industry has flourished. *The Economist,* February 25, 2012, 62.

10. The quotation is from "El Modelo Económico Chileno," *Mensaje,* January–February 2007, 8. This theme is taken up in great and convincing detail in *El Modelo Económico Chileno de la Concertación, 1990–2005* (Santiago: FLACSO-Chile Catalonia, 2007). Consider the statement of Mervyn King, at the time the governor of the Bank of England: "Never confuse the world with a model. The whole point of a model is to abstract from a wide range of factors in order to think clearly about one particular issue." From *The Guardian,* August 27, 2005, 15.

11. Apart from copper there were subsidies for planting forests, car manufacturing, and promotion of exports. I am grateful to Samuel Valenzuela for this point.

12. This paragraph draws on personal communication from Carlos Huneeus.

1

Political and Economic Life Under the Rainbow

Kirsten Sehnbruch and Peter M. Siavelis

The eyes of visiting dignitaries fearfully cast toward the ceiling when a 6.9 magnitude earthquake shook Chile's national congress in Valparaíso just as outgoing president Michelle Bachelet passed the presidential sash to the newly elected Sebastián Piñera of the right-wing Coalition for Change. The quake was merely an aftershock from the 8.8 magnitude earthquake that had caused widespread devastation in the south of Chile only weeks before the presidential handover. But it prompted jokes of divine retribution: "God's wrath for having elected a right-wing government!" After all, the general consensus in the media and among most scholars was that the center-left-wing coalition, referred to as the Concertación, had governed Chile successfully for twenty years, between 1990 and 2010, and sometimes looked as though it would be in power indefinitely.

How did the Concertación maintain its power for twenty years? How did it preside over what is commonly referred to as a "model" of democratic transition and development in the region? How was it that the outgoing and extremely popular president Michelle Bachelet, who enjoyed an approval rating over 80 percent, could not pass on this popularity to her coalition's candidate? And how did this remarkable governing coalition finally fall to electoral defeat? These questions lead to some of the deeper issues we seek to analyze in this book. From its 1988 victory in a plebiscite on the continued rule of Pinochet onward, the Concertación competed in elections employing a rainbow as a symbol of the many parties it comprised. This rainbow also symbolized the beginning of a new period of hope after the long and violent storm of the Pinochet dictatorship. But what was life like for Chileans "under the rainbow"? How was Chile transformed politically, socially, and economically during the four Concertación govern-

1

ments that followed the return to democracy in 1990? How did the coalition maintain itself in power for twenty years? Is the Concertación indeed a political "model"? An economic model? Did it transform Chile for the better? In what ways were Concertación governments found wanting? These are the questions this book seeks to answer. In doing so, we will also uncover some of the reasons for the coalition's defeat.

The metanarrative of the Chilean success story is embedded in an ongoing, profoundly emotional and ideological debate. For his supporters, modern Chile was built by Pinochet, who set the country on a course of political moderation and economic success. For his opponents, modern Chile is a creation of the Concertación coalition, which ruled prudently with a consensus model of politics, successfully and creatively building upon the constraining economic model inherited from Pinochet. A closer examination reveals a much more complex story than either side tells. However, this story cannot be told without a deep and thoughtful analysis of the Concertación governments.

This book provides such an analysis. Modern Chile is a creation of neither of these narratives, but rather a synthesis of both. The Concertación was certainly successful, but it was not the unqualified success story that one finds in many accounts of the country's contemporary political and economic evolution. When President Bachelet, who headed the fourth Concertación government, handed over the presidential sash to the new president, Sebastián Piñera, this symbolic act was a historic moment that marked the end of an era: it symbolized the end of the term of Chile's first female president. The country inaugurated the first right-wing president democratically elected in fifty-two years. It constituted the first democratic and peaceful handover of power from one governing coalition to another since 1970. Finally, it concluded twenty years of rule by the Concertación, the lengthiest and most stable democratic coalition in Chilean, and perhaps Latin American, history.

In this book, we seek answers to theoretical questions as well: What does the Chilean case tell us about why political transitions succeed? What are the limitations of consensus models of transitions and what are their implications for democracy? What does the Chilean case tell us about the interplay between processes of economic and political reform? How does the country's development strategy inform us with regard to the optimal policies and strategies for reform within the context of such transitions?

In essence, to presage many of the arguments set out in this book the Concertación was simultaneously a victim of its own success and the author of its own demise—both with respect to its political and economic model. In political terms, the coalition crafted a model for democratic transition and governance that relied on elaborate forms of consensus building between political parties, between the government and opposition, and between political parties and powerful social groups. This model of consensus government is interpreted by most as the key to the success of the coalition in managing the inevitable conflicts and tensions that arise in the course of democratic transitions. We argue that this model became entrenched and difficult to change for a number of political and institutional reasons. At the same time, however, the continued reliance on transition politics over the long term led Chileans to believe that elitist politicians were engaged in a process of government by negotiation and horse trading rather than true representative democracy and that citizen input mattered little. Presidential and legislative candidates were named by elites, parliamentary lists assembled by negotiation, and, once in power, elites negotiated policies that maintained the integrity of the transition, but often failed to meet the needs of average Chileans. While to a certain extent elite domination was also historically the case in Chile (and has been the case in many other countries of the world), the extent of elite domination and the sheer extent of power concentrated in the hands of elites is what sets Chile apart from its historical experience and other countries. As a result of this failure to respond to legitimate citizen demands, political participation and levels of engagement and confidence in the democratic system have declined precipitously, and citizen discontent has spilled onto the streets.

We make a parallel argument regarding the economic and social policy sphere. Chile's development model is widely lauded as a potential blueprint for the rest of Latin America, given consistently high levels of growth and very successful economic management. For Pinochet supporters, analysis of this economic success usually includes a discussion of the much vaunted University of Chicago–trained economists inspired by Milton Friedman, who, at Pinochet's behest, transformed Chile's economy into a free market success story. For the Concertación, however, the neoliberal experiment may have begun in a ham-handed way under Pinochet, but its taming and its transformation into a successful economic policy occurred during the democratic governments that followed the dictatorship. As is often the case, a closer examination reveals a much more complex economic story than either side tells.

On the subjects of economic and social policy we contend, once again, that the Concertación was both a victim of its own success and instrumental in its own demise. By maintaining the broad outlines of the neoliberal economic model bequeathed by Pinochet, the Concertación kept powerful actors and veto players in the business community and on the Right at bay, ultimately assuring its ability to continue to govern the country and generate positive macroeconomic outcomes. However, Chile's positive economic growth has been of little comfort to those at the lower end of Chile's notoriously unequal socioeconomic ladder: Chile remains one of the most unequal countries in the world. Twenty years of consistent economic growth have led to equally consistently declining absolute poverty rates, but they have also led to constantly increasing demands for consumption of goods and services among the poor that have outpaced their income growth rates.

Similar patterns emerge in the success story of Chile's social development: while health care services that can compete with the best in the world cater to the rich, the poor largely remain excluded from these private clinics. Similarly, Chile's privatized pension system replicates the inequalities generated by its labor market, with little redistribution between rich and poor. The education system is equally split between excellent standards for the rich and very low standards for the poor. Many Chileans sense a lack of social justice that fails to provide greater equity in the overall distribution of the country's wealth and access to opportunities. In essence, the twenty-year Concertación period has been dominated by the tensions of achieving social progress within the confines of an economy that still largely adheres to the principles laid out by a neoliberal dictatorship, which privatized social services as far as possible, reduced the size of the state, and limited its tax base. Thus, while the Concertación has been lauded for maintaining economic stability and growth, it is also continuously criticized for its lack of audacity in engaging in real reforms to the Pinochet model that could make Chile a more just and equitable society.

Whether we criticize or applaud the Concertación on its achievements largely depends on the perspective we take of Chile's development process. Very few countries in the world have successfully closed the "development gap" and raised the standard of living of their population to levels similar to those of industrialized countries. So far, no Latin American country has succeeded in this endeavor. In Latin America, Chile continues to stand out as a case of above-average economic, social, political, and institutional development, and must therefore be applauded as the region's success story. However, if we consider Chile's development record from the perspective of those countries that have successfully caught up with industrialized nations, we have to apply a more critical perspective. In particular, such an approach leads to the question of whether Chile has implemented the structural reforms necessary to achieve such a goal. This book discusses Chile's development process from these two perspectives, continually evaluating its absolute achievements (e.g., reduced poverty levels, expansion of health care and education) against the country's relative performance as compared to those countries that succeeded in bridging the gap between the status of "middle income" and "developed."

Four broad themes thus apply to all of the chapters in the book, and make for the volume's many theoretical contributions to more general literature on democratic transitions:

1. The delicacy of the democratic transition created restraints on the scope of political change and economic policy. Strong veto power of elements in the military and the Right created powerful limits on the potential for political change under the Pinochet-imposed 1980 constitution. Similarly powerful economic actors restricted the scope for significant economic and social policy reforms.

2. The economic and political models introduced by the Concertación were, indeed, the keys to the success of the transition and the "success" of the coalition, but they also created longer-term limits still felt today. In particular, and as developed fully by Siavelis in Chapter 2, certain entrenched norms and ways of doing politics eventually evolved into what he calls *transitional enclaves*. He builds on the work of Manuel Antonio Garretón (2003) who argued that certain *authoritarian enclaves* left over from Chile's authoritarian regime interfered with the optimal functioning of the democratic system. He argues that similar transitional enclaves have become entrenched and have limited the range of action and audacity of reforms. These include *el cuoteo* (the process of passing out positions based on partisan identification), elite control of candidate selection and electoral politics, party-dominated politics, elitist and extra-institutional policymaking, and the untouchability of the economic model inherited from the Pinochet government. We consider these enclaves to have deeply shaped the political, social, and economic development of Chile.

3. Crucially, toward the end of the Concertación governments the economic and political model of the transition *became the status quo* for both the governing coalition and the opposition—in effect freezing these enclaves, which have now become impediments to the realization of deeper economic reforms and a higher-quality democracy.

4. The challenge for the future of Chile and the Concertación is to leave behind the political and economic enclaves to devise a political model that is more legitimate, representative, and accountable, and an economic model that will allow the country to close its development gap.

In our book we analyze these tensions in three additional sections. Each author points to the relative success and failures of the Concertación, and how the constraints created by the democratic transition helped lead simultaneously to both success and limitations. Part 1 focuses on politics and policymaking and begins with an overview of the genesis and evolution of the Concertación by Peter Siavelis in Chapter 2. This chapter traces the development of the Concertación as a political entity whose very nature is tied to the conditions of its birth. In particular, it analyzes the genesis of the Concertación as a product of the characteristics of the democratic transition. It outlines the mechanisms, both formal and informal, that allowed the coalition to govern with high levels of effectiveness and governability. The chapter then turns to the variables that led to the entrenchment of these mechanisms and how they eventually undermined the effectiveness and popularity of the coalition. This chapter is fundamental to understanding the rest of the book's argument, as it sets down and analyzes what we contend are the transitional enclaves to which our contributors so often refer.

The point of departure for Chapter 3 is that we cannot understand the development of the Concertación without an exploration of how it was shaped by its main opposition, the rightist Alianza. Patricio Navia and Ricardo Godoy's chapter traces the development of Chile's right-wing coalition that later became known as the Alianza from its defeat in the 1988 plebiscite to the 2010 election victory of Sebastián Piñera. The authors recount how at first, the coalition was divided between two sectors: those who sought to modernize and adapt to the new democratic rules, and those who advocated for the status quo and defended the remaining authoritarian enclaves of the 1980 constitution that allowed the Alianza to exercise veto power in key areas despite its minority electoral support. The 2009 presidential victory by Sebastián Piñera was the culmination of a process that timidly began after the 1988 plebiscite with the gradual convergence of the Right toward a more liberal democratic stance. However, the authors do note that the tensions between a more liberal and pro-democracy wing and a more conservative current emerge in areas other than the convenience of the protected democracy framework. In this sense, just as the Concertación's political strategy and policy orientation were shaped by the transitional enclaves, so too were the Right's.

Chapter 4 takes up the institutional enclaves of the democratic transition (and some authoritarian ones left over from the military regime first identified by Garretón [2003]). In particular, Claudio Fuentes examines the Chilean political dynamics related to constitutional reforms since 1989. He argues that the Chilean case is an outlier in Latin America as the constitution was promulgated during the military regime and political changes have been negotiated as opposed to undertaken by decree or by executive fiat. By analyzing the process of reform, the chapter proposes two main cycles: in the first cycle, between 1989 and 2005, politicians focused on transforming the balance of power between executive and legislative and eliminating the authoritarian enclaves; in the second cycle, after 2005, politicians broadened their political agenda to include social rights and topics of rep-

resentation. The chapter provides a detailed account of the dynamics of negotiations and suggests that informal mechanisms of bargaining by the executive were crucial to set the agenda and timing of the reforms. In line
with the overall argument of this volume, Fuentes argues that given the political and institutional restrictions they faced, pro-reformer forces of the
Concertación chose a gradual strategy that avoided social and political confrontations with the opposition along with an elite-led bargaining process.
In essence, the Concertación initially accepted the institutional limits as a
guarantee to prevent veto powers from removing them from office and then
engaged in gradual reforms. As the political context changed and affected
the existing balance of power, the pro–status quo forces of the Right engaged in constitutional reforms to retain some power in congress.

The military was one of the crucial veto players during the democratic
transition, and one that was deemed the most dangerous. In Chapter 5, Gregory Weeks analyzes how Chilean civil-military relations changed considerably from the beginning to the end of the Concertación's twenty years in
power. This chapter chronologically traces the development of the civil-
military relationship from Patricio Aylwin to Michelle Bachelet, and argues
that a combination of creation and destruction of specific laws and institutions has fostered stronger formal connections between the armed forces
and the executive branch. Weeks argues that the Concertación was more
successful in reforming political rather than economic aspects of civil-
military relations, and that the military continues to wield important economic prerogatives and influence. At the same time, Weeks does note areas
of weakness in civil-military relations, particularly with regard to intelligence oversight and legislative accountability. Though less than is the case
in other areas, he argues that the practical effects of the transitional enclaves here made reform of the military slow, difficult, and plodding, and
that the military's potential veto power was central to the development of
the other transitional enclaves analyzed in the book.

Michelle Bachelet was one of the most, if not *the* most, popular Concertación presidents and the first woman not related to a powerful husband
or father who was elected president of a Latin American country. However,
her election was not necessarily an indication of progressive gender policies during the democratic transition. In Chapter 6, Liesl Haas and Merike
Blofield argue that policy reform on these issues also revealed the limits of
the possible, particularly when reform touched on any aspect of Catholic
doctrine or required redistributive measures. They argue that the lack of reform exposed stark divisions within the Concertación as well as the limits
imposed by the transition on the reach of reform. Using specific policy
areas as illustrations, they analyze how the battle for gender equality policy
within the Concertación exposed the ideological fault lines within the gov-

erning coalition, which had to balance the goals and platforms of individual parties with those of the coalition as a whole, while at the same time taking into account issues of the stability of democracy and consensus. They do note, however, that in the course of two decades of Concertación government, all the parties in the coalition strengthened their support for gender equality. They analyze the changing patterns of bill introduction as well as public opinion survey data to demonstrate parties' slow evolution on these issues, and how this slow evolution also reflects broad trends in Chilean society. Once again, the transitional enclaves set out here limited the scope and audacity of potential reforms in the gender arena.

Chile is still dealing with the legacy of terror and torture from its authoritarian past. In Chapter 7, Cath Collins provides an in-depth study of the struggle to obtain justice for human rights violations in Chile. She argues that public policy and political activity, with respect to dealing with the country's human rights legacy, display the kind of stability-oriented and risk-averse behaviors suggested by the transitional enclaves metaphor, perhaps more than any other area dealt with in this volume. She argues that the Concertación in essence allowed early constraints to permanently narrow its horizons thereby minimizing the reach of reform and the extent to which it would deal with the legacy of abuses. She contends that limited progress was made because presidents saw significant movement on the human rights agenda as politically unrewarding and too controversial. Collins shows how eventually the impetus for change came from below, which gradually supplanted elite resistance to change and culminated in a 2003 policy that expanded and built upon previous truth and reparations measures but stopped short of dealing with or providing restitution for private justice claims.

Part 2 of this volume discusses Chile's economic and social development under the Concertación. Though the transitional enclaves that shaped the policymaking arena are relevant here, the most important factor that limited socioeconomic progress was that the neoliberal economic model established by the military regime became a transitional enclave in its own right. Since the economic model was "untouchable," any structural reform that proposed fundamental change to its incentives, regulation, or fiscal mechanisms constituted an extremely difficult endeavor. In addition, though there is no separate chapter on inequality, the subject so clearly permeates every area in the socioeconomic realm that it is discussed by every author as a legacy of the military regime, and one that the Concertación has been least successful in confronting. In Chapter 8, Oscar Landerretche Moreno discusses the idea that Chile's development process constitutes a "model" that other less successful countries should copy from a critical perspective. He argues that if there is indeed a "Chilean model" that other countries should study, this model was shaped and developed by the Concertación, and not by the Pinochet dictatorship. This does not contradict what has been said up until now concerning the resistance of civilians to fundamentally alter the Pinochet economic model. Rather the argument is that democratic governments worked within the broad outlines of the model left from the previous regime, essentially optimizing economic performance within the constraints imposed upon them. Indeed, Landerretche argues that these legacies of the Pinochet regime and the resistance of civilians to deal with them constitute the major challenges facing Chile for the future in the economic and social policy realms: income distribution, labor market reforms, diversification of the country's export portfolio, the need for significant increases in spending on research and development and innovation policies, and the necessity of substantial improvements in productivity, vocational training, and educational performance. Furthermore, he argues that Chile's development model incorporates both evident strengths and important weaknesses, the combination of which has led to a significant increase of GDP per capita levels and improved social indicators, but not to a sufficiently diversified economy that can ensure continued high levels of growth over the long term, or to an improved income distribution structure.

These arguments are echoed in Chapter 9 where Ramón López presents an analysis that shows how the emphasis of the Concertación's fiscal expenditures on the provision of public and social goods, including health, education, and social programs, has been exemplary compared to many other countries in the region. The key problem he identifies is the reduced level of fiscal resources derived from a tax system that has lagged behind Chile's overall development process. He argues that these low revenue levels have negatively affected the expansion of human capital and the reduction of inequality on all levels. López's central hypothesis is that fiscal policy has been in part responsible for Chile's lack of progress toward developing an economy that is based more on knowledge-intensive and environmentally clean industries and has prevented the country from becoming less dependent on natural resource–based industries, and in turn from generating greater social equality.

In Chapter 10, Silvia Borzutzky, Claudia Sanhueza Riveros, and Kirsten Sehnbruch take up these arguments in their discussion of the evolution of poverty rates under the Concertación. They engage critically with one of the most frequently and widely cited achievements of the Concertación: its successful reduction of absolute poverty levels from 38.6 percent in 1990 to 15.1 percent in 2010. The authors argue that contrary to widespread belief and official rhetoric, this achievement is due more to economic growth rather than social policies, which have been fiscally constrained, ideologically timid, and resistant to existential reforms. The authors also show how current definitions of poverty in Chile are both outdated and methodologically limited. While a multidimensional approach to poverty demonstrates that the Concertación's social policies have been successful in almost all dimensions of social development (with the exception of employment indicators), this analysis also very much depends on the thresholds used to define poverty. The authors illustrate this point by applying Organization for Economic Cooperation and Development (OECD) standards of relative poverty to the subject, which lead to the conclusion that progress has been minimal.

Along similar lines, Dante Contreras and Kirsten Sehnbruch argue in Chapter 11 that progress on social issues in absolute terms has not been accompanied by structural changes in Chile's systems of social protection that go far enough to make real inroads into the difficult problem of inequality. In their chapter they examine the social policies of the Concertación from the perspective of welfare state theory and focus on the key question of whether Concertación governments really have laid the foundation for something that could develop into a liberal welfare state, as official government rhetoric has claimed. The authors present six initial arguments, which show that overall and despite its many achievements in the area of social policy, Concertación governments did not succeed in undertaking the necessary structural reforms that such an objective would require. The chapter examines this question by looking at the pension, health, and unemployment insurance systems, as well as at the benefit structures that the Concertación created. Once again in this area of policymaking, elites demonstrated a deep resistance to challenge audaciously the status quo with significant reforms. The chapter concludes by questioning whether Chile's social systems are sustainable in the long term.

Similar arguments emerge in the area of labor policy. In Chapter 12, Kirsten Sehnbruch argues that the Concertación essentially left employment issues—such as high levels of informality and unemployment as well as low levels of participation and of job quality—to the market, assuming that these problems over time would be resolved by high levels of economic growth. However, the empirical evidence over the last twenty years has not been consistent with the neoclassical theory on which Concertación governments relied. In fact, despite relatively high economic growth rates and a stable regulatory environment, employment conditions have deteriorated while the level of employment generation has not been sufficient to reduce the pressures of low employment rates and underemployment in any significant way. Thus, labor reform—and the development of the Chilean labor market—is one of the most important unresolved issues of the Concertación's legacy. Sehnbruch's chapter briefly examines the evolution of labor legislation under the Concertación before reviewing the economic performance of the Chilean labor market, labor policy, and the political situation of unions.

The issues of inequality that mark the chapters of this section also emerge in Chapter 13 where Gregory Elacqua and Pablo González Soto discuss the Concertación's education policies. The chapter discusses in detail the constraints faced by the four Concertación administrations in reforming the education system, and that have ultimately led to two powerful social movements, the "Pinguino" demonstrations of 2006, and the student movement that erupted in 2011, almost as soon as the Concertación left office. The subject of education, and its significance as a policy arena that has most motivated Chileans to popular protest, is one that has perhaps most demonstrated the Concertación's temerity in challenging the status quo inherited from Pinochet.

Unfortunately, no book of this kind can be an absolutely comprehensive analysis of a country's political, economic, and social development. We are conscious of the fact that there are many subjects, such as governance, trade, foreign affairs, infrastructure, sociocultural change, ethnic minorities, or social movements, that we do not cover in dedicated chapters. Our critics may argue that some of the Concertación's principal achievements lie precisely in those subjects that we do not cover: for example, in Chile's institutional capabilities and functioning where it outranks many developed countries or in its integration with international trade systems where it functions as one of the most open economies of the world. Similarly, others may argue that we are ignoring subjects that express deep levels of social discontent, such as the Mapuche conflicts in the south of Chile or the multiple social movements that have emerged since the advent of student protests in 2006. Unfortunately, time and space constraints limit the analyses in this book and have forced us to be selective in our approach. Nevertheless, many of these issues are included in the chapters that follow even if they are not analyzed in depth.

What the chapters of this volume hold in common is a critical evaluation of Concertación governments. We seek to avoid the simplistic notion that we can simply call the Concertación a success by pointing to political stability and impressive macroeconomic indicators. Nor can we take the route of the Concertación's critics and simply conclude that its governments represented simple continuity with the Pinochet regime. Our task is to elucidate how the coalition was a success, and at the same time provide a balanced analysis of the limits of the Concertación's room to maneuver in initiating more audacious policies. Our analysis leads to the conclusion that the Concertación failed to appreciate the extent to which and the pace at which it changed Chile. This is a problem that has emerged in many transitioning democracies, as, for example, in Spain: while the population comes to take democracy for granted and expects progress commensurate with its expectations, political elites remain stuck in the modus operandi of transition politics, and fail to adapt and change at the same pace as their electorate.

The constraints on the first transitional government were very real. Where the Concertación erred was in the routinization of the transitional political model and in its conception of the menu of social and political reform options. There were many constraints to moving beyond the transitional enclaves we discuss, and the legislative electoral system itself served as an important impediment to abandoning these enclaves, given that it forced the kind of elite negotiations necessary to maintain the coalition in the electoral arena. To win, the Concertación had to remain coherent electorally and the only way to achieve this was through purposeful elite negotiations on policy, candidate selection, and shared consensus-forming arrangements and institutions. From a theoretical perspective, we can draw important lessons from the case. Chile clearly shows how pacted transitions create real constraints for political actors. This has been recognized in much of the literature on democratic transitions. What has been less recognized is that the influence of the mode of democratic transitions goes beyond the politics and economics of the transition per se to leave a profound imprint on later ways of doing politics once democratic regimes become consolidated. The chapters that follow provide ample empirical evidence of this reality.

Part 1

Political Development

2

From a Necessary to a Permanent Coalition

Peter M. Siavelis

Throughout the 1990s Chile was routinely referred to as a country that experienced a model democratic transition and as one of the most successful democracies in Latin America. What is more, the Concertación coalition that governed Chile from 1990 to 2010 was one of the longest and most successful coalitions in Latin American history. As other chapters in this volume attest, the coalition presided over high levels of economic growth, impressive strides in eliminating poverty, and remarkable political stability, leading a democratic transition lauded as a model. The coalition grew from a disparate collection of Center-Left political parties who opposed the military government of Augusto Pinochet and devised a formula for governing based on consensus building among its many parties and negotiation with potential powerful veto players, including the military.

This chapter traces the development of the Concertación as a political entity whose very nature is tied to the conditions of its birth. The chapter begins by analyzing the genesis of the Concertación, pointing to the elements of the democratic transition that shaped its emergence and way of governing. The chapter goes on to outline the mechanisms, both formal and informal, that allowed the coalition to govern with high levels of effectiveness and governability. However, in line with the central thesis of this volume, the chapter argues that the very elements that allowed the coalition to govern so successfully also planted the seeds of its own defeat. Thus, in the third section the chapter turns to the variables that led to the entrenchment of these mechanisms and how they eventually undermined the effectiveness and popularity of the coalition. I refer to these entrenched realities as *transitional enclaves*, and the idea of these enclaves is the central one around which the entire argument of this volume is based. The chapter concludes with a discussion of the significance of these enclaves for the future of democracy in Chile.

The Birth of the Coalition

The conditions of the birth of the Concertación coalition would fundamentally shape its structure and the way it governed. The seeds of the Concertación were sown during Chile's lengthy democratic transition, which really began with the 1980 plebiscite. Pockets of fragmented opposition did exist before the plebiscite; however, it remained disorganized as a result of the traumas of repression and exile. As space for the opposition returned to the country with the easing of military repression, this fragmentation was reinforced by differing perspectives on what should be the tactics of opposition. Fundamentally, divisions between the Center and Left concerning the desirability of an insurrectionary route to defeat Pinochet prevented the coalescence of opposition (Garretón 1989; Siavelis 2009). In addition, there remained an underlying suspicion between the two sectors as a result of the centrist Christian Democratic Party's (Partido Demócrata Cristiano [PDC]) initial support for military intervention. Leftist socialist factions joined with the outlawed Communist Party's military wing, the Frente Patriótico Manuel Rodríguez (FPMR), while other leftists favored working within the framework established by the 1980 military constitution.

The 1980 plebiscite was an important turning point. Feeling pressure for a political opening, the military government sought to solve two problems. First, it sought to provide a purportedly "legal" formula to prop up a fatigued regime and an institutional framework to keep it in power. In addition, it sought to assure the future institutional structure of the country and provide protection for the military and parties of the Right for the longer term. To achieve these goals, in the 1980 plebiscite (despite its questionable democratic propriety) voters simultaneously approved a new constitution and a time line for transition that kept former dictator Augusto Pinochet in power. He would remain in power as president until another plebiscite would be held on his continued rule in 1988, followed by presidential elections in 1989 (A. Valenzuela 1995).

Two major attempts at unifying the opposition predate the ultimate establishment of the coalition. Both the National Accord for a Full Transition to Democracy of 1985 and the Civic Assembly of 1986 fell victim to political divisions and the half-hearted participation of the centrist (and relatively more conservative) elements of the opposition (mostly the PDC) (Garretón 1989). However, Pinochet's framework for a controlled transition unwittingly set the stage for more coordinated opposition to the military. In essence the regime committed a strategic error by casting the 1988 ballot as a yes or no vote on Pinochet's continued rule. Had Pinochet opted for a simple presidential election (in which he would be a candidate) the fractionalized opposition would not have to choose a party standard-bearer to face off against Pinochet. Now rather than discussing and agreeing upon candidates and platforms, all they needed to do was agree that they opposed Pinochet. They did so by forming the Concertación de Partidos por el No (Coalition of Parties for the No) and by defeating Pinochet by a margin of 55 percent to 42 percent in the plebiscite. This initial oppositional glue, ironically created by Pinochet, would later allow parties to coalesce into the Concertación alliance that ruled Chile for the next twenty years. The Center-Left Concertación coalition (which grew from the No forces in the 1988 plebiscite) comprised five major parties: the PDC, the Partido Socialista (PS, Socialist Party), the Partido por la Democracia (PPD, Party for Democracy), and the smaller Partido Radical (PR, Radical Party) and Partido Social Demócrata (PSD, Social Democratic Party). The latter two parties merged in 1994 to form the PRSD (Partido Radical Social Demócrata—Radical Social Democratic Party). The alliance went on to win every presidential and legislative election until 2011, putting four presidents in power and successfully overseeing what has now become a model transition based on multiparty power sharing and consensus.

Nonetheless, the victory in the plebiscite was only the beginning of a democratic transition whose characteristics would deeply mark the coalition and its pattern of government. First, it is important to note that the Concertación's initial victory was not absolute. Though successful in removing Pinochet, the alliance was forced to accept the constitution that he and his allies drafted in 1980. Chilean elites inherited an institutional structure that they did not design, and that was extraordinarily difficult to reform (Siavelis 2000). In most political systems elites craft institutions to serve their own interests, while in Chile democratic institutions were imposed by actors with a strong political agenda. The 1980 constitution provided for exaggeratedly strong presidential systems, effective veto power for the armed forces, the establishment of a strong and military-dominated National Security Council, and a number of appointed senators (named by the military or other forces sympathetic to the Right for most of the transitional period). To work within this system, constant consultation and negotiation were necessary to succeed, both among parties within the coalition and between the coalition and the opposition. The awkward combination of presidentialism and multipartism is well substantiated and fraught with disincentives for cooperation (Linz and Valenzuela 1994; Mainwaring 1993; A. Valenzuela 1994). If elites were going to sustain the transition, they needed to build in incentives for cooperation. In addition, reformers established a two-member district legislative electoral system, despite the fact that Chile was historically (and throughout the transition) characterized by a multiparty system. This would necessitate the formation of electoral coalitions (explored in detail in the following pages) and elaborate negotiations to share legislative seats.

The Concertación was successful in doing so. The coalition grew from a disparate collection of seventeen parties, which eventually whittled to five major parties, managing to overcome divisions to forge the longest lasting coalition in Chilean history, and one of the longest in South America. Four Concertación presidents followed: Christian Democrats Patricio Aylwin (1990–1994) and Eduardo Frei (1994–2000) and socialist Presidents Ricardo Lagos (2000–2006) and Michelle Bachelet (2006–2010). Beginning in 1989 the Concertación won every presidential and legislative election until bested by the Alianza with the victory of Renovación Nacional's Sebastián Piñera in 2010. As Table 2.1 shows, the Concertación also managed to win every subsequent legislative election at least with respect to the popular vote (it dropped below the Alianza in the number of seats in the 2009 election), and sometimes by margins as large as 18 percent.

However, despite this extraordinary success, it is important to bear in mind that the transition was also extremely delicate. The hindsight of success blurs the real potential threat that existed for a return to authoritarian rule. While most former dictators board a plane for exile, at the end of his term Pinochet left the presidential palace and literally moved across the street to the Ministry of Defense from where he could see the presidential palace. There were several close calls, where the potential for a military return to power was real. In 1990, in what became known as the *ejercicio de enlace*, Pinochet put troops on high alert in response to incipient investigations into human rights abuses and rumblings of trying the military. Similarly the stalling of military promotions and allegations of conflicts of interest in the business dealings of Pinochet's son led to the *boinazo* of 1993, where troops in full military gear surrounded the Ministry of Defense (for a full account see Chapter 5 by Gregory Weeks in this volume). Indeed, the first post-authoritarian president, Patricio Aylwin (1990–1994), underscored that his gravest political problems were the continuation of militarism and the possible return of Pinochet. Commenting on the *boinazo*, he noted, Pinochet "always thought we were going to fail and that the country was going to call him back to replace me."[1]

The combination of constitutional and legal measures and the delicacy of the transition deeply shaped the pattern of government. As will be noted throughout this chapter, the Concertación created elaborate power sharing arrangements among parties to assure widespread representation and avoid conflict. Party elites understood the difficulty of generating the majorities necessary to govern in a presidential system characterized by many parties.

Table 2.1 **Valid Votes and Seats Received by the Concertación and the Alianza in Chamber of Deputies Elections, 1989–2009 (in percentages)**

	1989 Votes/Seats	1993 Votes/Seats	1997 Votes/Seats	2001 Votes/Seats	2005 Votes/Seats	2009 Votes/Seats
Coalition						
Concertación	51.5/57.5	55.3/58.3	50.5/57.5	47.9/51.7	51.8/54.2	44.35/47.5
Alianza	34.2/40	36.7/41.7	36.3/38.4	44.3/47.5	38.7/45	43.45/48.3
Others	14.3/2.5	7.9/0	13.3/4.2	7.8/0.8	9.5/0.8	12.19/4.2
Concertación's margin	17.3/17.5	18.6/16.6	14.2/19.1	3.6/4.2	13.1/9.2	0.9/–0.8

Sources: Votes—author calculations based on Sitio Histórico Electoral at http://historico.servel .cl; seats—Congreso Nacional de Chile, www.camara.cl.

Cabinets and legislative slates were filled by multiple parties, but were negotiated at the elite level. To avoid antagonizing the opposition, the alliance engaged in extensive consultation with the opposition and with potential veto players (especially in the business community) that might derail the transition. These realities also had profound consequences for the reach of policy. The Concertación consistently governed with an eye to avoiding potentially destabilizing policies. This resulted in a piecemeal reform process. For example, presidents never challenged the fundamental economic model of Pinochet for fear of the potential backlash it might cause. All of these realities are what made the Chilean transition a success. However, ultimately, as will be argued here, many of these patterns of governing and policymaking that were created to respond to the exigencies of the transition came back to haunt the Concertación.

The Roots of Success

The chapter now turns to an analysis of the roots of the Concertación's success. To balance the goals of assuring the stability of the transition and working within the constitutional framework left by the military, the Concertación developed a series of ingenious formal and informal mechanisms. These include ministerial power sharing arrangements, creative mechanisms for legislative candidate selection, extensive executive outreach in executive/legislative relations, and informal consultation with social actors outside the executive branch.

Ministerial Power Sharing Arrangements

The significance of the distribution of ministerial portfolios for the performance of governments has been extensively analyzed in the literature on
parliamentary democracies (Austen-Smith and Banks 1988; Laver and
Shepsle 1990).[2] Less has been written on the significance of portfolio distribution in presidential democracies. While coalitions as institutions are the
political hearts of many parliamentary systems, they are not often associated with presidential governments. There is a good deal of literature that
attests to the disincentives for coalition government in presidential systems
(Mainwaring 1993; A. Valenzuela 1994). However, coalitions are much
more central to presidential systems than has been acknowledged. For example, in her study of nine Latin American presidential systems between
1958 and 1994, Deheza (1997: 67) shows that 69 out of a total of 123 governments were coalitions characterized by the multiparty distribution of
ministerial portfolios.

How was the actual cabinet formation and portfolio distribution
process used to provide incentives for coalition formation and maintenance? Concertación leaders struck an agreement that endured throughout
all of the post-authoritarian governments from the Patricio Aylwin administration (1990–1994) until the Bachelet administration (2006–2010). Fundamentally, this agreement assured that in each ministry the cabinet minister
was from a different party than the vice minister. What is more, throughout
the ministries, and particularly the "political" ministries, each of the post-
authoritarian administrations has also sought to balance the representation
of the complete constellation of members of the Concertación coalition in
the upper level staffs of each ministry.

Rehren (1992) correctly underscores that this was a key departure from
the pattern that had characterized the distribution of cabinet portfolios in
Chile's last socialist government, where entire ministries were controlled by
a single party, or what Rehren calls "vertical feudalism." In contrast, in dis-
tributing parties across ministries, the Concertación provided a pattern of
"horizontal integration" that prevented the establishment of ministries as
tools for the distribution of party patronage. Therefore, cabinet portfolio
sharing was a central component of a multifaceted power sharing arrangement whose elements in combination consistently reinforced the incentive
to remain together as a coalition. This form of distribution for ministerial
portfolios and high-level staff has also built trust, by ensuring widespread
party input into governmental decisionmaking.

Nonetheless, with the passage of time these power sharing arrangements, while at first well received, lost their luster. Reflective of this reality
was that they eventually became known somewhat derisively as *el cuoteo*
(suggesting a cynical distribution of spoils based on partisan identification

rather than merit). As I underscore later in this chapter, while initially a positive force, the *cuoteo* eventually came to undermine the very legitimacy of the Concertación.

In light of the very success of Concertación governments it is easy to forget the atmosphere that reigned in 1990 as democratic authorities inherited power for the first time in almost twenty years. During the initial election the Right campaigned on a platform suggesting that the victory of the Concertación would represent a return to the chaotic years of the Unidad Popular (UP) government of Salvador Allende (1970–1973), which ended in the disastrous military coup of September 11, 1973. One reason for this chaos was that parties selfishly and single-mindedly pushed their own agendas within the framework of the UP coalition. Outgoing dictator Augusto Pinochet often spoke of the evils of political parties and of venal party leaders who pushed their own agendas and this was a constant subtext used by the parties of the Right in campaigns against the Concertación. Parties of the Right consistently underscored that electing the Concertación (and later when Ricardo Lagos ran, a socialist government) would constitute a return to a formula where selfish partisan squabbling would get in the way of governing Chile. Following the return of the democracy, General Secretary of Government Edgardo Boeninger recognized this risk, noting the importance of party cooperation. In a then confidential internal memo circulated among the highest levels of the Concertación, he wrote, "The fear of a military regression, and the understanding of the risk of such an event occurring, will be directly determined by the level of conflict that exists between political parties" (Boeninger 1989). Unity was transformed into something near an ideology in the governing alliance. In this sense, as the Concertación moved into office, it sought to paint a picture of consensual party government, where petty partisan squabbles would not get in the way of governing. By constructing cabinets with cross-party representation the Concertación projected a public image of moving beyond the interests of party to put the interests of the democratic transition first.

Subsequent administrations have also used the *cuoteo* as a public relations tool (or, less cynically, have used the cabinet appointment process to send a message about the values, goals, and orientations of the government). The Frei administration (1994–2000) used cabinet appointments to send a very similar message of unity to that which characterized the Aylwin administration. However, after two governments the attitude toward the *cuoteo* itself began to change toward a more negative one in the eyes of the public, a reality discussed in more detail later. This change was largely a function of the fact that the novelty of the Concertación had begun to wear off and the delicacy of the democratic transition had begun to wane. With this transformed and more negative view of the *cuoteo* beginning to develop, presidents turned its use toward other public relations ends. The Lagos administration (2000–2006) for the first time focused on cabinet portfolio distribution as a way to send the message that his government would be one of "new faces" in terms of appointing a number of young people to his cabinet. The average age of cabinet ministers appointed by Lagos was 47.5, and women entered the upper levels of the Chilean government. He also sought to send a message regarding gender parity, putting five of the sixteen ministries under the direction of women (Siavelis forthcoming).

This attempt to use the mechanism of cabinet appointments to remake the Concertación's image reached its height under the Bachelet administration. Part of Bachelet's victory in the presidential election was based on her promise to remake the Concertación by introducing a *gobierno ciudadano* or citizens' government. As part of this campaign she pledged to appoint a cabinet with an equal number of men and women ministers. She also pledged even more clearly to appoint "new faces" to these positions, promising that the same ministers who served before would not serve again, or that "*nadie se va a repetir el plato*." Together these promises were an effort to send a strong symbolic message that there would be a renovation of political elites, which proved very popular with the electorate. Although Bachelet filled party quotas in ministerial and undersecretary positions, finding new faces, who were also women, and whom she trusted that also fit the party bill proved extremely challenging. The result was that President Bachelet appointed a cabinet that theoretically respected *cuoteo* rules but did not contain the people that the party presidents would have liked. This later translated into more difficulties and open conflict among the coalition when it came to governing. What is more, Bachelet's appointments and frequent subsequent cabinet shake-ups reinforced the gradual erosion in the public's perception of the *cuoteo*.

Thus, at first the strategy of using portfolio distribution as a public relations tool proved successful. The *cuoteo* was designed to assure the widespread and complete representation of all parties in the coalition. Without this representation and voice, parties would have had little incentive to remain loyal to the coalition, it would have likely fallen apart, and Chile would not be the textbook democratic success that it is today. In addition to all of the positive outcomes with respect to the actual outcomes of governing, survey data suggest that the Concertación also achieved a public relations victory in the initial years of the democratic transition with extraordinarily high levels of public support.

Legislative Candidate Selection

The process of legislative candidate selection is most illustrative of the ability of the Concertación to negotiate spaces for all parties, which ensured the unity of parties and underwrote the success of the transition. Faced with all of the challenges to coalition maintenance outlined above, and the additional challenge of the military's efforts at electoral engineering, Chilean political parties have been forced to reconcile a multiparty coalitional dynamic with a majoritarian electoral formula.

At the core of the military's project of social transformation was an attempt to reduce the number of political parties through electoral engineering and ensure an exaggerated political voice for parties of the Right. The adoption of a first-past-the-post system would appear to have been the best choice to reduce the number of parties. However, given that the Right could count on only about 40 percent of electoral support, this type of system would have potentially excluded it from congress. Thus, military reformers decided to adopt an electoral system with district magnitudes of two. Such a system (known in Chile as the binomial system) amounted to the best of both worlds for the military. It had the purported reductive tendencies of a marjoritarian system, while also benefiting the Right. The system creates powerful electoral thresholds. In order for a party to win one seat, it must garner at least 33.4 percent of the vote of the two largest finishers in each district, and in order to win two seats, it must win 66.7 percent of the vote. Thus, with 40 percent of the vote nationally, the Right could expect to garner about 50 percent of the congressional seats. At the same time, in theory, such a system would help lead to party system integration and a reduction in the number of parties.

Military authorities were correct to assume that the system would help the Right. However, in terms of party system integration, rather than reducing the number of parties, the electoral system has encouraged the development of an extensive array of agreements and negotiations to ensure the existence of a multiparty system in the face of the electoral system's powerful integrative tendencies.

First, despite the efforts of military authorities, Chile continues to be a multiparty system composed of four or five major parties and a number of minor parties (Scully and Valenzuela 1997; Siavelis 1997). Parties recognize the necessity of forming multiparty coalitions to pass crucial thresholds. So to underwrite their success in elections, parties must form some preelectoral coalitions. This is the case for both the governing parties of the Concertación and the opposition Alianza por Chile.

However, the reality that only two seats are available in each of the country's sixty electoral districts tremendously complicates negotiations, and has given birth to informal institutions and rules that respond to the well-understood incentives created by the electoral system. Each of Chile's major parties has formalized rules for candidate selection. However, the exigencies of negotiation and give-and-take inherent in cobbling together two member lists from multiparty coalitions mean that informal processes take over where formalized processes fail.

Each of the two coalitions is, in turn, broken down into two "sub-pacts" representing each ideological subsector within coalitions (for the Concertación, the Center and the Left, and for the Alianza por Chile, the Center-Right and the Right). The constituent parties of each coalition must negotiate sixty two-seat electoral lists. However, the thresholds of the system complicate negotiations. Two-seat victories in a particular district are rare, because in a context of two-coalition competition, a single coalition has to poll over 66 percent of the vote to win both seats. In the last six elections (1989, 1993, 1997, 2001, 2005, 2009) there were two-seat victories in eleven, twelve, twelve, five, five, and none of the sixty districts, respectively. This means that the pairing of candidates is crucial to victory. Being paired with a strong list partner almost guarantees an electoral loss even if one's list is victorious. Therefore, parties want to place their candidates with coalition partners that will contribute to their overall list vote, but not defeat their candidate. This is a delicate balance and, because all parties want to strike it, one that is very difficult to achieve. Thus, given the constraints of district magnitudes of two, parties must join and help maintain their coalitions, must seek to extract as many seats as possible from that coalition, and simultaneously be sure to pair their candidates with coalition partners that they can beat. The complexity and many levels of this candidate selection game prevent the use of genuine primaries, and push the real selection of candidates squarely into the hands of elites (the broader significance of which is discussed later).

Each party central committee begins with a set of between 60 and 120 candidates. While in the first parliamentary election of 1989 major parties simply negotiated candidacies at the elite level (an extraordinarily informal process), by 1997 some sort of party activist primary had been instituted in most parties. However, this reality is deceiving. Informality is the rule despite the apparent formalized process of candidate selection within parties. Usually party central committees or national councils propose the initial lists of candidates to local party activists, who are likely to approve candidates put forward by party elites, because these candidates tend to fare better in elections.[3] Also, party central committees nominate candidates with an eye to districts where they are going to attempt to negotiate their candidate "in."

As the candidate selection process becomes a multiparty affair it becomes more complicated, and informal processes and elite negotiations become even more important. While each of the party's national councils must approve candidate lists, elite negotiations in and outside of formal coalition structures determine the ultimate lists, taking into account the candidates designated by parties, but also sometimes overriding the choices of party activists (Navia 2008).

It would seem quite easy to simply divide candidacies based on the percentage of vote a particular party has polled in previous elections. However, with district magnitudes of two, a minor party candidate paired with a major party candidate often stands to lose. Those minor parties are crucial for coalitions to rally enough support for them to pass thresholds nationally, and to maintain single coalitional presidential candidacies. Thus, minor party candidates often lobby to be paired with weaker party partners, a counterintuitive logic, but one that makes sense. It means that candidates capable of garnering the highest number of votes in a particular district may not be placed on electoral lists (Siavelis 2002c). Even major party candidates will lobby to be placed either with very strong coalition partners that will allow them to pass the 66 percent threshold, or with weak partners who will contribute enough votes to pass the 33 percent threshold, yet not outpoll them.

In pre-authoritarian Chile, the multimember district PR system did not obligate parties to form multiparty electoral slates. Smaller parties could simply field a list of candidates, and the proportionality of the system allowed for a wider array of party representation. However, Chile's binomial system is at odds with its strong tradition of multipartism. To respond to this inflexibility, parties have devised a series of informal mechanisms to both ensure their continued existence, and to underwrite coalitional integrity.

What is more, the electoral system as a formal institution has created a series of commonly understood informal rules related to relative party strength and the placement of candidates. These rules have, in turn, shaped and affected the nature of the elaborate informal strategies designed to simultaneously balance the goals of promoting party interests, ensuring coalition survival, and winning political office.

Given the lack of congruence between the binomial electoral system and Chile's very institutionalized multiparty system, to ensure representation parties were forced to ally with ideological neighbors to pass the strong thresholds of representation established by the electoral system. The failure to strike a coalitional bargain could mean exclusion from parliament even for relatively large parties. For small parties the incentive to join with a larger coalition was even greater, as they would be absolutely excluded without joining a major list. Very clearly then, the adoption of informal mechanisms of candidate selection was a response to the lack of congruence between political reality and formal institutions.

In addition, congressional lists and presidential candidacies are intimately connected, given the irrationality and impracticality of separate presidential and parliamentary lists. A division between the Center and Left and the failure to choose a single presidential candidate would likely have resulted in the victory of a candidate on the Right. Similarly, the failure of the two major parties of the Right to coalesce behind a single standard-bearer would have subjected its candidate to defeat. In turn, joint lists were key to the maintenance of coalitions, which helped presidents succeed in the legislative arena and avoid the deadlock, immobilism, and problems of democratic governability that have been identified by critics of presidentialism. Ultimately, this complex constellation and network of informal institutions underwrote the smooth trajectory of Chile's democratic transition. However, it was also extraordinarily elite centered and not very representative.

External-Formal Relations: Executive Outreach

Chile returned to democracy with a weak congress and an extremely strong executive. Chile's president is the most important legislative actor in the country, and is universally recognized as a "co-legislator." Presidents have wide latitude to control the legislative process, broad urgency powers, a monopoly on the presentation of legislation having to do with social policy or expenditures, and effective decree power in budgetary affairs (Siavelis 2000: 11–31). The comparative literature suggests that this constellation of executive powers is problematic in terms of democratic governability, and may provide disincentives for interbranch cooperation with potentially negative consequences for presidents' ability to govern (Shugart and Carey 1992). This is the case primarily because executives are tempted to bypass congress and impose their own agendas when they lack majorities, or to abuse their privileges and simply compel congress to cooperate where they can rely on majorities.

However, in post-authoritarian Chile, if presidents had simply relied on their powers and enforced their own partisan agendas it is likely that legislation would have failed. Therefore, because different ministries were made up of a variety of parties, all parties had some input into the legislative process and through a variety of mechanisms could ensure that legislation was acceptable to the full range of parties within the coalition. What is more, simply relying on the presence of ministers from allied parties in the executive branch without outreach to the congressional parties of those ministers might have created a rift between the congressional and ministerial contingents of allied parties. Therefore, executives consistently attempted to structure formal relations with members of congress in an effort to transform an executive branch alliance into a working legislative coalition.

Under the Aylwin administration a series of interministerial commissions were formed to ensure the coherence of the government's program and legislative agenda given the multiparty scope of the coalition. Ministerial commissions are made up of high-level ministry officials in different ministries working in similar areas that require coordination. For example, officials from the Ministry of the Interior and the Ministry of the Economy necessarily need to coordinate with the Ministry of Planning when determining spending priorities and budgets. However, in informal terms, these interministerial commissions also serve as crucial mechanisms of communication. While coordinating their various activities, ministers and officials from distinct parties share information on the nature and status of activities of the government, providing widespread party input and ensuring both coordination and coalition-reinforcing trust.

President Aylwin relied on the Ministerio Secretaría General de la Presidencia (SEGPRES) most extensively to govern and promote his agenda. However, all post-authoritarian presidents have relied on the political division of this ministry to structure relations with congress. Officials at this ministry talk often with members of congress, paying careful attention to the preferences of legislators when drafting legislation. This is a surprising pattern where presidents are so powerful in formal terms, but one that has eased the legislative tasks of all presidents.

Presidents have also established a number of consultative mechanisms. Meetings between the representatives of the executive branch and legislators have been the norm. Legislators of governing parties meet with ministers, subsecretaries, and high-level officials within the ministries working in the same substantive area to discuss what type of legislation is necessary and should be incorporated into the executive's program. Also, at the beginning of legislative sessions, officials of the executive branch meet with members of congress to decide what the most important legislative priorities for the year will be. Representatives from ministries and legislative committees in the same substantive areas continue to meet after the proposal stage to discuss aspects of bills later in the legislative process. In cases where particularly important legislation is being considered, like the annual budget, the president often meets with legislators of the committee discussing the legislation. Presidents in the post-authoritarian period have also met weekly with the *jefes de bancada* (party whips) of the various parties of the Concertación to discuss the legislative agenda for the week (Siavelis 2000).

Ferraro (2008: 115) notes that with the passage of time these meetings, though initially instigated by members of the executive branch, have increasingly become part of the expected legislative process and that members of congress "demand frequent meetings with ministers and vice-ministers." He goes on to note that ministers and vice ministers spend a good deal of time in Valparaíso, where the congress is located, in meetings, in formal committees, or in simple consultation with individual members of congress.

All of these mechanisms, however, are based on the principle of extensive cross-party influence and are rooted in an assumption that the constituent parties of the Concertación would have input in policy formulation. Without a sharing of cabinet portfolios, this promise of true cross-party policy formulation and implementation would have been impossible and presidents would have likely been much less successful in passing legislation. However, with just portfolio sharing without extensive relations with congress, presidents' legislative tasks would have been much more difficult.

External-Informal Relations: *Democracia de los Acuerdos*

Outside of the executive branch presidents also sought to reach agreements to ensure coalitional peace and maintenance.[4] Legislation was even more complicated for post-authoritarian presidents in Chile given the initial intransigence of conservative social forces who reacted negatively to the Concertación's electoral success. With the return of democracy, powerful conservative social groups expressed concern that a Concertación government would upset the positive record of Chilean economic performance and threaten private property (Boylan 1996; Weyland 1997). Thus, in addition to legislating and making good on their promises of redressing inequality, presidents sought to put to rest the idea that the Right, and the powerful groups backing it, should have something to fear from Concertación governments.

To overcome this threat to legislative success, presidents consistently engaged in a pattern of informal negotiations that have come to be known as *democracia de los acuerdos* (democracy by agreement). The model of *democracia de los acuerdos* allowed presidents to advance their legislative agendas while consistently assuaging the fears of a potentially reactionary Right. These negotiations have consistently been carried out with the congressional opposition, and with powerful social groups outside of congress.

Examples of the pattern of informal negotiations and the reaching of *acuerdos* abound. The tax reform of 1990 is perhaps the most cited, but it is simply one example of a regularized and normalized pattern of informal pact-making. Key members of the executive branch sought links with the business community and producer groups to neutralize any potential opposition to the tax reform, which passed with very limited congressional input. Boylan shows how the tax reform itself was designed to assuage "powerful business interests in an environment of uncertainty"; however, more importantly in terms of the argument advanced here, she shows that the "reform was characterized by a series of extra-parliamentary negotiations in which the government clinched the support of the chief opposition party, thus defusing any potential opposition to the reform and ensuring its rapid passage" (1996: 15, 23). Indeed, President Aylwin's behavior led many to contend that he had "gone over the heads" of his own congressional contingent to precook a deal that powerful interest groups and, thus, rightist members of congress would support (Siavelis 2000: 57). Officials in the executive branch also have met and consistently negotiated with members of the opposition in relation to legislation on tax reform, labor standards, and the minimum wage.

That said, contrary to what one would expect given the extent of presidential powers in Chile, all four Concertación presidents have been circumspect in their use. This is intriguing in an age where delegative democracy is the norm in countries with formally far weaker presidencies than Chile's. As noted, Chilean presidents have almost complete control over the budgetary process. The president presents the national budget every year, and if congress fails to approve it, the president's budget enters into force (Article 64, Constitution of the Republic of Chile). However, scholars of budgetary politics have noted that though deputies are barred from formal consultation on the budget, in reality members have a good deal of informal input in its formulation stage (Baldez and Carey 1999). Their influence continues during negotiations in legislative conference committees of the two houses, and in negotiations outside of formal congressional institutions. Presidents routinely consult with legislators of their own parties and members of the coalition to reinforce coalition unity and ensure that the budget is acceptable to coalition partners.

More importantly, informal negotiation has also been central to securing the votes of the *opposition* to pass budgets, even though presidents do not necessarily need these votes. During negotiations on most budgets the Concertación's various ministers of finance have met and negotiated with opposition leaders. Formally, presidents have the capacity to simply implement their budget, but it makes little sense to do so because of the consequences this would have for the long-term capacity of presidents to legislate. Because budget negotiations are only one piece of presidents' legislative agendas, they must avoid completely alienating the opposition to continue to be able to legislate (Siavelis 2002a). Hence, despite their impressive formal budgetary powers, presidents consistently choose informal avenues of negotiation and consultation to come to budget agreements that are acceptable to members of both the presidents' coalitions and the opposition. This is a stark departure from the familiar model of "delegative democracy" and the image of Latin American legislatures as compliant rubber stamps (O'Donnell 1994).

Chile's four post-authoritarian executives also have engaged in a series of regular, yet informal, consultations with the business community, producer groups, and members of the conservative media.[5] Silva (1992: 103) is correct in noting that capitalists were granted privileged access to the executive branch to stem the fears of business elites that the neoliberal model would be abandoned. He goes as far as to characterize this influence as "institutional veto power." He notes that business elites lobbied directly with the executive branch in relation to key legislation that affected business, and that Chile's main business lobby, the Confederación de Producción y Comercio (CPC), was particularly influential in derailing initiatives that were perceived to be antibusiness. While Silva characterizes this relationship as one that sacrificed potentially progressive economic reform in exchange for political democratization, these relationships also granted executives the power to persuade conservative forces in congress that business interests had been taken into account in elaborating budgets and controversial economic legislation.

Democracia de los acuerdos, then, helped to stave off potentially destabilizing conflicts both within the coalition and between the coalition and the opposition. By ensuring that the fundamental interests of allied parties, the opposition, and key social groups were not threatened, Concertación presidents have succeeded in governing and in passing legislation in what is, in formal institutional terms, a very infertile environment for consensus politics. This was possible in large part because of successful coalition formation underwritten by the careful construction of formal and informal relationships within and outside of the executive branch.

Transitional Enclaves

Chilean elites constructed an impressive array of mechanisms to rule successfully.[6] How is it then that a coalition whose final president left power with an approval rating of over 70 percent went down in defeat? While coalitional exhaustion is often offered as an explanation, few have considered the possibility that the very model of transition that has been lauded as so successful might actually be at the root of the difficulties that plague both the Concertación and Chilean democracy today. To make this argument this chapter develops the idea of transitional enclaves that is used throughout this volume. Building on the work of Manuel Antonio Garretón (2003), who argued that certain *authoritarian enclaves* left over from Chile's authoritarian regime interfered with the optimal functioning of the democratic system, this chapter argues that interaction of the electoral system and the structure of post-authoritarian competition have created a similar set of transitional enclaves. In particular, the chapter points to five transitional enclaves: the *cuoteo*, elite control of candidate selection and electoral politics, party-dominated politics, elitist and extra-institutional policymaking, and the untouchability of the economic model inherited from the Pinochet government.

The Cuoteo

The *cuoteo* was one of the keys to success of the democratic transition. Nonetheless, despite the centrality of the *cuoteo* to the success of the democratic transition, this arrangement has outlived its usefulness. Though initially seen as a positive effort at building consensus, the *cuoteo* has come to be viewed derisively by the Chilean public and leaves the impression that ministerial positions are not awarded based on the talents or experience of a would-be minister, but rather on the exigencies of party politics. Chileans increasingly view the *cuoteo* as a form of *politiquería* and as a way to ensure political positions for politicians, some of whom have been unsuccessful in winning elections.[7] Indeed, Carey and Siavelis (2005) show that political positions within the public administration are often given as consolation prizes to those who are willing to run under the coalition banner in risky electoral districts. Rather than a measure to build and maintain the coalitions, the *cuoteo* has gained a reputation as a form of corrupt dealmaking. Perhaps more seriously, from the level of the cabinet (and especially the recent cabinets of President Bachelet) down to the level of public administration, the *cuoteo* has been blamed for government incompetence given the lack of preparation of officials appointed for partisan reasons. In November of 2008, several politicians on the Right called for elimination of the *cuoteo* in the Ministry of Health because of a series of errors and irregularities in the nation's hospitals (Renovación Nacional 2008).

Thus, though the *cuoteo* emerged as a successful informal tool to manage coalition building and maintenance during a democratic transition, this transitional enclave has become an impediment to the establishment of more representative patterns of political recruitment in Chile, with important consequences for the ability of citizens to hold their leaders accountable. Perhaps more troubling, there are strong disincentives among politicians to eliminate this enclave given how central it has been to maintaining such a successful coalition and managing the often difficult combination of presidentialism and multipartism. Without these types of power sharing arrangements it will be difficult to continue to operate as a coalition, meaning parties (none of which is currently capable of generating majority support) will have to govern alone, with all of the difficulties this entails. In addition, the *cuoteo* is reinforced by the existence of a parliamentary election system that, as will be explored below, obliges parties to form electoral alliances to win. Deals struck in the executive branch are tied to a wider dynamic of coalitional deals related to presidential candidacies and joint legislative lists. The *cuoteo* has been an important glue that helps keep this electoral alliance together and there are very strong disincentives to eliminating it.

Elite Control of Candidate Selection and Electoral Politics

The process of candidate selection and the dynamics surrounding electoral politics are the second transitional enclave. While the election system itself was bequeathed by the Pinochet government and is an authoritarian enclave, the political dynamics with respect to interparty negotiation and candidate selection were a response to the election system, which was profoundly conditioned by the transition and can, thus, be considered a transitional enclave.

While the democratization of candidate selection processes has the potential to loosen elite control, the dynamics of the electoral system have also prevented any significant democratization of the process. The complexity of this negotiation process necessitates strategic coordination that can effectively only be handled by elites, working at cross-purposes with any efforts to democratize the candidate selection process (Navia 2008). The complexity of this negotiating environment in a multilevel game where considerations of coalition maintenance also come into play necessitates very purposeful intervention if parties are to achieve their goals. Party leaders become much more influential than the rank and file in choosing candidates. The incentives provided by the binomial system make a reform of the candidate selection process virtually impossible given the current pattern of partisan competition.

One could argue that voters could reassert control by ousting incumbents nominated by party elites. However, the binomial system also makes it almost impossible to defeat incumbents. Barring incompetence or extreme indiscipline, Chilean parties consider incumbents to have a right of renomination (Siavelis 2002c). The election system in the context of two coalitions strongly limits the ability to unseat an incumbent. Rarely will one list contain two candidates from the same party, providing incumbents the luxury of not facing intraparty competition at least in the electoral arena. More importantly, if a voter seeks to unseat an incumbent there are two potential strategies. The voter can either completely abandon his or her ideological convictions and vote for an opposition list, or cast a likely more ideologically sincere vote for the list partner of the incumbent. However, because votes are pooled in determining seat distributions, a vote for one candidate on a list is in many respects a vote for both. Therefore by voting for an incumbent's list partner, a voter may actually be contributing support to the very incumbent the voter aims to defeat (Navia 2005). Further, as Navia notes, because of the thresholds of the system a candidate who loses support in a district could conceivably go from a level of 60 percent support to 35 percent without losing the congressional seat. Accountability is central to democracy. The current coalitional configuration combined with the properties of the binomial system does not provide voters the opportunity to hold their representatives accountable.

Once again, the election system created very strong and positive incentives for coalition formation, and the selection of candidates by way of negotiations assured political voice for all members of the coalition in congress. Though this enclave has outlived its usefulness and become arguably counterproductive to representation, it is difficult if not impossible to eliminate. The simple reality of reconciling the political goals of multiple parties within the context of an extraordinarily strategically complex electoral system virtually guarantees the continued existence of this enclave of the transition.

Party-Dominated Politics

Strong and well-institutionalized parties are often central actors in high-quality democracies (Mainwaring and Scully 1995). Indeed, strong parties were central to the success of the Chilean transition, because only strong parties with the capacity to discipline members could negotiate and enforce the agreements that sustained the democratic transition. However, increasingly, the domination of the Chilean political system by parties with low levels of popular adhesion is bordering on the development of a *partidocracia*. This argument may come as a surprise to those who have followed the coverage of the progressive erosion in support for parties among the Chilean population, both in the press and in academic literature (Luna 2008; Ruiz 2006). However, while popular support has eroded for parties, they continue to be, in part as a legacy of the democratic transition, the major organizational actors in Chilean politics.

What is more, parties continue to operate within the same patterns that they did during the transition, despite the fact that the population has gradually abandoned identification with them. In this sense, and as Luna has argued, there remains a highly institutionalized and stable party system at the level of elites, but it has very weak ties to the population (Luna 2008). This is a problematic enclave of the transition and a form of political activity that is also difficult to dislodge. Strong party government has underwritten a successful transition and strong party control continues to be necessary to strike the deals that have held the Concertación coalition together.

When surveys began immediately following the return of democracy in 1990, 62.5 percent of the Chilean public attested to identifying with a political party. By 1992, the number of Chileans self-identifying with political parties increased to 87 percent. From there this percentage has registered gradual declines, to the point that in 2008 only 43 percent of Chileans said they identified with a particular political party, and none of the parties registered a level of adherence above 10 percent.[8]

Nonetheless, at the elite level, parties—and in particular party elites—remain the most important political actors in Chile. First, parties are recognized as one of the central policymaking actors. Party elites in concert with the president bypass congress to work out legislative deals with major social actors and veto players before they are presented to congress for approval. Members of parliament also recognize the centrality of party leaders to legislation. A series of questions drawn in three waves of surveys of members of parliament undertaken by the University of Salamanca (for the Parliamentary Elites in Latin America [PELA] survey), asked whether the structures of deputies' parties "were continuous" or "merely mobilized for elections." Over the three waves of questionnaires deputies pointed to the continuing structural importance of their parties by wide margins: 94.7 percent (1994–1998), 88.8 percent (1998–2002), and 85.2 percent (2002–2006). With respect to the power and influence of party elites in particular, Chile is the only country of the fifteen included in the PELA study where party leaders are ranked as most important ahead of voters and party militants in terms of whose opinions deputies take into account when making decisions (Marenghi and García Montero 2008).

Second, party elites are remarkably powerful actors within their own parties. As already noted, party elites exercise almost complete control over the legislative candidate selection process and in the few cases where primaries are undertaken party elites have overridden the decisions of popular contests to satisfy other deals related to coalition politics. With respect to internal party democracy, legislators perceive it as quite low, albeit growing, when measured in terms of the power and influence of party militants. During the first three legislative periods of the democratic government, 16 percent of deputies termed levels of party democracy as "high" or "very high" during the first (1994–1998), 31 percent during the second (1998–2002), and 44.4 percent during the third (2002–2006). Overall, among the fifteen countries included in the PELA study, Chile ranked third from the bottom in terms of perceived internal party democracy, behind only Argentina and the Dominican Republic (Ruiz 2006).

Finally, and as has been detailed throughout this chapter, parties and considerations of party identification are central in determining which posts people receive, where parliamentary candidates run, and how the spoils of Chile's coalition government are distributed. In writing on pre-Chavez Venezuela, a country previously touted as a "model" and island of stability in Latin America, Coppedge (1994: 2) contended that "The institutions that make Venezuela a stable polity also tarnish the quality of its democracy." Coppedge noted that Venezuela's highly institutionalized parties had come to completely dominate the political system in the form of a "partyarchy" or *partidocracia.* In a very similar way, the institutions and political dynamic that made Chile's transition to democracy a success have also tarnished the quality of democracy, and many of these are tied to a developing *partidocracia.*

This is not to say that party institutionalization is a bad thing. Just as Coppedge noted the different forms of institutionalization and partisan power, Chile's parties can play the vital role in democracy that they played in the past. In their study of Uruguay, Buquet and Chasquetti (2004) refer to the *partidocracia de consensos,* noting the extraordinary strength of Uruguayan parties. However, the crucial difference is that Uruguayan parties demonstrate many of the same prerogatives as Chilean parties, but unlike in Chile, they enjoy extraordinarily high levels of cohesive support among the mass public. Therefore, while parties in Chile are strong and influential at the elite level, they increasingly lack deep roots in society, which characterized parties in the past and have been recognized as central to effective party representation (Luna 2008; Ruiz 2006).

Clearly, this pattern of party domination then can be considered an enclave. The electoral system has obligated parties to stand together if they have any chance of winning, and purposeful action in building coalitions and alliances is at the core of continuing to win. Without strong party elites who structure and enforce agreements, it is difficult to forge the types of collaborative efforts that have been central to maintaining the Concertación. As noted, the election system is key, because the striking of coalition agreements is necessary to maintain the type of electoral alliances necessary to win under the binomial system. Perhaps the clearest demonstration of this reality was the decision by the Center and the Left to run separate lists in the municipal elections of 2008—this option was only possible because of the existence of a proportional election system that provided a different constellation of incentives than that which underwrites this enclave. With a different legislative electoral system it is likely that the party elite stranglehold will be moderated in a number of ways. The political dynamic of party domination grew out of the basic correlation of political forces characteristic of the transition period, coupled with the dynamics of the binomial system. There are very strong practical limitations to reforming this enclave, not the least of which is the potential for electoral disaster for major parties and ideological sectors if party elite negotiations for joint lists fail.

Elitist and Extra-Institutional Policymaking

The post-authoritarian policymaking process has been dominated by elites, and given the weakness of congress, mostly by executive branch elites negotiating deals with the opposition and extraparliamentary actors. This model of *democracia de los acuerdos* described above is once again a transitional enclave that was crucial to the success of the democratic transition. Given the number of parties involved in the coalition, it could facilitate agreement among parties. In addition, the fragility of the transition during much of the early years of democracy coupled with the controversial nature of many political issues and the existence of veto players made direct negotiation with those players a very smart strategy. However, over the years this politics of elite accommodation has created a perception among the public that citizen preferences matter little, and that politics is a negotiated rather than representative game. Finally, in negotiating directly with social actors outside of the congress, presidents have consistently ignored the country's principal representative institution and created the perception (even among legislators) that the president bypasses congress. Elite and extra-institutional negotiations of this type grew out of the dual imperative of maintaining policy coherence for a coalition forced to compete together to win elections, and of maintaining a consensus form of democracy that could stem a negative reaction of potential veto players. These imperatives remain and, once again, are reinforced by the election system and the dynamic of partisan competition, making the reform of this enclave quite difficult.

Untouchability of the Economic Model

Even more than its political model, Chile's economic model has been lauded around the world for its success, with high rates of growth and impressive achievements in eliminating poverty. Still, the county's neoliberal economic model has been a contentious issue. The question of the underlying roots of economic success and where to place the credit or blame are still divisive in Chile. For supporters of Pinochet, it was his neoliberal economic policies that transformed Chile into the free market dynamo that it is today, and Concertación governments have managed success without altering the Pinochet model. Many of Pinochet's critics, on the other hand, acknowledge that he set the country on the economic course it is on today, but are more critical of the process of reform and its outcome. They contend that Concertación governments have improved the imperfect model that they inherited from Pinochet, but the fundamentals of the model remain intact. In addition, they argue, despite impressive macroeconomic indicators,

Chile is one of the most unequal countries in the world, and the Pinochet government's comprehensive privatization of the health, education, and social security systems has created an effectively two-tiered system where those with access to privatized social goods enjoy much higher standards of quality and access.

In essence, political actors across the spectrum agree that part of the unwritten deal underwriting the transition was that the neoliberal economic model inherited from Pinochet should remain untouched in its essentials (Silva 1992). Early democratic leaders recognized that the economy was the Achilles' heel of the transition. Had a substantial change in economic course taken place, the integrity of the democratic transition would have been compromised. The commitment of presidents to leave the economic model untouched calmed powerful economic elites whose reaction to a potential change in policy could have been extraordinarily destabilizing. International investors were assured of economic stability and a dependable investment panorama. Finally, the process of veto player consultation on the economy later facilitated more widespread agreement on other issues with groups whose sympathies lay with the Right. In sum, this enclave, like all of the others, was central to maintaining the democratic transition.

Nonetheless, the unwillingness of democratic governments to enter into a discussion of the economic model (beyond some minor piecemeal reforms like the plan AUGE—a limited reform of the health care system undertaken by President Ricardo Lagos to address the most egregious inequalities in the system) has left the Concertación open to charges that nothing has changed with democracy. Despite success at fighting poverty, levels of inequality in Chile are among the highest in the world, and weaknesses in lines of citizen representation underscored throughout this chapter leave citizens with few avenues to affect the political economy of the country. Once again, high-level negotiations, rather than popular or legislative consultation, have been the norm in making economic policy.

The political system shows signs of dissatisfaction with the lack of fundamental economic change. President Bachelet campaigned on a platform of social inclusion. However, despite words to the contrary—and a number of citizen commissions largely convened for show—she continued to pursue the elitist pattern of policymaking that has characterized the entire transition. Bachelet's contention to be in touch with the real demands of the people with respect to their social and economic needs was quickly belied early in her administration. Indeed, nagging inequality in the educational system turned into newly elected Bachelet's first major crisis, abruptly ending her administration's honeymoon. In May of 2006, and only weeks into her term, small-scale student protests began in response to an increase in the price for college aptitude tests and rumored limitations on the free student-transport pass. Protests quickly escalated to focus on inequality and the poor state of public education more generally. An estimated half million students participated in the first protests, and in subsequent protests in early June the numbers swelled to over 700,000 as high school students were joined by parents, university students, and unions. Throughout 2006 and 2007 labor, popular, and student protests continued, often ending in violence and hundreds of arrests. Bachelet and her government failed to grasp the nature and scope of dissatisfaction with economics as usual in the country.

The unwillingness or inability of governments to address severe inequality and devise more inclusive patterns of economic policymaking has contributed to the wider pattern of dissatisfaction noted here. The student protests that began in 2006 and continued into 2013 and labor unrest are the first indications of public disgust with inequality and the lack of fundamental economic reform. Pragmatic policies aimed at addressing economic problems now can help to avoid the emergence of a more troubling form of conflict, which is increasingly common across Latin America.

With such clear signals of trouble with the inherited economic model, why did governments not act more aggressively to fundamentally transform its key aspects? Once again, the economic policymaking process since the return of democracy has been based on two sets of tacit agreements that are enclaves of the transition and that are underwritten by the interaction of political party context and the election system. The first is a tacit agreement between the Concertación and the Alianza. The Concertación has agreed to preserve the economic and social security structures set up by the Pinochet dictatorship. Although the Concertación governments have significantly increased fiscal expenditure on social policies, for example, they have not in any way touched the privatized structures of health care and pensions, or attempted any form of redistribution that would even out the highly unequal structure of income distribution or educational opportunities. They have kept the state out of economic activities as far as possible, precluding the discussion or implementation of any kind of development strategy. What is more, even today the Concertación must avoid charges of irresponsible economic policymaking or populism, and an unwillingness to engage in fundamental economic transformations is deeply entrenched in a habitually risk-averse group of political elites.

The second agreement was within the Concertación. As repeatedly noted, the parliamentary election system obliged the Concertación to run as a coalition, which requires at least limited policy consensus. Engaging in fundamental structural economic reforms risked fracturing the Concertación among its various ideological flanks—a disastrous outcome, for either the Center or the Left—given the dynamics of a parliamentary electoral system that will exclude at least one ideological sector in the context of three-bloc competition.

Conclusion

The Concertación devised an admirable model for managing the democratic transition and for making Chile the success story that it is today. However, at the same time, the very roots of success of the coalition also planted the seeds for its defeat. While all of the elements used by the Concertación to manage the transition and politics were functional and contributed to the success of Chile's model democratic transition, they are double-edged swords. The success of the Concertación coalition (and, in turn, the democratic transition) was based on a complex power sharing arrangement; but it is one that increasingly brings charges of elite domination and politics by quota. At the system level, the dynamic interaction of coalition politics and the electoral system provided strong incentives for coalition formation, but in the process have provided Chile's two major coalitions an effective lock on power, where citizen preferences mean little. Each major coalition is provided an effective assurance of one of the two seats in each electoral district. The sharing of electoral spoils through negotiated assignment of legislative candidacies guaranteed peace among Chile's parties, but could only be undertaken through elite selection of candidates and precluded significant citizen input. Chile's highly institutionalized parties are credited with underwriting the success of the democratic transition and the stability of Chilean democracy. However, while party institutionalization has provided presidents workable legislative majorities, strong parties, and powerful party leadership, party elites dominate decisionmaking and candidate selection, with little citizen input. Party elites exercise strong control over legislative behavior. With respect to the policymaking process, party elites in concert with the president bypass congress to work out legislative deals with major social actors and veto players before they are presented to congress. This was certainly a stabilizing phenomenon, but one that sidelined congress and the public.

When it comes to economic change, elites avoided destabilizing change, but have been loath to address deep public dissatisfaction by engaging in any reform of any of the fundamentals of the economic system inherited from Pinochet. While forming a central part of the success of the democratic transition, it is important to underscore that all of the enclaves explored here interact and combine to provide strong limits on representation and accountability.

One might argue that the enclaves set out here have always character-ized politics in Chile, and characterize democratic politics in the rest of the world. While there is certainly a grain of truth to this contention, I argue that these enclaves are distinct from politics as usual historically in Chile and in other democracies. What sets these enclaves apart and makes them much more than "ways of doing things" is their depth and entrenchment and the difficulty in reforming them.

Further, because this set of institutions, behaviors, values, and beliefs is rooted in the legislative electoral system, Chilean presidential system, and the deeply entrenched post-transitional political partisan context they will be very difficult, if not impossible, to eliminate without electoral reform or a substantial exogenous political shock to the extant party dynamic.

As long as the underlying conditions that led to the formation and maintenance of authoritarian enclaves persist, those enclaves are likely to remain with negative consequences for representation.

There are additional less tangible variables that also contribute to the maintenance of these enclaves. Undoubtedly the transitional model of poli-tics was successful, and regularized patterns that are successful in the past tend to be repeated. Until a new political model is devised, elites continue to rely on what has worked in the past. The Concertación has only experi-enced one defeat in national elections, and, as such, has had little occasion to reflect on a model that up until defeat has been sufficiently effective to win over voters. The entire elite political generation governing Chile was forged during the pre-authoritarian period and profoundly shaped by the process of democratic transition while most of the mass public was born after Pinochet came to power. The spectacular triumph of the democratic opposition over Pinochet provided the fundamental narrative on which the Concertación based its government. The problem is that as Chilean elites look back, the Chilean public is looking forward to a post-transitional pat-tern of politics that will shed these transitional enclaves.

The remainder of the chapters in this volume explore how these en-claves have affected the policy process in a number of areas. The conclu-sion to the volume takes up the potential for moving beyond the transi-tional enclaves that have both underwritten its success and proven to be its undoing.

Notes

1. Interview with the author, August 20, 2008.
2. Portions of this analysis are drawn from Siavelis (2006).
3. These contentions are based on a series of interviews carried out with elites charged with candidate selection in every major Chilean political party during the summers of 1999 and 2000.

4. Portions of this section appeared in Siavelis (2006).

5. Concertación leaders also often engaged in direct negotiations with influential actors on the Left, primarily trade unions, when drafting and advocating the passage of controversial legislation, pointing to a consistent pattern of pact-making even when attempting to satisfy the coalition's natural constituencies.

6. For a complete elaboration of this argument see Siavelis (2009).

7. Salvador Valdés Prieto, *La Tercera,* January 7, 2006.

8. Data collected from the Centro de Estudios Públicos. See www.cepchile .cl/dms/lang_1/home.html.

3

The Alianza's Quest to Win Power Democratically

Patricio Navia and Ricardo Godoy

The electoral victory of right-wing presidential candidate Sebastián Piñera in January 2010 put an end to twenty years of Center-Left Concertación governments. After having supported the Pinochet military dictatorship and its neoliberal reforms, right-wing parties struggled to accommodate the new reality forged by the restoration of democracy in 1990. In the 1988 plebiscite, right-wing parties supported General Pinochet's bid for a new eight-year term, despite a division between the extreme Right party and enthusiastic supporter of the Pinochet regime, the Unión Demócrata Independiente (UDI), and the more catch-all right-wing party, Renovación Nacional (RN). In RN, a liberal wing committed to democracy advocated for an alternative candidate that would keep the market-friendly economic policies implemented by Pinochet but, at the same time, leave behind the painful legacy of human rights violations and authoritarianism. The tension between the hard- and soft-liners evolved into a permanent conflict within the Chilean Right. In fact, the evolution of the political Right can be characterized as an ongoing battle between those who have held on to the legacies of the dictatorship and those who favor a democratic Right. Both groups embrace the market-friendly economic model implemented, but differ on policy issues and on their conception of democratic institutions. While the conservative Right feels more comfortable with a protected democracy framework, the liberal Right embraces democracy free of authoritarian enclaves. Piñera's victory in 2009 represented a victory for the soft-liners. However, because part of the Right is not fully committed to democracy, right-wing parties might still be tempted to embrace some of the authoritarian features that characterized it during the dictatorship. For-

43

tunately, since voters have become increasingly moderate, drifting to authoritarian positions will hurt the Alianza in elections.

A central tenet of this volume is that the evolution of the Concertación was shaped by an ongoing political bargaining with the Right. This combination of challenging the Right, engaging it, and sometimes adopting its policies was a key to success for the Concertación. Therefore, for a volume of this type, to understand the Concertación, it is also necessary to understand the genesis and evolution of the contemporary Chilean Right. Furthermore, just as the much discussed transitional enclaves fundamentally underwrote the behavior of the Concertación, they also did so for the Right, albeit from the other side of the partisan divide.

Since the restoration of democracy, the two right-wing parties consolidated distinct political identities, ideologies, and electoral bases. While UDI derives its electoral support from popular sectors, "RN draws its support from middle and upper class voters . . . it also has a captive electorate in rural popular sectors, which despite being admittedly not a large voting bloc, offer a solid electoral base, and present a clear continuity from the old National Party whose strength was precisely in rural areas" (Barozet and Aubry 2005: 27). Though both parties differ in their ideological beliefs and on key policies, there is mixed evidence on their distinct electoral bases. The claim that UDI's electoral growth can be associated with its penetration in urban popular sectors cannot be squarely based on polling data or electoral results. The two parties differ more on the party elites than among their voting blocs.

Despite the tension over how to deal with the authoritarian legacy, the Alianza became a viable electoral alternative in the 1999 presidential election. Ten years later, it won a presidential election. In what follows, we discuss the evolution of the Alianza, intertwining the debates on the two right-wing parties' distinct electoral base, on their policy differences, and on how they have dealt with contentious issues of the authoritarian legacy. We question the alleged different electoral bases for both parties and show that the tension between conservative forces favorable to the authoritarian enclaves and liberal forces committed to a new democratic Right has been slowly but surely resolved in favor of the latter. We conclude by suggesting that the Alianza is a democratic coalition and that, in fact, makes Chile a full-fledged democracy. Chilean voters can freely choose between at least two fully democratic options.

The Party System in Chile

Historical social cleavages explain the existence of political parties in Chile. Aligned on a Left-Center-Right continuum, the party system consolidated in the mid-twentieth century (Angell 2003, 2007; Drake and Jaksic 1999; Izquierdo and Navia 2007; Siavelis 2000, 2002c; Tironi and Agüero 1999; S. Valenzuela 1995, 1999). According to some, the old three-way divide reemerged after the transition to democracy (Angell 2003; Huneeus 1998; S. Valenzuela 1995, 1999; Valenzuela and Scully 1997). Others argue that after the dictatorship, voting patterns have been determined by a new authoritarianism-democracy cleavage that has shaped party alignment (Tironi and Agüero 1999; Torcal and Mainwaring 2003). Be it a two- or three-way divide, the political system has been remarkably stable since 1990. Two coalitions, the Concertación and the Alianza, have combined to receive around 90 percent of the vote in all elections since 1989.

The electoral rules in place since 1989 have forced parties to form coalitions. The across-the-board two-seat proportional representation system used for the Chamber of Deputies and the Senate (the binomial system) makes it difficult for third parties to win seats, but it also imposes high thresholds for a coalition to win both seats. A coalition can secure a seat with one-third of the votes. Thus, parties lack incentives to adopt moderate positions. To win both seats, a coalition must get twice as many votes as the other coalitions. The incentives of the electoral rules have induced parties to form two large coalitions: the Center-Left Concertación and the right-of-center Alianza (see Chapter 2).

Though they initially formed for the 1988 plebiscite to oppose and support Pinochet's eight-year presidential bid, the Concertación and Alianza evolved into stable multiparty coalitions. For those who claim there is a three-way divide, the Concertación brings together the Left and Center, while the Alianza represents the Right. For those who believe there is an authoritarian-democratic divide, the Alianza represents the former and the Concertación embodies the latter. To be sure, the names used to refer to both camps are not appropriate. The Alianza is as democratic as the Concertación. No coalition advocates the authoritarianism that characterized the military dictatorship. Though it has an illegitimate authoritarian origin, the 1980 constitution has been repeatedly modified to eliminate authoritarian enclaves and protect democratic features.

The Divided Right

Since the early twentieth century, the political Right has been represented by two parties. The Conservative Party had a strong rural and pro-Catholic presence while the Liberal Party had a more urban industrial and less Catholic, but still oligarchic, electoral base. During two brief periods, the Right coalesced into a single party. In 1967, the Liberal and Conservative parties formed the National Party (PN) after a disastrous electoral performance in the congressional elections of 1965, when the centrist Christian Democratic Party (PDC) did exceptionally well, drawing strong support from areas where right-wing parties had been traditionally strong (Correa 2005; Morales 2004; Scully 1992; Walker 1999). Since the PDC originated two decades earlier from a division in the Conservative Party championed by young leaders, its rise affected the Conservative Party more notably. Because it formed as a response to an electoral defeat and not out of ideological proximity, the PN quickly dissolved after the 1973 coup, heeding the military demand for the suspension of party politics.

The second moment of unity in the political Right took place in 1987, when a number of right-wing groups formed a single political party, Renovación Nacional (RN) (Allamand 1999; Cavallo 1998; Cavallo et al. 2004; Durruty 1999). The formation of RN and its subsequent division in 1988 set in motion the dynamics that would characterize the evolution of the Right after democracy was restored. The events that led to the dissolution of the PN in 1973 and to the formation of RN in the late 1980s help explain why a unified right-wing party did not survive.

In 1973, most right-wing politicians supported the coup against the socialist government of Salvador Allende. The PN welcomed the coup and self-dissolved to comply with the demand of the junta. However, there were significant disagreements within the PN on the duration of authoritarian rule and on the type of democracy that should follow. A moderate wing wanted a quick restoration of democracy, while a more conservative group feared that communism would threaten the stability of any democratic order and, consequently, favored a prolonged period of military rule.

The moderate wing was overshadowed by the PDC, a centrist party that also opposed Allende. The PN and PDC formed an electoral coalition for the March 1973 legislative elections. Thus, even though several right-wing leaders favored the quick restoration of democracy, that position was led by the indisputable PDC leader, former president Eduardo Frei.

A vocal leader in the conservative group was Jaime Guzmán, a conservative lawyer and sympathizer of the Franco regime in Spain (Cristi 2000; Huneeus 2001a). As a student in the Catholic University in the 1960s, Guzmán joined a far-right political group, Fiducia. Guzmán shared the group's anticommunist beliefs and was dissatisfied with the progressive role played by the Catholic Church and the PDC. At the Catholic University, Guzmán founded his own group, the gremialistas, characterized by anticommunism, strongly conservative Catholic views, and an overt mistrust of democratic rule (Cristi 2000). As a motivating organizer, Guzmán attracted young conservatives who shared his displeasure with the PDC. Guzmán became an influential political voice due to his regular participation in a televised political debate program. Under military rule, Guzmán's influence over the regime allowed the gremialista movement to take control of the Catholic University (Huneeus 2001a).

After the coup, the military government suspended party activity and banned left-wing parties. Pinochet did not establish a one-party system. Instead, he fostered the formation of recruitment organizations to mobilize political sympathizers (Huneeus 2001a: 328). The anticommunist military junta had a clear idea of the kind of government they opposed. Intelligently, Guzmán seized the opportunity to influence the type of government the regime eventually created. Guzmán encouraged gremialista sympathizers to join the government in the Commission for the New Constitution, the planning agency ODEPLAN (Oficina de Planificación Nacional), the General Secretariat of Government, and local governments (Huneeus 2007).

Guzmán's influence increased as Pinochet became the dominant figure within the military junta and the authoritarian government consolidated. In 1977, following Guzmán's advice, Pinochet outlined a vision for a transition to a protected democracy in the Chacarillas Speech (Cristi 2000; Loveman 1991, 1999). For the first time, Pinochet established a calendar for the end of the dictatorship. That speech was widely considered an antecedent of the 1980 constitution. Imposed by the military, the constitution was also apparently forced upon other junta members by Pinochet, who had concentrated power. Because Guzmán successfully sought to influence Pinochet directly from day one, as Pinochet acquired power so did the leader of the gremialista movement.

The 1980 constitution established a framework for protected democracy. In transitional articles, it also outlined the mechanism to cede power to a democratically elected, but highly constrained, government after an eight-year presidential period for Pinochet. The 1980 constitution came into effect on March 11, 1981, with Pinochet as the constitutional president—more powerful than the junta—and with the gremialistas occupying key government posts. More liberal and traditional right-wing leaders supported but did not join the government.

Among the most important features of the new constitution, the prohibition of Marxist parties and a set of electoral rules that sought to foster a two-party system reflected both the military's mistrust of party activity and its intent to nurture the formation of a unified right-wing party. The constitution also established an institutional tutelary role for the military and gave the armed forces a prominent role in the powerful National Security Council. It established the appointment of nine nonelected senators (in addition to twenty-six elected senators) and introduced other authoritarian enclaves to restrict the power of democratically elected authorities (Constable and Valenzuela 1991; Garretón 2003; Huneeus 2001a; Loveman 1991, 2001).

An economic crisis in 1982 produced massive popular discontent. Social protests and renewed party activity forced Pinochet to speed up the transition away from authoritarian rule by allowing political parties to openly organize. Moderate opposition parties quickly moved from underground activity to leading the emerging opposition. As right-wing groups also openly organized, divisions between liberals and conservatives reemerged in the form of soft-liners in favor of a negotiated transition to democracy, and hard-liners—including Guzmán and his group—committed to upholding the 1980 constitution.

The economic crisis weakened the dictatorship. Pinochet sacked his cabinet and replaced many of the young technocrats—the so-called Chicago Boys. Though the Chicago Boys were neoliberal and the gremialistas were mostly anticommunist Catholic conservatives, the two groups developed growing links during the late 1980s. When the regime signaled that it would tolerate opposition parties, Guzmán formed a political group in favor of the transition to a protected democracy. The Unión Demócrata Independiente was created in September of 1983. UDI attracted many Chicago Boys who feared that Pinochet's political concessions would undermine neoliberal policies.

Pressured by growing popular discontent, Pinochet made concessions to the opposition and to the moderate right wing. He appointed Sergio Onofre Jarpa as minister of the interior. A former member of the National Party and strongly anticommunist, compared to other supporters of the dictatorship, Jarpa was a soft-liner. Though he was not openly in favor of a transition to democracy as other soft-liners, like up-and-coming leader Andrés Allamand, Jarpa was willing to depart from the transitional calendar established in the 1980 constitution. His appointment reflected Pinochet's acceptance that political activity was inevitable and that, just as leftist and centrist parties were reemerging, right-wing parties would also resurface. Since he had distant—if not hostile—relations with Guzmán and the gremialistas—Jarpa encouraged the formation of moderate groups that could represent the Right after the dictatorship ended. Under the leadership of Andrés Allamand, a young moderate lawyer who opposed Allende as a student leader, the Movimiento de Unión Nacional (MUN) was formed in July of 1983, three months before UDI.

Political differences between MUN and UDI were evident from the start. MUN supported a negotiated transition to democracy. UDI favored the protected democracy framework of the 1980 constitution. Despite social protests, the dictatorship resisted pressures to alter the transition calendar. When it became evident that Pinochet would complete his eight-year term, the two right-wing factions agreed on a political ceasefire in late 1986. In the view of the military and of right-wing groups, the preferable political party system would have few parties. In early 1987, UDI, MUN, and a few smaller right-wing groups formed RN. The party sought to bring together all groups supportive of the dictatorship, regardless of their views on transition to democracy.

Maintaining unity in the new party was not easy. UDI and the liberal MUN struggled to gain control of the party apparatus. MUN was far more heterogeneous than UDI, with different leaders advocating different positions. Allamand was among the most liberal leaders. Others, like Jarpa, were conservative. Allamand was closer to UDI in his support for market-friendly economic policies. Jarpa and other traditional right-wing leaders were sympathetic to protectionist policies, but were in tandem with UDI in supporting the authoritarianism of the military regime. Thus, while UDI was more ideologically homogeneous and identified with the dictatorship and the neoliberal economic model, the rest of the Right—grouped into RN—was heterogeneous, bringing together neoliberals with advocates of protectionist policies and grouping staunch supporters of authoritarianism with advocates of an orderly transition to democratic rule. In social beliefs, UDI was also more homogeneously conservative and Catholic while RN had more diversity, ranging from extreme conservative views to more tolerant views championed by Allamand and others.

The nonaligned RN president, Ricardo Rivadeneira, an elder figure charged with keeping unity and building a party, was unable to prevent disputes between the different branches from escalating. The RN party election in early 1988 was a moment of rupture for the short-lived single right-wing party. UDI defined the 1988 internal RN election as a contest between pro- and anti-Pinochet right-wingers. The conflict escalated to the point of breaking the new party (Allamand 1999: 138). After the election, the Pinochet government intervened in favor of UDI. The conflict resulted in the expulsion of Jaime Guzmán from RN in 1988. Most UDI leaders and militants resigned in solidarity, putting an end to the unified right-wing party (Angell and Pollack 1990; Cavallo 1992; Otano 1995). Since then, RN and UDI have remained the two leading right-wing parties, with UDI being more ideologically cohesive and RN having a more diverse base of support, from a liberal wing to a very conservative one that includes advocates of protectionist policies in the agricultural southern regions of the country and faithful supporters of the Pinochet dictatorship.

The division within the Right in 1988 came at the worst possible moment for Pinochet and for the Right. That was the year of the plebiscite on a new eight-year term for the candidate proposed by the military junta. As expected, Pinochet was named candidate and a plebiscite was called for October 5, 1988. UDI and RN supported Pinochet, but RN made it clear that it would have preferred a civilian candidate. Moreover, RN signaled its willingness to hold competitive presidential elections. In addition to being a more democratic mechanism, RN believed that the opposition would find it easier to unite against Pinochet than to unite behind a single opposition candidate. UDI, on the other hand, supported Pinochet and campaigned in favor of the protected democracy framework of the 1980 constitution.

The opposition united behind a Center-Left coalition, the Concertación of Parties for the No Vote. After having been rivals during the Allende government, centrist and leftist parties, led by the PDC and the Socialist Party (PS), united to oppose Pinochet. The contrast between a united opposition and a divided Right was damaging for Pinochet. The opposition seemed more politically responsible and more mature than the parties that supported the military dictatorship.

After Pinochet lost the plebiscite, divisions within the Right worsened. While RN was amenable to an agreement with the opposition to reform the constitution and eliminate authoritarian enclaves, UDI remained committed to the preestablished transition calendar. RN openly negotiated with the Concertación a constitutional reform package to eliminate authoritarian enclaves. UDI stood by the protected democracy framework and the transitional calendar. Pinochet agreed to some reforms—but not to the entire reform package negotiated by RN and the Concertación. The dictatorship called for a plebiscite in July of 1989, with the reluctant support of UDI and the enthusiastic support of RN. The Concertación acquiesced to the reforms, though it promised to further reform the constitution after its expected victory in the December 1989 election (Andrade 1991; Ensalaco 1994; Heiss and Navia 2007).

The reforms brought about positive changes, but the new institutional status quo was more favorable to the protected democracy framework preferred by the Right than to the concept of democracy without qualifiers (*democracia sin apellidos*) promoted by the Concertación. Though the number of elected senators increased from twenty-six to thirty-eight, the nine appointed senators and the binomial system almost made it impossible for the Concertación to transform its electoral majority into a seat majority in the Senate. Thus, the Concertación could not impose constitutional reforms. At the same time, by adopting the binomial system, the outgoing military practically forced UDI and RN to form a coalition for the 1989 election. Since the Concertación had a unified ticket, it would be suicidal for UDI and RN not to run together.

Since the electoral system distributes only two seats per district, and the Concertación was likely to secure at least one seat in most districts, due to its overwhelming popularity, the binomial system became both a blessing and a curse for the unity of right-wing parties. On the one hand, the system guaranteed one seat for the Right if that sector got more than one-third of the vote. On the other hand, it automatically forced the two right-wing candidates in every district to fight against each other to win that seat. Thus, though it provided overrepresentation for the Right, the binomial system also turned that overrepresentation into a zero-sum game for UDI and RN. Every seat for one of those parties would mean one fewer seat for the other.

Choosing a presidential candidate for the first election turned out to be a difficult task for the Right. In the eyes of RN, UDI support for Pinochet as the plebiscite candidate helped the victory of the No vote. UDI believed that RN did not show sufficient support for the protected democracy framework. Interparty tensions remained high. Seeking to strengthen right-wing unity, and also because the party had no clear front-runner, RN agreed to support the popular finance minister of the Pinochet dictatorship, Hernán Büchi. Given his pro-military credentials and his proximity to the Chicago Boys technocratic government elite, Büchi was a UDI favorite.

As expected, the Concertación won the presidency and a majority of elected seats in the Senate and Chamber of Deputies in 1989. An independent right-wing candidate, businessman Francisco Javier Errázuriz, further eroded support for the UDI-RN candidate. Büchi only managed to receive 29.4 percent of the vote. Still, RN and UDI consolidated as the two dominant right-wing parties. In the Chamber of Deputies election, UDI won 9.8 percent of the votes while RN received 18.2 percent, securing eleven and twenty-nine deputies, respectively. Altogether, the Alianza (named Democracy and Progress at the time) obtained 34.2 percent of the vote and forty-eight deputies. Though most seats in the Chamber went to RN and UDI candidates, in the Senate RN got five seats, UDI two, and nine seats went to independents. Together with the nine senators appointed by the outgoing dictatorship, the nine right-wing independents controlled the balance of power in the upper chamber. The conflict between UDI and RN turned to attracting the support of the independent right-wing senators.

In the Senate, the sixteen Alianza-elected senators (42 percent of the elected seats) and the nine right-wing appointed senators had majority control. The Alianza could veto any legislation sponsored by the Concertación government and passed by the Concertación-controlled Chamber of Deputies.

During the Aylwin administration, the Concertación used disagreements between RN and UDI to negotiate legislation separately with each party. The institutional constraints that prevented the Concertación from transforming its electoral majority into a majority in the legislature facilitated the emergence of the *democracia de los acuerdos* (see Chapter 2), the need for pacts and negotiations to advance the Concertación's legislative agenda. Even before the new government was inaugurated, UDI surprised RN by privately negotiating the presidency of the Senate with the Concertación. With UDI votes, PDC Gabriel Valdés became president of the Senate—and thus handed the presidential sash to Patricio Aylwin. In exchange, the Concertación ceded UDI the Senate vice presidency, a vice presidency in the Chamber of Deputies, and key positions in the Chamber of Deputies. UDI and RN raced to be the bargaining partner of the Concertación. While UDI was willing to bargain over power sharing, RN was ready to bargain over constitutional reforms. The *llaves de la transición* (keys to the transition) argument assumed that democracy could not consolidate with the authoritarian enclaves in place. In the eyes of RN leader Andrés Allamand, RN facilitated "consensus on tax reform and labor reform during the Aylwin government, guaranteeing economic stability and social peace" (Allamand 2007: 246).

UDI senator Jaime Guzmán emerged as the leading defender of the protected democracy framework. When Guzmán was assassinated in 1991 by an extreme left-wing paramilitary group, several right-wing independent senators joined UDI in solidarity. The crime strengthened the UDI's political agenda and brought many young conservatives to the party. At the same time, RN reproduced the traditional lack of organization that characterized right-wing parties before 1973. Given its weak national organization, RN leadership could not deliver votes in the legislature after it negotiated key reforms with the Concertación.

With Pinochet still in charge of the army, and many constraints of the 1980 constitution in place, the Concertación nonetheless had high popular support and was able to govern successfully. A negotiated tax reform in 1990 with liberal RN legislators—despite UDI opposition—gave the Aylwin government additional funds to combat poverty and increase social spending. After another negotiation with the Alianza allowed for the democratic election of council members—*concejales*—and the indirect election of mayors in 1992, the Concertación confirmed its electoral dominance with 53.3 percent of the vote while the Alianza—under the Participación y Progreso label—only obtained 29.7 percent. The combined vote for all right-wing parties was 40 percent.

Tensions between RN and UDI destroyed the right-wing coalition's chances in the 1993 presidential election. A phone-hacking scandal in late 1992 increased tensions between UDI and RN. The conflict involved two liberal RN rising stars with presidential ambitions, Senator Sebastián Piñera and Deputy Evelyn Matthei, the daughter of a junta member. Piñera's phone was hacked and a recording of a private conversation was put on a live television program where Piñera was a guest. In the conversation, using foul language, Piñera asked a friend to get a television journalist to ask Matthei tough questions in an interview. The scandal destroyed the presidential aspirations of both politicians. It also uncovered the influence of military intelligence, espionage, and foul play between the two parties. RN leader Andrés Allamand famously referred to the "de facto power" that sought to influence right-wing politics. In essence, Allamand argued that Pinochet—with the help of UDI—sought to control right-wing politics.

The scandal led to the Alianza defeat in the 1993 elections. In an Alianza convention, UDI maneuvered to prevent the RN presidential candidate from getting the Alianza nomination. Instead, an independent senator was named as the Alianza candidate (under the Unión por el Progreso de Chile label). UDI preferred to concede the election rather than allow RN to nominate a moderate right-wing candidate. The Concertación presidential candidate, Eduardo Frei, won with 58 percent of the vote. The Concertación also won a majority in the Chamber and retained a majority among the elected seats in the Senate. The appointed senators gave the Alianza control in the Senate. RN remained the dominant Alianza party, with twenty-nine deputies and seven senators. UDI increased its presence in the Chamber from eleven to fifteen and had three senators.

After 1993, there was a change in the balance of power within the Right. The phone-hacking scandal badly damaged RN. With its higher discipline, UDI strengthened its influence. Ideological and tactical division weakened RN's bargaining power. Notoriously, in 1996, the Concertación government of Eduardo Frei and RN leaders reached a constitutional reform agreement to eliminate appointed senators. Though it was supported by RN's national council, the agreement failed to pass when RN senators voted against it, contravening the agreement reached by the party. While UDI defended protected democracy, RN was split between a liberal wing in favor of eliminating authoritarian enclaves and a conservative group that voted with UDI.

In the 1996 municipal election, RN and its affiliated independent candidates received 18.4 percent of the vote, while UDI and affiliated candidates obtained 14.0 percent. The two parties reduced the power and influence of independents, but RN was no longer the indisputable dominant partner in the coalition. UDI militant Joaquín Lavín, the mayor of Las Condes, one of Santiago's most populous and wealthy districts, won reelection with an overwhelming 77.8 percent of the vote. For the first time, a UDI militant was a serious contender for the presidency.

UDI's rise consolidated in the 1997 parliamentary election (when the Alianza ran under the Unión por Chile label). UDI increased its vote share to 14.5 percent and elected seventeen deputies. RN had 16.8 percent of the vote and won twenty-three seats. Independent Alianza candidates won six additional seats. In the Senate, UDI had eight seats and RN had six, with four additional seats for independent Alianza candidates. In addition, the Right commanded the support of six of the nine nonelected senators (for the 1998–2006 period). RN no longer dominated the Alianza. UDI had more senators and a more disciplined contingent in the Chamber of Deputies. The shift in the balance of power in the Right was symbolized by the defeat of RN's Andrés Allamand, who lost the senatorial race in Santiago to UDI's Carlos Bombal.

Another defining moment for the Alianza was Pinochet's retirement as chief of the army and the granting of his lifetime seat in the Senate. After he was sworn in, in March of 1998, the aging former dictator sought to reinvent himself as the leader of the Right. During his short tenure in the Senate, Pinochet controversially negotiated with the PDC Senate leadership regarding the abolition of the September 11 holiday, established to commemorate the coup—in place since 1974. The Alianza had blocked previous Concertación efforts to abolish that holiday. When Pinochet negotiated the end of the controversial holiday, right-wing senators acquiesced. A few weeks later, when he traveled to London to undergo back surgery, Pinochet was arrested on charges of crimes against humanity. A Spanish judge, Baltasar Garzón, issued an arrest warrant that, after a series of legal battles, kept Pinochet under house arrest in London for seventeen months, until he was released on humanitarian grounds by the British government and sent back to Chile.

The arrest of Pinochet had two distinct effects. It was the end of the tutelary role for the military over Chilean democracy. Though the former dictator had already lost influence, his arrest confirmed that he was not a relevant actor in contemporary democracy. During the months Pinochet was held under arrest, his remaining power vanished. As it lobbied to secure his return, the Right implicitly accepted that Pinochet would no longer be a relevant actor. After his return, Pinochet resigned from the Senate for health reasons—the same health reasons used to slow down the judicial cases against him in Chilean courts. When a corruption scandal uncovered secret bank accounts in the United States in 2006, Pinochet's image was further damaged. By the time he died in late 2006, he had long stopped being a relevant political figure. Pinochet's 1998 arrest helped the liberal wing in the Alianza that wanted to build a political Right devoid of the authoritarian legacy.

The second effect of Pinochet's arrest was felt strongly in the Alianza. RN was divided among conservative pro-Pinochet defenders and a liberal dominant wing. UDI voiced its defense of Pinochet, with references to the protected democracy framework. However, the arrest also provided an opportunity for Joaquín Lavín, the rising star in UDI, to distance himself from Pinochet's legacy and to center his presidential message on the economic crisis and high unemployment that Chile began to experience in 1998. The arrest of Pinochet also provided an opportunity for many right-wing leaders to claim that they were unaware of human rights violations when they supported the military regime. Lavín himself qualified his support for Pinochet by condemning human rights violations committed under military rule.

The economic crisis had a stronger impact on the 1999 presidential election than Pinochet's arrest. The Concertación failed to win an absolute majority in the first round. Ricardo Lagos—the founder of PPD, a leftist Concertación party—struggled to defeat Lavín. The fact that the Concertación had a leftist candidate, and not a PDC one like in 1989 and 1993, made it easier for Lavín to embrace moderate positions. Also, the economic crisis and the low support for outgoing president Eduardo Frei made it an uphill battle for Lagos. The nonconcurrent presidential election made it more difficult for the Concertación to attract moderate voters. In 1999, the Alianza believed, for the first time since democracy was restored, that it could actually win a democratic election.

Lavín lost, but UDI consolidated itself as the dominant Alianza party (the coalition began to use that label in 1999). In the 2000 municipal election, the Alianza got just above 40 percent, with UDI receiving more votes than RN, 16 percent to 15.5 percent. The relative weight of Alianza independents declined. In the 2001 legislative elections, the Alianza received its highest vote share yet, with 44 percent. UDI received 25.2 percent of the vote, securing thirty-one seats. RN got 13.8 percent and only eighteen seats. The other eight seats went to Alianza independents. UDI became the largest party in the country, relegating the PDC to second place. The increasing power of UDI over RN was evident when RN leader Sebastián Piñera withdrew a Senate bid in a district that UDI wanted for a retired admiral who was a strong advocate of the military dictatorship.

The increasing power of UDI within the Alianza did not prevent RN from negotiating institutional reforms unilaterally with the Concertación. In 2002, with UDI voting against, RN and Concertación legislators passed a reform to separate the election of council members and the election of mayors. In a number of key votes, including the end of film censorship and the legalization of divorce, some RN legislators voted with the Concertación, while UDI and most RN legislators voted against.

A corruption scandal that affected the Concertación government in 2002 provided UDI an opportunity to negotiate with the government not just on power sharing agreements, but on institutional reforms as well. The MOP-Gate scandal, which forced the resignation of the public works minister, allowed UDI president Pablo Longueira to negotiate with President Lagos a set of reforms to regulate campaign spending—and provide public funds for campaigns—and reduce the number of positions in the public sector appointed at the president's discretion by creating a nonpartisan civil service board to handle high-level technical appointments.

Differences between RN and UDI persisted. Yet, more than the ideological and policy differences, political divisions damaged the Alianza coalition. A scandal involving accusations of pedophilia against unnamed

UDI legislators, made by an RN liberal deputy, triggered a civil war within the Alianza that would again derail its efforts to win a democratic election. The conflict and two-way accusations of wrongdoing damaged Lavín, who was forced to mediate between UDI and RN in early 2004. Lavín's popularity fell as a result of his involvement in trying to bring peace to the two parties after what became known as the Spiniak pedophile scandal.

The 2004 municipal election was devastating for the Alianza. With 44.8 percent of the vote, the Concertación won 203 of the 345 municipalities. UDI and RN elected only fifty-one and thirty-eight mayors, respectively. Five years after Lavín's impressive performance, the Alianza had a bad outlook for the 2005 presidential election. Part of the Alianza municipal defeat was due to the fact that mayors were elected separately from city council members. Unlike previous municipal elections, where it found it difficult to secure the unity of its council member candidates, the Concertación nominated a single mayoral candidate in every municipality in 2004. President Lagos's high approval ratings also facilitated the coalition's overwhelming victory in 2004.

After the Alianza defeat, Lavín's falling popularity created an opportunity for Sebastián Piñera's presidential aspirations. A successful businessman who made his fortune during his eight-year term as senator and who had embodied the spirit of *democracia de los acuerdos*, Piñera was considered too liberal by UDI leaders. Because Piñera came from a well-known PDC family and because he had openly opposed Pinochet in the 1988 plebiscite, some conservative RN leaders considered Piñera too centrist. However, since Chilean voters are moderate, a moderate Alianza candidate has a good chance of winning. Lavín's close run in 1999, despite being well right-of-center, was partially explained by the economic crisis. Many voters punished the Concertación for the high unemployment and difficult economic conditions. In 2005, instead, the economy was growing and unemployment was low, thus a protest vote would not make the Alianza competitive.

In mid-2005, with the support of RN and the acquiescence of UDI leaders, the Concertación government of Ricardo Lagos promulgated a set of constitutional reforms that eliminated most remaining authoritarian enclaves—like appointed senators and the National Security Council. Reforms to the Constitutional Tribunal and more powers and attributions ceded to the legislature led many Concertación leaders, including President Lagos, to claim that Chile had a new constitution. Symbolically, Lagos had his signature on the replacement of Pinochet's constitution. Though UDI was initially opposed to the constitutional reforms, RN's decision to support the elimination of authoritarian enclaves eventually forced UDI to the bargaining table. UDI was able to safeguard some authoritarian enclaves—like the binomial electoral system—and get concessions on other reforms—like the composition of the Constitutional Tribunal. UDI and RN defended the binomial electoral system, which had given them significant overrepresentation in both chambers.

Even though the Alianza put together a unified slate of legislative candidates for the 2005 election, divisions within the coalition resulted in RN and UDI naming different presidential candidates. RN nominated Piñera and UDI nominated Lavín. The presidential campaign was marked by mutual accusations and reflected the long-term tensions between UDI and RN. The first-round vote became a primary between the two Alianza candidates. The Concertación candidate Michelle Bachelet came in first, with 46 percent of the vote. Piñera came second (25.2 percent) and Lavín ended up third (23.3 percent). For the first time since democracy was restored, the two Alianza candidates received more votes combined (48.5 percent) than the Concertación candidate (46 percent). Bachelet defeated Piñera in the runoff by 53.5 percent to 46.5 percent. Some low-income voters—and many women—who had supported Lavín in the first round voted for Bachelet in the runoff.

UDI retained its electoral dominance in the Chamber, with thirty-three seats to RN's nineteen. In the Senate, UDI had nine senators, two more than RN. For the first time since 1989, the Concertación had a majority of seats in both chambers. Though not sufficient to reform the constitution at will, the Concertación no longer needed to negotiate with the Alianza on every bill. The loss of Lavín and the end of the Alianza's veto power in the Senate represented the end of UDI's growing hegemonic cycle. After he defeated Lavín in the first round, Piñera became the early favorite for the 2009 presidential election.

Under the Bachelet administration (2006–2010), the Concertación continued to negotiate separately with RN and UDI to advance some reforms. An educational reform, triggered by the student protests in 2006, was negotiated with RN, despite the opposition of UDI legislators. A pension reform championed by Bachelet was negotiated separately with UDI and RN legislators. While UDI and RN agreed to defend the market-friendly economic model, the two parties regularly had differences on the regulatory power of the state on constitutional and legal reforms.

In the 2008 municipal election, the Alianza celebrated its first electoral victory since democracy was restored. Anticipating its political demise, the Concertación incomprehensibly ran under two different slates. In the council members race, the two Concertación slates received more votes than the Alianza, but in the mayoral races, the Alianza received more than the two Concertación slates combined (40.7 percent to 36.6 percent). The Concertación did win more mayoral races than the Alianza (147 to 144), but the Alianza won in an overwhelming majority of the most important and populous cities. As he actively campaigned for Alianza mayoral candidates,

Piñera consolidated his lead to secure the Alianza nomination for the 2009 presidential election. Though UDI received more votes than RN, the two parties almost equally split the number of mayoral races, with UDI winning in fifty-eight cities and RN winning in fifty-five. The other thirty-one Alianza mayors elected were independents.

After the 2008 municipal election, it became clear that UDI could not stop Sebastián Piñera from becoming the sole Alianza presidential candidate. For different reasons, UDI had been able to prevent RN from fielding a presidential candidate in 1989, 1993, and 1999. After Piñera edged out Lavín in the first-round vote in 2005, UDI no longer was in control of the presidential candidate nomination process in the Alianza. Despite losing to Bachelet in 2005, Piñera was able to remain as the most popular right-wing figure during the entire Bachelet period. When RN and UDI fared similarly well in the 2008 municipal election, Piñera successfully consolidated as the most viable presidential candidate in the Alianza.

Piñera's victory in the runoff election in 2009 represented at the same time a vindication within the Alianza of the more moderate strategy championed by the liberal wing that dominated RN and the opportunity for a right-wing coalition to govern democratically and leave behind the memories of the authoritarian legacy. The position advocated by UDI—in favor of retaining authoritarian enclaves because the Concertación was likely to retain an electoral majority—proved unnecessarily pessimistic. With Piñera or other moderate candidates, the Alianza has been electorally competitive. During the twenty-year Concertación rule, despite UDI resistance to disband the protected democracy framework, constitutional reforms negotiated between the Concertación and the more liberal wing of RN have slowly but surely strengthened democratic institutions and eliminated the oversight power of the military. Tax reform in 1990, the reform that allowed for municipal elections in 1992, direct election of mayors in 2000, and the 2005 constitutional reform package facilitated the consolidation of democratic rule. These reforms were achieved despite initial UDI opposition and with support from the liberal wing of RN.

Expanding the Electoral Support Base

Since the mid-1980s, Jaime Guzmán was committed to expanding the UDI electoral base into the popular sector. He sought to "go beyond the class struggle framework imposed by the Marxist dialectic" (Soto Gamboa 2001: 13). Guzmán encouraged his gremialista sympathizers to use the strategic positions the movement had in the dictatorship—especially in ODEPLAN and local governments—to build support for his movement. Guzmán believed the Right could build support among groups that were historically inclined to support Christian Democrats and leftist parties.

During the dictatorship, the gremialista movement built support in the popular sector using the state apparatus, constructing youth networks in *poblaciones* (low-income neighborhoods) and promoting the organization of shantytown dwellers. Guzmán's gremialista movement recruited popular sector dwellers for the party. Guzmán's leadership was central in designing and implementing the gremialista strategy. Guzmán would normally end outreach meetings in the popular sector with a stump speech: "I am not here seeking votes. We are interested in people. We want UDI to be an instrument for your personal growth, a tool for your own development and progress as human beings" (Soto Gamboa 2001: 14). Guzmán realized the need to build support for the Right among the low-income sectors and the poor. It was the only way the Right could potentially be electorally competitive after the dictatorship ended (Arriagada 2005; Huneeus 2001a; Soto Gamboa 2001).

UDI *población* work provoked tensions with left-wing parties and the PDC as UDI used the state apparatus to strengthen its popular presence. The 1986 assassination of UDI popular sector leader Simón Yévenes at the hands of the left-wing Manuel Rodríguez Patriotic Front evidenced the growing presence of UDI in traditional left-wing areas. The UDI strategy was not necessarily in sync with the views of the military. In fact, the Pinochet dictatorship notoriously chose not to send a representative to the Yévenes funeral (Soto Gamboa 2001).

The work of UDI in the *poblaciones* was more clientelistic than ideological. UDI "offered resources in exchange for political support" (Arriagada 2005: 5), while RN showed "limited links with its electoral support base since it lacks social aid networks and has no foundations dedicated to helping the poor" (Barozet and Aubry 2005: 21). UDI work in popular sectors was accompanied by an electoral penetration strategy that allowed it to position candidates. UDI focused first on getting municipal council members elected in 1992, 1996, and 2000, and then deputies starting in 1997 (Morales and Bugueño 2001). In seeking to expand its base, UDI leaders sought to prevent RN's growth just as they built the party from below (Barozet and Aubry 2005; Joignant and Navia 2003; Morales and Bugueño 2001).

The binomial system also helped UDI grow without risking an Alianza breakup. RN and UDI had to stay together to remain competitive. Just as RN lacked party discipline, UDI grew steadily. The binomial system discouraged competition between coalitions and induced competition within coalitions. It also discouraged coalitions from going after the support of the median voter. The system had centrifugal incentives, as it allowed parties to secure half of the seats with one-third of the votes in every district. Since the Alianza had little chance of winning both seats, RN and UDI occasionally abstained or ran weak candidates in certain districts in support of the other Alianza party. However, because of its organization, RN tended to protect political heavyweights while UDI protected candidates in areas where the party was expanding its presence in the popular sector. Thus, while RN protected legislators who sought reelection, UDI fostered the growth of the party where left-wing parties and the PDC were strong.

Figure 3.1 shows the evolution of the vote share for RN and UDI from 1989 to 2009. Two trends stand out. First, the vote for right-wing parties has remained stable. The Right has received around 40 percent in all legislative elections since 1989. Its lowest support has been in municipal elections (1996 and 2008), while its highest vote was in 2001, when right-wing parties received 44 percent. Second, the number of right-wing officeholders not affiliated with UDI or RN has decreased over time.

Never between 1989 and 2008 did the Right get an absolute majority in an election. The January 2010 runoff victory by Piñera following the 2009 first-round presidential election was the first time the Right won an absolute majority. The unpopularity of Concertación candidate Eduardo Frei and the divisions between the Concertación and the former-Concertación-turned-independent candidate Marco Enríquez-Ominami facilitated Piñera's victory. Had the Concertación named a more attractive candidate and had the Center-Left coalition made a more vigorous effort to secure the support of Enríquez-Ominami in the runoff, a Piñera victory would have been

Figure 3.1 Vote Share for Right-Wing Parties in National Elections, 1989–2009

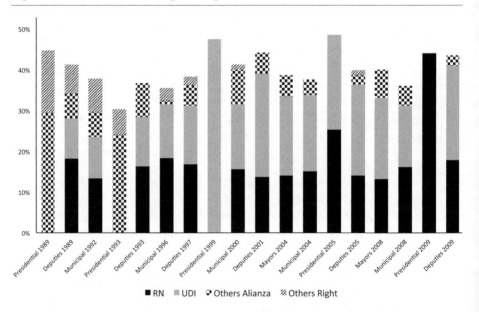

Source: Authors' compilation of data from www.elecciones.gov.cl.

highly unlikely. Yet, the Alianza came very close to winning in 1999 and 2005—when Piñera and Lavín combined to get more votes than Bachelet in the first round. Elections have been highly competitive since 1999.

The Right has greater support than what the "three-thirds" arguments about the division of the Chilean electorate seem to indicate. The right-wing coalition has consistently received around 40 percent of the vote since democracy was restored in 1989. Over time, the two right-wing parties, UDI and RN, have been able to capture most of the right-wing vote. Within the Alianza, support for independents has declined, UDI's strongest support was observed in 1999–2001, while RN has seen its support grow since Piñera's first presidential bid in 2005.

Figure 3.2 shows the seat share for RN and UDI for all elections held between 1989 and 2009. UDI remains a highly centralized party with high levels of discipline. Since democracy was restored in 1989, UDI has seen its presence grow among elected officials, while the percentage of RN elected politicians has declined at all levels of government. The presence of right-wing independents among elected Alianza representatives has also declined, which highlights the increasing power of right-wing political parties but also the growing dominance of UDI militants. Though RN is no longer dominant in the Alianza, Sebastián Piñera was the first president elected in

Figure 3.2 Seat Share for Right-Wing Parties in National Elections, 1989–2009

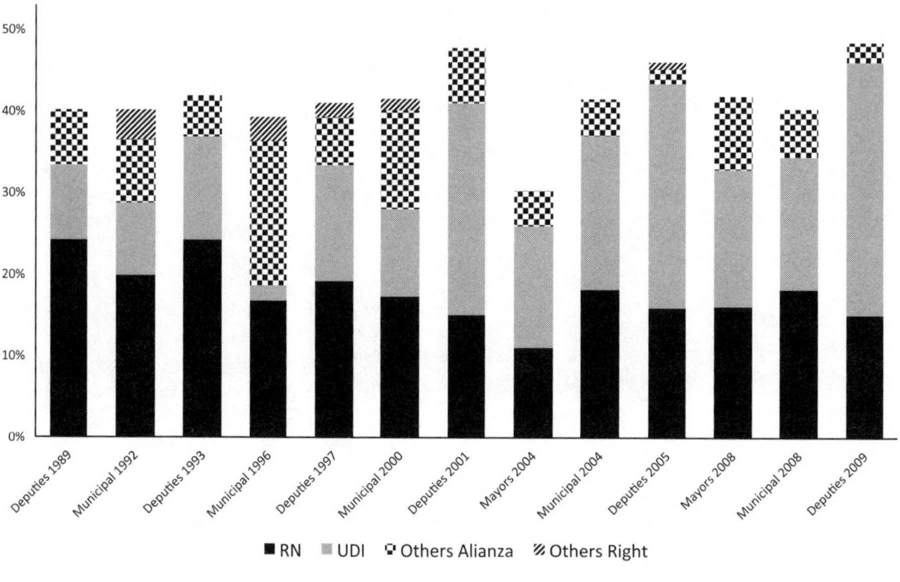

Source: Authors' compilation of data from www.elecciones.gov.cl.

the Alianza. The fact that Piñera has more moderate positions than most UDI leaders helped him attract support among moderate voters.

Figure 3.3 shows the seat share in the Senate for UDI, RN, and independent Alianza legislators from 1989 to 2009. The percentage of seats the Alianza held in the Senate was higher than its vote share. This was in part due to the presence of appointed senators until 2005, but also the result of the distortions produced by the binomial electoral rule. Though the Alianza had a minority vote in most senatorial districts, it received half of the seats in most senatorial elections.

That overrepresentation in the Senate gave the Alianza effective veto power during most of the years the Concertación was in power. When that overrepresentation diminished after the elimination of appointed senators, the position advocated by conservative Alianza leaders who wanted to hold

Figure 3.3   Senate Seat Share for Right-Wing Parties in National Elections, 1989–2009

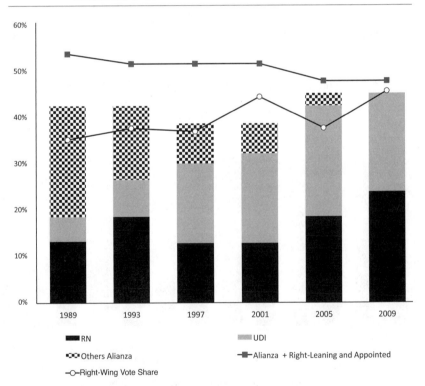

Source: Authors' compilation of data from www.elecciones.gov.cl.

on to the authoritarian enclaves in the 1980 constitution weakened. Many of those enclaves have now been eliminated and, thus, the only road to exercising political power is through electoral victories.

The overwhelming electoral support for the Concertación kept the Alianza seat share among elected senators around 40 percent during the first decade of post-Pinochet rule. However, as the Concertación lost support and the Alianza began to expand its electoral base, it was able to increase its seat share in the Senate. When appointed senators were eliminated in 2005, the Alianza already had slightly less than half of the elected members of the Senate. Starting in 2005, the Alianza has seventeen of the twenty-eight elected Senate seats, with an additional independent regularly voting with the Alianza.

Are Chileans Moving Right or Is the Alianza Moving to the Center?

Support for the Alianza parties has remained stable since 1990. After a decline in the early 1990s, Alianza parties have consistently received around 40 percent of the vote. Identification with the two right-wing parties has evolved over time. There have been sharp increases in the percentage of Chileans who identify with UDI. From a low of less than 6 percent in the early 1990s, UDI's party identification grew to more than 15 percent in 2001, after Lavín's good 1999 presidential run and UDI electoral success in the 2000 municipal elections. Identification with UDI has fallen since 2001. Identification with RN has not varied much over time. Since the early 1990s, it has fluctuated between 6 and 11 percent. In 2011, it was 7 percent.

The combined support for UDI and RN has fluctuated between 15 and 20 percent for most of the period. When UDI has peaked, support for RN has fallen. Conversely, when RN has seen its support rise, UDI has experienced a decline. Altogether, identification with the Alianza reached its peak in late 2001, but it has steadily declined since.

The electoral dominance of RN in the early 1990s and the growth of the seat share in elected offices held by UDI in the last decade are not reflected in popular identification with both parties in polls. As Figure 3.4 shows, though a slightly higher number of Chileans identify with RN than with UDI, UDI does have a higher vote share and a higher seat share in elected offices.

When poll identification is broken down by socioeconomic status, there are no significant differences between RN and UDI. Contrary to the "popular UDI" argument, UDI does not have a stronger support base among lower-income Chileans. Thus, UDI's electoral penetration in popular sec-

Figure 3.4 Chilean Self-Identification with RN and UDI, 1990–2011

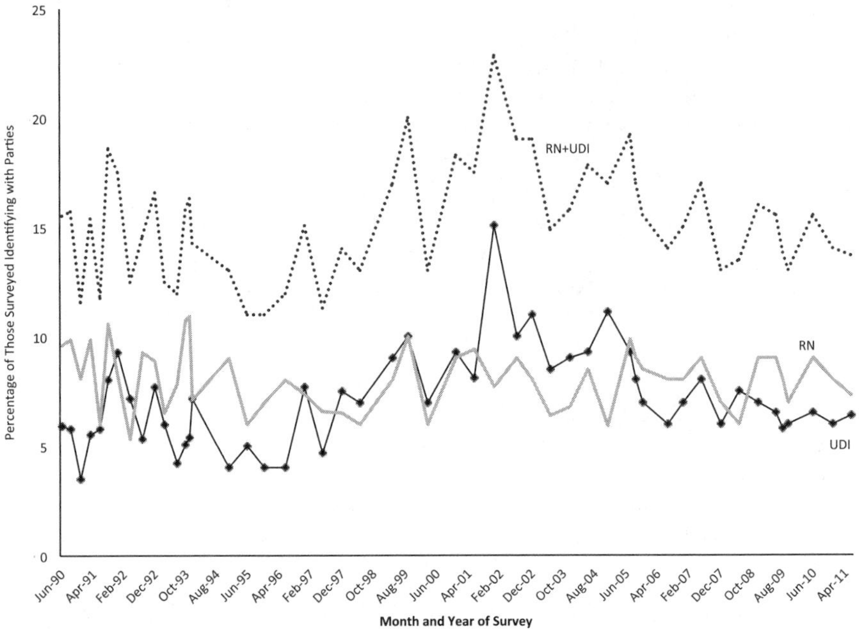

Source: Authors' compilation with data from CEP Polls (1990–2011).

tors, winning seats in districts that were traditionally held by left-wing parties and the PDC, is not reflected in popular identification with UDI among
the lower class. Figures 3.5 and 3.6 show the identification with UDI and
RN in 2009 (before the presidential election) and 2011 (two years into the
Piñera administration). Among the upper class (about 6 percent of the sample), levels of identification vary substantially. Overall, between 40 and 45
percent of high-income Chileans identify either with RN or UDI. The high
fluctuation between both parties is due to the small sample size of high-
income people in the poll. Among the middle class (49 percent of the sample), identification with RN is slightly higher than identification with UDI
in 2009 and 2011. Among those classified as the low socioeconomic group
(45 percent), fewer identified with UDI than with RN in 2005. In 2009, the
level of identification with RN and UDI was similar. Overall, more people
identified with RN than with UDI in 2009 and 2011. For earlier years, the
level of identification with UDI among those in the lowest socioeconomic
levels increased when overall identification with UDI increased as well.
However, the claim made in the late 1990s that UDI penetrated the popular
sector and built a strong party base can no longer be sustained with data
after 2005. The vote share for the Alianza has remained stable since 1989.

Figure 3.5   Identification with RN and UDI by Socioeconomic Group, October 2009

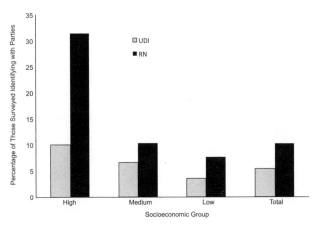

Source: Authors' compilation of data from CEP Poll 61 (October 2009), www.cepchile.cl.

Figure 3.6   Identification with RN and UDI by Socioeconomic Group, December 2011

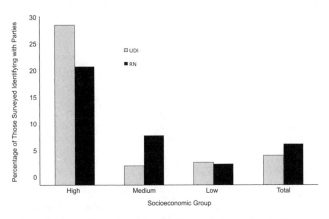

Source: Authors' compilation of data from CEP Poll 65 (December 2011), www.cepchile.cl.

Though the breakdown between UDI and RN has varied over time—in part due to the incentives of the binomial electoral system—the overall vote for the Alianza has not grown. The growth in electoral support for UDI has come at the expense of the former right-wing independents who were elected on the Alianza ticket.

Finally, Figure 3.7 shows Chileans' self-positioning on the ideological scale (1–10, Left to Right) before the 2009 presidential election. When asked about sympathy toward political parties or identification on the Left-Center-Right axis, half of Chileans identify as none. However, when asked to place themselves on the ideological scale, more than 70 percent do so. Figure 3.7 shows that two-thirds of Chileans who position themselves do so between the values 4 and 6. So, even though they might reject the classification of centrists, a majority of Chileans are moderate. Figure 3.7 also shows electoral preferences for the 2009 election. The line in Figure 3.7 shows the distribution of voters in each point in the Left-Right (1–10) scale. The bar shows the electoral preferences of those who voted. As expected, Piñera received the overwhelming support of those who placed themselves right of center. Piñera also received a third of the vote among centrists. The Concertación candidate Eduardo Frei also received a third of those votes, while Marco Enríquez-Ominami had the support of slightly less than a third of centrist voters. Piñera also attracted some support from left-of-center

Figure 3.7 Chileans Self-Positioning on Ideological Scale, 2009

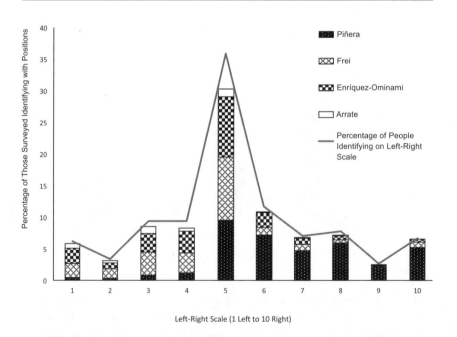

Left-Right Scale (1 Left to 10 Right)

Source: Authors' compilation of data from CEP Poll 61 (October 2009), www.cepchile.cl.

voters. Figure 3.7 shows voters perceiving Piñera as a moderate candidate capable of attracting support beyond the traditional right-wing constituency.

Conclusion

Since the restoration of democracy, a liberally oriented Right has sought to build a democratic Right free of the authoritarian legacy and committed to democratic principles. A more conservative Right has sought to build political power using the authoritarian enclaves of the 1980 constitution. As democracy consolidated and authoritarian enclaves were eliminated, the liberal position gained ground when it also became clear that the Right could be electorally competitive when adopting moderate positions.

It might have been the case that democracy consolidated despite the initial resistance of the Right, especially UDI, to eliminate authoritarian enclaves. However, as the protected democracy framework weakened, right-wing parties acquired political power by adopting moderate positions. That made the Right electorally competitive. The 1999 economic crisis made the Concertación vulnerable. The Alianza candidate, Joaquín Lavín, moved to the Center to take advantage of the opportunity. After 1999, all presidential elections have been fiercely fought as Concertación and Alianza candidates have championed moderate positions.

After being competitive in 1999 and 2005, the Alianza won a presidential contest in 2009, when Sebastián Piñera became the first democratically elected right-wing president since the end of the dictatorship. His victory represented a clear victory for the more liberal wing of the Alianza. To be sure, there are powerful groups within the Alianza, mostly associated with UDI, that continue to resist the adoption of more moderate policy positions championed by the more liberal wing of the Alianza. The government of President Piñera has found strong UDI opposition to some of its moderate reforms, from legislating on civil unions for same-sex couples to tax reform. The conservative forces have found an effective veto power in congress, as the electoral system is not sufficiently competitive and conservative legislators can secure a veto without majority electoral support. However, the Piñera administration has shown that, when aspiring to secure majoritarian electoral support and strong approval numbers in polls, the Alianza also responds by adopting positions that will be supported by voters who have overwhelmingly shown their moderation in post-Pinochet Chile.

As the Alianza builds the new political Right, tensions between a liberal pro-democracy wing and a conservative current will probably emerge in areas other than the convenience of the protected democracy framework. On social issues and modernizing reforms there are conflicting views among right-wing parties. As long as the electoral system forces RN and UDI to remain in an electoral coalition, those tensions will be played out in the same confrontational and occasionally self-destructive fashion observed since 1989.

Nonetheless, in terms of the themes of this volume, it is crucial to recognize that the Right was the other side of the Concertación coin when it came to the transitional model that dominated politics. Part of the temerity of the Concertación in pursuing more reforms was a product of fear of the potential reaction of the Right. In addition, many of the institutional and political limits on reform (including the binomial system and the high quorums for legislative reforms) were staunchly defended by the Right until the Alianza parties perceived that they could actually win power democratically and not just hold on to power by clinging to the authoritarian enclaves in the institutional setup. What is more, just as the transitional enclaves were the principal bases that shaped the Concertación's behavior, so too did the Right adapt and pursue a very similar set of transitional enclaves in its behavior, sometimes on the other side of negotiations, and sometimes reacting to the exigencies of the electoral system. Just as the combination of presidentialism, a multiparty system, and an electoral system with only two seats per district conditioned certain types of behavior for the Concertación, it also did so for the Right. Indeed, all of the enclaves (*el cuoteo*, elite control of candidate selection and electoral politics, party-dominated politics, elitist and extra-institutional policymaking, and the untouchability of the economic model inherited from the Pinochet government) were equally used and accepted by the Right. Thus, the enclaves of the transition pose just as much of a challenge for the Right as it moves forward as they do for the Concertación.

Note

This chapter was partially funded by FONDECYT Project No. 1120638, "How Electoral Preferences, Institutional Incentives and Internal Party/Coalition Politics Determine Who Wins and Who Loses in Legislative and Municipal Elections in Chile, 1989–2009."

4

Democratizing Chile Through Constitutional Reforms

Claudio A. Fuentes

In this chapter, I explore the political dynamic of democratizing political institutions in Chile, focusing on the Concertación. In 1980, the military regime imposed a constitution, establishing a set of antidemocratic institutions and procedures, which were rejected by most political actors at that time. The transition to democracy, therefore, implied two interconnected processes: a formal transfer of power from the military regime to a democratically elected government and the modification of essential features of the military regime's constitution to establish a free and open political system.

In sharp contrast to the overall trend of complete constitutional replacement, seen across South America as nations have transitioned to democracy, Chile has undergone a rather moderate and gradual process of constitutional amendment. We did not see political actors mobilizing their constituencies or calling for the abolition of such antidemocratic law immediately after the transition. Even within left-wing political parties, we observed moderate views about transforming the constitution and making it more democratic. Contrary to all intuitive expectations, during the transitional period in Chile neither political elites nor social actors addressed the subject head-on. Both opted instead for a very cautious, gradual strategy.

Indeed, within the South American context, Chile and Peru became the exceptions to the rule, as they both experienced a transition to democracy without the replacement of authoritarian provisions.[1] But what makes Chile truly unique is the absence of an open debate on the subject as soon as democracy was reestablished, as happened in other countries. Even in Peru, immediately after Fujimori left power in 2000, a commission for the study of constitutional reforms was established by the provisional government.[2] Thus, although we observe reforms in Chile, they were primarily the result of an elitist bargaining process.

Another characteristic of the Chilean case is that institutional barriers that were meant to hinder constitutional reform did not preempt political actors from changing the constitution. Indeed, several of the intuitive conditions predicted by the literature are not present in this case: no significant social groups pressured for reforms; no relevant political party in congress used the issue as a platform for mobilizing its constituency against the 1980 constitution; no significant economic or institutional crisis affected the country; and no significant change occurred in the balance of power between the main political forces in congress between 1990 and 2010. The story of constitutional reform in Chile is characterized by agreements among the elite, the influence of a few academic experts, and a lack of citizen engagement.

Summarizing this chapter, I argue that facing political and institutional restrictions, the pro-reform forces of the Concertación chose a gradual strategy that combined the avoidance of social and political confrontations with the opposition along with an elite-led bargaining process. As the political context changed and affected the existing balance of power, the pro–status quo forces of the Right engaged in constitutional reforms to retain some power in congress. Following the argument underlined by the editors of this volume, political restraints and patterns of behavior internalized during the transition resulted in an incremental process of reforms. However, as the political and social context changed after 2000, these restraints affected the latitude of leaders to engage in deeper reforms. I suggest three distinctive periods: from 1984 to 2000 in which actors "played by the rules"; from 2000 to 2005 in which actors decided to eliminate the authoritarian enclaves; and from 2005 to 2010 in which actors pushed for, and became more receptive to, democratic institutions. Gradualism and top-down bargaining processes are the two main features of this political process, which embody, I will argue, the essence of the political strategy designed by the Concertación. Paradoxically, this strategy was a key feature explaining the Concertación's success at the beginning of the transition and a lost election twenty years later. Despite variations in the depth and pace of reform throughout these periods, the enclaves of the transition did limit the capacity of leaders to formulate a completely new constitution.

Playing by the Rules, 1984–2000

Soon after the military coup in 1973, the military regime decided to reshape the Chilean institutional framework by promulgating a new constitution that was eventually approved by the military junta in 1980.[3] This arrangement established a combination of strong presidentialism, autonomy of the armed forces, and a complex system of checks and balances between different state institutions. In the original version of the constitution, presidential powers included a presidential term of eight years without the possibility of reelection; the power to dissolve the chamber once per presidential term; the power to nominate ministers, regional governors, provincial governors, ambassadors, and mayors; and the exclusive power to propose bills on issues concerning the budget, collective bargaining, social security, and the creation of new public services. At the same time, the constitution established greater levels of autonomy for some institutions, including the Constitutional Tribunal, the armed forces, and the Contraloría General.

Moreover, the constitution aimed to diminish the influence of political parties. First, it reduced the power of political parties at the local level by replacing elected officials with appointed mayors, and allowed for the creation of local and regional development councils in which members of the armed forces and the police had guaranteed seats. Second, it established a binomial electoral system, a unique device that, in practice, forces all parties to collaborate with one or two established coalitions to obtain a seat in congress. Third, it established a system of senatorial appointment, thereby increasing the influence of the armed forces within the political system. In the original scheme, appointed senators accounted for 25.7 percent of the Senate.[4] Finally, former presidents who had served terms of more than six years had the right to serve as senators for life.

Framers aimed to make constitutional reform extremely difficult for future authorities. For instance, in certain strategic areas the constitution established a special quorum of three-fifths or two-thirds for any constitutional reform.[5] Additionally, for certain chapters of the constitution, the approval of two consecutive legislatures was required. Finally, the constitution established so-called Leyes Orgánicas that also required a special quorum for approval (four-sevenths) and that involved a wide range of crucial themes, including institutional, political, social, and economic issues (Siavelis 2000).[6]

A concrete example may help to illustrate the distortions of the political system under this new rule. The constitution established that the head of the armed forces and the chief of police had fixed appointments of four years. The president could not remove them without the approval of the National Security Council (NSC); however, the military controlled the majority of votes (four out of seven votes). Two members of the NSC could also call a meeting if they considered the state to be under threat. Moreover, through the NSC, the head of military institutions appointed four senators and two members of the Constitutional Tribunal. Military institutions also held seats in regional and municipal development councils, the Council of Cinematography (responsible for revising and censuring movies and TV programs), and the National Mining Company (CODELCO) (see summary in Fuentes 2006).

Politicians had strong incentives to alter the existing balance of power prior to the transition but the story of reform was characterized by moderate and gradual changes. When the military regime called a referendum to ratify the constitution in September 1980, the opposition rebuffed this attempt by General Pinochet to perpetuate the armed forces' influence in the political process.

The opposition rejected the constitution on two grounds. First, it opposed the establishment of several antidemocratic clauses within the constitution that ran contrary to Chile's republican tradition. Second, it objected to the ratification process organized by the military dictatorship, which failed to incorporate basic conditions of fairness, freedom of expression, and transparency. As a matter of fact, the military regime called the referendum just one month in advance without allowing those who had rejected the new constitution to express their concerns or criticisms. Moreover, no independent electoral tribunal oversaw the referendum and vote counting was extremely irregular (Cavallo, Salazar, and Sepúlveda 2004).

The Christian Democratic Party (PDC), the only political party allowed to take part in political activities at that time, strongly rejected the plebiscite, stating, "this is an act of extreme violence and an offense to all the country. Under these conditions, the so-called plebiscite has no validity whatsoever and, as a consequence of that, all acts and powers originating from the new text are equally illegitimate and worthless" (in Cavallo, Salazar, and Sepúlveda 2004: 443–444).[7]

Despite the less than democratic characteristics of the plebiscite and the protestations of the then opposition, the 1980 plebiscite moved forward, being approved by a margin of 66 percent to 30 percent. With victory, the military government effectively set down the institutional and constitutional rules of the game.

Social protests against the military regime intensified, and in 1983 a group of moderate-center and leftist leaders signed a "Democratic Manifesto" offering a conciliatory path toward democracy. Through several proposals, they called upon the regime to provide a set of basic rights and securities "in order to create the necessary conditions for the reestablishment of democratic institutions, particularly through the establishment of a constituent assembly that included diverse political perspectives and the adoption of an electoral system that guarantees a free, informed and authentic expression of citizens' will."[8] Thus, until the early 1980s, most leaders of the opposition (even moderate actors) favored the idea of replacing the constitution as a condition for the establishment of a truly democratic political system.

But due to increasing levels of social unrest against the military regime, these actors were strongly divided on the best strategy for confronting the Pinochet regime. Three segments existed within the opposition. Some radical left-wing sectors believed that the only exit strategy available was to make the country ungovernable, through monthly social protests as well as the use of violent methods of challenging the regime. A more moderate Center-Left segment of the opposition believed strongly in social mobilization as the best strategy to push for change. This faction increasingly tried to distance itself from the radicals because the use of violent protest methods was seen as unacceptable by civil society and ineffective in weakening the regime.

Finally, a third segment within the opposition believed that the only option for advancing a peaceful transition to democracy was through negotiation with the military regime.

Across these groups, the question of the constitution was at the heart of the debate. Indeed, exit strategies were tightly related to the acceptance or rejection of the existing rules of the game. The debate within the opposition on whether to accept a negotiated solution intensified when, in 1983, moderate sectors of the opposition engaged in an informal but intense political dialogue with the minister of interior, Sergio Onofre Jarpa. While the opposition explicitly proposed the establishment of a constituent assembly, Jarpa stated that such an option was unacceptable for the military regime (in Cavallo, Salazar, and Sepúlveda 2004: 579).

By 1984, Patricio Aylwin, one of the most prominent leaders of the PDC, publicly recognized that the only way to promote a peaceful transition was to avoid the question of the legitimacy of the constitution, and therefore accept the armed forces as a veto player:

> The only advantage that he [Pinochet] has over me is the fact that the constitution is ruling—like it or not. This is part of a reality that I accept. How can we solve this impasse without suffering any humiliation? There is only one way: to deliberately avoid the question of the constitution's legitimacy. (Patricio Aylwin in Otano 1995: 18–19)

In August 1985 moderate sectors of the opposition and some right-wing political sectors supportive of the military regime signed the National Accord, calling for a peaceful and orderly transition to democracy, including free and fair elections. But this political document explicitly abandoned the idea of replacing the constitution. Instead, the document suggested a "constitutional accord" based on the approval of certain fundamental democratic principles including the popular election of congressional representatives, a more flexible mechanism for reforming the current constitution, the popular and direct election of the president, an autonomous constitutional tribunal, the regulation of states of exception, and the denouncement of any party that promoted the use of violence as "unconstitutional."[9]

Another crucial moment came in September 1986 after a failed attempt by a radical group called the Frente Patriótico Manuel Rodríguez (FPMR) to kill General Pinochet. This provided an impetus for the military regime to justify its repression of the opposition. The increasing political confrontation in the streets prompted several political actors to search for more peaceful options to end the regime. As José Joaquín Brunner pointed out at that time, "we need to make an explicit affirmation that the exit [from the military regime] cannot be found outside the limits imposed by the 1980 Constitution" (Brunner 1986: 5).

The same year Edgardo Boeninger, another influential PDC leader, sent a document to the head of his party, outlining what he considered the essential features of the path toward democracy. He underlined the need for "a political proposal based on the minimum number of constitutional reforms needed to ensure the transition to democracy, and the acceptance of the 1980 Constitution as a concrete fact from which reforms shall be materialized" (in Aylwin 1998: 319). After 1986, the debate within the opposition forces was not so much about the legitimacy of the constitution but about what kinds of reforms were likely to be proposed in the short term. Thus, the acceptance of an imposed institutional framework was the first limitation pro-reform forces had to face early in the transition. Any change would imply a political negotiation with veto powers once democracy would be reestablished.

Moreover, playing by the rules implied a high level of risk for the opposition; the military regime imposed a strict itinerary, which included a national plebiscite to ratify General Pinochet's appointment for eight more years. In Brunner's words (1990: 7), the opposition became a "constitutional force" as they agreed to play by the military regime's rules. The opposition accepted this challenge and in October 1988 it defeated Pinochet in the plebiscite. This allowed the opposition to gain some political momentum, which it could leverage into an extensive set of reforms to the constitution. Indeed, the Concertación, together with some of the more liberal segments of right-wing parties, organized a commission and proposed a set of essential reforms to the military regime.

Even though the regime invited representatives of the opposition to send their proposal to the government, the Junta Militar only submitted a limited set of reforms to a national referendum in July 1989. These reforms included a slight reduction in quorums for constitutional reforms in Leyes Orgánicas;[10] the elimination of the requirement that two consecutive legislatures approve issues covered by certain chapters of the constitution; the elimination of the executive power to dissolve the chamber; the establishment of a transitional government of four years without the possibility of reelection; the incorporation of the *contralor* in the National Security Council to help balance the relationship between civilians and the military; the indirect election of mayors by elected council members; the elimination of the clause proscribing parties that promote "totalitarian" doctrines; and an increase in the number of elected seats in the Senate from twenty-six to thirty-eight, reducing the portion of appointed senators from 25.7 percent to 19.1 percent, thereby reducing their power. Thus, this moderate reform allowed for the establishment of better conditions for future constitutional reforms (Heiss and Navia 2007).

According to the head of the Concertación's technical commission, Francisco Cumplido, several aspects remained untouched, including the electoral system, the appointed senators, and the mechanisms for constitutional reforms (Andrade 1991). The reform actually increased the military's autonomy by addressing the issues of military pensions, social security, and budget under the rules of a Ley Orgánica, thereby making it more difficult to approve changes to these systems. Moreover, the approved proposal actually increased the required quorums for reforms from three-fifths to two-thirds in certain sensitive areas, such as Chapter III (constitutional rights and duties) and Chapter XV (constitutional reform).

Even though the 1989 constitutional reform addressed fifty-six areas, the core features of the constitution remained practically untouched. Thus, in preparing the political platform for the 1989 presidential elections, the Concertación focused heavily on reforming the constitution. In fact, the first chapter of the Concertación programmatic document specifically addressed twelve constitutional reforms needed for the country.[11] The Concertación emphasized the need for a broad agreement among all social and political forces within the country to reform the constitution, even though any attempt to reform the constitution would still require foremost a political agreement in congress.

Did the Concertación's programmatic commitment translate into real action? The Concertación won four consecutive presidential terms but its approach toward the subject was quite different during the first two versus the third and fourth administrations. As soon as new Concertación political authorities took power in March 1990, they decided not to set political reforms as a priority. According to Edgardo Boeninger, Aylwin's secretary of the presidency, one of the programmatic goals of the new authorities was the democratization of political institutions. However, "if we acted like that [promoting reforms], it would produce a difficult and confrontational congressional debate with a high probability of rejection, given the signals sent by the most moderate rightist party Renovación Nacional, in the sense that the reforms were inappropriate at that time" (Boeninger 1997: 389). Thus, the first democratic government chose to look for the support of right-wing parties in economic subjects (tax reform, for instance), postponing its political reform platform.

Politically, President Aylwin chose a less confrontational strategy and accepted the relative autonomy of the armed forces. Just after Aylwin took office, Ricardo Lagos—his minister of education—suggested the idea of announcing just one critical reform: the reestablishment of the presidential power to remove high-ranking officers from the armed forces. Facing a tense moment at the beginning of the transition, President Aylwin responded, "I believe that doing something too strong is not convenient at this moment" (Ricardo Lagos in Politzer 1999: 149–150).

On May 21, 1990, just two months after taking office, President Aylwin delivered his first speech before congress. It was the new government's first opportunity to underscore its main priorities for the next four years. In an open contradiction to what previously had been an integral part of his political platform, President Aylwin excluded major political reforms, including the abolition of appointed senators and the reduction of the autonomy of the armed forces. Instead, he suggested that there was an auspicious political climate for promoting three specific reforms. The first was the democratization of municipal and regional administrations. The lack of political support from right-wing parties and the pragmatic decision to postpone more conflictive issues made by the executive branch explain this change. The second concerned the establishment of a truth and reconciliation commission to investigate human rights violations committed during the military regime. The third was the establishment of a commission to promote a comprehensive reform of the justice system.[12]

Thus, the government opted for a strategy that combined pragmatic agreements with right-wing parties in congress, and informal conflict resolutions with the military. The presence of the former dictator, General Pinochet, as commander in chief of the army increased political tension, and by the end of 1990 the country faced the first military challenge to civilian rule. Military officers complained about the government's investigation of an illegal business transaction between the army and Pinochet's son. Informal talks between key actors within the government and army officials helped reduce the level of hostility, but also reaffirmed the special status the armed forces had within the political process (Fuentes 2006).

One may think that in a political context of transition, and with Pinochet explicitly pressuring the new government, democratic authorities might look for the support of the general population to change certain rules. Even though the agenda of constitutional reforms was a potentially powerful political tool for bargaining with right-wing parties in congress, Aylwin was committed to avoiding the issue of reform. At the heart of this decision was a fear of provoking a strong military reaction, as well as the executive branch's early assessment that the Right would strongly support any military demands. Acting as veto players, right-wing parties made it clear to the new authorities that they would not make concessions regarding the institutional framework inherited from the military regime (Fuentes 2006). According to Manuel Antonio Garretón, the Aylwin administration was not guided by a comprehensive agenda for social democratization of the country, but rather by a case-by-case strategy of trying to obtain circumstantial majorities in congress to pass some legislation (Garretón 1993).

But did all leftist sectors within the governing coalition accept such a strategy? As one might expect, left-wing parties within the governing coalition (the Socialist Party [PS] and Partido por la Democracia [PPD]) emphatically rejected authoritarian enclaves such as appointed senators, the institutional involvement of the armed forces through the National Security Council, the existence of Leyes Orgánicas, and several constitutional clauses to protect military autonomy from civilian control, among others.

However, there were two factors that made political actors on the Left more hesitant to advance a reformist agenda. First, several representatives of the more moderate Left held key positions within the executive branch, which encouraged leftist parties to support the executive branch's viewpoint. Second, in a presidential system such as Chile's, it is hard to advance a reformist agenda without the sponsorship of the executive branch. Indeed, as several authors have pointed out (Morgenstern and Nacif 2002; Shugart and Carey 1992), in presidential systems the executive branch plays a key role in terms of legislative outcomes. Concerning the case of Chile, Siavelis correctly asserts that "the president has always been an important legislator, with the ability to dominate the legislative process given his agenda-setting ability, budgetary dominance, and areas of exclusive initiative. . . . In postauthoritarian Chile the president has been the most important legislative actor and perhaps the most important legislator" (2002a: 83–84). He adds though that these strong presidents often need to moderate their policies to satisfy coalition partners.

The executive branch in Chile enjoys strong powers, such as exclusive initiative in all legislation involving the provision of fiscal resources, including taxation; automatic approval of the budget if congress fails to approve it; the right to define what is being discussed in congress through the mechanism of "urgencies"; the existence of an "extraordinary period" in which congress can debate only the proposals sent by the executive branch; and access to a high level of expertise and important institutional capacities within the Ministry of the Presidency, which are used to write proposals and keep track of law-related issues (Siavelis 2002a). Another relevant executive power is the ability of ministers and their advisers to sit in on the assembly (particularly in congressional committees) and actually solicit the support of the chamber on any given piece of legislation (Cox and Morgenstern 2001).

Thus, any attempt at even minimal reforms was inhibited by both a strong executive branch that had clearly refused to address the constitution issue, and highly disciplined political parties within the governing coalition. The early decision made by key actors within the Concertación not to prioritize constitutional reforms along with the lack of social pressures to push for deeper reforms allowed the governing coalition to electorally succeed over time. The tally of bills submitted to congress between 1990 and 1994 is probably the best example of the Aylwin administration's success in advancing its political goals. Senators from the Concertación introduced only two bills aimed at eliminating authoritarian enclaves (the elimination of appointed senators and the presidential power to remove military officers). In both cases, the executive branch refused to sponsor the proposals, thereby significantly reducing the options of approval.[13] In June 1992, the executive branch introduced a bill in congress suggesting the modification of the electoral system, including the elimination of appointed senators. Along with the democratization of municipal elections, this was the only initiative led by the executive branch that addressed a fundamental aspect of the authoritarian enclaves. The proposal was rejected, three to two, in the Senate Commission of Constitution, Legislation, and Justice.[14]

The second democratic administration (Frei, 1994–2000) developed a relatively similar strategy with only some minor changes. After several overt cases of military insubordination in 1995, the government decided to signal its commitment to constitutional reform by introducing a legislative package that proposed the elimination of appointed senators, the modification of the Constitutional Tribunal, a significant reduction in power of the NSC, and the reestablishment of the presidential power to remove officers from the armed forces.[15] Several months later, the executive branch withdrew the proposal as no agreement could be reached in congress. In sum, the initial political commitment made by the governing coalition leaders toward a pragmatic and gradual approach became the source of success at the beginning of the transition and the source of discontent after the most significant constitutional reform was approved in 2005. Pro-reformers assumed that the only possible strategy was to promote an elite-led compromise with the right-wing opposition. Therefore, the only solution was to wait for a change in the political context to allow veto power players to open up to further reforms. As the Concertación chose not to actively change the political conditions (through mass mobilization, for instance), the chances for change heavily relied on pro–status quo forces. And this is what happened between 2000 and 2005.

Eliminating the Authoritarian Enclaves, 2000–2005

As previously mentioned, several political and strategic conditions made the first two post-transitional democratic governments more cautious about pushing an extensive agenda of constitutional reform.[16] Key actors within the executive branch decided not to address constitutional reforms, and political parties of the Concertación decided not to put political pressure over this chosen gradual strategy. But after 2000, during the Ricardo Lagos administration (2000–2006), Chile witnessed a more proactive executive branch. Although facing a similar balance of power in congress, the behavior of the executive branch differed significantly in the periods of 1990–1999 and 2000–2005. This difference is due to strategic as well as contextual conditions.

Indeed, the most relevant reform came—after five years of negotiation in congress between the Concertación and the right-wing coalition Alianza—in 2005, during the Lagos administration. The change included the elimination of appointed senators, including lifelong senatorial appointments for former presidents; a reform of the states of exception; the elimination of several prerogatives of the armed forces; restoration of the power of the president to remove the head of the armed forces and the chief of police by submitting a perfunctory report to congress; and a substantial reduction in the power of the National Security Council. Moreover, other institutional features were affected. These included a reduction of the presidential term to four years without the possibility of reelection; the elimination of the "extraordinary" period of sessions in congress, which reduced the executive branch's power to control congress's legislative agenda; the establishment of a congressional mechanism to summon members of the cabinet; an increase in congress's power to create investigative commissions; and the reform of the composition of the Constitutional Tribunal, among others.

The strategic shift happened after Lagos took office in March 2000. The political context helped him pursue a proactive strategy of encouraged agreement with the opposition. In 1998, General Pinochet left the army and was appointed senator for life. In October 1998 he was arrested in London and in March 2000 he returned to Chile after his release on medical grounds. In his inaugural speech before congress, Lagos addressed the constitutional issue by suggesting that "It is time to submit the constitution to an integral evaluation in order to adapt it to modern times as well as to give it all the legitimacy a superior law like this deserves."[17]

A few weeks later the president, attempting to promote a political agreement in the Senate, spoke to the president of the Senate, Christian Democrat Andrés Zaldívar. After an informal period of political consultations with key senators from the Concertación and Alianza, both parties agreed to submit two independent congressional bills in July 2000.[18] This was a key moment in setting the agenda for reform. While the Concertación's original proposal involved the elimination of most authoritarian enclaves, the Alianza submitted a more moderate set of reforms. Essentially, both segments agreed upon eliminating the appointment of senators, reforming the Constitutional Tribunal, increasing the legislature's oversight of the executive branch, and making probity a duty for public servants.

The Concertación proposed a bill that incorporated the elimination of enclaves, the reduction of military powers, and the proposal of a proportional electoral system. But the Concertación introduced other topics as well, such as making national citizenship easier, transitioning from a mandatory toward a voluntary voting system, reducing the presidential term from six to four years, and promoting the recognition of indigenous rights. The Alianza, in contrast, did not make any reference to military powers, although it did try to reduce the power of the executive branch. The Alianza did this by incorporating into its bill proposals such as reducing the executive branch's ability to transfer resources from one agency to another without congressional approval, and increasing the required quorums on subjects concerning public spending. Moreover, the Alianza attempted to reduce the influence of international law in Chile by mandating the enactment of a constitutional amendment before the president could sign any international treaty that would affect national norms (see Table 4.1).

Proposals were debated in the Senate for more than four years, until November of 2004. Different versions of the proposals were sent to the Senate Commission on the Constitution, Justice, and Legislature (SCCJL) three times and were discussed on the floor the same number of times. A critical juncture took place in November 2001, when the SCCJL delivered a report of over 600 pages addressing the basis for the agreement between the Concertación and the Alianza. In November 2004, the proposal was transferred to the Chamber of Deputies, and six months later it was sent back to the Senate.

The constitution does not make any provision for the type of conflicts that arose between the two chambers during the negotiation of this bill in November 2004. To solve this political impasse, the executive branch introduced twenty-seven presidential vetoes for those subjects that the two chambers did not agree upon. Then, between June and August of 2005, the executive branch and the legislature established an informal commission to solve all pending issues.

The executive branch played a crucial role in setting the agenda, promoting informal agreements on divisive issues, and proposing alternative courses of action for legislators. Indeed, even though the proposals formally emerged from the Senate, the executive branch took a leading role in setting the agenda by promoting specific initiatives and by restricting the scope of issues to be considered on the floor.

Table 4.1 Concertación and Alianza Proposals Submitted to Congress, 2005

	Concertación	Alianza
Similarities in original proposal	Elimination of appointed senators[a] Modification of Constitutional Tribunal composition[a] Empowerment of Constitutional Tribunal Mechanisms to fulfill vacancies in the legislature Increased legislative oversight of the executive branch[a] Incompatibility of certain professions with being a legislator Probity	
Discrepancies negotiated in congress	Citizenship Control over the military[a] Regulation of civil society organizations Presidential term reduction	Regionalization
Discrepancies that ended with no agreement	Proportional electoral system[a] Indigenous rights Voluntary voting	Presidential power to make budget transfers Increased quorums in areas affecting public spending Public safety definitions International law

Sources: Bulletins 2534-07 and 2526-07, Chilean Congress.
Note: a. Proposals traditionally considered the "authoritarian enclaves."

The acting government knew that any constitutional amendment would require the opposition's cooperation. It also knew that the best place to achieve a minimum consensus was in the Senate. During the entire negotiation, the executive branch's strategy was to narrow down the scope of issues to be addressed in deliberations. In introducing the goals of the executive branch, the chief of cabinet, José Miguel Insulza, clearly stated that "the purpose of this reform is not to promote new improvements to the constitution but to take care of what is the essential core of the original 1980 constitution, that is, the idea of a protected democracy."[19] He rejected the attempts of some Concertación senators to increase the number of issues discussed in the reform, such as probity, freedom of expression, referendum initiatives, and other relevant subjects. Insulza stated that "all these issues are of great importance for the improvement of the constitution, but we need to address them once we have changed the essence of this agreement."[20]

During the first debates at the SCCJL some senators explicitly recognized the need to broaden the scope of constitutional reforms. Senator Boeninger, for instance, mentioned that if the idea was to draft a text that endures over time "we cannot exclude some relevant issues, such as the executive power to remove an officer or the reform of the military justice system. The purpose should be to achieve stable texts that resist long periods without significant reforms. My concern is that after approving these reforms, new voices may emerge asking for new amendments. This would be a diminished result, a failure."[21] Moreover, Senator José Antonio Viera-Gallo (PS) introduced the need to regulate states of exception, an issue that was not considered in the original proposal.

The executive branch followed the entire debate in congress very closely. Minister Insulza personally attended most sessions during discussions in the Senate and his advisers acted as colegislators by introducing amendments to ongoing proposals, submitting new indications,[22] and making informal recommendations to representatives in congress. Table 4.2 shows the number of proposals submitted to the SCCJL, where the original proposal of the constitutional reform had been outlined. Appointed senators were the most active but at the same time the least successful actors. The most successful institutional actors in getting proposals approved were the Concertación followed by the executive branch and the Alianza.

The Ministry of the Interior established a team of constitutional lawyers who followed the debate in the Senate closely and proposed alternatives to the discussion through formal indications to ongoing debates in different commissions.[23] Minister Insulza personally briefed the president on a regular basis and negotiations were discussed during Sunday presidential meetings with the executive political committee.[24] The executive branch established informal contacts with key actors in congress to negotiate agreements and propose consensual drafts on specific articles. According to deputy Jorge Burgos (PDC), a member of the Commission on the Constitution in the Chamber of Deputies,

Table 4.2 Proposals Submitted to the SCCJL, July 2000–June 2001

	Proposed	Withdrawn	Inadmissible	Rejected	Approved[a]
Executive	41	7	5	23	6 (14.6%)
Concertación senators	78	0	26	37	15 (19.2%)
Alianza senators	110	1	34	59	16 (14.5%)
Appointed senators	115	4	26	81	4 (3.4%)
Total	344	12	91	200	41 (11.9%)

Source: Historia de la Ley 20.050, Biblioteca del Congreso de Chile.
Notes: N = 344.
a. Percentage of total amendments presented by actor.

> I debated the topic with two key actors within the executive branch: Gonzalo García and Jorge Correa—both at the Ministry of the Interior. But I spoke with them as constitutionalist lawyers and comrades of the same political party [the Christian Democratic Party]. . . . I remember I stayed with them, debating specific topics many times after the commission's sessions. We always informed Minister Insulza, though. I think Carlos Carmona was also relevant in this exchange of views.[25]

By early 2005, more than two hundred indications were pending approval. The government supported the creation of an informal advisory group including academic lawyers close to the Concertación and the Alianza. In one expert's words,

> At some point toward the end of 2004, Carlos Carmona called me and asked me to be part of a plural group of constitutional experts, to promote an agreement in the Chamber of Deputies concerning particularly, but not exclusively, the reforms of the Constitutional Tribunal. . . . I personally talked with the President of the Commission on the Constitution at the chamber several times. We talked privately with several deputies. We sent draft proposals back and forth to the presidency, and then to our deputies in order to achieve an agreement.[26]

A second crucial moment came in June 2005 when the Chamber of Deputies sent the proposal back to the Senate. As previously mentioned, the constitution does not contain any provision to address eventual discrepancies between the two chambers concerning constitutional amendments. The executive branch proposed the use of vetoes to solve this impasse, and established an informal commission in which members of both chambers as well as the executive branch participated to achieve a final agreement. As Gonzalo García—one of the Minister of the Interior's key advisers on this reform—explains, twenty-seven objections needed to be resolved:

> I headed up some of the last informal negotiations on the vetoes on behalf of the executive branch. I participated in several more private meetings with members of Congress and of the Constitutional Tribunal. It was not properly a "negotiation" but a high-level scrutiny of the constitutional correctness of the reforms. . . . We needed to establish a balance between the Chamber of Deputies and the Senate. . . . Some vetoes were related to more stylistic issues and others to more substantive issues. Plus, two more issues were incorporated within the vetoes concerning freedom of expression and professional associations.[27]

By drafting the final proposals through the use of vetoes, the executive branch obtained a critical advantage. This informal mechanism also allowed members of the executive branch to request the opinion of experts and other state powers. For instance, right-wing parties asked the executive branch that some of the members of the Constitutional Tribunal have access to the final draft. Gonzalo García mentions that,

> indeed, congressional representatives delegated to us the power to write the final draft of the constitutional agreement. At some point, the opposition requested that members of the Constitutional Tribunal check one of the drafts, which was very complicated from an institutional point of view. But we accepted that proposal since right-wing parties trusted the judges' advice on the subjects we were negotiating.[28]

To gain understanding about who the key players were, I created a ranking system based on the number of indications approved by congress during the first debate at the SCCJL, as well as actors' perceptions of who was most relevant to this reform. As shown in Table 4.3, fewer than thirty people—including government representatives, legislators, and experts—are recognized as key players in the reform. Interestingly, during most of the negotiation, the subject of key players was not part of the debate in the national press. Additionally, very few actors from civil society were involved in the extensive process of negotiations in congress, confirming this volume's contentions concerning the very elitist form of policymaking that became the norm as a result of the transitional enclaves that characterized Chilean democracy during the years of the Concertación.

Thus, the executive branch had institutional as well as political tools to push its agenda. Facing the end of the government in 2005, and with more than two hundred pending indications, the government pressured for the quick closure of an agreement that omitted several of the programmatic issues the Concertación had promoted.

A wide range of substantial topics was left out of the political discussion in 2000 since none of the political parties represented in congress introduced them. These topics included revising quorums for constitutional reforms, the existence of eighteen Leyes Orgánicas with high quorums, the constitutional prohibition of union leaders' running for public office, the elimination of the constitutional clause making abortion illegal under any circumstance, the acceptance of the death penalty in the constitution under a qualified quorum, and the consideration of the "family" as the essential institution of the society along with the duty of the state to promote and strengthen it. The executive branch's strategy of narrowing the reform to a limited number of subjects, combined with the absence of required quorums for approval in congress as well as the lack of active social support for these reforms made it very hard for progressive forces to even suggest these proposals.[29]

Progressive sectors of the coalition attempted, unsuccessfully, to work certain topics into the debate, including a more substantial reform of the electoral system, the constitutional recognition of indigenous rights, and the

Table 4.3 Key Players in the 2005 Constitutional Reform

	Executive Branch	Senators	Deputies	Experts
First level	Carmona, C. (PDC) Correa S., J. (PDC) García, G. (PDC) Insulza, J. M. (PS) Lagos, R. (PS)	Boeninger, E. (PDC) Chadwick, A. (UDI) Espina, A. (RN) Larraín, H. (UDI) Viera Gallo, J. (PS) Zaldívar, A. (PDC)	Ascencio, A. (PDC) Burgos, J. (PDC) Bustos, J. (PS) Paya, D. (UDI)	
Second level	Kleissac, J. (PDC) Vidal, F. (PPD)	Diez, S. (RN) Hamilton, J. (PDC) Romero, S. (RN)	Ceroni, G. (PPD) Guzmán, P. (RN) Riveros, E. (PDC)	Cumplido, F. (PDC) Gómez, G. (Ind) Nogueira, H. (PDC) Zuñiga, F. (PS)

Sources: Fifteen author interviews with key actors.
Note: This is a qualitative scale (listed in alphabetical order within each group) based on (a) the number of congressionally approved indications each senator or deputy submitted, ranking them as high, medium, or low; and (b) key actors' perceptions of each other's influence within the process.

recognition of Chile not just as a democratic but as a "social and democratic state, inspired in principles of freedom, equality and pluralism."[30]

One of the most sensitive areas was the reform of the electoral system. The Concertación originally proposed replacing it with a proportional system of representation, but the Right was simply not willing to discuss the topic. By 2005, the Concertación and the opposition in congress still had not reached an agreement regarding the subject. As a way to demonstrate his own commitment to change, President Lagos began to pressure political actors to reform the electoral system.[31]

Negotiations ended with the Alianza's accepting elimination of reference to the binomial system in the constitution, transferring it to the Ley Orgánica of electoral procedures. This changed the quorum for approval of an eventual reform from three-fifths to four-sevenths. However, the new version of the constitution also dictated the number of deputies in the chamber. As a result, any significant change to the electoral system (anything that would alter the total number of deputies) would be considered a constitutional reform, and would require three-fifths of the votes. In President Lagos's words,

> I did not consider it acceptable that the reference to the binomial system would be in the constitution. The final arrangement was the typical "Chilean way": we took the subject out of the constitution and reduced the quorum to reform the system but we left some subjects in the constitution. I did not like this part because the agreement was taken by the incumbents based on strategic calculus. The agreement was done with a calculator.[32]

Overall, during the Lagos administration the executive branch was particularly proactive about collaborating on a legislative agreement with the opposition. It invested the time and resources needed to reach an agreement and to advance a substantial transformation of the constitution. The executive branch acted as colegislator, taking advantage of the political circumstances, setting the agenda, limiting the scope of topics to be discussed, and promoting agreements through formal and informal mechanisms of consensus building among political actors.

Obviously, the outcome of the reform also depended on the willingness of those with veto power to accept a change to the status quo. As previously noted, the balance of power in congress has not changed dramatically since the transition to democracy, so why did the opposition accept the proposed constitutional changes? The answer is that some key actors within the right-wing opposition decided to start negotiations with the government using a "forward-looking" strategy as they perceived that it was in the interest of the Right to agree to changes. Equally important, with the passage of time the presidential appointment powers that once had benefited the Right by allowing the dictatorship to appoint officials throughout a series of governmental institutions began to benefit the Concertación as the latter's appointees worked their way up through the ranks of various institutions.

The 1999 presidential election was a key moment for the opposition. In December 1999, the right-wing candidate Joaquín Lavín almost tied candidate Ricardo Lagos in the first round and trailed by 2.62 percent of the votes in the second round (a difference of approximately 190,000 votes) (see Table 4.4). At the same time, public opinion supported the reform of the armed forces' role, as the arrest of General Pinochet in London had substantially increased support for human rights and diminished military prestige (Fuentes 2006; Varas, Fuentes, and Aguero 2008).

Programmatically, it was hard for the Alianza to support reform in areas they had defended since the beginning of the transition. The Alianza also faced internal pressure from former collaborators of the military regime, such as UDI senator Sergio Fernández (former minister of the interior) and military officers appointed as senators in 1998, such as former chief of the navy, Jorge Martínez-Busch; former chief of the air force, Ramón Vega; former general, Julio Canessa; and former director of the police, Fernando Cordero.[33]

However, key leaders from both of the parties in the Alianza (Renovación Nacional and UDI) decided to support reforms in critical areas such as the reduction of military power and the elimination of appointed senators. From a political perspective, approving these reforms would put the Alianza more in tune with overall public opinion, which called for the reduction of military powers and demanded recognition of the human rights abuses committed during the military regime. Indeed, a survey published in May 1999 showed that even though the society was highly polarized on the past human rights violations, 69 percent of respondents supported the idea of bringing Pinochet to justice. The overall rates of public approval toward the opposition remained practically the same between 1996 and 2001 (an av-

Table 4.4 Presidential Election Results, 1999 (percentage of votes received)

	First Round, December 1999	Second Round, January 2000
Ricardo Lagos (Concertación)	47.96	51.31
Joaquín Lavín (Alianza)	47.51	48.69
Other candidates	4.53	N/A

Source: Data from www.elecciones.gov.cl.

erage of 17.3 percent), half of what the Concertación obtained in the same period (34.4 percent on average).[34] Moreover, by 1995 public opinion was particularly favorable toward making important reforms to the constitution (66 percent support), and by 2004, 68 percent of respondents agreed upon the idea of approving the constitutional reforms discussed in congress.[35]

Between 2000 and 2004 three critical factors made the Alianza distance itself from the armed forces, and particularly from General Pinochet. First, a 2001 roundtable on human rights sponsored by the government established several important recommendations. One of these was that the armed forces provide more information on the location of thousands of detained citizens who had disappeared during the military regime. Second, the Lagos administration pushed for a second Presidential Commission on torture and imprisonment. The commission's final report had a significant and positive public impact on the national debate on human rights. In fact, a survey conducted just after the report was delivered showed that 70.7 percent of respondents thought the report had a positive impact.[36] Finally, the reputation of General Pinochet was seriously damaged after an investigation was carried out in the United States. It revealed that Pinochet had more than US$13 million in several bank accounts at the Riggs Bank in Washington, DC (Fuentes 2006).

The Alianza also considered eventual shifts in the future balance of power in congress. After the initial appointment of senators by General Pinochet (nine appointed senators in 1990) the balance of power gradually started to favor the Center-Left coalition. If this trend were to continue, by 2005 President Lagos would be able to appoint three of his supporters directly to the Senate. Lagos, along with former president Frei, would also merit the personal right to serve as senator for life. Even though this shift would not be sufficient to promote constitutional reforms, it would eventually give the majority of the Senate to the Concertación.

Alianza representatives quickly understood the new political reality. In July 2000 they recognized that, "In our opinion, ending this period of transition would allow us to respond to the message sent to us by the majority of the electorate in the last presidential election, which is a demand for the reestablishment of social peace in this country."[37] Following the party's new message, Senator Andrés Chadwick stated, "our political sector has reconsidered some of its positions, as political circumstances now favor new steps [toward constitutional reform]."[38]

Thus, within right-wing parties a forward-looking decisionmaking process was at play. Because of the political context, the Right was more open to reducing the power of the armed forces. It was also more open to critical reforms related to the Pinochet regime's legacy. The most sensitive of these issues was the institution of appointed senators, which the Right was willing to eliminate as early as 2000. The Alianza's strategy was to accept the elimination of some authoritarian enclaves (appointed senators and reduction of military powers), increase the legislature's oversight of the executive branch, and reduce some of the executive branch's fiscal powers, such as its ability to reallocate resources.

The final outcome of the reform was less than the Concertación had aimed for but certainly more than what right-wing parties originally proposed in 2000. Overall, this outcome can be attributed to the combination of a proactive executive branch that was willing to use its political power to achieve a compromise between the governing coalition and the opposition and key actors within the opposition who were willing to transform the status quo. As we will observe in the next section, this significant constitutional reform created divisions within the Concertación as some pro-reformers thought more substantive changes needed to be addressed. Moreover, for the first time after the transition, some sectors of the coalition demanded not just further reforms but the rewriting of the entire constitution through a participatory process. Thus, even though the elimination of most authoritarian enclaves was highly significant, the actual process of reforming the constitution revealed the attachment of the political elite to the same practices that dominated the transition period: an elite-led bargaining model with practically no popular input.

Deepening Democracy, 2005–2010

Gradualism was an essential component of the Concertación's strategy to reform the constitution. After the elimination of the most significant authoritarian enclaves in 2005, a new agenda emerged within the coalition. During the Bachelet administration, new proposals were sent to and approved by congress. This inaugurated a new period of reforms, which included the approval of the Statute of Rome creating the International Criminal Court, a reform of regional government that permitted greater levels of decentralization, a constitutional shift from compulsory to voluntary voting, the declaration of Easter Island as a special territory, and reforms on the quality of politics and probity among public administrators.

Looking at the big picture we see two crucial moments: 1989, when congress enacted a set of relatively unsubstantial reforms, which were nevertheless critical in paving the way for future agreements; and 2005, when congress eliminated the authoritarian enclaves and reshaped certain state institutions, thereby producing a slightly different balance of power more favorable to the congress and the Constitutional Tribunal. Between 1990 and March 2010 the executive and legislative branches submitted a total of 342 bills, in the form of messages (*mensajes*) by the executive branch or motions (*mociones*) by legislators. On average, 17.1 constitutional reform proposals were debated in congress every year (see Table 4.5).

Some characteristics of this political process are worth noting. First, the executive branch's role in submitting and sponsoring bills is an integral component of the Chilean political system. Seventy-one percent of the proposals approved by congress were originally submitted by the executive branch. Of the remaining 29 percent of the proposals, the executive branch also played a significant role in sponsoring them.

Second, as the democratic transition evolved, themes crucial to reform were increasingly debated. It was during the Lagos administration that more substantial, and therefore divisive, issues were discussed in congress. That is why, on average, a proposal submitted during the Lagos administration took almost four years to be approved. Long periods of negotiations led to the approval of the Statute of Rome (eighty-five months), the reform of regional governments (seventy months), the crucial 2005 reform eliminating the authoritarian enclaves (sixty-one months), and the elimination of the compulsory voting system (fifty-eight months).

Third, we would expect political activity to decrease following the crucial August 2005 agreement, which eliminated authoritarian enclaves. However, figures show a rather significant increase in the number of proposals, particularly those submitted by congressional representatives. In this section, I will examine the conditions that led to this abrupt change.

The election of Michelle Bachelet as president in January 2006 brought new hope for the Concertación coalition. For the first time since the reestablishment of democracy, the governing coalition held not only the presidency but also a relative majority in both chambers (see Table 4.6). Even though the legislative majority was not large enough to pass constitutional reforms without the support of the opposition, the political climate still favored a new political agenda. From the very beginning, President Bachelet proclaimed her government as a "citizens' government."

In terms of the executive branch's initiative to send bills to congress, Bachelet's was not much different from previous administrations, sending an average of 2.75 proposals per year (eleven in total). What was different was the tone of the new government's political agenda, which proposed fundamental changes to the electoral system, the elimination of the fixed number of deputies written into the constitution (to allow for future reform of the electoral system), increased access to information and government transparency, a process whereby citizens could initiate bills, recognition of indigenous people's rights, and protection of water rights. Most initiatives were aimed at empowering citizens vis-à-vis other powers of the state and citizen empowerment became a key topic for the new administration.

Table 4.5 Constitutional Proposals Debated by Congress, 1990–2010

	Bills Introduced by Executive Branch	Bills Introduced by Congressional Representatives	Total Bills (average per year)	Bills Approved (executive initiative)	Average Duration Bills Were Debated
Aylwin, 1990–1994	8	33	41 (10.2)	3 (3)	4.3 months
Frei, 1994–2000	13	78	91 (15.2)	10 (6)	20.8 months
Lagos, 2000–2006	8	58	66 (11.0)	8 (5)	41.8 months
Bachelet, 2006–2010	11	133	144 (36.0)	3 (3)	20.3 months
Total	40	302	342 (17.1)	24 (17)	25.6 months

Source: Legislative Database, Biblioteca del Congreso.
Note: In this case, proposals are considered single bills submitted to congress that deal with one or more issues. Under "Bills Approved" we consider the year of the submission of the proposal when counting the bill, irrespective of when it was passed.

**Table 4.6 Balance of Power in Congress, 1990–2014
(percentage of seats)**

	Concertación	Alianza	Independent
Chamber of Deputies			
1990–1994	60.0	40.0	–
1994–1998	58.3	41.7	–
1998–2002	58.3	41.7	–
2002–2006	52.5	47.5	–
2006–2010	54.2	45.8	–
2010–2014	47.5	48.3	4.2
Senate			
1990–1994	46.8	53.2	–
1994–1998	44.7	55.3	–
1998–2002	50.0	50.0	–
2002–2006	50.0	50.0	–
2006–2010	52.6	44.7	2.7
2010–2014	52.6	44.7	2.7

Sources: Data from www.elecciones.gob.cl and www.bcn.cl.

A detailed analysis of the proposals submitted under different administrations reveals some interesting features. As one may expect, there was a shift in the topics that the governing coalition parties aimed to address through congressional initiatives (see Table 4.7). While during the Aylwin, Frei, and Lagos administrations the governing coalition mostly emphasized the removal of the authoritarian enclaves, during the Bachelet period there was greater attention to issues concerning representation and civil, social, and political rights. In this sense, the strategy of acting in gradual steps (removing the authoritarian enclaves first, and addressing other social and political reforms second) permeated the whole coalition. Between 1990 and 2005 moderation was at the core of the governing coalition's political agenda. By 2006, congressional representatives of the Center-Left coalition began to address more emphatically new issues including social, labor, property, environmental, and sexual and reproductive rights.

If the balance of power did not change significantly before or after the constitutional reform of 2005, what are the factors explaining renewed interest in reforming the constitution in key areas during the Bachelet administration? There are institutional as well as political incentives accounting for this shift. From an institutional point of view, at the end of 2005 the executive branch promoted a procedural change in the approval of new legis-

Table 4.7 Constitutional Reform Bills Submitted to Congress by Concertación Representatives, 1990–2010

	Total	Aylwin (1990– 1994)	Frei (1994– 2000)	Lagos (2000– 2006)	Bachelet (2006– 2010)
Total number of constitutional reform bills submitted	273	20	74	80	99
Reforms concerning balance of power, Constitutional Tribunal, armed forces, states of exception, and probity (%)	56.8	60.0	67.6	58.8	46.6
Reforms concerning electoral systems, representation, parties, citizen participation, decentralization, and intermediary groups (%)	17.2	30.0	14.9	13.8	19.2
Reforms concerning civil, political, and social rights; "social democratic state"; taxes; and role of the state in administering the economy (%)	24.9	10.0	17.6	25.0	33.3
Public safety (%)	1.1	–	–	2.5	1.1

Source: Elaborated by the author using database of bill proposals on constitutional reforms at www.camara.cl.

lation that allowed the authors of proposals to be recognized in new laws. Thus, legislators had a stronger incentive to propose bills to increase their political visibility and gain recognition.

But this alone does not sufficiently explain the shift in the legislative agenda. Legislators know that bills proposed by congressional representatives are still much less likely to be approved than those proposed by the executive branch. Another important factor is the change in the political environment that took place within the coalition. Relevant actors in the Concertación were disappointed by the 2005 constitutional agreement, arguing that a new wave of reforms was required to fully democratize the country.

Indeed, after the reforms were approved in congress, President Lagos stressed that "Chile now has a constitution that is not dividing us; what we have now is a shared institutional setting from which we can continue making improvements to our democracy. . . . Chile deserved a democratic constitution, according to international standards, and this is what the Congress has just ratified."[39] But soon after this declaration, Senator Andrés Zaldívar (PDC) mentioned the need to discuss new constitutional reforms, including the reform of the electoral system and the required quorum to reform laws. Moreover, Senator Carlos Ominami (PS) suggested the establishment of a constituent commission to propose a new constitution by 2010, the bicentennial anniversary of Chilean independence.[40]

Then, in April 2008, the Chamber of Deputies established a special commission to study the Chilean political system. The commission, led by Deputy Marco Enríquez-Ominami (PS), proposed several modifications to the political system, although it failed to reach a consensus in crucial areas such as the establishment of a semipresidential system, the attenuation of presidential powers, and changes to the duration of the presidential term. In September 2008 senator and former president Eduardo Frei (PDC) took the political establishment by surprise when he proposed the ratification of a new constitution: "We have tried to amend this constitution but it has not been enough. This constitution was designed with an authoritarian logic, in fear of liberties."[41] Following this declaration, the centrist and leftist political elite engaged in an intense debate on the need to establish a new constitution. As a result the political platforms of the three candidates running during the 2009 presidential election—representatives of centrist and leftist parties—each included some reference to a new constitution.

Running as the Concertación's presidential candidate in 2009, Senator Frei reiterated his proposal for a national debate on the establishment of a new constitution (see quote in Fuentes 2010: 68–69). His political platform comprised a significant set of reforms, including increasing the power of the legislative branch, increasing the length of the president's term in office, a popular initiative for lawmaking, implementing mandatory primary elections, incorporating new social and economic rights into the constitution, merging certain ministries together, creating a new ministry of social policy, and increasing accountability of the Central Bank and the Constitutional Tribunal, among others.

Even though the Concertación political elite supported substantial reforms, they disagreed strongly on the best way to achieve that goal. For instance, some political actors wanted to continue the strategy of promoting reforms through congressional consensus. Others instead suggested the formation of a presidential commission, composed of experts and party representatives who would draft a proposal for a new constitution. Still others demanded a national referendum on the subject.[42]

The internal division within the Concertación's political elite is another factor in the story. Certain political actors in congress, who generally supported the coalition, had still adopted a critical stance toward many of the coalition's approaches to key issues. However, following the coalition's new agenda in 2005, dissent among certain senators and deputies from the more conservative or most leftist sectors of the coalition increased. This trend resulted in four senators' and eight deputies' abandoning the coalition between 2005 and 2009. A group of Christian Democrats joined the Partido Regionalista Independiente (PRI), one senator joined Chile-Primero, and several others supported Marco Enríquez-Ominami's presidential candidacy.[43] As a result, political actors strove to distinguish themselves from one another, inaugurating a period of more individualistic party politics. The traditional approaches of Concertación leaders were criticized by leftist actors, who demanded social and political rights, as well as by conservative actors, who focused on the demands of the middle class.

These changes did not automatically translate into less cooperation within the coalition. As a matter of fact, an analysis of the proposals concerning constitutional reform submitted by legislators demonstrates two collaborative trends within the Concertación parties (see Table 4.8). First, there is a decrease in the percentage of bills presented by single parties (from 56.3 percent during the Aylwin period to 10.5 percent during the Bachelet period). Second, during the Bachelet period, Concertación legislators maintained the strategy developed during the Lagos administration: cosponsoring bills with other parties within the coalition (28.6 percent) and cosponsoring bills with at least one of the opposition parties (25.6 percent).

In such a fragmented political environment, one may expect the emergence of traditional cleavages in the coalition, such as increasing levels of

Table 4.8 Constitutional Reform Bills Submitted by Individuals and Alliances, 1990–2010

	Bills Submitted Individually		Bills Submitted with Other Parties Within or Outside the Coalition			
	Alianza	Concertación	Alianza[a]	Concertación[b]	Mix[c]	Total
Aylwin	6 (18.7)	18 (56.3)	1 (3.1)	4 (12.5)	3 (9.4)	32
Frei	27 (34.6)	20 (25.6)	3 (3.8)	9 (11.5)	19 (24.4)	78
Lagos	17 (29.3)	10 (17.2)	4 (6.9)	17 (29.3)	10 (17.2)	58
Bachelet	38 (28.6)	14 (10.5)	9 (6.8)	38 (28.6)	34 (25.6)	133
Total	88 (29.2)	62 (20.6)	17 (5.6)	68 (22.6)	66 (21.9)	301

Source: Compiled by the author using database of bill proposals on constitutional reforms at www.camara.cl. It includes all bills submitted in congress by deputies and senators.

Notes: Percentages are in parentheses.

a. Proposals introduced by UDI and RN.

b. Proposals introduced by more than one party from the Concertación (PDC, PS, PPD, or PRSD).

c. Proposals introduced by at least one party of the Alianza and one party of the Concertación.

cooperation between Christian Democrats and rightist parties on issues concerning family and values. But at least until March 2010 this was not the case. In very few instances (five out of fifty-six proposals) Christian Democrats sponsored bills with UDI or RN—the two rightist parties. Thus, while the political dynamics after 2005 were much more divisive, this did not translate into a significant change in patterns of alliances and cooperation in congress. Overall, the governing coalition was able to develop a collaborative strategy within the coalition and with individual parties from the opposition. In contrast, the parties comprising the Alianza developed a rather uncooperative strategy, preferring to act individually.

Conclusion

In this chapter, I delineate the process of transition to democracy in Chile employing three distinct periods: from the mid-1980s until 2000, a period in which the Concertación decided to play by the rules inherited from the military regime; from 2000 to 2005, when basic features of the constitution were reformed but following the same strategic features defined in the previous period; and post-2005, a period in which a new agenda of democratizing institutions was debated.

Studying the way constitutional reforms have been enacted allows us to understand some of the key features of the governing coalition's strategy. First, an essential characteristic of the reform process has been a methodical, step-by-step approach to reform (removing authoritarian enclaves first, democratizing the constitution second). On the one hand, gradualism has allowed actors to break through impasses imposed by the constitution. On the other hand, this strategy has led to a set of political institutions with little coherence. The never-ending process of reform negotiations is partially explained by the fact that the political elite lack a comprehensive agreement on the basic rules of the game. One moment the elite support a four-year presidential term with no possibility of reelection, and the next they suddenly argue that such a term is too short to carry out any meaningful work.

In this sense, the strategy developed by the Concertación allowed it to overcome the strong veto power of the military and right-wing parties that acted cohesively at the beginning of the transition period. Indeed, the political strategy designed early in the transition partially explains the success of the governing coalition.

A second feature of the coalition's strategy is the elite-led process of bargaining and agreement on fundamental political reforms (a reality underlined in both Chapter 1 and Chapter 14, as well as in Siavelis's Chapter 2, of this volume). Political reforms have involved a relatively small group of politicians and policy experts, most of whom are constitutionalist lawyers. They were present during the 1989 reform negotiations and at several important junctures after the democratization in 1990. They also played key roles in the 2005 constitutional reform. Facing a political opportunity for reform after 2000, political leaders of the governing coalition followed the very same path of the transitional period, including a moderate set of proposals and an elite-led strategy in congress. For instance, political actors did not seek the support of new or old constituencies to advance reforms. The changing conditions of the political environment since 2005 make it less likely that future reforms will follow that path. Political and social actors have been demanding more participation within the political system and have been very critical toward the Concertación precisely because the coalition lost connection with its social base.

The election of right-wing Sebastián Piñera in 2010 brought a backlash in terms of reforms, as the government did not make such reforms part of its plan. Until the end of 2012, congress passed just one minor constitutional reform concerning a change of the date of the presidential election. However, there is a growing social and political debate on the desirability of a completely new constitution through the establishment of a constitutional assembly.

Thus, under a relatively similar institutional framework, the political model developed in the early stages of the transition was deeply affected by the transitional enclaves noted by the editors of this volume, reinforcing certain ways to solve conflicts during the last two decades. Indeed, the process of reforming the authoritarian enclaves was deeply affected by the transitional enclaves. This chapter shows that during the initial stages of the transition, pro-reformers opted for a gradual strategy that implied two assumptions: first, change would come only if veto players would support it; and second, only a significant change in the balance of power in congress would open options for constitutional reforms. In this sense, extra-institutional negotiations with veto players were how reform was advanced. The level of confidence in the pro-reformer coalition declined as leaders of the Concertación dismissed social and political engagement as valid and viable strategy to advance citizens' demands.

However, there are some indications of change in this dynamic. After 2005 two new interesting trends emerged: a decline in party discipline and more proactive citizens demanding collective and individual rights. This may anticipate a more democratic and accountable political system.

Another characteristic of the democratization period was the way coalition parties have handled reforms collaboratively. While the coalition parties in power progressively "learned" how to cooperate with each other as well as with parties outside the coalition, the two opposition parties (UDI and RN) opted for a more individualistic approach, each negotiating directly with the governing coalition rather than working together. At the beginning of the 1990s liberal members of the RN's legislative contingent supported important Concertación initiatives such as tax reform in opposition to UDI's position. Similarly, by 2003 UDI supported a relevant agenda on transparency and modernization of the state. Transforming the fundamental rules of the game in Chile implied both a serious commitment by the governing coalition to eliminate the authoritarian enclaves, and the cooperation of at least one, if not both, of the parties on the Right. The Right and the Center-Left played the elitist game of politics.

Finally, in presidential systems, a crucial agent of change is the executive branch. Actors within this branch have important political and institutional tools for influencing political outcomes. The Chilean case illustrates just how powerful informal and formal mechanisms are for building consensus within a highly constrained political environment, as well as the influence of entrenched patterns of political activity and norms left over from the democratic transition period.

Notes

This chapter is revised from an article that is part of FONDECYT research project no. 1100255. The author thanks Brian Tauzel for editing work. Translations of interviews and books published in Spanish quoted in this chapter are by the author.

1. New constitutions were promulgated after transitions to democracy in Brazil (1988), Paraguay (1992), Argentina (1994), Ecuador (1998, 2008), and Bolivia (2009). Significant changes were ratified by popular referendum in Uruguay (1996, 2004).

2. Even in Peru, provisional president Valentín Paniagua (2000–2001) called a Commission for the Study of the Constitutional Reform. The National Congress under Toledo's administration (2001–2006) took into consideration the conclusions from that commission and proposed a reform, which also included the consultation of more than one hundred civil society organizations. However, the debate in congress was highly divisive as some congressional representatives thought a new Constituent Assembly was necessary (Bernales 2005).

3. The military regime organized a referendum but did not comply with any of the basic conditions to be considered legitimate, including freedom of press, freedom of speech, freedom of association, the existence of an independent body controlling the electoral process, acceptance of the opposition's call to explain their views to the public, etc.

4. Four of these appointed senators had to be either former commanders in chief of the armed forces or former chiefs of police. They were appointed by the National Security Council in which the armed forces and the police hold a majority. Three were appointed by the Supreme Court and two were appointed by the president.

5. The 1980 constitution established a special quorum for Chapter I (essential basis of institutionalism), Chapter VII (Constitutional Tribunal), Chapter X (armed forces), and Chapter XI (National Security Council).

6. Areas covered under Leyes Orgánicas included the Constitutional Tribunal, Central Bank, military justice, states of exception, investigative and national police,

armed forces, political parties, regional administration, voting and electoral system, electoral court, electoral service, education, municipalities, national congress, and mining franchise.

7. The declaration was signed personally by Andrés Zaldívar, Jaime Castillo, Raúl Troncoso, Tomas Reyes, and Carmen Frei. The military regime sent Zaldívar to exile after he strongly criticized the procedure concerning the plebiscite.

8. "Manifiesto Democrático," March 14, 1983, signed by Patricio Aylwin, Hugo Zepeda, Enrique Silva Cimma, Julio Subercaseaux, Fernando Luengo, Luis Bossay, Ramón Silva Ulloa, Dubenildo Jaque, Hernán Vodanovic, Gabriel Valdés, and Julio Stuardo.

9. The National Accord proposed nineteen specific measures. It was signed by representatives of the liberal Right, Center, and moderate left-wing parties. The Communist Party and other radical left-wing parties rejected the agreement. The conservative UDI was invited to be part of this accord but it refused to sign it (Cavallo, Salazar, and Sepúlveda 2004: chap. 43).

10. The quorum to reform Leyes Orgánicas was reduced from three-fifths to four-sevenths of congressional representatives.

11. Proposals included the establishment of a proportional electoral system, the abolition of appointed senators, the elimination of the clause forbidding the Communist Party to participate within the political process, a reform of the National Security Council to reduce its influence within the policymaking process, the reestablishment of the presidential power to remove commanders in chief of the armed forces, allowing union leaders to take positions within political parties' leadership, democratization of municipal elections, promoting effective measures to decentralize the country, increasing congressional powers, reducing existing quorum requirements for reforming laws, incorporating a section on crimes against humanity into the constitution, increasing amparo rules to protect all constitutional rights, altering the composition of the Constitutional Tribunal and Elections Supervisor Tribunal to make them more autonomous, and the reform of the justice system through the creation of a National Council of Justice.

12. See Patricio Aylwin, *Mensaje Presidencial, 21 de Mayo de 2010* (Santiago: Ministerio Secretaría General de la Presidencia).

13. On September 13, 1990, a bill proposing the elimination of appointed senators was introduced by Concertación deputies (Bulletin 148-07). On April 9, 1991, a bill proposing a reform to reestablish presidential powers to remove officers was introduced by Concertación senators (Bulletin 319-07).

14. The bill was introduced by the executive branch on June 9, 1992, and it was rejected by the Senate in January 1993 (Bulletin 720-07).

15. Bulletins 1680-07 and 1682-02 of August 22, 1995, www.camara.cl.

16. A significant part of this section was previously published by the author in Fuentes (2010).

17. Ricardo Lagos, "Mensaje del Presidente de la Republica al Congreso Nacional," May 21, 2000 (Biblioteca del Congreso, Chile). Lagos proposed the need to eliminate appointed senators, change the binomial system, reform the Constitutional Tribunal and the National Security Council, reestablish presidential power over the armed forces, increase legislative powers to oversee the executive branch, and promote an electoral campaign finance system for the first time in Chilean political history.

18. The Concertación proposal was signed by Senators Sergio Bitar, Juan Hamilton, Enrique Silva-Cimma, and José Antonio Viera-Gallo. Francisco Zuniga and Francisco Cumplido played a significant role during the early stages of this

process by helping senators with their first drafts and by actively participating in the Senate discussions as experts. Interview with Francisco Zuniga (August 25, 2010) and José Antonio Viera Gallo (June 4, 2010). Senators Hernán Larraín, Andrés Chadwick, Sergio Diez, and Sergio Romero sponsored the Alianza.

19. José Miguel Insulza, *Historia de la Ley* 20.050, Biblioteca del Congreso Nacional, 52.

20. Ibid.

21. Edgardo Boeninger, *Historia de la Ley* 20.050, Biblioteca del Congreso Nacional, 63–64.

22. In Chile, the executive branch has the legal option to submit modifications to ongoing bills that are being discussed in congress.

23. Interviews with Gonzalo García (March 26, 2010), Jorge Correa Sutil (August 8, 2010), and Jorge Burgos (August 27, 2010).

24. President Lagos established a regular Sunday meeting including the political committee of the cabinet (ministers of interior, communications, presidency, and finance). They briefed the president on the coming week's agenda. Interview with Ricardo Lagos, June 1, 2010.

25. Interview with Jorge Burgos (Santiago), August 27, 2010. Jorge Correa was undersecretary of the interior, Gonzalo García was adviser to the minister of the interior for constitutional subjects, and Carlos Carmona was the chief of the legislative division at the Ministry of the Presidency.

26. Interview with advisory lawyer (anonymous) (Santiago), August 2010.

27. Interview with Gonzalo García (Santiago), March 26, 2010.

28. Ibid.

29. A review of printed press during the period 2000–2005 reflects that the whole legislative process received very little media attention. Most are op-ed articles by experts and congressional representatives arguing in favor of or against very specific portions of the reforms. Active social actors did not participate in congressional debates, with three exceptions: in 2000–2001 indigenous organizations were invited to give their opinions concerning indigenous rights; representatives of professional associations attended some of the congressional sessions in 2001; and in 2005 the association of journalists (Colegio de Periodistas) did some lobbying to have protection of freedoms included within the package of reforms.

30. This can be seen in the record of indications presented by congressional representatives. See *Historia de la Ley* 20.050, Chile.

31. Interviews with Jorge Burgos (Santiago), August 27, 2010; Jorge Correa Sutil (Santiago), August 4, 2010; and Gonzalo García (Santiago), March 26, 2010.

32. Interview with Ricardo Lagos (Santiago), June 1, 2010.

33. Most indications presented by those appointed senators linked to the armed forces and the police aimed to protect the status quo or even increase military autonomy from political control (see *Historia de la Ley* 20.050, Biblioteca del Congreso Nacional, Chile).

34. Public support for Alianza was 18.6 percent (1996), 15.1 percent (1997), 13 percent (1998), 18 percent (1999), 18.9 percent (2001), and 20.7 percent (2002). In comparison, support for the Concertación was 36.4 percent (1996), 34 percent (1997), 35 percent (1998), 38 percent (1999), 30.9 percent (2001), and 32.1 (2002). In 2000, the Centro de Estudios Públicos (CEP-Chile), a nonprofit think tank, did not include the question in its survey. See national surveys at www.cepchile.cl (accessed on February 25, 2011).

35. There are few surveys addressing the issue of constitutional reforms. The 1995 CEP-Chilean national survey showed that while 66 percent of respondents

supported the idea of making important changes to the constitution, only 19 percent supported the idea of leaving it untouched or making few changes. In 2004, 68 percent agreed on reform issues' "being discussed in Congress, like allowing the president to remove commanders in chiefs of the armed forces, eliminating appointed senators and establishing simultaneous presidential and congressional elections." See www.cepchile.cl.

36. See CEP-Chile national survey conducted in December 2004, www.cep chile.cl.

37. Alianza proposal submitted in congress. *Historia de la Ley* 20.050, Biblioteca del Congreso Nacional, 51.

38. Senador Andrés Chadwick (UDI), *Historia de la Ley* 20.050, Biblioteca del Congreso Nacional, 37.

39. "Con discurso político, Lagos firma nueva Constitución," *La Tercera,* September 18, 2005.

40. *La Nación,* October 15, 2005.

41. *La Nación,* September 9, 2008.

42. *La Nación,* September 14, 2009.

43. Christian Democrat deputies Araya, Mulet, Olivares, Sepúlveda, and Díaz del Rio as well as Senator Zaldívar (Adolfo) joined the PRI. Deputies Enríquez-Ominami (PS), Valenzuela (PPD), Escobar (PPD), and Senator Ominami (PS) left their parties to join Marco Enríquez-Ominami's presidential candidacy. Senator Navarro (PS) left his party to create a social movement called Movimiento Amplio Social (MAS). Senator Flores founded a movement called "Chile-Primero."

5

The Military and Twenty Years of the Concertación

Gregory Weeks

The relationship between elected civilian officials and the armed forces in Chile changed considerably from the beginning to the end of the Concertación's twenty years in power. In 1990, civilian-military relations were antagonistic and marked by a high level of distrust. Chile experienced a unique situation since former dictator and president Augusto Pinochet retained his position in the army along with a high public profile. By 2010, the context was quite different, with more positive interaction. This chapter traces the development of the civil-military relationship from the administrations of Patricio Aylwin to Michelle Bachelet, arguing that the Concertación was more successful in reforming political rather than economic aspects of civil-military relations. Overall, the practical effects of the enclaves of the transition discussed in Chapter 1 made reform slow and difficult. In particular, there was some trepidation regarding rapid and far-reaching reform. This chapter analyzes the difficulties of enacting reforms, and the ways important areas of military autonomy still exist.

The chapter divides the twenty years into three distinct time periods, each characterized by changes in reform opportunities and concluding with a decrease in power for important veto players. The first, 1990–1998, corresponds to General Augusto Pinochet as commander in chief of the army. His retirement paved the way for younger leaders to slowly change the institution's political course. The second, 1999–2005, begins with a new commander in chief and concludes with important constitutional reforms undertaken by President Ricardo Lagos. As the Concertación demonstrated that it would not alter the status quo significantly, the military and the Right accepted democratizing the constitution. The last period, 2006–2010, involves the aftermath of the reforms. The chapter concludes with an analysis of the legacies inherited by Sebastián Piñera when he assumed office in 2010. The Concertación's efforts ultimately made it possible for a president on the Right to extend civil-military reform.

In each period, the Concertación had certain opportunities and constraints that allowed it to advance more in some areas and less in others, yet the transitional enclaves noted in this volume prevented deep reform until 2005. Despite important progress, by the end of President Michelle Bachelet's term in March 2010 limitations remained on the complete exercise of civilian authority. As Table 5.1 illustrates, reform was uneven throughout the entire period of Concertación rule. There were clearly different levels of progress made politically over time, but in areas related to economic policy the military successfully resisted the efforts of all Concertación administrations.

General Pinochet and Democracy, 1990–1998

After nearly seventeen years in power, in 1990 General Augusto Pinochet ceded the presidency to democratically elected Patricio Aylwin. This was a transformational moment in Chilean history, since it marked the end of an especially violent and divisive period in a country that had experienced far less of such tumult than other Latin American countries. However, the balance of civilian-military relations still weighed heavily in favor of the armed forces. The restraints on the new democratic government were strong and imposed precisely because Pinochet and other military leaders did not trust civilians to govern responsibly. The 1980 constitution granted broad authority to the armed forces, and between 1988 and 1990 civilian and military leaders negotiated the extent of those and other authoritarian legacies. In addition, the transitional enclaves noted earlier in this volume provided a model for reform through extra-institutional negotiations with veto players. Although some of the more extreme laws were revoked or diluted, many others remained as the military regime's price of democratization.

There were numerous and serious constraints on the new elected leaders. The incoming president had limited, or in some instances zero, power over the military budget, promotions, the National Security Council (which the military leadership could force the president to convene), military intelligence, the autonomy of military courts, and prosecuting human rights abuses (Weeks 2003). Each branch of the military—army, navy, air force, and national police—even had an appointed seat reserved in the Senate for a retired commander in chief. All of these formal links between civilian authorities and the armed forces were dysfunctional and antidemocratic.

Table 5.1 Military Reforms During Concertación Rule, 1990–2010

Extent of Reform	Political Policy	Economic Policy
Full	Designated senators Constitutional role Firing commanders in chief National Security Council	n/a
Partial	Intelligence oversight Pursuing human rights cases	n/a
None	Revoking 1978 amnesty Military justice system	Copper law Military budget floor law Legislative oversight

Source: Author compilation from Biblioteca del Congreso.

For example, the armed forces could (and did) force the president to convoke the National Security Council (though they generally told the president ahead of time as a courtesy so that he could claim he was doing so himself) for any reason even if the president did not deem it necessary—or even desirable at all—himself. Aylwin held five such meetings during his four-year term. Further, the president did not have the authority either to name or to fire commanders in chief (though the executive did have the right to block promotions of more junior officers). Since General Pinochet was still army commander, this meant that he could say or do anything and the executive was powerless to rebuke him formally or to force his resignation. At that point, the military leadership believed firmly that it had saved the country from destruction in 1973, that all its actions were justified, and that civilians had not yet proven themselves trustworthy to govern. It was, as Pinochet himself said, democracy that was "tied, and well tied" (for a complete review of constitutional constraints, see Chapter 4 in this volume; Loveman 2005: 309).

An important, though generally less examined, element in civilian-military relations is economic policy. Maintaining the military government's economic model was an explicit part of the transition, and the Concertación agreed with the military and the Right that the market model would remain largely unaltered. Pinochet considered the economic model to be an essential aspect of his legacy, one that was diametrically opposed to Marxism and therefore optimal. Ironically, however, Pinochet also ensured that the market would not be able to infringe upon the military budget. Indeed, protecting the military's budget was an important part of the regime's economic calculus. The political and economic legacies of the dictatorship were intended to foster consensus in the post-authoritarian era. The bino-mial system would—in theory—protect the Right and create incentives to form coalitions (see Chapter 2 in this volume). Meanwhile, market-oriented policies would eliminate or at least reduce what the Right believed was the class war mentality of the Left. The Right, meanwhile, was set against any economic reform and, given the binomial system (and until 2006 the desig-nated senators as well), consistently enjoyed veto power.

The Concertación itself was forged in the spirit of consensus, as parties from the Center and Left set aside long-standing and sometimes bitter pol-icy differences to defeat Pinochet in the 1988 referendum and then win the presidential election. It came to power with the goal of proving to the Right (and to the armed forces) that it could govern from the Center, and would not engage in any aggressive measures intended to weaken or antagonize the military (which included economic policy). For that reason, there were strong political incentives to offer virtually no challenge to the civilian-military status quo in the immediate post-authoritarian period.

This did not mean the Concertación did nothing, but rather it worked very cautiously. Not surprisingly, the issue of human rights violations was immediately a source of friction. President Aylwin quickly established what became known as the Rettig Commission (named after Raúl Rettig, the well-respected former politician who led it) to investigate political murders. Aylwin had to strike a balance between what many members of the Con-certación wanted, namely, truth and justice, and what he felt was politically feasible, which was partial truth—for example, withholding the names of accused—and very limited justice. In particular, the military government had decreed an amnesty in 1978, and since the lion's share of repression had taken place within a few years of the 1973 coup, it meant that many cases simply could not be prosecuted. In Aylwin's oft-repeated phrase, this was "justice to the extent possible."

The 1991 Rettig Report did not include any names of those who com-mitted crimes, though some of the information was sent to courts trying specific cases. Eventually, however, Aylwin publicly called for a *ley de punto final*, referring to a law that would specify a date beyond which human rights cases would no longer be pursued. The military was strongly in favor of such a law, since it would limit the number of prosecutions and ensure they did not drag out over time. Given strong resistance from within the Concertación, however, Aylwin backed off. Judges did not change their dictator-era interpretation of the amnesty, which was that it blocked even beginning investigation of cases. For most of the 1990s, human rights cases would be sporadically tried, which angered the armed forces since they never seemed to stop, but also exasperated human rights advocates who felt too few prosecutions were taking place. This was democracy within the possible.

Friction surfaced frequently during the Aylwin presidency (1990–1994). For example, congress launched an investigation into a check fraud scheme involving Pinochet's son. That, plus Pinochet's belief that the government was trying to force his resignation, led him in late 1990 to call every soldier to the barracks, an action often associated with military rebellion. This so-called *ejercicio de enlace* was peacefully resolved in Pinochet's favor as the government agreed to quash the investigations. The weakness of formal points of civilian-military contacts was also evident with what became known as the *boinazo*, when the guards outside army headquarters wore camouflage and war paint. This was a symbolic move, obviously intended to send a message to the government that Pinochet wanted investigations to end and had the army behind him in support. At that point there was little civilian concern about an authoritarian reversion, but such actions were highly distracting and embarrassing for the government, since the demonstrations of force made clear the military's success in bullying the elected government.

Thus, while Pinochet remained as commander in chief the Aylwin and Frei administrations (1994–2000) often walked on eggshells, not knowing precisely when the mercurial general would make his demands known through informal channels. Their tentative approach to policies reflects that tension. Within a short time, few believed there would be an authoritarian reversion, but civilian-military tension, especially when it spilled into the streets, served as a severe distraction for governments intent on addressing important socioeconomic challenges.

Because of restrictive laws, military budgeting was very difficult to change. Although hampered by restrictive defense spending laws, civilian authorities continued to cut budgets. Defense spending fell from 2.98 percent in 1990 to 1.65 percent in 2005 (Huneeus 2007: 437).[1] Yet congress was prohibited from cutting spending below 1989 levels, adjusted for inflation. Debates over budgets reflected the strength of the Chilean executive, since congress could not modify the president's proposed defense budget and could not call for additional cuts. The almost total lack of influence over resources undercut congressional power and made it even more peripheral to civilian-military relations. The budgetary process primarily involved negotiation between the president and the commanders in chief.

The copper law, however, ensured that civilian governments would be unable to block the transfer of state funds into military coffers. In 1973, the military government expanded an already existing law tying part of the military budget to copper earnings, the Ley Reservada del Cobre. The revised law granted 10 percent gross sales—instead of net earnings—to the military budget for equipment, with a floor to ensure it could not fall too low. The law was deemed too sensitive to address seriously while Pinochet was commander in chief, and for many on the Right it was a symbol of protection for those who in turn protected la Patria from internal or external threats. In practice it meant that budget cuts could only go so far. Billions of dollars still flowed toward munitions.

Nonetheless, the Aylwin and Frei governments made steps toward normalization, which required demonstrated civilian interest and expertise in defense. To that end, months of meetings led to the 1997 Libro de Defensa Nacional, a narrative of the state of Chile's national defense. The document was quite vague and general, but its purpose was less a firm blueprint than an avenue for more interaction. The process was repeated in 2002, with more agreement on specifics that reflected a greater level of trust. The most recent version, from 2010, also acknowledged the constitutional reform enacted in 2005, discussed below. Overall, the process of creating these defense documents was much more important than their details. By the third iteration, the participants were comfortable with their respective roles, which was not the case in the early 1990s.

Pinochet finally retired from the army in 1998, and passed the baton to General Ricardo Izurieta. Not only did this represent an obviously important symbolic moment, but it also reflected generational change. Pinochet was born in 1915, and Izurieta in 1943. By 1993, officers at the rank of lieutenant colonel were only about twenty years old at the time of the coup, and Izurieta was part of a new generation with less emotional attachment to the military regime and less direct connection to repression than its older counterparts (Atria 2002). In fact, Izurieta and his successors were specifically interested in maintaining the army's prestige, which meant gradually distancing the institution from the legacies of the military government. Pinochet's retirement further opened the door to improved relations.

Nonetheless, according to his own constitution, as a former president Pinochet immediately became a lifetime appointed member of the Senate and so retained a relatively high political profile. Fatefully, soon after becoming a senator he traveled to Great Britain in late 1998 for back surgery. Spanish judge Baltasar Garzón had issued a warrant for his arrest, charging him with torture and conspiracy to commit torture against Spanish citizens. Pinochet obviously felt he was untouchable in Britain, a country to which he felt great personal and diplomatic attachment. Instead, Scotland Yard complied with the Spanish request to arrest him in the hospital. As Chileans started thinking about their third democratic election in 1999, the nondemocratic past remained in the spotlight.

For most of the 1990s, then, substantial reforms of the constitution or military-related laws were extraordinarily difficult. Civilians were able to chip away at human rights abuse cases, though even these were fraught with political risk because of the immense backlash they produced. Pinochet was consistently successful in mobilizing the army (and to a lesser extent, the navy, air force, and national police) and the two main parties of the Right in the legislature to effectively veto any proposal deemed too radical.

Once Pinochet hobbled home, however, he retreated from the public eye and his political strength fell dramatically, a process that accelerated when news of financial improprieties emerged. Since his entire defense centered on his ill health, he had no choice but to retire from the Senate as well. However, as a way to facilitate his departure, congress approved an official status as "ex-president" that granted him immunity.

Civil-Military Normalization, 1999–2005

General Pinochet's detention in Great Britain put a tremendous strain on the Frei government. In response, President Frei was forced to hold multiple National Security Council meetings of an indignant military leadership. They considered the arrest not only an affront to the general, but also an assault on Chilean sovereignty, which enjoyed broad agreement even among many members of the Concertación. During the fifteen months Pinochet was in London, Frei convoked the NSC four times, and did so eight times total during his six-year presidency. He was put in the unusual position of agreeing vehemently (to the extent that Frei was capable of being vehement) with Pinochet, asserting that the general should be returned to his homeland.

At the same time, the crisis also allowed Commander in Chief Ricardo Izurieta to stake out a more pro-democracy position for the army, as he resisted retired officers as well as the Pinochet family, who felt he was not exerting nearly enough pressure on civilians and was therefore being disloyal to his former commander (Huneeus 2003). He was caught between needing to support a former commander in chief while also demonstrating that the army was no longer perfectly aligned with its authoritarian past. Those months were tense, and ultimately the British government released the general, claiming humanitarian reasons based on his poor health.

Pinochet's arrest did have the salutary effect of opening sufficient political space to hold discussions about human rights. The painful legacies of the military government were once again making headlines, and the government took the opportunity to engage the armed forces. As noted in Chapter 1, the Concertación's maintenance of the political and economic status quo meant that the military was willing to accept dialogue (as long as it entailed no punitive measures). In 1999, Defense Minister Edmundo Pérez-Yoma launched the Mesa de Diálogo, a series of meetings with military officers, academics, politicians, lawyers, journalists, Catholic Church officials, and even psychologists to discuss the issue of the detained and disappeared and to establish guidelines for moving forward with dialogue.

In its official declaration, the Mesa emphasized the importance of a "re-encounter" between civilians and members of the armed forces as a means of coming to terms with the past and addressing human rights more frankly.[2] It was important largely for its symbolic value, but it also established a precedent for opening lines of civilian-military communication.

Human rights cases also advanced, though primarily through the persistence of private actors rather than elected officials. First the Catholic Church Vicariate of Solidarity, then later a number of national and international nongovernmental organizations, assisted Chileans in bringing cases to the courts. Though the Vicariate closed once the transition began, these organizations, and eventually Chilean-based lawyers themselves, picked up the slack. Lawyers found innovative ways to deal with the amnesty with regard to the detained and disappeared. If an individual had never been found, then they were not technically deemed deceased. So cases could be investigated and witnesses called to testify, although if a body were eventually found, no prosecution could move forward. By 2009, 554 agents of the dictatorship were under active investigation, while an additional 276 had been sentenced (Collins 2010a).

There is no consensus about precisely why the courts accelerated the human rights cases so much after Pinochet's detention. At least in the post-authoritarian era there had never been so much international attention focused on Chilean human rights, so international factors were critical. It may have been judicial guilt about their complicity with the dictatorship that motivated the courts to restore their positive image (A. Huneeus 2010). Judges even accepted cases that presidents argued should be set aside. But Pinochet's detention itself could have been a key catalyst for the government more so than the courts themselves, speeding up official support for a process that was already under way but very slow until European courts stepped in (Hilbink 2007; Pion-Berlin 2004). Judicial reforms were part of the domestic shifts in 1997 and 1999 that both modernized the Supreme Court and created the equivalent of an attorney general. All of this also coincided with generational changes already taking place, as a conservative court stuffed with Pinochet appointees began to change in the 1990s (J. Correa 1999: 281–315). For all of these reasons, the Chilean Supreme Court was a different institution by the time Eduardo Frei left office.

President Ricardo Lagos (2000–2006) came to office just after Pinochet returned to Chile. He argued that Chilean courts, rather than foreign courts, should become more active and put the general on trial (Lira 2006: 3–25). In 2003 he supported reparations legislation for former political prisoners. As Aylwin and Frei had done, he expressed interest in completing the process of democratic transition. Although rumors periodically surfaced that he would support a *ley de punto final* (full stop law—one barring further investigations and prosecutions), ultimately he did not. Lagos wanted his legacy to be that he ended the transition by modifying authoritarian elements of the constitution.

Lagos initiated the National Commission on Political Imprisonment and Torture, which issued the Valech Report on torture (named after the bishop who headed it).[3] It catalogued 27,255 people who were detained and tortured, and who were held an average of 180 days in prison. As with the Rettig Report, the intent was not to facilitate prosecutions, as the testimonies were kept secret for fifty years. Instead, President Lagos viewed it as a vehicle for reparations, which slowly were being made. The military's response was not unified, and the army revealed generational splits. The Circle of Retired Generals and Admirals criticized the report, but army commander Juan Emilio Cheyre publicly accepted institutional responsibility for abuses that occurred. Such a declaration was important because it recognized that orders were coming in an organized manner from above, and so torture and murder were not merely the work of a few bad apples, which had previously been the official stance of the army.

Chilean courts also advanced against Pinochet himself. His arrest seemed to puncture the sense of invincibility that had always surrounded him. By the time of his death in 2006, he had been named in hundreds of cases, some of which—such as his role in the 1973 Caravan of Death and the 1974 murder of former army commander in chief Carlos Prats—even led to interrogations and house arrest in 2004. The Supreme Court ruled in these cases that his immunity be stripped. Meanwhile, authorities in the United States revealed in 2004 that Pinochet had laundered upward of US$30 million and stashed it in foreign banks. This tarnished his image even more than human rights abuses, since his allies had long insisted that he was no dictator because he never benefited personally from being in power. While his funeral did generate a large crowd of admirers, a majority of Chileans were more disillusioned. A 2004 poll found that two-thirds did not believe the story that the money came just from savings and investments, and 59 percent believed he stole it from the treasury. Further, 63 percent rejected the statement that he was "a man with good intentions who did not know what his collaborators were doing."[4] This was very damaging since it brought him down to the level of a common autocrat, using the state for his own personal gain.

In 2005, President Lagos was finally successful in passing constitutional reform that changed the balance of civilian-military power. Designated senators (including one former commander in chief from each branch) were abolished, the president was given the right to fire commanders in chief and full authority over the National Security Council, and the constitutional wording itself was changed to remove the military's duty to protect "institutional order." These reforms had important practical and symbolic effects. Since 1990, for example, presidents had resented the fact that the armed forces could force them to convoke meetings of the National Security Council, and indeed they had done so with regularity. Symbolically, they demonstrated a commitment on the part of the Right and the military to accept greater democratic civilian prerogatives, thus showing greater civilian-military trust. The army in particular had repositioned itself away from the dictatorship's institutions and accepted a more democratic defense structure (Agüero 2006). Generational change was critical in this regard. In the wake of controversies surrounding Pinochet, younger army commanders such as Izurieta and Cheyre consciously worked to modernize the army and depoliticize it. Knowing that practical limitations prevented civilians from making "rash" decisions (such as slashing military budgets) created confidence that otherwise might have been lacking.

Indeed, the acquiescence of the Right was essential to the reforms, because the Concertación otherwise could not muster the supermajorities required to get them passed. Organic constitutional laws like the copper law require four-sevenths majorities in both houses to pass. Fifteen years had convinced the Right that the Concertación could govern "responsibly" and therefore that reducing military prerogatives would not threaten the system itself. That recognition on the part of conservative politicians is part of the double-edged sword of the Chilean political transition, because trust came at the expense of many potential changes

Normalized and Incomplete, 2006–2010

The passage of the constitutional reforms prompted President Lagos to proclaim the transition to be over (Weeks 2010). Yet these changes concentrated almost exclusively on political issues related to the executive branch. In particular, the legislative branch continues to play virtually no role in providing horizontal accountability to either the armed forces or the executive branch. The absence of knowledgeable congressional staff, a constant in Chilean (and Latin American more broadly) legislative history, still poses a challenge. Overall, there remains a striking absence of horizontal accountability, as decisions about the military are made almost entirely in the executive branch.

President Michelle Bachelet (2006–2010) seemed an ideal candidate to categorically leave the transitional model of civil-military relations behind. She had suffered tremendously at the hands of the dictatorship, as her father (an air force general) was detained and died of a heart attack in prison, and then she was also detained and tortured in Villa Grimaldi, a Santiago torture center. Yet after 1990, she worked to become an expert in defense, including earning a master's degree at the Army War College and taking courses at the United States Inter-American Defense College. She already had cabinet-level experience as minister of health (2000–2002). With that pedigree, Lagos named her minister of defense, where she won the respect of the military leadership.

Ultimately, though, Bachelet's policies toward human rights were very close to those of her predecessors. She emphasized the importance of memory, which included funding museums dedicated to the detained and disappeared, and she spoke frequently about the topic. She did not support a *ley de punto final* but neither did she call for more prosecutions. In 2008, the Agrupación de Familiares de Detenidos Desaparecidos (the Association of Relatives of the Detained-Disappeared, a nongovernmental organization that allows for coordination of those seeking information about and justice for their family members) criticized her for not being more of an advocate for human rights.

Further, the 1978 amnesty was untouchable and still remains untouched. That sets Chile apart from other cases where the issue is at least on the table. For example, the Argentine Supreme Court overturned the dictatorship's amnesty in 2005. In 2009 Uruguayan voters voted no on repealing the amnesty, while in 2010 the Brazilian Supreme Court upheld the country's amnesty. Even when the amnesty remained in force, there was political debate about its legality and purpose. In Chile that discussion took place largely within the confines of human rights organizations, and was too controversial to get a broader public airing. Even for Bachelet, who had suffered personally at the hands of security forces, the amnesty was too divisive to become a priority. For both the military and the Right, the amnesty was a security-building measure that prevented politically motivated witch hunts. This did not mean no prosecutions took place. The law does not cover crimes committed after its implementation, and Chilean judges have interpreted disappearances in ways that allow prosecutions, for example, by labeling them as "permanent crimes," which are exempt from the amnesty.

She was also not successful in making changes to military courts, which had been a powerful instrument of repression for the military government. The military believed the status quo was important for maintaining order, and there were far too few legislators who disagreed to make reform viable. The Code of Military Justice dates to 1925, but retains many features of both the colonial justice system and the immediate post-independence period. It allows for broad jurisdiction, with the ability to try civilians in military courts, where their rights are limited. That was even utilized by the Concertación itself. The Lagos government used Pinochet-era antiterrorism statutes for military courts during land disputes with the Mapuche in southern Chile, which resulted in ten-year sentences for arson, which was defined as terrorism (Human Rights Watch 2004). Others were held by military authorities for up to a year before being released. The purpose of the Chilean military justice system is "less the administration of justice than the protection of the armed forces' interests in hierarchy, discipline, and order" (Pereira and Zaverucha 2005: 115). Bachelet created a commission in 2007 to study the issue (a strategy that she repeatedly employed) and it released a report the following year proposing reforms, but these were not enacted before she left office.

Her efforts at civil-military reform were lower profile and more professional in nature. In defense, she supported creation of a Joint Chiefs of Staff structure—with the head chosen by the president—and rationalization of the Ministry of Defense, which were introduced in 2005 and then passed in 2008. These would be useful for improving lines of communication and reducing redundant positions in the ministry. They also emphasized civilian leadership in the formation of military doctrine, which historically had been abdicated by civilians and therefore determined almost entirely by the armed forces themselves.

Intelligence, which was so highly controversial during the military government, has been changed only cosmetically. The infamous Dirección Nacional de Inteligencia (DINA) was replaced in 1977 by the Centro Nacional de Inteligencia (CNI), which in turn was dismantled in 1990. Once intelligence was no longer wielded as a tool of repression, popular support for reform evaporated. As a result, politicians lacked incentive to address highly complex questions of intelligence organizations and instead deferred to the armed forces (Weeks 2008). After years of inaction, the Lagos administration did create a new organization, the Agencia Nacional de Inteligencia (ANI), in 2004. The law creating it, however, explicitly made it only a coordinating and information-sharing body. The intelligence services of each military branch would still maintain full control over its own activities. Further, each could undertake covert operations such as wiretapping and surveillance, and was required only to obtain the permission of a military—not civilian—court to do so. This had important implications, particularly in the context of various intelligence scandals involving spying on both politicians and on a foreign consulate (Argentina).

The Concertación was also never able to convince the Right to make changes to the military budgeting process, despite offering proposal after proposal in the legislature. Between 2005 and 2009, with high copper prices, the military budget exceeded US$1 billion a year. That money has been spent on fighter planes, tanks, frigates, submarines, and other equipment in addition to upgrades on existing equipment. The law was revised in 2004 to grant the Ministry of Defense discretion to use funds in excess of the minimum amount (Ruiz-Dana 2007). The "reserved" nature of the law means its full text was literally secret and accessible to relatively few officials. As a result, accountability was virtually impossible (though it increased through a 2011 reform, discussed later in the chapter). Such a reform has been a topic of both executive and legislative discussion since

1990, and as of October 2012 a reform had passed the lower house and was being debated in the Senate. The military and its political allies have always viewed it as an important obstacle to indiscriminate budget cutting, and so feel great reluctance to dismantle it until an acceptable alternative has been devised.

Oddly enough, reform of the copper law became more likely under a Center-Right government. Some have argued that politicians would erode military prerogatives because these would conflict with politicians' self-interest. In other words, politicians would want to dole out those resources themselves (Hunter 1997). The Chilean case, however, did not evolve in that manner. There was definitely both political and economic interest on the part of the Concertación, but it was blocked at every turn. With the Right in power, however, fiscal conservatism has facilitated more discussion about access to hitherto untouchable sources of revenue. Reducing military expenditures could give President Sebastián Piñera more resources to address economic difficulties without affecting the current budget. As noted above, reforms are imminent.

The memory of the dictatorship does, however, still loom. When a major earthquake hit Chile in 2010, President Bachelet deployed only the police for the first two days, choosing not to send other armed forces. Article 41 of the reformed constitution granted the president power to designate a head of national defense (Jefe de la Defensa Nacional) to take charge of any area designated a state of catastrophe. Only when looting and crime were obviously a serious problem did she sign an order allowing military control. Although she denied it, the immediate perception was that her administration was reluctant to bring the army into the streets because of its past history. She denied the claim, but there is no doubt that the legacies of the dictatorship cast a long shadow.

That episode once again raised a conundrum that is central to Latin American civil-military relations more generally, namely, how to define a military role in the absence of an external enemy. Although there was a serious conflict with Argentina in 1978 that threatened the use of arms, the War of the Pacific (1879–1884) is the last example of a Chilean war. In the context of a history of internal repression, the Concertación sought to steer the military away from domestic policing and instead moved toward international peacekeeping, combating drug trafficking, preserving the environment (particularly by the navy), and other similar missions.

From a generational perspective, just the length of time in power helped the Concertación stabilize civilian-military relations and establish more trust. The last army commander in chief of the Concertación era, General Oscar Izurieta, was only twenty-three at the time of the coup. This does not mean that younger officers were not deeply involved in the regime's repressive apparatus, but for most their long-term commitment to protecting the status quo—as well as protecting retired officers facing charges—has been weaker.

By the end of the Concertación's years in power, what did Chileans think about democracy and civil-military relations? The Chilean military left power roughly a generation ago and there is no longer support for military intervention as a way to mediate political disputes. Chileans are not necessarily happy with their elected representatives, but they view them as the only political game in town. According to the 2010 Latinobarómetro poll, only 15 percent of Chileans have a positive impression of the military government. Sixty-three percent of Chileans believed democracy was preferable to any other type of system, which has remained more or less stable since the question was first asked in 1995, while 56 percent were satisfied with democracy. At the same time, 69 percent would not accept an authoritarian government under any circumstances. Meanwhile, 11 percent preferred an authoritarian government, which was the lowest percentage since 1995 (though, oddly enough, it had shot up to 21 percent in 2007).

Conclusion: The End of a Civil-Military Era

After twenty years in power, the relationship between Concertación governments and the armed forces improved notably. Saber rattling in the early 1990s gave way to sustained dialogue, and a number of substantive constitutional reforms were put in place. The end of each period laid out in this chapter was marked by veto players seeing their power gradually decline. The reasons for this include Augusto Pinochet's retiring and then becoming enmeshed in scandal; generational change in the armed forces; and increased trust in the Concertación as it proved it would not pursue radical civil-military reform. Civilian-military relations in 2010 were utterly different, as they were routinized and channeled through formal institutions. Nonetheless, successive presidents had extreme difficulties enacting political reforms, and were wholly unsuccessful at making economic changes that affected the armed forces. Human rights violations kept hitting national headlines, which made activists and many officers indignant for different reasons.

It is noteworthy that the administration of Sebastián Piñera rather quickly made some important strides in civilian-military relations, both rhetorically and concretely. Although during the campaign Piñera promised to limit prosecutions and to expedite those that did occur, his government continued to pursue human rights violators, to the point that the association of retired generals expressed its displeasure. The Chilean Conference of Bishops asked him to grant amnesties, in the spirit of the 2010 Bicentennial, to members of the military who showed repentance and Piñera refused. He fired his ambassador to Argentina when he praised the military government, and then publicly argued that ex-members of the CNI should not be in the military. From an economic perspective, he moved control of the copper revenues from the Defense Ministry to the Finance Ministry, and promised to abrogate the copper law entirely. Clearly, Piñera was committed to protecting the economic model inherited from the military government, but he saw no political benefit from defending the armed forces' economic privileges.

These positive steps are possible only because the Concertación laid the initial groundwork by very slowly making reforms while maintaining political and economic stability, thus accepting many of the restraints placed on the political system by the outgoing military regime. Particularly after Pinochet's arrest, the military gradually became less overtly political, and its allies in congress were less concerned about protecting its prerogatives. The pace of reform, however, has been very slow and in some areas virtually nonexistent. Piñera's latitude to make public statements and to successfully push for reform of the copper law highlights the legacy of fear that the Concertación governments were compelled to accept. Bachelet had made the copper law a priority, yet was never able to garner the necessary legislative support from the Right.

A final appraisal of progress in civilian-military relations during the 1990–2010 period may well have to wait until the Right has been in power longer. That will shed more light on whether there are certain transformations that the Right can successfully foster that were impossible for the Concertación. It will also offer more insight into whether there are any reforms that are impossible to pass, either because of resistance or lack of interest, regardless of the type of government in power. The road to civilian control over the armed forces in Chile has been a very long and winding one.

Notes

1. It should also be noted, however, that the Pinochet government had also been gradually reducing the defense budget since the final agreement about the end of hostilities with Argentina in 1979.

2. See *Declaración de la Mesa de Diálogo sobre derechos humanos,* www.ddhh.gov.cl/filesapp/Declaracion_Acuerdo_Final.pdf.

3. *Informe de la Comisión Nacional sobre Política y Tortura,* www.comision valech.gov.cl/InformeValech.html.

4. Quoted in "Pinochet's Secret Millions Tarnish His Image," *Reuters,* October 19, 2004.

6

Political Reform and Gender Equality

Liesl Haas and Merike Blofield

On January 15, 2006, Socialist Michelle Bachelet was elected president of Chile. Her presidency marked both the continuation of Concertación governance as well as a clear break with the past. An avowed feminist, she signified the progress that Chilean women had made since the transition to democracy in legitimizing issues of women's rights and in gaining greater political voice. In many ways, Michelle Bachelet's political success seemed to represent the public face of a deeper transformation of women's status in Chilean society.

However, behind Bachelet's success lay a more complicated story of women's political influence in Chile since the transition to democracy. At the moment of the transition in 1990, the state of women's legal rights in Chile lagged far behind most of Latin America. During twenty years of Concertación government, women joined political parties and won elections in greater numbers than at any time in Chile's history. Feminist representatives and their supporters—men and women—together with the newly created National Women's Service (Sernam) successfully pushed for policy reforms on a wide range of gender equality issues, touching on education, health, marital and property rights, violence against women, labor rights, and constitutional guarantees of equality.

This chapter evaluates the degree to which the Concertación promoted public policies that increased gender equality. The conflicts about women's rights that took place over two decades within the Concertación mirrored larger societal debates about gender equality and women's "proper" place in Chilean society. In practice the evolution of Chile's political parties on issues of gender equality, particularly within the ruling Concertación, represented a microcosm of Chilean society in transition.

Efforts to promote gender equality exposed stark divisions within the Concertación between left-wing parties that largely supported gender equality policies and the Christian Democratic Party, which was deeply ambivalent about the proposed reforms, within the context of vocal opposition from the political Right.[1] The battle for gender equality policy within the Concertación revealed the ideological fault lines within the governing coalition, which struggled to balance political unity with the desire of its individual parties to pursue distinct policy agendas. More fundamentally, the struggle for policy reform on these issues revealed the limitations of the transition itself, which empowered precisely those political and economic actors most opposed to gender equality. The obstacles to far-reaching reform became apparent whenever proposed reforms touched on Catholic doctrine or required redistributive measures. Despite these challenges, in the course of two decades of Concertación government, all the parties in the coalition strengthened their support for gender equality. We analyze changing patterns of bill introduction together with public opinion data to demonstrate that the parties' slow evolution on these issues reflects broad trends in Chilean society at large. At the same time, the combination of real and self-imposed limits to reform inherent in the enclaves of the transition are starkly evident with respect to gender legislation.

We illustrate these dynamics through brief examples of the evolution of laws on women in the workforce, divorce, and reproductive rights. While the first involves increasing women's status in the economy (and hence can elicit economic opposition), the latter two involve conflicts between women's rights and secular definitions of family in contrast to Catholic doctrine, and hence elicit religious opposition. They thus represent some of the substantive conflicts feminists have faced in improving women's status in post-transition Chilean laws and society (see Blofield and Haas 2005, 2011; Htun and Weldon 2010).

A Society in Transition

Since the 1970s, Chilean women and families underwent significant sociodemographic changes. The fertility rate declined from 4 children per woman in 1970 to 2.6 in 1990, and down to 1.9 in 2010, which is below replacement level (OECD Family Database 2012). At the same time, out-of-wedlock births increased from 19 percent of children in 1970 to 51 percent by 2000, and female-headed households went from 24 percent of households in 1990 to 32 percent by 2006 (CEPAL 2009: 174). Women's labor force participation, while low by regional standards, increased from 32 percent in 1990 to 42 percent by 2009 (Chioda 2011). In the early 1990s, the abortion rate in Chile was roughly one for every three live births (Requena 1990; Alan Guttmacher Institute 1994).

At the time of transition, however, many laws limited women's rights. Both abortion and divorce were illegal; as one of its last acts in office, the military regime outlawed therapeutic abortion in 1989. Laws also failed to protect Chilean women from domestic violence, rape laws were limited and underenforced, "illegitimate" children had fewer rights than "legitimate" children, married women had little control over marital property and even their salary, and women faced widespread discrimination in the workplace (domestic workers, in particular, lacked protection). There were, thus, significant deficits in women's rights as well as contradictions between the laws that governed women's and men's lives, and social reality.

In addition, public opinion was not in line with the conservative laws. Since the late 1980s, the majority of Chileans consistently supported legalizing divorce and therapeutic abortion, and popular support for legalization of abortion under some conditions such as rape and fetal deformity also existed by the late 1990s (Blofield 2006: 99). Moreover, over 80 percent of Chileans in 1990 were accepting of single mothers and out-of-wedlock children (World Values Survey 1990).

However, as feminists and members of the Left began to push for reform of these laws, they faced mounting conservative opposition from within and outside the government. The moment of transition to democracy was one of significant social tension, exacerbated by fears of instability that were stoked by the outgoing regime and the new parties of the Right. The Chilean women's movement, which played an influential role as part of the opposition to the dictatorship, struggled to position itself as an influential player in the new democratic government.[2] During this critical period, the women's movement tried to transcend ideology to "model unity" for the Concertación. Feminists and their allies on the Left consciously downplayed issues like legalizing abortion to facilitate the transition and the Left alliance within the Concertación. The decision to moderate their political agenda eased the transition itself, but feminists soon found themselves marginalized from the new policymaking centers within the democratic government. Despite their influence at the moment of transition, women in Chile struggled over the next two decades to turn the power of their social movement into concrete influence over public policy.

The Legislative Influence of the Catholic Church

At the time of the transition, the role that progressive sectors of the Catholic Church played in supporting human rights during the dictatorship gave the church as a whole renewed moral authority following the transition (see Fleet and Smith 1997; Haas 1999). At the same time, the prioritization by the Vatican of issues related to sexual morality and the family since Pope John Paul II also resulted in a shift of focus in the church hierarchy. On issues such as gender equality and women's rights, the church is the most influential extragovernmental actor in opposition. The Catholic Church has exerted significant influence over post-transition politics, particularly on contentious issues of social reform.

At the same time, on a societal level the church had to contend with decreasing church attendance rates throughout the decade—lower than in Italy, Spain, or the United States—and a decreasing share of Chileans who identified themselves as Catholics (World Values Surveys; Lehmann 2002). In 1990, the World Values Survey showed that more than half of Chilean adults (53.4 percent) attended church rarely (e.g., only at holidays) or never. Only 27.7 percent attended once a week or more (Blofield 2006: 21).

The Catholic Church has translated its cultural power into political influence through a variety of mechanisms. Buoyed by its historical links to the Christian Democratic Party and its strong post-democratization links to the political Right, the church uses pastoral letters, public sermons, and personal ties with economic and political elites to influence public debate on contentious social issues. The church's significant media ownership allows it to suppress public debate on controversial topics and to obscure the gap between public discourse and public practice in Chile (Blofield 2006; Haas 2010).

The continued influence of the church in society and politics has been cemented by the active growth of links between right-wing Catholic groups, such as Opus Dei and the Legionaries of Christ, and the Chilean economic elite. These links need to be understood in the context of the high concentration of income and wealth in Chile.[3] During the Pinochet regime, the top quintile of the population increased its share of income from 52.3 percent in 1971 to 62 percent in 1994 (Deininger and Squire 1996). This trend, along with privatizations of formerly state-owned corporations, as well as social security, education, and health care programs (see Borzutzky 2002; Castiglioni 2005), has concentrated economic power in the hands of a small but cohesive and conservative elite. This elite has invested in private schools and universities run by the conservative Catholic groups, and has promoted its values through its ownership of the media and by funding conservative political campaigns (Blofield 2006: 108–112).

Under Concertación government, the strong role of the church, combined with the inherited tenets of the neoliberal model, the concentration of wealth, and a powerful political Right, meant that any reforms on women's rights that challenged church doctrine or fundamentally challenged the neoliberal model were likely to elicit significant political opposition in congress. The Left's ability to counter this influence was complicated by the internal political dynamics of the Concertación itself.

Jockeying for Power Within the Concertación

The return of electoral democracy in 1989 ushered in a new institutional structure to Chilean politics, one that complicated interbranch relations and gave disproportionate representation to the political Right. Supporters of women's rights had to learn over time how to maneuver within this new institutional arena.

As detailed elsewhere in this volume, the creation of binomial districts necessitated the creation of multiparty electoral coalitions. In current democratic politics, issues of internal party discipline are therefore complicated by the need for parties to find areas of compromise among one another to maintain the stability of these broad alliances. The bicameral system creates additional veto points. Until 2005, the appointed senators[4] tended to tip the balance of power in favor of the political Right. This increased the need for members of the governing coalition to compromise on issues to prevent legislation that had passed the Chamber but was rejected in the Senate. These social and institutional dynamics have affected attempts to legislate on women's rights within the governing Concertación. Within the governing coalition the relationship between the PDC and the Left, as well as executive-legislative relations, have defined the dynamics of women's rights bills.

At the level of the Concertación coalition, there exists significant disagreement on gender issues between the Left and the Christian Democrats. This creates a policy distance within the coalition significantly greater than is the case with other issues examined in this volume. The Left has been much more supportive of gender equality policy in general than the Christian Democrats, and within the Left, there is greater willingness to discuss issues of women's rights. The presence of more feminists in the parties of the Left than in the other parties and the existence of networks of feminist organizations in civil society with their own lists of policy priorities make gender equality policy a logical one for the Left to pursue. These factors offer an ideal opportunity for the Left to make a unique contribution to the policy process. While this does not imply that all representatives from the Left have been highly proactive in introducing legislation in this area, it does mean that, with only a few exceptions, those members of the Left who have taken the initiative in introducing legislation on women's rights have been able to count on a solid backing of support from the Left for their efforts. There is thus a higher degree of ideological unity on these issues than among Christian Democrats. This cohabitation presents both opportunities and obstacles for the Left to influence policy.

The PDC is deeply divided on women's rights. Broadly reflecting the social teachings of the Catholic Church, the policy positions of the Christian Democratic Party tend to be more reformist on economic issues and conservative on issues that refer to sexuality, gender roles, or the family. Church opposition causes particular conflict for the Christian Democrats, whose liberal wing often supports proposed legal reforms on women's rights but whose historic ties with the church make it difficult for the party to vote in opposition to official church teaching. Hence, while the Christian Democratic Party has publicly expressed its recognition of women's inequality, the party is also hesitant to introduce legislation on issues that will bring it into conflict with the church. Therefore, on bills that seek to improve women's economic position (for example, access to day care, breastfeeding breaks), the majority of Christian Democrats will likely ally with the Left against the Right. However, if an issue causes conflict along the gender dimension, and challenges church doctrine specifically, gaining the support of the Christian Democrats will be more difficult. A solid sector of the Christian Democrats will identify with the Right more than the Left on such issues (Lehmann 2002; Blofield and Haas 2005).[5]

On the other hand, the Christian Democratic Party has become less programmatic over time (Scully 1996), and there is diversity of opinion within the PDC on these issues (Baldez 2001; Londregan 2000). This diversity allows for the possibility that a controversial proposal by the Left on women's rights, properly drafted, may gain sufficient votes from PDC legislators to pass congress. However, the conflict that these issues cause within the PDC means that members of the party will rarely introduce such topics, and winning PDC support for Left initiatives will be difficult. Given this, with the diminution of disagreement over economic policy between the PDC and the Left, social policy became the issue that distinguished them.

These tensions play out within congress, and also between congress and the executive, where the Center-Left coalition divides the leadership of government ministries across the parties of the coalition (see Baldez 2001). The PDC controlled the presidency and Sernam for the first administrations (1990–2000), and it was also the largest party in congress (see Table 6.1). Lacking a majority, the PDC still needed Left support for its policies, but provided the Left room to advocate for its own issues.

Despite being constrained by both the dominance of the executive over policymaking and the Left's secondary position within the governing coalition for the first decade of Concertación government, the Left was successful in influencing policy in this area.

Table 6.1 Congressional Representation by Party and Coalition, 1990–2010

Coalition and Party	1990–1994 Chamber	1990–1994 Senate[a]	1994–1998 Chamber	1994–1998 Senate	1998–2002 Chamber	1998–2002 Senate	2002–2006 Chamber	2002–2006 Senate	2006–2010 Chamber	2006–2010 Senate
Concertación coalition										
PDC	39	13	37	13	39	14	22	12	21	6
PS	18	4	15	5	11	4	12	5	15	8
PPD	7	1	15	2	16	2	21	3	19	2
PR[b]	5	3	2	1	4		6		7	3
PSD		1								
PH	1								3	
IND concert			1				2			
Coalition total	70	22	70	21	70	20	63	20	65	19
Right coalition										
RN	32	13	29	11	23	7	19	7	20	8
UDI	14	2	15	3	17	5	34	9	33	9
UCC			2							
IND Right		1	4	3	9	6	4		1	0
Coalition total	46	16	50	17	49	18	57	16	54	18
Other	4				1			2	1	2
Congress total	120	38	120	38	120	38	120	38	120	38

Sources: Haas 2010 and National Congress of Chile, www.congreso.cl.
Notes: a. Until 2005, in addition to elected representatives, there were nine appointed senators.
b. The PR and PSD combined to form the PRSD in the second administration.

On the other hand, the Concertación was slow to increase the representation of women. As Table 6.2 shows, the share of women in congress has been consistently low, from 5.8 percent in 1990 to 15.8 percent in 2008 in the Chamber, and from 2.6 percent to 5.2 percent in the Senate. In the first congress (1990–1994), the three main parties of the Concertación had only one female deputy each in the Chamber, and two female Concertación senators. Ten years later, in 2000, there were three women from the PPD and two each from the PS and PDC, and five from the Alianza. By 2006, coinciding with Michelle Bachelet's election, ten women were elected to the Chamber (and just one to the Senate) from the Concertación, and seven from the Alianza. These numbers are below the regional average, which was 10.7 percent in 1997 and had increased to 19.3 percent in 2006 (Schwindt-Bayer 2006).

Female leadership in political parties, which have a strong role as gatekeepers in Chilean politics, was also low, from 9 percent across all parties in 1995, to 17.2 percent in 2000, dipping to 8.3 percent in 2006, and up to 16.7 percent in 2008 (Valdés 2010: 254). The low numbers of elected women reflect the difficulties women have had in rising into positions of power through the political parties and in being elected. Much has been written about the ossified nature of the political parties and their difficulties in opening up to women and to youth (see, for example, Luna and Mardones 2010). Women's representation was higher in the cabinet, where they were appointed by presidents rather than elected, from 15.8 percent of ministerial posts under Aylwin to parity in Bachelet's cabinet in 2006. Despite their low numbers, female politicians in the Concertación have been important players in promoting women's rights. The majority of legislative bills on women's rights were initiated by women on the Left, for which they then sought to build broader support.

Given the strong constitutional powers of the executive, the president and executive ministries are crucial players in agenda-setting on women's rights. The National Women's Service, Sernam, was created in 1991, immediately following Chile's transition to democracy. As an arm of the executive, Sernam is the specific political institution that crafts executive bills on women's rights. Sernam is meant to oversee the policies developed by other government agencies, but the ministry also develops its own projects, largely independently of the rest of the government.

Under the Concertación, the superior legislative strength of the executive was evident in the greater success of Sernam's bills, most notably those like domestic violence, sexual assault, or the reform of paternity laws that proposed similar policy reforms to earlier, unsuccessful congressional bills. At the same time, the fate of Sernam was closely linked to the politics surrounding the democratic transition itself. Sernam's top positions are politically appointed. Reflecting the power balance within the Concertación, the first two ministers were Christian Democrats and the subdirectors were So-

Table 6.2 Women's Representation in Congress by Party and Coalition, 1990–2010

Coalition and Party	1990–1994 Chamber	1990–1994 Senate[a]	1994–1998 Chamber	1994–1998 Senate	1998–2002 Chamber	1998–2002 Senate	2002–2006 Chamber	2002–2006 Senate	2006–2010 Chamber	2006–2010 Senate
Concertación coalition										
PDC	1	1	1	2	2	1	3	1	1	1
PS	1		2		2		1		3	
PPD	1	1	3		3		5		5	
PR[b]										
PSD										
PH	1									
IND concert									1	
Coalition total	4	2	6	2	7	1	9	1	10	
Right coalition										
RN	2		2		4		2	1	3	
UDI					1	1	2		4	1
UCC					1					
IND right	1		1				1		7	1
Coalition total	3		3		6	1	5	1	7	1
Other							1		1	
Congress total[c]	7	2	9	2	13	2	15	2	18	2
	5.8%	4.2%	7.5%	4.2%	10.8%	4.1%	12.5%	4.2%	15%	5.2%

Sources: Haas 2010 and National Congress of Chile (2010), www.congreso.cl.

Notes: a. In addition to elected representatives, from 1990 to 2006, there were nine appointed senators. In 2005 the system of designated senators was abolished. One woman was appointed, Olga Feliu Segovia, from the Contraloría General de la Republica. A political independent, she served from 1990 to 1998 and did not support gender equality legislation during her tenure.

b. The PR and PSD combined to form the PRSD in the second administration.

c. The number of senators changed during the period in question due to the existence of appointed senators, deaths, and constitutional reforms. There were 47 senators (from 1990 to 1998), 48 (from 1998 to 2000), 49 (from 2000 to 2002), and 48 (from 2002 to 2006). The higher number from the period in question is used to calculate percentages.

cialists. After his election in 2000 Socialist president Ricardo Lagos appointed a Socialist to head the ministry. As political appointees, Sernam's top directors must strike a rather precarious balance between the agenda of the feminist policy community and the more conservative agenda of the Concertación. The strongest political support for Sernam comes from the Left, but under Christian Democratic administrations, Sernam was largely tied to the social policy agenda of the PDC, which limited the Ministry's ability to support the more controversial gender equality policies introduced by the Left.

This political tension meant that there were certain issues, like the legalization of divorce, that Sernam favored but would not explicitly support while under Christian Democratic leadership. In these cases Sernam was limited to speaking informally in favor of a bill and offering limited degrees of informal support to representatives. There were also issues—most notably the legalization of abortion, which, due both to the general political atmosphere and to the personal ideologies of the Christian Democratic ministers of Sernam, were not supported in any way by the ministry. PDC minister Josefina Bilbao (1994–2000) joined feminists in protesting the imprisonment of women who have abortions, but she stopped short of advocating the decriminalization of abortion. During the 2000 presidential campaign, Ricardo Lagos indicated his willingness to reconsider the ban on therapeutic abortion, but in the face of strong opposition backed down from this position. Even under the administration of Michelle Bachelet, Sernam declined to speak publicly about liberalizing Chile's abortion law.

Legislative Reforms on Women's Rights
Under Concertación Governments

Drawing on the policy agenda developed by the feminist community under the dictatorship, early in the first post-transition democratic administration congressional advocates for women's rights and the leadership of Sernam began to develop a wide-ranging policy agenda, touching on a number of critical women's rights issues. Under two decades of Concertación government, scores of legislative proposals were introduced to expand women's legal equality, across policy areas as diverse as the rights of domestic workers, intrafamily violence, sexual harassment and assault, sex and wage discrimination, the educational rights of pregnant students, protections for pregnant workers, day care, paternity law, marital property rights, therapeutic abortion, and divorce.[6]

While the range of gender equality proposals introduced under Concertación government was impressively broad, only a minority of proposals became law. Issues of gender equality expose deep divisions within Chilean society, and these divisions are reflected in the ideological debates within the political parties. The minority position of the Left within the governing coalition limited Left influence over policy for the first decade of Concertación government. Beginning in 2002, Left representatives outnumbered Christian Democrats in the Chamber of Deputies, and combined with executive support from Socialist presidents and more progressive ministers in Sernam, the Left began to assert a more ambitious policy agenda on women's rights, especially under Bachelet.

The evolution of gender equality policy within the Concertación exhibits several distinct phases. Following the transition, feminist representatives from the Left developed an ambitious legislative agenda on women's rights, introducing bills that touched on core issues of gender inequality and that were often deeply controversial. The failure of these early bills led representatives to alter their legislative strategies, working more closely with Sernam and with Christian Democrats to moderate the content of their bills to broaden support for the measures. While the legislative success of gender equality proposals increased, feminist representatives and their supporters became discouraged in the face of entrenched opposition, and efforts to promote gender policy waned. Finally, the election of Socialist presidents, who appointed progressive ministers to Sernam and publicly supported gender equality policies, prompted renewed congressional efforts to legislate on these issues. Below, we outline these broad dynamics in more detail and then illustrate them with case studies of three legislative topics: women and work, divorce, and reproductive rights.

An Ambitious First Congress

The first phase in the evolution of gender equality policy under the Concertación coincides with the first democratic congress (March 1990–March 1994). Despite their strength as a social movement at the moment of transition, women did not fare well in the first administration, either in numbers run as candidates, elected to office, or appointed to executive positions. The creation and staffing of Sernam was controversial. The first ministers came from the PDC, were not feminists, and had little connection to feminist organizations in civil society.[7] In the Chamber of Deputies, only four women were elected overall, and only the three elected from the Left self-identified as feminists. Only two women from the Concertación were elected to the Senate, and here, too, only the senator from the Left (PPD) self-identified as feminist.[8]

Despite their low numbers, feminist legislators from the Left, many of whom had their political roots in the women's movement, were eager to pursue a progressive social agenda. They introduced twelve gender equality bills, ranging from paternity reform[9] to domestic violence, the property rights of married women, abortion, divorce, and sexual assault. Only one of these bills eventually passed: a 1991 bill criminalizing "intrafamily" violence (it became law in 1994). Over this same period, Sernam introduced three bills, all of which eventually passed.[10] Sernam's bills addressed critical areas of gender inequality, paternity reform, and sexual assault. Sernam's sexual assault law, which in addition to increasing the penalties for sexual assault decriminalized consensual homosexual relations, provoked strong opposition from the Right and conservative Christian Democrats. Nevertheless, the clear majority of bills, and the most controversial proposals, including bills on abortion and divorce, were introduced by the Left. The range of bills that Left representatives introduced during this period illustrates the Left's strong desire to impact the social policy agenda of the Concertación, and reflects the relative support for these issues within the parties of the Left. Significantly, none of these bills was cosponsored by Christian Democratic representatives or received support from the PDC at the drafting stage.

Building Alliances Around Moderate Bills

The second phase of policymaking coincides with the second congress, from March 1994 to March 1998. The presidency and Sernam continued under PDC leadership, although the Left made small gains in the Chamber of Deputies.

During this period, the Left largely abandoned independent attempts at gender equality policy and instead pursued broader alliances with the PDC (and a few representatives from the Right). The cost of these alliances was a moderation of the agenda, and fewer controversial bills were introduced. Gender equality bills in the second congress focused, for example, on marital property rights, the right to nurse infants at work, day care, prohibiting pregnancy tests as a condition of work contracts, prohibiting the expulsion of pregnant students from public schools, electoral quotas, and violence against women. Each of these bills addresses an important area of gender inequality, but it became clear during this phase that a more radical gender equality agenda was off the table. The one notable exception to this pattern is the 1995 divorce bill, which was introduced by two Christian Democratic deputies, Mariana Aylwin and Ignacio Walker, and is discussed below. The most controversial gender equality policy, abortion liberalization, was not revisited during this period (the only abortion-related bill introduced and debated in congress came from the Right, to increase penalties for abortion).

This strategy of building broader alliances around more moderate bills increased the legislative success of gender equality bills during this period. Six of fourteen congressional bills eventually passed, as did each of Sernam's four bills.

Frustration and Retreat

During the third phase, from March 1998 to March 2002, the number of representatives from the Left decreased slightly, and the introduction of gender equality bills decreased dramatically. While the total number of deputies from the Concertación held steady at seventy, the Socialists lost four seats, and the Christian Democrats gained two (the PPD gained one seat, and the PRSD gained two). The number of female Socialist and PPD deputies remained the same, at two and three, respectively, and the number of female representatives from the PDC increased from one to two.

The decrease in the number of gender equality bills introduced cannot be attributed simply to the slight decrease in the number of Socialist deputies. Rather, the strength of the opposition to gender equality policy, from conservative Christian Democrats, to the Right and the Catholic Church, left proponents of reform frustrated and demobilized. This period corresponds to the third democratic congress. From March 1998 to March 2000, the Christian Democrats held the presidency and the leadership of Sernam; from March 2000 to March 2002, the Socialists controlled the presidency and headed Sernam. During this four-year period, only six bills were introduced: one from Sernam and five from congress, two of which passed. Despite the overall lull in the introduction of gender equality legislation, it is important to note that three of the four congressional bills were introduced after Lagos's election. These bills dealt with reproductive rights and sexual harassment, and they enjoyed broad cross-party support, including a few members of the Right. Thus, while the end of Christian Democratic leadership coincided with a sense of exhaustion on the part of supporters of gender equality, following the election of a Socialist to the presidency, the pace of legislative efforts began to increase once again.

Renewed Efforts Under Bachelet

The final phase of gender equality policymaking stretched from March 2002 until the end of Bachelet's presidency in 2010. This period coincides with a small increase in female representatives from the PS and PPD, but more female representatives were also elected from the Right, and the latter were more likely to oppose than support feminist initiatives. These shifts in female representation reflect the changing electoral fortunes of the parties overall, with both the Left and Right gaining seats at the expense of the PDC. When Bachelet took office in 2006, she appointed women to 50 percent of cabinet positions,[11] significantly broadening support for gender equality policies within the executive branch. Thus, the last congress under Concertación government presented new opportunities for gender equality policy as well as strengthened opposition to these proposals.

Under the Bachelet administration we saw a remarkable increase in the introduction of gender equality bills. Bachelet spearheaded the development of a broad gender equality agenda, which resulted in significant reforms in a number of areas. In addition, congressional representatives attempted to take advantage of the presence of a feminist president and more supportive ministries to push forward on a more ambitious agenda, which included the reintroduction of multiple bills covering abortion and reproductive rights. We also saw the emergence of a legislative dynamic in which Sernam (at times together with other ministries) played a supporting role in congressional legislative efforts.[12] Sernam introduced only one bill during this period, a gender quota bill that was cosponsored by the president. By contrast congressional representatives introduced forty-nine bills.

The congressional bills spanned the breadth of gender equality legislation that had been introduced previously and pushed into new, and controversial, issues. Representatives introduced bills addressing sex discrimination, sexual harassment and assault, violence against women, electoral quotas, marital property rights and minimum marriage age, various rights of women workers, and wage equality. Several bills addressed the rights of gay and lesbian individuals, from antidiscrimination laws to proposals for civil unions. Finally, representatives introduced a number of measures expanding the right to divorce and establishing reproductive rights.

While only four of the forty-nine congressional bills had become law as of March 2011,[13] the sheer number of new proposals and the widening base of support for gender equality legislation signaled an important new dynamic around these issues. To begin, ten of the forty-nine bills originated in the Senate, which previously had been relatively inhospitable to these issues (between 1990 and 2006 only five gender equality bills had originated in the Senate). The bills introduced under Bachelet also reflected a much broader base of support for gender equality. Whereas similar congressional bills in the previous periods were usually the product of a small group of feminist legislators, either working alone or with a small group of male colleagues, many of the more recent bills were introduced only by men, or by a relatively large number of male representatives together with the usual feminist female representatives. Bills introduced by male representatives alone included some of the most controversial issues, covering reproductive rights and abortion, and equal rights for same-sex couples. These intriguing dynamics suggest both that sectors within the Concertación are willing to push back against the policy dominance of the executive and that interest in gender equality is expanding, particularly within the Left. We return to this theme in our conclusion.

In contrast to the 1994–1998 period when feminists reached out to more moderate colleagues at the drafting stage, under Bachelet the Left renewed its efforts to legislate alone (although it did not abandon the idea of cooperation on legislation). Furthermore, where cross-party alliances were made, they were increasingly likely to include representatives from the Right. This was the case with multiple bills on reproductive rights, violence against women, and the rights of women workers. Most interesting, perhaps, is the fact that the Christian Democrats remained noticeably absent from much of this legislation. Many of the cross-party bills were authored by representatives from the Left *and* the Right, but did not include the PDC. This dynamic reflects the ongoing divisions within the Christian Democratic Party over issues of gender equality.

The Role of Bachelet in Supporting Gender Equality

An avowed feminist, Bachelet signaled her support for gender equality in a number of concrete ways, including the appointment of more women to executive office, increasing Sernam's budget,[14] introducing sweeping gender equality reforms in several critical policy areas, and by providing funding and structural support for gender equality laws that had been insufficiently implemented. Bachelet's policy of gender parity in cabinet and governor posts represented a radical departure from past Concertación administrations, where, with some notable exceptions,[15] few women had held high-level positions.[16] In practical terms, increasing the number of progressive women in high office broadened the base of support for gender equality policies, and it increased the pool of experienced women leaders. On a symbolic level, seeing more women in powerful government positions changed public perceptions of women's roles and provided powerful role models for young Chileans.

We see Bachelet's support for gender equality policies reflected in a number of areas. In the area of early education and care (ECEC) policies, a notable policy success under Bachelet was the program Chile Crece Contigo (Chile Grows with You). This integrated program coordinates care for pregnant women and ECEC services for children until they enter preschool, targeting specifically the lowest income quintiles. The policy was enshrined into law by congress in 2009 and now establishes free access to ECEC services as a right for children three years and younger from low-income families (Staab and Gerhard 2010: 15). Bachelet focused particular attention on the issue of domestic violence, providing needed executive support for weakly enforced existing policies. The 1994 Intra-Family Violence law, while groundbreaking in some respects, was widely criticized for its narrow scope, lack of protection for victims, and the lack of a viable victim support system, such as shelters for victims of domestic violence, that would make the law workable in practice. When Bachelet assumed office, there was only one domestic violence shelter in Santiago. Bachelet created new shelters and established a domestic violence hotline. Bachelet's emergency contraception policy, discussed below, was particularly controversial and a major advance in Chile's reproductive rights policy. Perhaps most significant among Bachelet's gender equality policies was her reform of Chile's private pension system (Law 20.172), which, among other changes, makes it easier for nonbreadwinners (usually women) to gain access to the spouse's pension and incorporate single mothers more effectively into the pension program.[17]

Bachelet's forceful advocacy of women's rights and her active engagement on gender equality issues emboldened congressional representatives to renew their efforts at legislative reforms. This is reflected in the increased attempts to legislate on issues related to women and work, divorce, and reproductive rights, as illustrated in the case studies that follow.

Case Studies

Women and Work

Gender equality in the workplace includes a wide range of issues. Between 1990 and 2010, congressional representatives or Sernam introduced numerous bills on the topic. These bills addressed workplace discrimination and salary equity, workplace harassment, the rights of mothers to breast-feed their babies at work, the banning of pregnancy tests as a condition of work contracts, and day care. Compared to divorce and reproductive rights, which cause conflict with the Catholic Church and therefore create divisions within the PDC, most issues of workplace equity are relatively uncontroversial. Nevertheless, while most of these issues do not conflict with Catholic doctrine, they do require government outlays and as a result will create opposition from conservatives on economic grounds.

Despite the lack of inherent controversy in most of these bills, this was not an area of significant cooperation within the Concertación between the Left and the Christian Democrats in the first congress. Left representatives introduced three bills banning sex discrimination, one of which (Bill 1065) explicitly focused on employment discrimination. The PDC failed to cosponsor any of these bills, and none were debated in committee.

During the second congress, there was increased cosponsorship of legislation addressing women and work, and this reflects the overall trend for gender equality legislation during this period. Six bills related to women and the workplace were introduced. Sernam's bill to ban pregnancy tests as a condition of work contracts and to expand day care options passed the congress in 1998. Three of the five congressional bills enjoyed cross-party support. Senators from the Left and the PDC cosponsored a day care bill, which became law in 1995. In the lower house, Christian Democratic deputies joined their colleagues from the Left in sponsoring a bill banning wage discrimination, which failed to pass the congress. A law banning sexual harassment and assault in the workplace was coauthored by deputies from the Left, the PDC, and the Right.[18] The Left introduced two additional bills on its own. A bill allowing mothers to nurse infants at work passed the congress in 2007,[19] twelve years after its introduction (and with a strong push from President Bachelet). A Senate bill expanding day care options was never debated in committee.

Reflecting the decrease in gender equality legislation between 1998 and 2002, only one bill was introduced on women and work during this time. Left senators introduced a bill banning age and sex discrimination in employment, which passed the congress in 2000. With President Bachelet's support, beginning in 2006 congressional representatives addressed workplace equality with renewed force. Thirteen bills introduced between 2006 and 2010 directly addressed various aspects of workplace discrimination or inequality. Chief among these were Bachelet's pension reform, mentioned above. In the area of day care, a law passed in 1995 (Law 19.408) failed to make day care available for most working parents as it only obligated companies with more than twenty female (excluding male) employees to provide day care. Under the auspices of Chile Crece Contigo, the Bachelet government increased the number of public day care centers from 700 in 2006 to 4,000 by 2009 (Staab and Gerhard 2010:15).

Of eleven work-related congressional bills initiated under Bachelet, half were cosponsored by parties outside the Left. The PDC coauthored a bill establishing pay equality, and the PDC and the Right cosponsored a Left initiative expanding the right of female workers to take breast-feeding breaks. Interestingly, the three other cosponsored bills enjoyed the support of the Left and the Right, but were not cosponsored by any Christian Democratic representatives. Three of these bills became law: a proposal to extend day care rights to male workers, the establishment of a four-day paternity leave following the birth or adoption of a child, and the equalization of public holidays for live-in domestic workers. Five additional bills by the Left failed to pass the congress. These initiatives sought to prohibit the firing of pregnant workers, expanded the right to pregnancy and family leave, and allowed women workers to miss work for medical checkups.

Legislation addressing workplace discrimination and women's equal participation in the labor force reflects the complex dynamics at work within the Concertación. These bills make it clear that the PDC and the Left were not only divided on gender equality legislation that conflicted with Catholic teaching; rather, there was disagreement over the very priority of gender equality within the larger social policy agenda of the government.

While policymaking in this area improved under Bachelet, her support could not eliminate these basic divisions within the Concertación.

Divorce

Despite high public support, the legalization of divorce took fourteen years after the transition to democracy, and spanned three Concertación governments. In 1991, 1993, and 1994, legislators from the Left introduced liberal divorce bills, but the executive, including Sernam, did not support them, despite tacit acknowledgment that legislation was needed. These bills never left committee. They paved the way, however, for a more conservative bill in 1995. On this bill, several liberal Christian Democratic deputies lent their support to the efforts and also became the most vocal spokespersons for the bill in the media. Given the necessity for partial PDC support, a shift from a more openly secular and pragmatic bill to a Catholic based bill was an expected result of coalition politics. The bill did not allow for divorce on the basis of mutual consent, but required a waiting period of at least five years, if aggravating circumstances (such as homosexuality or domestic violence) were not proven.

In this case, the church and the political Right launched an aggressive lobbying campaign against the bill that was influential but ultimately unsuccessful in preventing the bill's passage. It was lengthily debated and approved in 1997 in the Chamber along party lines. In the Senate, the Right shelved it until President Lagos forced a Senate debate and vote on an executive-modified version of the bill in 2004. This version is more liberal; it allows for couples to file for divorce on the basis of mutual consent after a one-year separation, with some qualifications. The bill passed the Senate in 2004, instituting civil divorce for the first time in Chile's history (see Blofield 2006: 95–120; Haas 2010).

Under Bachelet, congressional representatives undertook several attempts to improve the divorce law, initiating multiple bills that sought to facilitate the process of divorce. Five bills were introduced between 2007 and 2010, three originating in the Chamber of Deputies and two in the Senate. The most moderate of these bills, which would make the process of filing for divorce easier, originated in the upper house and was the only bill that was coauthored by Christian Democratic deputies. The other bills were sponsored only by the Left. Three sought to institute a system of no-fault divorce, and the fourth sought to create civil unions for same-sex couples. None of the bills introduced since divorce was legalized have passed the congress. However, the introduction of bills in both houses of congress, and the proposal to create civil unions, illustrated a desire, particularly on the Left, to use the 2004 divorce law as a stepping stone to more progressive reforms.

Reproductive Rights

Abortion is the most controversial gender equality issue in Chile, and attempts to decriminalize even therapeutic abortion provoke strong opposition from the Right, conservative Christian Democrats, and the Catholic Church. When a left-wing deputy proposed a bill to reinstate therapeutic abortion in 1991—two years after it was repealed—she was vilified by the political Right and by the media. The Right declared the bill would signify the "death of the defenseless and the innocent" (*El Mercurio,* October 5, 1991). The PDC leadership made it clear it had no interest in broaching abortion because it went "against Christian Democratic values." No one in the Concertación would touch it, and the bill died in committee despite supportive public opinion (Blofield 2006: 97–105; Haas 2010).

In the 1990s, agenda-setting on this topic was in the hands of the Right, as UDI legislators proposed bills to increase penalties for abortion. One was debated in the Senate in 1998 and failed by just two votes. The church and conservative Catholic organizations and the political Right dominated framing and agenda-setting on abortion (Blofield 2006: 95–120). Concertación efforts during this decade were limited to modest attempts to address the equally important issue of prevention of pregnancies. Here, too, such efforts faced significant opposition. For example, the sex education program developed under the Frei administration (the first comprehensive sex education program attempted in Chilean public schools)[20] was widely characterized by conservatives and church leaders as a government attempt to undermine traditional moral values (see Haas 1999).

Indeed, expectation of opposition from the church—and the effect that would have on the Concertación as well as the Right—was a main reason why representatives in favor of the decriminalization of abortion would not support bills on the topic, even ones that merely reverted back to the pre-1989 abortion law. However, in recent years congressional representatives from across the political spectrum have shown increased willingness to legislate on this issue, and on reproductive rights more broadly (Haas 2010).

After the failure of the 1991 therapeutic abortion bill, no reformist bill on abortion or reproductive rights was introduced until 2000. Since that time, representatives have initiated eleven bills attempting to reform laws in this area. The Left was the primary support for each of these bills. Only two of these bills were coauthored by Christian Democratic representatives, and they were the most conservative bills. They sought merely to recognize that the concept of reproductive rights exists and to clarify that women should have control over certain aspects of their reproduction, but the bills do not clarify what these rights are. Two other bills were coauthored by members of the Right (but not by the PDC), and these bills sought to decriminalize therapeutic abortion under narrowly defined circumstances. The remaining bills were supported only by the Left. Some sought only to decriminalize therapeutic abortion, some would have decriminalized abortion under a broader set of circumstances, and other bills proposed a broader establishment of reproductive rights that included abortion. None of these bills was debated in committee during the Bachelet government, but the last one introduced during her administration (Bill 6845) was approved in committee for Senate debate in 2011.

An examination of these bills indicates that representatives tried to breach the powerful opposition to reproductive rights by approaching the subject in a variety of ways. These efforts illustrate the continuing reluctance of Christian Democrats to legislate on reproductive rights, but these bills also reflect the growing acceptance of these issues beyond the Left, as members of the Right demonstrate a growing interest in reforming laws on this subject.

Bachelet's support for reproductive rights has been critical to the increased willingness of congressional representatives to revisit the issue. Arguably Bachelet's most controversial policy decision in the area of women's rights was her executive decision to provide free emergency contraception to women fourteen and older. This decision deepened divisions within the Concertación and provoked strong opposition from the Catholic Church. Bachelet withstood enormous pressure from the PDC, the Church, and the Right and refused to rescind the policy. The program withstood a court challenge in 2008 and became law in 2010. The emergency contraception policy stands as one of the most significant pieces of social legislation of Bachelet's presidency. In future years, we may see positive effects from this policy in multiple social indicators, including improvements in health and education levels and reductions in poverty. Bachelet's victory in this area also carries political importance beyond the practical impact of the policy. Her willingness to defend the reproductive rights of Chilean women in the face of strong opposition within and outside her governing coalition demonstrated the possibility of progress on gender equality in Chile, even on the most controversial issues.

Conclusion: Gender Equality Under a Right Government

The elections of 2009 and 2010 were the Concertación's to lose, and they did. The unparalleled popularity of Bachelet upon leaving office was largely based on the way her administration handled the economic crisis, and the inability of the governing coalition to renovate itself ultimately led to its defeat and the victory of President Sebastián Piñera (see, for example, Luna and Mardones 2010). This heralded a new era in Chilean politics, and the first time the Right had won the presidency at the ballot box since 1958.

It does not represent a seismic shift to the right among the Chilean electorate, however, and Piñera himself comes from the more liberal wing of the Chilean Right. While the longer-term impact of these political changes on gender equality remains to be seen, the Piñera administration has shown that it is not interested in a radical reversal of policy on gender equality. While the Left tends to be the initiator of women's rights reforms, often with considerable opposition, once such reforms are in place, they tend to become an accepted part of reality even by many of those who most ardently opposed them. Today, the discourse of the governing Right on gender equality accepts many of the reforms that elicited so much opposition twenty, ten, or even five years ago.

Recognizing the reality of Chile's very low women's labor force participation rates as well as below-replacement fertility rates, the priority of the Piñera government has been to promote public policies to both increase women's participation in the workforce and to reconcile the family-work nexus. Piñera's administration, with Sernam at the forefront, sent a project to congress to extend maternity leave to six months, including a publicly provided subsidy, in March 2011.

Carolina Schmidt, the minister of Sernam under Piñera, reflects the evolution of the Right's thinking on gender equality. While Schmidt affirms that she does not support same-sex marriage, she declared herself willing to consider some benefits for same-sex couples. While she asserted that she was against therapeutic abortion, she also stated that saving a mother's life with the effect of the baby dying was not an abortion. She also argued the morning-after pill should be available, although only with parental authorization for minors. These positions, while not liberal, nevertheless signal a willingness to break with church teaching, and with the position of much of the Right, on critical areas of gender equality.

Despite these signs of progress, this overview of gender equality policy under the Concertación makes clear that like many of the themes discussed throughout this volume, more progressive gender reform and increased women's representation in political institutions have been hampered by the political constraints of the transition. On the one hand, the overall goals of maintaining stability and peace and legislating through negotiation have diluted the scope and content of reform. On the other hand, the transition, as we have noted and as has been the case with respect to other issue areas in this volume, empowered the very economic and political actors most opposed to reform.

Yet the period of Concertación government also reveals significant progress on policy reform on gender equality. The remarkable increase under Bachelet in the number of representatives interested in introducing gender equality legislation reflects a new political reality in Chile that counterbalances political gains by the Right. Over the last decade, the willingness to initiate gender equality legislation has moved from a small, committed group of feminist representatives on the Left to a growing cohort of male as well as female legislators from across the political spectrum. The Left remains at the forefront of these efforts, and the Christian Democrats as a whole remain noticeably disengaged from many of the bills. But support within the PDC, and within the Right, is growing. Buttressed by the continuing evolution of public opinion on issues of gender equality, the expansion of congressional support for reform suggests that efforts to address these issues outlived the end of Concertación government.

Compared to other policy areas, gender equality has been a particularly uncomfortable fit for the parties of the Concertación. To a large degree the parties that formed the coalition came together despite their differences on these issues, not because of them. Conflict within the Concertación over gender equality policy was clearly reflected in debates within the congress, as well as between the strongest advocates for gender equality in congress, who hailed primarily from the Left, and an executive under Christian Democratic control for the first half of Concertación rule. In the course of almost two decades of Concertación government, it also became clear that public policy on gender equality was increasingly out of step with liberalizing public opinion. Given these pressures from within and outside the governing coalition, the dramatic change in policy dynamic we see under Bachelet is not entirely surprising. The broadening of interest in gender equality policy across the Left, together with congressional efforts to retake the legislative dynamic from Sernam, suggest that, in this important policy area, Chile may be making significant progress despite the temerity of reform that grew, in part, from the enclaves of the transition.

Notes

1. Here, *Left parties* refers to the Socialist Party (PS), the Party for Democracy (PPD), and the Humanist Party (PH). Each of these parties elected women to the Chamber of Deputies during the period covered by this analysis, and the PS and PPD were critical in providing support in committee and on the floor for gender equality legislation. The PRSD elected few representatives overall and no women in the period covered (see Tables 6.1 and 6.2). For the legislation covered here, PRSD representatives tended to vote with the Left during floor votes, but the party was not central to either the development of or support for gender equality legislation and is therefore not a focus of our analysis. The primary legislative dynamic on these issues, and the focus of our analysis, centers on debates over these issues within the Concertación between the Left and the Christian Democratic Party (PDC).

2. On the role of the women's movement during this period, see, for example, Frohmann and Valdés (1993) and Waylen (2000).

3. These inequalities slightly declined in the 2000s (see CEPAL 2009), but remained high even by regional standards.

4. In addition to thirty-eight elected senators, nine senators were appointed.

5. This "gender dimension" touches on a wide range of public policy. While the Left is more supportive of policies that increase gender equality, the broad scope of such policies, and the fact that many touch on deep-seated cultural beliefs about gender roles, means that the gender dimension is not reducible to a simple Left-Right dimension. For this reason we will not see unified support for gender equality policies even within the Left, and parties such as the PDC, with ideological links to the Catholic Church, will be starkly divided on these issues. For a more detailed discussion of these dynamics, see Blofield and Haas 2005.

6. For purposes of this study, we define gender equality legislation as legislation whose primary purpose is to address some aspect of gender inequality. Pending legislation can be searched through the website of the Chilean Senate, available at http://sil.senado.cl.

7. In fairness, both PDC ministers Soledad Alvear (1991–1994) and Josefina Bilbao (1994–1998) developed closer links to the feminist community during their time in office (see Haas 2010).

8. Those representatives not identifying as feminist supported some of the gender equality legislation after it was introduced, but they were not involved in initiating such proposals.

9. Prior to the reform of paternity laws in 1998, children born outside of marriage had fewer rights to parental care and to inheritance than children born within marriage, and men had few obligations to their extramarital children. In addition to the discrimination faced by these children, the previous laws left women to be the sole caretakers of children born outside of marriage.

10. One bill—a bill increasing the penalty for sexual assault in a narrow range of circumstances—was introduced by a female representative from the right and did not pass.

11. She also appointed women to 50 percent of governor posts.

12. Support took the form of technical assistance in the writing of bills, support during committee and floor debates, and lobbying of representatives.

13. These laws extended day care rights to male workers (Law 20.399), granted paternity leave to fathers (Law 20.482) and to mothers with disabled children (Law 20.535), and extended equal holidays to live-in domestic workers (Law 20.336).

14. Sernam's budget increased by 67 percent between 2004 and 2006 (Valdés 2010: 262).

15. Most significantly, Michelle Bachelet held the positions of health minister and later defense minister under Lagos, and Soledad Alvear was justice minister under Frei and foreign minister under Lagos.

16. After two years in office, Bachelet reshuffled her cabinet, but by the end of her term almost 45 percent of cabinet posts were still held by women.

17. Pribble (2011: 190) explains, "In accordance with the 2008 law, the Chilean state will make a contribution worth 10 percent of 18 minimum wages for the first two children born to each woman. This is important because many women accumulate much lower savings because of the fact that they exit the labor market following the birth of a child."

18. Despite the breadth of support at introduction, this proved a controversial bill, as representatives struggled to define the legal limits of harassment. The bill was introduced in 1994 and became law in 2005.

19. Law 20.166.

20. This program was termed JOCAS (the Spanish acronym stood for Conversations About Sexuality and Affection).

7

Human Rights Under the Concertación

Cath Collins

In Chapter 5, Greg Weeks discusses how civil-military relations under the Concertación were for a long time conducted in the long shadow cast by Augusto Pinochet. The same could of course be said of Chile's uncomfortable, and still unresolved, legacy of past human rights violations. This rumbled on through the 1990s, making periodic reappearances in "irruptions of memory" (Wilde 1999), whose military dimension is ably analyzed by Weeks in the aforementioned chapter. The extent to which such legacies can ever be considered fully resolved is of course limited, and this chapter does not aim to classify Chile's transitional justice performance as laudable or lacking according to any rigid external referent or ideal type. Rather, it explores how public policy and political activity along this dimension of post-1990 national life display the kind of stability-oriented and risk-averse behaviors suggested by the transitional enclaves set out in Chapters 1 and 2. The argument made there, that the Concertación in essence mistook early constraints for a permanent narrowing of horizons, is nowhere more in evidence than in regard to its treatment of the human rights legacy of the Pinochet years.

A succession of four Concertación presidents, each with firsthand experience of the appalling human costs of the seventeen-year military regime, nonetheless proved unwilling or unable either to reverse the regime's deep and abiding transformations of the country's economic, social, and political culture or to force an unequivocal acknowledgment and repudiation of its worst crimes. The prevailing mood of deference to the sensibilities of outgoing authoritarians largely ruled out insistent reference to crimes committed during the construction of a model now upheld by all,

143

and the issue of past human violations seems to have been viewed by successive Concertación presidents as largely politically unrewarding and socially controversial, best avoided or downplayed. Once Aylwin (1990–1994) had tested and established the very narrow limits of what seemed sensible to push for, none of the subsequent Concertación presidents—Frei Ruiz-Tagle (1994–2000), Lagos (2000–2006), or Bachelet (2006–2010)—seemed tempted to make human rights any kind of flagship cause, in either its narrow or broader possible interpretations. Many factors other than solely military opposition or pressure militated against their doing so: these included the formidable combination of public indifference with the political Right's implacable intransigence and buoyant electoral and legislative strength. A left-wing political elite haunted by the memory of personal defeat and sobered by encounters with actually existing socialism in its declining years proved no match for a still combative military establishment and a self-confident private sector that demanded, and largely obtained, guarantees of business as usual under the new dispensation.[1] Tables 7.1 and 7.2 summarize human rights–related policy innovations and major reparation measures, respectively, by president for the Concertación era. The tables support this chapter's contention that the horizons for reform were quite restrained. Indeed, far from planning significant inroads into transition-era impunity, the Concertación seemed if anything to be fighting constant rearguard actions against opposition proposals seeking to refine, perfect, and extend the 1978 amnesty law.

The chapter illustrates and analyzes this persistent, and ongoing, tension between moral imperatives and pragmatic politics in Concertación human rights policy between 1990 and 2010. The first sections discuss initial constraints and show how these led to the entrenchment of dictatorship-era ideological differences about the validity of human rights discourse. Next, the Frei presidency of 1994–2000 is discussed as a largely missed opportunity for more assertive Concertación action over human rights policy. The chapter goes on to describe how reluctance to pursue change from above was gradually supplanted by growing pressures for change from outside and below, culminating in a 2003 policy announcement by Ricardo Lagos that expanded previous truth and reparations measures but stopped well short of underwriting private justice claims. The final sections discuss the limits and contradictions of advances in memory politics under Bachelet, before drawing conclusions that show just how comprehensively Concertación-era action and inaction over human rights fit the overarching thesis of this book: that a penchant for stability can, and in this case did, become a serious impediment to real and lasting transformation. The self-limiting nature of the transition is particularly evident in the area of past atrocities, with even Bachelet, the most sympathetic of the four Concertación

Table 7.1 Human Rights–Related Policy Innovations by Presidential Period, 1990–2010

Policy Innovation	Disposition
Aylwin (1990–1994)	
First national truth commission: National Commission on Truth and Reconciliation (Comisión Nacional de Verdad y Reconciliación [CNVR]), "Rettig Commission"	Created by Supreme Decree No. 355, April 1990; report published March 4, 1991
"Aylwin Doctrine" Exhortation to the Supreme Court, March 1991	Failed
Truth commission followup: National Corporation for Reparations and Reconciliation (Corporación Nacional de Reparación y Reconciliación [CNRR])	Created by Law 19.123 of February 8, 1992, which also assigned reparations (see Table 7.2)
Framework agreement (acuerdo marco), April–June 1990	Failed
Leyes Cumplido: Legislative package introduced in April 1990 to modify existing terror legislation, state security laws, death penalty statutes, and due process guarantees	Partially successful Law 19.027, January 24, 1991, modified terror legislation; Law 19.055, April 1, 1991, constitutional reform to allow pardons to be granted even to those condemned under antiterror laws (expressly excluded from potential pardons under the existing 1980 constitution)
Frei (1994–2000)	
Reception of CNRR report	CNRR presented its final report, and ceased to exist, on December 31, 1996.
Creation of the Human Rights Program, Programa continuación de la ley 19.123	Created by Supreme Decree No. 1.005 of 1997, under the Ministry of the Interior
Beginning of the round table, Mesa de Diálogo	Convened August 21, 1999, by then defense minister Edmundo Pérez Yoma
Judicial reform package including changes to the Supreme Court	Law 19.374, February 18, 1995 began migration from a written investigative magistrate system to an oral trial system. Importantly, the reforms had a modernizing rubric and had been agreed through a long process of cross-party negotiation.
"Frei project" and Figueroa-Otero proposal	Failed

(continues)

Table 7.1 continued

Policy Innovation	Disposition
Lagos (2000–2006)	
Closure of the round table and reception of results of its information-gathering phase	
Second national truth commission: National Commission on Political Imprisonment and Torture (Comisión Nacional sobre Prisión Política y Tortura), "Valech Commission"	Created by Supreme Decree No. 1.040, operated November 2003–November 2004; initial report published November 28, 2004, appendix in 2005
Legislative package "No hay mañana sin ayer" (Without yesterday, there can be no tomorrow)	Announced on August 12, 2003
Bachelet (2006–2010)	
Creation of a second-round truth commission: "Valech II"	Law 20.405, December 10, 2009, and Supreme Decree No. 43, January 27, 2010, established the Comisión Presidencial Asesora para la Calificación de Detenidos Desaparecidos, Ejecutados Políticos y Víctimas de Prisión Política y Tortura. Operated between February 2010 and August 2011
Creation of a special presidential advisory commission on HR, the Comisión Asesora Presidencial de DDHH	
Recognition of adverse Inter-American Court ruling, case Luis Almonacid	The Inter-American Court of Human Rights issued its final ruling in *Almonacid Arellano y otros vs. Chile* on September 26, 2006, finding against Chile. The verdict ordered the state to ensure that the 1978 Amnesty Law did not continue to impede justice obligations in cases of disappearance.
Law instituting the legal status of "absent through forced disappearance"	Law 20.377 of September 10, 2009
Construction of the National Museum of Memory and Human Rights	Approved by Law 20.405 of December 10, 2009; inaugurated on January 11, 2010
Design of the National Human Rights Institute (Instituto Nacional de Derechos Humanos [INDH])	Law 20.405, December 10, 2009, gave the institute legal existence, but it was not inaugurated until July 20, 2010, under the subsequent presidency.

Sources: Loveman and Lira (2000, 2002); research assistance by Boris Hau.

Table 7.2 Major Reparations Measures by Administration, 1990–2010

Measure	Purpose
Aylwin (1990–1994)	
Office for Returnees (Oficina Nacional del Retorno); created by Law 18.994, August 20, 1990	To promote return from exile overseas, offered validation of professional qualifications, waiving of duty on imported personal effects, and some educational scholarships for those willing to commit to return within a specified time frame
Health Program (Programa de Reparación y Atención Integral en Salud [PRAIS]); began 1991, officially established by Resolución Exenta no. 729, December 16, 1992	Access to the public health system and to specialized mental health support for those directly and indirectly affected by grave violations
Reparations for relatives of Rettig victims; Law 19.123, February 8, 1992	Established pensions, health care access, educational scholarships, and exemption from military service for immediate family members of those recognized in the Rettig report as victims of disappearance or political execution
Program for victims of politically motivated dismissal (Programa exonerados); created by Law 19.234, August 12, 1993, extended by Law 19.582, August 31, 1998	Restoration of missed pension contributions and other social protections for individuals dismissed or "blacklisted" for political reasons. Some receive a specific top-up pension from the program.
Victims' memorial (Memorial del Detenido Desaparecido y del Ejecutado Político)	
Frei (1994–2000)	
Grace and favor pensions for dispossessed farmers (exonerados de tierra), 1995– 1996	
Compulsory purchase of Villa Grimaldi memory site, 1996	The state ceded to pressure and prevented an emblematic former clandestine torture center from being sold for a housing development
Restitution of confiscated assets, Law 19.568, July 23, 1998	Orders the state to return all major assets confiscated for political reasons during the dictatorship period
Additional legislation for victims of political dismissal (exonerados); Law 19.582, August 31, 1998	Extends the definition of exonerados to include former judicial branch personnel, military, and congressional representatives
Derogation of September 11 as a public holiday; Law 19.588, November 11, 1998	Replaced with a self-styled official Day for National Reconciliation

(continues)

Table 7.2 continued

Measure	Purpose
Lagos (2000–2006)	
Law 19.740, June 30, 2001	Reduced debt burden on returnees from exile
Law 19.881, June 27, 2003	Extended the application period for cases of politically motivated dismissal
Law 19.962, August 25, 2004	Wiped the prison records of those considered to have been unfairly or illegitimately jailed during the dictatorship
Law 19.980, November 9, 2004	Improved Rettig reparations (Law 19.123 of 1992) by increasing amounts of pensions for relatives of the dead or disappeared and/or by incorporating new categories of individuals
Law19.992, December 24, 2004	Established a monthly pension, health care access, and educational scholarships for those recognized by Valech as survivors of torture and political imprisonment
Bachelet (2006–2010)	
Inauguration of memory sites, 2006–2009	Bachelet agreed to preside over the inauguration of a series of memory sites or memorials built with (some) public funds
Declarations of the National Day of the Disappeared and Day of Victims of Political Execution (Día Nacional del Detenido Desaparecido y del EjecutadoPolítico), 2006, 2010	
Law 20.134, November 22, 2006	Established a one-off lump sum payment for victims of politically motivated dismissal whose cases had already been recognized
Law 20.405, December 10, 2009	Created the National Institute for Human Rights and reopened the Rettig and Valech lists; also made educational scholarships transferable to grandchildren and expanded exemptions from military service

Sources: Lira Loveman (2002); INDH (2011); research assistance by Boris Hau.

presidents to the issue, prioritizing expressions of empathy with victims over open confrontation with perpetrators.

Setting the Tone:
Early Muting of the "Human Rights Question"

One notable feature of the trajectory of human rights in Chile is a persistent conceptual and definitional narrowness whereby the term is predominantly or even exclusively employed to refer to abuses committed under the 1973–1990 dictatorship (INDH 2011). Another is its remarkably swift relegation to a secondary role in public life. Despite having been a key mobilizing and discourse frame uniting national and international opposition to the Pinochet regime in the 1980s (Ensalaco 1999), after the initiation of transition in 1989, human rights soon became a minority interest for civil society despite remaining a major trope of governmental-military relations throughout the 1990s and beyond. The change of emphasis was in part deliberate: as Garretón (1996) describes, in its keenness to show its governability credentials the Concertación was both determined and effective in deactivating radical projects or potentially contentious issues, of which human rights was undoubtedly one. Accordingly, after an initial valiant foray by the newly inaugurated Aylwin into truth and memorialization politics,[2] official attention focused on economic and social fine-tuning designed to offset the dictatorship's "social debt" rather than highlight its more dramatic iniquities. Chile's dead and disappeared faded from view for many of those not directly connected to them, and other preoccupations perhaps naturally took their place. A glimpse at comparative regional politics suggests that path-dependency theorists may find Chile particularly suitable for the contention that initial conditions overdetermine initial policy choices, particularly in the highly sensitive area of possible actions against outgoing authoritarians. On a spectrum with Argentina's 1983 transition by collapse at one end, Chile clearly stood at the other extreme (see Figure 7.1). At the same stage at which Argentina had busied itself putting the military junta members on trial, Chile was facing up to the reality of eight more years of Pinochet at the head of the army. Certain issues were off limits: in particular, those with potential to affect Pinochet's image and that of the institution over which he still presided.

Chile's human rights legacy question was never, therefore, resolved in any remotely definitive manner, and by the time of Pinochet's 2006 demise it had moreover entered a significant new incarnation. It became a prime site of the judicialization of politics, an issue played out in the courts rather than in the presidential office or legislative chamber. It also increasingly

Figure 7.1 Typology of Permissiveness of Transition Type for Prospects of Early Human Rights Accountability

Chile——Uruguay——Brazil——El Salvador——Guatemala——Peru——Argentina
1990   1984   1985   1992   1997   2000   1983

Highly controlled transition	Negotiated transitions	Transition by collapse

Low accountability prospects		Higher accountability prospects

Note: This typology considers factors including residual military strength, institutional and political replacement or continuity and, in the case of Central America, UN involvement in peace negotiations.

shifted away from the parade ground (Huneeus 2007; Loveman and Lira 2000; Collins 2010a)[3]: successive new commanders in chief seemed as happy as some of their politician counterparts to leave the question to judges, finally distancing themselves from the increasingly tarnished image of their former supreme commander. After revelations in 2004 of a family fortune consisting largely of dollars of dubious precedence held in secret US accounts, the image of Pinochet as the old soldier who had reluctantly shouldered the heavy burden of office in the name of rectitude was definitively exploded. The armed forces began to observe that they were "not the inheritors of any particular regime," and the high command took noticeably to the habit of referring in public at every opportunity to the "civil-military regime" of the 1970s and 1980s. This was a way of highlighting the intimate involvement of right-wing civilian politicians in installing, running, and propping up a regime for which the military was no longer prepared to take full credit, once credit appeared at least in some quarters to be turning into blame.

This largely welcome "civilianization" of the human rights framing, allowing at least the possibility of its reformulation as a discussion about correct state-society relations rather than predominantly a question of past military wrongdoing, might have happened earlier had Chile developed any semblance of a broad-based understanding or definition of human rights over the 1990s. Instead it is notable how through the 1990s, human rights nonetheless continued to be identified almost exclusively with their past systematic and massive transgression. Indeed, new groups wanting to organize or lobby around emerging environmental, indigenous, or gender issues were often explicitly reluctant to adopt a rights discourse, correctly diagnosing that to be associated in the public mind with human rights meant the risk of considerably reducing possible broad appeal.[4] In the circumstances, politicians of all stripes but particularly in the Center-Left Concertación had little to gain and much to lose by pursuing a politically unrewarding or even actively unpopular issue. With notable but few exceptions—legislators prepared for personal or moral reasons to make common cause with relatives' associations—human rights issues were shied away from by most mainstream politicians. As the relative narrowness of the Concertación's victories in the 1988 plebiscite and 1989 presidential elections graphically illustrated,[5] unease about the regime's human rights record was by no means universal, and did not in any case translate into mass popular repudiation of the regime or right-wing political movements associated with it. Indeed, as Carlos Huneeus and others have shown and other chapters in this volume also make clear, the apparent political alternation represented by replacement of a right-wing authoritarian regime by a Center-Left elected one in fact masked remarkably high levels of continuity in pre- and post-transitional Chilean politics (Angell 2007; Barros 2002; Huneeus and Ibarra forthcoming; Siavelis 2000).

In this setting the personal histories of many incoming Concertación politicians—as direct or indirect victims of regime repression or, when in exile, outspoken critics of its abuses—had to take second place to a Weberian "ethic of responsibility" that privileged consolidation of the still-narrow democratic opening. Rather than insist on the pursuit of unequivocal social repudiation of the authoritarian period as a whole or its human rights violations, the coalition accordingly allowed the politically motivated 1991 assassination of right-wing senator Jaime Guzmán to overshadow and finally foreclose its plans for national promotion of the findings of the official Truth Commission (Rettig Commission). This undoubtedly significant, but limited, early truth measure was largely left to stand as the high water mark of official Concertación protagonism over the issue. Vigorous rebuttal by perpetrating institutions of its sober and cautious conclusions was left to stand publicly unchallenged.[6] One official monument to victims was inaugurated in 1994, in a muted ceremony with no high-level government representation, and a reparations package for some relatives and survivors was introduced quietly so as not to attract too much unfavorable attention on the Right.[7] But justice measures were a definite no-go area, with Aylwin's campaign promise to seek repeal of the 1978 self-amnesty law dropped before he even took office.

"Rights Talk" and the Left-Right Divide

This pattern of cautious, self-limiting official behavior seems to have entered the Concertación's genes, as it demonstrably outlived the objective conditions that may once have made it necessary. As Chapter 1 of this volume suggests, through the 1990s and the early 2000s, Concertación governments avoided as far as possible legislating, pronouncing, and acting not only over the understandably controversial issue of impunity for the past but over a host of associated rights issues. Profoundly conservative or openly retrograde in questions of "public morals," Chile was one of the last countries in the world to pass a divorce law, does not countenance abortion, and has still not come to terms with the question of same-sex civil partnerships. The kinds of judicial activism and rights-guaranteeing behavior that have served to advance rights protections elsewhere in the region have also been notably absent: one of various outstanding complaints against Chile before the Inter-American Court of Human Rights concerns a serving judge denied custody of her children on the grounds of her homosexuality, and the judge who later became associated with domestic prosecutions of Pinochet had previously made his public mark by upholding censorship laws.[8] In sharp contrast to relatively progressive constitutional courts in the rest of the region (Sieder, Schjolden, and Angell 2005),[9] in 2009 Chile upheld an Opus Dei–inspired attempt to outlaw public funding of the morning-after pill. Through to the present day, Chile is one of only two South American countries not to have a human rights ombudsman's office. It has several adverse Inter-American human rights system opinions or verdicts outstanding,[10] made unilateral reservations to its signature of the International Labor Organization treaty (ILO 169) on indigenous rights, and ratified the Rome Statute of the International Criminal Court only after a decade of protracted negotiation during which the political Right insisted on a constitutional reform and unnecessary[11] domestic legislation as a precondition.

Recent steps toward a long overdue basic human rights infrastructure share both this "form without substance" quality and a certain air of having been rushed into existence once it became clear that the Concertación's electoral days were numbered. The national Museum of Memory and Human Rights, inaugurated in the last weeks of Bachelet's 2006–2010 presidency, draws on public funds but is not technically a state institution. Its present director acknowledges that it is seen as "the museum of one side" (*de un bando*), and considers it primarily to be a reparations measure for victims and survivors rather than the embodiment of any genuine shared national narrative or sentiment of *nunca más* (never again).[12] The National Human Rights Institute (INDH),[13] virtually the only state body with a rights brief that goes beyond the past, nonetheless falls well short of ombudsman status and does not quite meet the relevant international standards for a fully autonomous body capable of exercising genuine horizontal accountability.[14] Moreover, an inaugural survey of social attitudes toward human rights published by the INDH in December 2011 showed that respondents continue to value civil and political rights more highly than identity-based or economic, social, and cultural rights, and even in regard to the former found that over half of Chileans support banning homosexuals from the teaching profession and continuing to prohibit same-sex marriages. The same survey diagnosed a hard core of approximately 20 percent of respondents who appear impervious to the gradual acknowledgment of past violations described below and continue to deny validity to rights discourses past or present (INDH 2011).

A broad-based national opinion survey by the Universidad Diego Portales (UDP) in Santiago found in 2009 a relatively high tolerance for authoritarian and restrictive public order actions. Approximately 25 percent of respondents agreed both that the authorities ought sometimes to break the law to guarantee public safety and that the police would be justified in violating a suspect's rights if they believed the person had knowledge of a crime. Comparative results for 2010 showed little movement on this issue.[15] Chile, in other words, falls well short of offering the same kind of model of progress in human rights promotion and defense as in the macroeconomic advances or absolute poverty reduction that earned it coveted entry to the OECD in 2010.This shortfall has earned it repeated cross and apparently frustrated mentions in the annual reports of major international human rights organizations,[16] and seriously imperiled both its election and 2001 reelection to the revamped UN Human Rights Council.[17]

This pattern is one predictable outcome of the fact that until well into the 2000s, and arguably still today, human rights are traded and interpreted in Chile along an inflexible Left-Right ideological axis. To be "pro–human rights" is accordingly taken to mean to be left-wing and radically so, an association partly fed by the fact that the Communist Party was the only political party to keep the issue of justice for past violations prominently on its official policy agenda after 1990. The association is also probably strengthened by the fact that the Catholic Church, the main agent of human rights defense and promotion in dictatorship-era Chile (aside from the political parties), abruptly vacated the human rights field at the beginning of transition.[18] This action removed one of the main nonpartisan transmission belts whereby pro–human rights ideas could be socialized and publicly proposed in Chile, leaving a largely vacant field whose dwindling population was disproportionately made up of individuals who had come to human rights via left-wing ideals or direct victimization based on presumed or actual left-wing leanings. The hierarchical church's subsequent migration toward prioritization of a socially conservative moral agenda has made it an ever stronger cultural referent for the political Right, but the simultaneous abandonment of social doctrine or other "popular church" practices has emptied this engagement of any rights promoting content or associations (Huneeus 2011).

To profess a right-wing political identity or affiliation in Chile for a long time implied denying or downplaying of the existence of serious violations during the Pinochet regime at all, support for continued amnesty for alleged perpetrators, and insistence on consideration of economic success and the "political context" (meaning supposed justification for the resort to dirty war tactics) in drawing up a full balance sheet of the "military regime" (never "dictatorship").[19] Although these hard-and-fast associations finally showed some signs of loosening by 2010, with a modernizing faction of the right-wing governing coalition prepared to countenance rights-based reforms rooted in an essentially classical-liberal political philosophy,[20] the instinct of senior politicians on both sides still seems to have been to react to "rights talk" in the time-honored way: the Left saw it as its exclusive preserve, and the Right was suspicious of the motives of those who used it. To democratize, for this version of the right, may certainly have meant much more than just cosmetic change but did not necessarily entail enthusiastic embracing of a rights agenda, at least not over the touchstone issue of past abuses.

These continuing fault lines, gaping rifts even, in Chilean public life were never, and probably still are not, a feature exclusive to high-level politics. If anything, the exigencies of office have muted their expression among the higher echelons, at least in public and certainly for international consumption. But drilling down into the strata of everyday life in 1990s Chile made it abundantly clear that old hatreds died hard, if at all, and that they were preserved as if in aspic when it came to using human rights as a shield of virtue or a term of abuse, respectively.[21] The UDP opinion poll discussed above showed that pro-rights views are more scarce on the Right than on the Left side of the ideological spectrum, but also diminish significantly in both lower socioeconomic quadrants. Consistent public opinion work over time by political scientist Carlos Huneeus shows that the percentage of Chileans who believe Chile's "human rights problem" could be solved actually fell during the Concertación's first three terms. By the end of the third term, 72 percent of people felt that the divisions that gave rise to the military regime in 1973 had not yet been overcome, although right-wing voters were more likely than those on the Left to believe reconciliation was possible (CERC data from 2006). Support for a *punto final* law[22] dropped slightly from 47 percent in 2001 to 45 percent in 2003, but between 1995 and 2003 the percentage of people declaring themselves in favor of both truth and justice measures (as opposed to truth plus amnesty or inaction) dropped from 62 percent to 52 percent.

Huneeus's results suggest little if any readiness to abandon hardened views for or against the Pinochet regime or the political Right just because of inconvenient revelations about past atrocities. The percentages of respondents who believed Pinochet was responsible for the human rights violations of his regime were 65 percent in 1998 and 68 percent in 1999, amid the flurry of intense media attention and discussion of these provoked by his continuing detention in London. However, only 57 percent were prepared to actually declare Pinochet guilty of human rights–related crimes in 2000, while 27 percent thought him innocent. Even in 2003, with his financial and legal disgrace almost complete, 74 percent of people still believed Pinochetismo to be "very" or "somewhat" influential in Chile, although the numbers of people who believed Pinochet would go down in history as a dictator grew from a 1996 baseline of 63 percent to 78 percent in 2005 and again to 82 percent in mid-2006. Disillusionment was most pronounced among right-wing voters, although in 2005 around 40 percent of these still placed him among Chile's "best ever" leaders (Huneeus 2003b; Mendelson and Gerber 2006).[23] In December 2011, fully 12 percent of Chileans were still prepared to agree that "the deaths that took place under the military government were a necessary evil in order to save the country from communism." Among right-wing voters, support for the statement rose to 23 percent (UDI) and 18 percent (RN) (CERC 2011).[24] A total of 11 percent of respondents held that Miguel Krassnoff, a former regime agent currently serving sentences for twenty-seven homicides and disappearances, had not committed human rights violations (CERC 2011).[25]

How We Got Here:
Frei and the Consolidation of Human Rights

However, and against a certain tendency to portray Concertación politicians' inertia over the country's human rights legacy as entirely a product of popular feeling or adverse circumstance, personal disinclination seems also to have played a part. Frei Ruiz-Tagle, particularly, liked to be seen as a pro-business president. The beginnings of still unresolved, and now sharpened, clashes with mainstream civil society issue groups over large hydroelectric and agribusiness projects in the country's southern regions provoked him to observe that he would not allow growth figures to be imperiled by "environmental terrorists." He also famously repeatedly refused to grant an audience to Chile's main relatives' association[26] throughout his six-year term. Frei was nonetheless occasionally ambushed by human rights–related events beyond his control. These included the landmark 1995 imprisonment of Manuel Contreras, former director of the feared DINA secret police. Undoubtedly a very senior figure to fall, Contreras's fate owed much to exceptional circumstances, which were unlikely to be replicated. The DINA (National Intelligence Directorate, in English) had operated early in the dictatorship and under Pinochet's personal direction. Responsible for a large proportion of the fatal violence and disappearances occurring over the entire period, the DINA nonetheless made a serious miscalculation in 1976 when its sophisticated overseas assassination operations were extended to the United States. Cuban anti-Castro activists and a dual US-Chilean citizen were recruited to plant a car bomb that killed exiled former Chilean foreign minister Orlando Letelier and a US think-tank colleague on Washington's Embassy Row.

The DINA had seriously miscalculated the indulgence with which its activities were seen in Washington: US anticommunism and support for the Pinochet takeover did not include welcoming with open arms what would until 9/11 represent the worst fatal foreign-led terrorist attack on US soil in modern times. In the ensuing diplomatic furor, a vigorous US investigation saw the bombmakers jailed. Pinochet was forced finally to put some distance between himself and his former henchman. Chile's 1978 self-amnesty law suspending criminal responsibility for crimes committed up until that date became part of a wider triage operation after the Letelier blunder. At US insistence the law included a clause ruling out amnesty for the Letelier crime. Domestic investigations by a compliant Chilean military court had predictably gone nowhere during the dictatorship period itself. After transition, however, they offered the next closest thing to a chink in the wall of impunity the regime had managed to construct around itself. Family members—including Letelier's sister, a noted human rights lawyer—pressed executive and judicial authorities to reopen the case, and successful convictions were achieved in 1993 against Contreras and his then second in command. Disputed in the Appeals and Supreme Courts, the verdict and sentences were not finally confirmed until 1995. This meant that the unwelcome task of overseeing implementation of the closest thing to a bold independent decision made by the judicial branch in over two decades fell to Frei rather than to Aylwin.

The affair led to a tense public standoff between the military and the civilian authorities to whom in theory they now answered. Amid outraged reactions at this "politically motivated" assault, Contreras took refuge in a military hospital and finally on a rural estate, pleading ill health—a ruse that would later become a favored defense strategy of his former comrades in arms once accountability cases finally took off in Chile after 2000. The incident evoked disturbing parallels with the military saber-rattling that had cost Aylwin dearly in the early part of his presidency.[27] Then, as now, a perceived threat to military impunity had provoked immediate and vigorous reaction and the result presented the risk-averse Frei with a serious dilemma. To back down would show weakness and risk making the supposedly model transition look like a thin veneer pasted over authoritarian realities. It would also of course have required blatant intervention in a judicial branch decision, hardly a proper pastime for a newly minted democracy whatever the exigencies of circumstance. Contreras deigned to serve his sentence, but only in a specially constructed military prison facility guarded by his peers. There were persistent rumors that the Frei government had also had to offer explicit guarantees that a number of other senior regime figures would not be similarly pursued (Cavallo 1998). The whole debacle also helped derail a delicate attempt to seek cross-party consensus for a "reconciliation package" involving strengthened amnesty guarantees but with constitutional reform (see Table 7.1).

The fact that anyone at all was in danger of being held to account might seem puzzling, given the prevailing culture of impunity and the 1978 amnesty law. However, the law was and is only valid up until the date of its introduction in early 1978. Although this covers most of the regime's most egregious crimes—perhaps explaining why a new and updated version of the law was not considered necessary by the regime as an "exit clause"— certain atrocities committed after 1978 fell outside the remit of amnesty and could therefore in theory be investigated. But this required finding an investigative magistrate willing to take up and pursue such a case. This was no mean feat in a highly unreformed judicial system where human rights cases were predominantly under the control of the separate military justice system. Almost all such cases had been jealously appropriated by military courts from early on, using the first suggestion of armed forces or police involvement to claim jurisdiction. Military courts went on to preemptively apply amnesty where the date of the crime allowed them to do so. Where it did not, military judges creatively put cases on ice, using all kinds of delaying devices and temporary suspensions designed both to avoid investigating properly and to prevent the case's being reclaimed by the civilian court system (Collins 2010b). Even where the civilian system did manage to assert jurisdiction, almost all senior judicial figures were pretransition appointees who sought basically the same outcomes as their military colleagues.

Over the course of Frei's six-year term (1994–2000), the human rights accountability scene accordingly consisted of this virtually barren justice wasteland, picked over by relatives and those human rights lawyers and organizations who managed to survive. These were relatively few, as Chile's post-transitional equivalent of the post–Cold War "peace dividend" saw such organizations reduced to a shadow of their former selves as external funding almost disappeared.[28] Truth and memorialization initiatives were equally few and far between, at least in the official sphere, and Rettig and the single state-sponsored memorial had to suffice. Rettig's official victim total was complemented and extended by the report of a follow-up body, the National Corporation on Reparations and Reconciliation. This was also entrusted with the task of continuing to trace the remaining disappeared, but its efforts were carefully shorn of judicial effect at least in the pursuit of criminal responsibility. Both entities were instead enjoined to pass any relevant information to the courts.[29] The continued absence of the term "justice" in the names of any of these official bodies is perhaps symptomatic, and so too is the appearance center stage of reparations. These were perhaps the most substantial and most complete of the Concertación's early transitional justice offerings. Health care access was offered to a range of directly affected individuals, including former human rights defenders, and economic and educational incentives were extended to those wishing to return from exile. Direct economic reparations in the form of pensions, however, were restricted to relatives of those named in Rettig's accumulated 1991 and 1996 lists as victims of death or disappearance. Survivors were still largely invisible in official policy, a striking absence in retrospect given their later forceful irruption onto the scene (see below).

In a certain sense Frei's rather pedestrian six-year term could be construed as the turning point that never was. Emerging from immediate transition-era worries about authoritarian regression, Frei might reasonably have expected or sought a freer hand than Aylwin in charting a distinctive course for Chile's post-authoritarian future. A more daring project, constructing a Concertación identity and vision capable of awakening popular enthusiasm and adherence beyond calculation of the *mal menor*, did not, however, take shape. Instead, the characteristic desire to preserve the status quo described by Sehnbruch and Siavelis in Chapter 1 of this volume won out: the transitional enclaves were not subjected to significant and deeper change. In a prescient 1998 paper, Huneeus describes the first visible manifestations of the generalized malaise and discontent that finally sunk the Concertación in the 2010 presidential election (where, and surely not uncoincidentally, Frei was again its candidate). Discussing 1997 parliamentary election results, Huneeus (1998) shows how massive youth disaffection (reflected in a hike in levels of abstentions and spoiled ballots) underlay a derailing of the Concertación's pretensions to consolidate itself through improved legislative majorities that would finally allow escape from the straitjacket of the 1980 constitution. Even more presciently, Huneeus detected a complete lack of the kind of critical self-reflection that would have allowed party elites to learn from rather than simply lament this misfortune. The response was retrenchment to try and salvage the 1999 presidential elections, instead of any radical rethink or consideration of whether mass support might be attracted by the offer of more, rather than less, change.

Despite this generalized reluctance to innovate, a human rights irruption even more colorful than the Contreras affair awaited, and two specific actions taken by the Frei administration were to prove instrumental in later accountability change. Both can safely be claimed as examples of the law of unintended consequences: they certainly did not respond to any master plan to foreground the human rights issue, and only one was initially seen as a human rights–related measure at all. This was the preservation of the

National Commission on Reparations and Reconciliation, the Truth Commission follow-up body (mentioned above) that held official victim classification lists and associated records. On expiry of the commission's limited mandate, it was transformed into the imaginatively entitled Programa de Continuación de la Ley 19.123. The mandate preserved record-keeping functions and assigned a skeleton legal staff whose task was exclusively to locate victims of disappearance. The Programa played a secondary role in its early years, but as will be seen below it was to acquire new relevance after a 2003–2004 revamp under subsequent president Ricardo Lagos (2000–2006).The Frei presidency's second and even less intentional contribution to future human rights accountability was an ambitious judicial reform program. Mooted under Aylwin and coming to full fruition only toward the end of Frei's term, the program addressed long-standing modernization questions. It was to involve a new criminal code, the reshaping of criminal justice proceedings (Collins 2010b),[30] and, crucially, incentives for the retirement and replacement of Pinochet-era appointees to the Supreme Court. The resultant renovation of personnel and the introduction of a second, nonspecialist recruitment mechanism for high judicial office are often credited with having brought a breath of fresh air to Chile's traditionally stultifying higher courts. Though the impact of the changes should not be overstated,[31] it is true that these new judges were the ones who would begin to rule in a slightly more permissive manner over accountability claims from the end of the 1990s.

1998 and Beyond:
What the Pinochet Case Did and Did Not Change

Frei's final and probably least welcome human rights ambush was one unanticipated by all domestic parties: the dramatic UK detention of Pinochet in October 1998 on an arrest warrant requested by Spanish judge Baltazar Garzón. Much has been written about the case and its national and international importance. For present purposes it is most instructive to note that both Frei and his foreign secretary chose to treat the matter as a strictly diplomatic issue. Explicit discussion of the detention's human rights dimensions was strictly avoided in official pronouncements, which did, however, unquestioningly recognize the legitimacy of Pinochet's status as a (self-declared) former head of state. As the diplomatic and legal wrangling continued, the protracted exposure of Chile's human rights legacy to international comment made it increasingly clear that the prevailing view from without was much less flattering than the occasionally self-serving view from within. Chile's political Right discovered a Europe less inclined than previously to be all forgiving in the cause of anticommunism, and was pained to discover that the European fascism Pinochet had so openly admired no longer won friends or influenced the right people. Outside of Chile, if not inside, Pinochet seemed a figure more generally reviled than revered and Chile's 3,000 dead or disappeared were inescapably, symbolically present at every stage of the drawn-out extradition battle. Their faces, images, or silhouettes were assiduously rendered visible by relatives, former exiles, and campaign groups at every public hearing and mentioned in almost every press report.

A somewhat simplified narrative easily took hold among less initiated observers in Europe, whereby a charismatic and undoubtedly photogenic Spanish judge allied with the forces of good would finally be the one to stand up against the exotic evils long practiced by Latin American generals. The sudden revelation that for purposes of stereotyping Chile could be treated as just one more banana republic was a nasty blow to elite Chilean exceptionalism of all political colors. This deeply rooted trait made it unconscionable for Chileans to see themselves treated like just another developing country state, supposedly unable or unwilling to uphold basic rule of law principles or emerging global norms. The United States, although rightly fearful of what the universal jurisdiction precedent could mean closer to home, was not prepared to go out to bat for Pinochet, a now deeply unpopular figure who had never in any case been a particular friend of Washington. The Clinton administration accordingly ordered the release of US State Department documents relating to the Chilean coup, and even allowed the reinvigoration of domestic investigation of the Letelier case. The hot potato of a final decision on Pinochet's fate was left squarely in the lap of Spain and the United Kingdom. Both governments were decidedly unenthusiastic about the turn of events, forced on them by their respective judicial branches and international civil society's campaigning.

Although in the final analysis diplomatic pragmatism won out, Pinochet's eventual release on medical grounds was far from being the triumphant vindication he and his supporters could have wished for. The thorough airing of his alleged misdeeds over the course of the 500-day debacle did little for his image, and the foregrounding of the issue of torture left his regime's reputation irrevocably tarnished. Despite the rapturous welcome given to the returning "hero" on his March 2000 touchdown in Chile, the hard-line Right and unabashed Pinochetismo would never really recover their former strength. Cooler heads within the Concertación had had the presence of mind to demand Pinochet's withdrawal from the national political front line as the price for their otherwise unpalatable protection of the former dictator. Accordingly, and to bolster the official version of his failing health, shortly after his return he resigned from the honorary Senate seat he had held since 1998.[32] Right-wing 1999 presidential candidate Joaquín Lavín had meanwhile been struggling to project a fresh, modernizing, and relatively moderate image in pursuit of the Right's first genuine chance to wrest the Chilean presidency away from the Concertación. The Pinochet arrest forced Lavín to negotiate a somewhat complex path between principled defense of the Right's historical icon and an accommodation of new national and international realities. But although the Pinochet affair harmed the ancien régime, it may in the last analysis have played midwife to the renewed Right that finally became electable in 2010. The crisis after all catalyzed a jettisoning of the most unacceptable parts of the Pinochet-era baggage, facilitating a final metamorphosis into an acceptable democratic alternative. If anything, the Center-Left, or at least its elite, may have paid an equally substantial political cost. Defending the indefensible played badly not just with the same convinced human rights constituency of old but with potentially more numerous and more influential floating voters. These sensed yet another example of the compromising, bargaining, and pact-making logic of which some had begun to tire.

Accountability and Its Limits
in the Concertación's Second Decade

In this finely balanced and rapidly evolving political scenario the Concertación only narrowly held on to the presidency in 1999. The change of decade moreover heralded a definite shift of political gears in which the coalition would need to actively seek out future election victories rather than relying on the assumption that their opponents were still unelectable. Incoming president Lagos (2000–2006), the country's first avowedly Socialist president since Allende, was far from being a radical firebrand in human rights or in anything else. Although he did in fact make a major human rights policy announcement in 2003, his 1999 presidential campaign had demonstrated a notable lack of enthusiasm for joining the fray over Pinochet's continued sojourn in London and he cannot have relished taking over the presidency just days after the former strongman's return. His early years in office were moreover marked by repeated efforts to rein in sudden judicial enthusiasm for domestic prosecutions (Collins 2010a).[33] Two major human rights policy events did take place during Lagos's term, but only the second of these (the Valech Commission, see below) was initiated on his watch. The first, known as the Mesa de Diálogo (dialogue round table), was instead inherited from the Frei period. Generally regarded as a crisis management response to the Pinochet arrest,[34] the round table was mooted by the Ministry of Defense in 1999 as a way of broaching the subject of the remaining disappeared. Pointing to the ongoing diplomatic crisis as evidence that the human rights problem would not, after all, go away without some kind of concession or action on the part of the military, the government persuaded the armed forces to sit down with some human rights community representatives under the auspices of the Catholic Church.[35]

The round table's sole explicit aim—a neat reduction of Chile's remaining human rights legacy conundrums to a truth, rather than a justice, problem—was to find the remaining disappeared. Adding to the sense of a lowest common denominator proposal, the instance would preserve previous elite-bargaining fig leaves. These included the widely disbelieved proposition that the armed forces did not hold any institutional information about the practice of forced disappearance or other "individual excesses" possibly committed by their members. As a result, intense and sometimes bad-tempered negotiations produced an agreement to guarantee absolute anonymity and legal immunity to individuals coming forward with reliable information. The required suspension of disbelief proved altogether too much for most grassroots human rights organizations. Those from the human rights community who participated in the Mesa did so in a personal capacity and were heavily criticized or even reviled for doing so, while relatives' associations opted to noisily boycott the whole initiative. This fact and the rudimentary and highly flawed information finally produced weigh significantly against official claims of success for the initiative as a historic bringing together of opposing sides. Long-term effects included the accentuation of deep and wide rifts among civil society activists, setting back prospects for concerted legal action or advocacy in domestic courts after Pinochet's return. They also included the resignation of the head of the air force after his wife deliberately withheld information destined for the final report. Moreover, traces of individuals named in the January 2001 report as having been "thrown into the sea" were subsequently discovered in inland mass grave sites, casting further doubt on the integrity of the initiative and reinforcing the perception that justice, rather than truth-telling, channels were a better bet for unsatisfied relatives.

The Mesa accordingly did little to stem the tide of criminal complaints brought by private citizens against Pinochet in Chile's domestic courts, and may indeed have served to fuel existing justice demands. The human rights lawyers who had agreed to participate in the Mesa wrote to Lagos in mid-2001 to complain about the lack of delivery on official promises made in the Mesa agreement. These had included the provision of legal advice to relatives of those whose remains were eventually identified. The lawyers, however, complained that although the courts had almost immediately named special judges to work on Mesa cases, the government had proved content to monitor the course of events rather than to take the initiative. Partly in response, the Lagos administration began to prepare a relaunch of the existing Human Rights Program with an expanded legal staff (though still restricted to the location of remains rather than the attempted prosecution of perpetrators). Support for a renewed wave of commemoration and victims' memorials was also mooted. These and other measures were finally bundled together into a major new policy announcement on human rights. Coming in August 2003, the No Hay Mañana Sin Ayer (no future without a past) proposal certainly signaled a welcome new seriousness in Concertación attention to the historic human rights question, but should not be mistaken for a visionary effort to set the rights agenda.

Indeed the official measures came somewhat after the fact, as social and particularly judicial re-irruptions had already gathered significant momentum. Legal cases had certainly not waited on the government's pleasure during the Mesa process, and had come about despite rather than because of any discernible state belief in the desirability of criminal prosecution. Initiated in early 1998 in response to Pinochet's imminent retirement, criminal complaints against the former dictator were being actively investigated even before the dramatic events of October that year. The Spanish warrant and UK arrest had only served to swell the early trickle to a tide, as domestic activists fought to prove that Chile could deal with its unfinished authoritarian-era business and that they themselves could be the ones to make it happen. Finding unexpected allies in the judiciary, grassroots groups and lawyers abandoned unfruitful political lobbying and began to make common cause with investigative magistrate Juan Guzmán Tapia and the team of detectives assigned to work with him. By the beginning of 2000 at least 300 separate private complaints had been registered, and Guzmán was busy accumulating and classifying them into a series of major episodes whose investigation would eventually grow to encompass almost every facet of dictatorship-era repression in Chile. The common feature of all Guzmán's cases, collectively known by the judicial code or rubric of 2182-98, was that each could be traced back to privately sponsored complaints naming Augusto Pinochet as the suspected author of a criminal offense. The old cases described above, which had languished in the civil or (more usually) military justice system for years, were accordingly dusted off and resubmitted under this rubric by lawyers, relatives, and survivors keen to have them taken up by the newly active Guzmán.

The post-Mesa activation of a certain number of disappearance investigations, and expansion of judicial capacity to deal with them, thus dovetailed with an existing and already expanding universe of legal activity, beyond the government's control and much more ambitious in seeking criminal punishment, not just the recovery of remains. With the 1978 amnesty law still being respected, cases were not yet producing convictions but were certainly making the military individually and collectively extremely uncomfortable. In January 2003 army commander in chief Juan Emilio Cheyre had published an open letter distancing the institution from the previous regime and pointing out the inherently individual rather than collective nature of criminal responsibility. In April, judge Alejandro Solís delivered the first sentence of the new era against Manuel Contreras, long at liberty after his lenient Letelier case sentence but now once again sentenced to a jail term, this time in a disappearance case.[36]

Lagos's No Hay Mañana speech embodied some of this zeitgeist and was bold at least in one aspect: he announced a new Truth Commission to deal specifically with political imprisonment and torture. Although these practices had been discussed in general terms by the Rettig report, individual cases had not been documented and survivors had not received recognition or reparations. The new National Commission on Political Imprisonment and Torture, which soon became known as the Valech Commission, was about to change all that. In the twelve-month period between its inauguration in November 2003 and the publication of its official report in November 2004, a series of Appeals and Supreme Court decisions went against Pinochet, rescinding both his putative senatorial or presidential immunities and previously granted stays on medical grounds. Next came the Riggs Bank scandal: US Senate money laundering investigations uncovered secret foreign bank accounts held by the Pinochet family, and in a final indignity Pinochet was accordingly subjected to a domestic investigation for tax fraud and corruption. Even amid such a dramatic succession of events, publication of Valech was a major bombshell. Based on 35,000 individual testimonies received, it found that over 28,000 people had suffered illicit politically motivated detention and torture in over 1,000 clandestine detention centers nationwide. A later appendix recognized 1,000 additional cases, including eighty-seven children under the age of twelve.[37] Deliberately shorn of legal effect by omission of perpetrators' names and the placing of a fifty-year embargo on individual testimonies, Valech nonetheless provoked intense national debate and disquiet. Right-wing think tank Fundación Futuro's end-of-year opinion poll, designed to measure public reactions to Valech, showed relatively high levels of acceptance. Although 15 percent of respondents claimed to "reject" the report's findings, 74 percent chose to "accept" them. Equally or even more significantly, this total was significantly higher than the 54 percent who reported that they had given similar credence to the Rettig report back in 1991 (Fundación Futuro 2004).

The following year, the final year of Lagos's term, saw a steady stream of pro-accountability judicial decisions moving toward a more definitive setting aside of the amnesty law (Hilbink 2007; Huneeus 2010). Moving beyond the cases or portions of a case that clearly fell outside the law's remit, lawyers began to argue and courts began to accept that certain crimes were not subject to amnesty at all. Due to their constituting war crimes or crimes against humanity, ran the argument, international treaty and customary law made domestic amnesty laws irrelevant or inapplicable. This principle was applied—though not without contradiction and occasional reversal—to produce the first convictions and jail sentences for otherwise *amnestiable* crimes. Judicial progress should not, however, be confused with executive enthusiasm. The breakthrough was made in the judicial rather than in the executive or legislative arenas, and over time was to put the judiciary increasingly at odds with the other branches of state.[38] Juan Guzmán and other designated human rights case judges reported consistent executive attempts to interfere with their investigations, and the much-hyped Human Rights Program launch stopped short of actually helping relatives—much less survivors—to bring criminal complaints.[39] Despite managing to negotiate significant cumulative constitutional reforms in 2005, the Lagos administration's legislative agenda left intact major accountability obstacles such as the amnesty law itself. The recurrent desire to limit or even oppose change had not, in other words, been overcome despite the apparent promise of No Hay Mañana Sin Ayer. Lagos bowed out in late 2005 with high approval ratings on both Right and Left, an outcome difficult to imagine had he taken a more robust line on accountability questions or other rights issues.

Bachelet and the Politics of Memory

Incoming (and, as it would prove, final) consecutive Concertación president Michelle Bachelet was the candidate considered most likely of any over the preceding decade and a half to show particular sensitivity to the question of past human rights violations. This perception was based on her closeness to many of the leading members of Chile's historical human rights community, and on her personal history as a onetime detainee and subsequent exile. Perhaps unwisely, it may also have been colored by the same gender stereotypes that led both supporters and detractors to assume that she would concentrate on social issues requiring the "personal touch"—notably lacking under Lagos, whose generally stern public persona had occasionally degenerated into plain awkwardness. However, Bachelet's identity as a survivor of repression was mentioned more often, and much more enthusiastically, in overseas media coverage of the campaign. Inside Chile it was generally played down. Her own camp seemed to prefer to refer to her time as defense minister under Lagos, believing it would do more for her appeal to the Center-Right public than would any suggestion of human rights victimhood, still tainted for some by automatic associations with unsavory radicalism. The portion of her exile spent in the United States—rather than in the former German Democratic Republic (GDR)—was accordingly emphasized. Bachelet's victory rally speech in December 2005 was also revealing: far from including any resounding call for justice, she reminded the crowd that "violence irrupted into my life, destroying the things I loved . . . and that is why I've dedicated my life to promoting understanding, tolerance and—why not say it—love."[40]

Once in office Bachelet was positively viewed by most human rights groups as far more sympathetic than her predecessors, and she chose to make a national Museum of Memory and Human Rights—inaugurated in 2010—the personal signature project for her presidency. Forced to deal at the end of her first year with the highly charged and long-anticipated demise of Pinochet, she pleased the human rights constituency by denying him a state funeral and associated honors. Most of these actions were nonetheless in the relatively "soft" area of symbolic politics (Hite and Collins 2009),[41] and even in this arena she proved erratic in her desire to placate, if not quite to please, all sides. Bachelet was dissuaded from inaugurating a private monument to Jaime Guzmán after it was forcefully pointed out that doing so would suggest acceptance of the tit-for-tat logic in which he represented the Right's equivalent of the 3,000-plus victims on the other side of the political divide (Hite and Collins 2009).

Bachelet also failed to keep an explicit commitment to act upon a 2006 adverse Inter-American Court ruling declaring continued use of Chile's 1978 self-amnesty statute to be unlawful. The Concertación was actually responsible for withdrawing an initial legislative bill to this effect, drafted by one of its own most respected jurists. In other related issue areas, although Bachelet emphasized gender questions and social welfare, she did not explicitly embrace a rights-based development model. Backing down or simply failing to take the lead on the same-sex marriage and morning-after pill issues that arose during her term, she also failed to reverse a decade-long tendency to tolerate or even actively embrace highly authoritarian responses to public order questions. Secondary school student protests at the very beginning of her term, and more serious and occasionally violent indigenous activism against logging and fishery companies, were each met with escalating and finally deadly force. A personal verbal commitment by Bachelet not to apply leftover dictatorship-era antiterrorism laws to subsequent prosecutions[42] was simply swept aside, with the weak justification that she had only promised abstention on behalf of her government, and was not in a position to insist upon the same from the state prosecutor's office.

On the whole, Bachelet's extremely positive final approval ratings and undoubted personal empathy for past and present rights issues were not matched by steady or consistent advances in institutionalization. The on-off National Human Rights Institute proposal discussed above was allowed to drag on: first mentioned in the 2003 Lagos policy announcement, it did not materialize until 2010. Its gestation period was, additionally, fraught: controversy with the Right over the extent of its legal powers turned rapidly into arguments with the Left over the concessions given to the Right to get the project through. Both the Institute and the Museum of Memory and National Institute of Human Rights were nonetheless duly installed at the end of Bachelet's term. Each recruited a full complement of personnel over the course of 2010 and 2011, drawing in a significant number of established human rights professionals from existing NGOs and civil society organizations. This "brain drain," while positive for state human rights capacity, has left the civil society rights field notably overstretched and thinly populated. As far as the question of formal accountability is concerned, the Bachelet period was moreover not markedly different from the previous Lagos administration. Judicial advances were neither particularly sought after nor overtly applauded, though they were perhaps slightly less evidently discouraged.[43]

Conclusion

Chapter 1 discusses Chile's consensus model of transition and of subsequent politics. Wilde (1999: 476) goes even further in describing a "conspiracy of consensus" manifesting itself as a "widespread aversion to conflict." Concertación attempts to change Chile's prevailing sociopolitical and economic arrangements back in 1990 would unquestionably have triggered such conflict, hence the elite conservatism described above. Holding a steady course was the principal task of the post-1990 leadership, and the plotted coordinates of that course were under no circumstances to be dramatically reset. Felipe Agüero has argued persuasively that in this sense the classification of Chile as a "pacted" transition is misleading, underrepresenting the high levels of control exercised by the outgoing regime well beyond the initial handover period.[44] It is, however, difficult not to sense that initial constraints were hardened into permanent shibboleths as to what could or could not be done about rights, with or in the judicial system. It took civil society action, motivated by largely symbolic politics, to discover that objective conditions, accepted by elites as a given, had changed to the point that in 1998 investigations had finally at least become possible. The glacial pace of subsequent motion may be understandable, but the apparent desire of the Concertación to push back against it is less so.[45]

Certainly every issue within the human rights canon has its own particular charge and acceptability quotient in public opinion, whatever the government. Neither sporadic inconsistencies nor a failure to fully meet international commitments or human rights movement expectations make Chile unique, nor do they automatically constitute evidence of a dictatorship-era deficit never rectified. However, combined with the tendencies to pro- or antirights partisanship mentioned above, and accentuated by a failure of human rights organizations born in the dictatorship era to broaden their membership, update their campaign agenda, or even to survive at all, they continue to ensure that any moderately ambitious or eager political leader or other socially influential figure in Chile will almost certainly look elsewhere for a suitable cause to take up. In Chile human rights still seem far from the prospect of becoming a transversal or cross-sectoral commitment shared by new Left and new Right. Nor is it easy to see how rights talk might position itself as a cornerstone of a reframed understanding of state-society relationships, one based on the language of citizenship, with rights as the grammar regulating the mutual transmission of ideas and demands. If this were to happen—and perhaps particularly if it were to happen under a right-wing administration—we might finally be able to declare an opening up of transition-era enclaves, with a commitment to basic rights and their universality replacing stasis and continuity as underpinnings of social and political stability.

Notes

1. The right-wing civilian business elite that had done so well under Pinochet fared no worse under his Center-Left replacement. The author is grateful to Carlos Huneeus for foregrounding this point in comments on an early draft of this chapter.

2. For details, see the section on the Rettig Commission in Chapter 5 in this volume.

3. Human rights violations in Chile evoked a strongly legally framed response from the very beginning, as many analyses of the period show. However, as will be seen below, the reactivation of formal criminal and civil cases for past crimes after 1998 notably reshaped the balance of legal, legislative, and social mechanisms that had previously served to contain the issue.

4. Author interviews over the course of the early 2000s with civil society lobby groups and external funders associated with them.

5. The Concertación's margin of victory over the mainstream Right was 12 percent and 17 percent, respectively, of valid votes cast.

6. Including an infamous speech given by Pinochet on March 27, 1991, three weeks after the publication of the Rettig report, during which he defended the "legitimate use of force" by his regime and declared that the injunction "never again" would be better directed at those still tempted to pursue leftist politics.

7. Or, indeed, among the public at large. The generally unsympathetic attitude of the Chilean populace to economic reparations is periodically expressed and reinforced by right-wing press exposés of individuals portrayed as living the high life at public expense.

8. By banning national distribution of the film *The Last Temptation of Christ*.

9. Examples include the Colombian and Venezuelan Constitutional Courts' successful efforts to rein in or strike down executive decrees on rights grounds, and the rapid recovery by sectors of the Peruvian judiciary from Fujimori-era intervention.

10. Notably the 2006 anti-amnesty law verdict discussed below.

11. Since simple recognition of the supraconstitutional rank or self-executing status of international law obviates the need for domestic legislation to enact regional and international treaty and customary law.

12. Interview with Ricardo Brodsky, director, Museum of Memory and Human Rights, Santiago, June 2011.

13. The National Human Rights Institute (Instituto Nacional de DDHH [INDH]). The negotiating process for setting up the institute was, moreover, protracted and contested, with the Right's insisting at committee stage on withdrawing the institute's faculty to independently initiate legal action. The faculty was eventually reinstated in the final draft bill; see Table 7.1.

14. Known as the "Paris Principles." See the UN High Commissioner for Human Rights (UNHCHR), www2.ohchr.org/english/law/parisprinciples.htm.

15. See UDP Encuesta Nacional, www.encuesta.udp.cl, for full results and the database of the Instituto de Investigación en Ciencias Sociales, www.icso.cl /observatorio-derechos-humanos, publications section for results and analyses of the poll's human rights segment.

16. See the annual reports available at www.amnesty.org and www.hrw.org, respectively.

17. In 2008 and 2011, respectively.

18. After closing the iconic Vicaría de la Solidaridad in early 1992.

19. This linguistic sleight of hand reached its maximum expression in early 2012 when the right-wing administration's education minister defended use of the term "military regime" rather than "dictatorship" in the national school curriculum.

20. Examples include the readiness of the right-wing coalition's first justice minister Felipe Bulnes (2010–2011) to resist a *mano dura* (heavy handed) logic in proposing early release and noncustodial sentencing to reduce prison overcrowding. Counter examples also abound, however, and much will depend on which faction gains ascendance as the coalition's first presidential term (2010–2014) plays itself out.

21. Assertion about how issues are felt or lived day to day are necessarily subjective and notoriously difficult to demonstrate, but for this author they have been graphically illustrated time and again over sixteen years of residence in and careful study of Chile in this particular area.

22. "Full stop" law, designed to truncate ongoing investigations by setting a maximum time limit by which investigations not fully completed must be abandoned.

23. All data compiled from Huneeus (2003a) and www.cerc.cl.

24. The figures are for those who declared themselves supporters of current right-wing coalition government parties UDI or RN, respectively. Twenty percent of supporters of the centrist Christian Democrat party that is part of the Concertación coalition held the same view.

25. CERC (2011).

26. The Relatives of the Disappeared (Agrupación de Familiares de los Detenidos Desaparecidos [AFDD]).

27. The *boinazo* and *ejercicio de enlace* incidents described in Chapter 5.

28. A process perhaps inadvertently accelerated by Aylwin, whose crusade to ameliorate seventeen years of neoliberal austerity had included appeals for outside benefactors to reroute their previous support for regime opposition groups through official state channels.

29. Whom Aylwin had attempted to persuade at least to investigate, albeit with no initial success. The suggestion stopped well short of seeking full prosecution for perpetrators, stating only that courts should determine what crimes had been committed, and if possible the whereabouts of victims of disappearance, before invoking amnesty.

30. Toward an adversarial oral trial system rather than the written, investigative magistrate–driven one. The detail of the arrangements for transition from one system to the next meant that human rights cases continue to be seen under the old system.

31. As one illustration, the introduction of legislative ratification of senior judicial appointments, in the context of a persistent right-wing majority in the Senate, initially served only to further politicize senior judicial appointments and keep Milton Juica out of the Supreme Court for a time due to his perceived pro-accountability stance.

32. Membership of the higher chamber granted him an additional layer of legal protection (*fuero*), impeding the bringing of criminal or civil prosecution against him. Designated senator seats were finally abolished in 2005.

33. According to well-placed justice system sources who hold that between 2000 and 2003 behind-the-scenes executive pressure sought an accelerated closure of domestic investigations of Pinochet and other former military officers.

34. Alternative accounts do exist, suggesting that the idea had in fact been floated previously. In this version the Pinochet arrest represented something of a setback to delicate negotiations resulting from gradual civil-military rapprochement in the 1990s.

35. The instance was chaired by Monsignor Sergio Valech, a somewhat patrician senior cleric who would later chair Chile's second Truth Commission and had directed the Vicaría de la Solidaridad at one point during the 1980s. Valech was reportedly the military's preferred choice, after they objected to initial nominee Christian Precht, another former head of the Vicaría, as too radical.

36. Disappearance was being treated by the courts as kidnapping and, the reasoning went, in disappearance cases the kidnapping had continued as victims had not yet been found. Meanwhile, amnesty only covered the period between September 1973 and March 1978, therefore a sentence could be passed for kidnapping committed from March 1978 up to the date of sentencing.

37. A final round of classifications in 2010 and 2011 gave accumulated totals of 38,254 recognized survivors. See Table 7.1.

38. Symptomatic perhaps, at least at senior level, of a newly self-confident air in the traditionally beholden judiciary as much as of any wholesale conversion to rights principles.

39. Arguing that the program's mandate restricted it to disappearance cases and, within these, to the location of remains, the Interior Ministry refused to grant the necessary authorizations. Program lawyers were forced to bring cases in a private capacity or limit themselves to referring their clients to private lawyers with more freedom to act.

40. From a clip in the 2009 documentary film *The Judge and the General* (Westwind Productions/PBS).

41. Such as inaugurating or visiting (privately impulsed) memorial initiatives, rather than intervening significantly in support of pro-justice activities.

42. Of activists, rather than of the police officers responsible for the fatalities, all of whom were cleared of any wrongdoing.

43. See the Verdad, Justicia y Memoria chapters of the Universidad Diego Portales's annual human rights reports for tracking of specific incidents and verdicts year on year at www.derechoshumanosudp.cl (in Spanish).

44. Remarks made to the International Political Science Association conference in Santiago, Chile, 2009 and in conversation with the author.

45. See www.icso.cl/observatorio-derechos-humanos for up-to-date case numbers and recent judicial news.

Part 2

Economic and Social Development

8

Economic Policy and the Ideology of Stability

Óscar Landerretche Moreno

One of the many double-edged legacies that the Chicago Boys have bequeathed to Chile is the idea that Chile's development process constitutes a model that other less successful countries should copy. To this end, José Piñera, one of the architects of the Chilean model and brother of the current president, has even established a website entitled "The Economic Transformation of Chile: A Model of Progress."[1] We may scoff that it is probably not surprising that one of the chief policymakers of the dictatorship should consider his own policies a model for other countries. However, the idea of the Chilean model has surfaced time and again in the policymaking and academic literature, while it is an even more frequently mentioned sound bite in media articles. During a 2011 visit to Chile, Colombia's President Santos, for example, told one of Chile's main daily newspapers, "In Colombia, we want to copy the Chilean model."[2]

Beyond the sound bites, the question of whether Chile's development process constitutes a model has also preoccupied serious analysts from all areas of the policymaking spectrum. As Alan Angell indicates in the preface to this book, interpretations frequently incorporate the idea that the Concertación followed, administered, and even deepened economic and social policies initiated under the Pinochet dictatorship, according to the precepts of what is commonly known as the Washington Consensus.[3] Given this context, this chapter cannot avoid engaging with this debate from a critical perspective. However, it will argue that if there is indeed a Chilean model that other countries should study, this model was shaped and developed by the Concertación, and not by the Pinochet dictatorship. Furthermore, this chapter argues that Chile's development model incorporates both evident strengths and important weaknesses. This combination has led to a significant increase of GDP per capita levels and improved social indicators, but not to a sufficiently diversified economy that can ensure continued high levels of growth over the long term, or to an education and vocational training system that can help the country transit toward the next phases of development, or to an improved income distribution structure. This chapter therefore examines the strengths and weaknesses of Chile's development model, partly to lay the foundation for the other chapters on Chile's development process in this book, which discuss the country's social and economic progress during the last twenty years, and partly also to contribute to the debate about whether Chile really is such a good model for other countries to follow.

Closely tied to this question is an empirical fact that is well known among development economists: countries that reach Chile's GDP per capita levels are rarely able to continue to grow at a pace sufficient to overcome the gap between them and developed countries. This empirical regularity that has, as they all do, many exceptions is known as the middle-income trap. So far, the only countries that have been able to overcome this trap are a handful of East Asian countries (Hong Kong, Singapore, South Korea, and Taiwan) and some European countries that were less developed during the 1980s (such as Spain and Ireland). In the Latin American region, there is not a single country that has successfully closed the development gap. Moreover, those countries that came close at different points in history have usually ended up regressing and even imploding economically and politically. Argentina is probably the best-known example of this, but the same could also be argued for Venezuela and Uruguay. One of the most important questions that this chapter therefore must raise is whether the Concertación's period of macroeconomic management has given Chile a genuine chance of escaping the middle-income trap. We will agree that it has given the country the opportunity to do so but not necessarily the instruments to achieve it. The Concertación prioritized and consolidated macroeconomic Keynesianism as a bedrock of Chilean policy with its emphasis on stabilization, and combined this with a strategy of slow reconstruction of the welfare state. These central policy elements, clearly directed at stabilizing the development process and softening its social consequences, constitute the Concertación's legacy so much that they have continued to be central during the first post-Concertación administration.

These policies were the concrete expression of the strategic option that dominated the Chilean Center-Left for a quarter of a century: the stability imperative. It is this strategic option that is being questioned within the Left today, and, consequently, so are the policies that are associated with it.

The Political Psychology of the Model:
The Stability Imperative

To understand the origins of the policies implemented by the Concertación one must understand the political psychology of the stability imperative that was the cornerstone of policymaking and politics for two decades.

Chile's history during the twentieth century is full of utopian political and economic experiments. All of these experiments ultimately failed, but many left very important structural legacies that have shaped Chilean society and culture. Examples of this radical approach to policy and politics abound. For example, consider the Popular Front of the 1930s and 1940s that competed in ambition and scope with Roosevelt's reconstruction policies and actually anticipated Beveridge's policies in the United Kingdom by setting up one of the most ambitious national health services in the world (Corkill 1976; S. Correa 2001; Meller 1996; Milos 2008; Salazar 2009; Stevenson 1970, 2004).[4] As a result of this effort Chile still has the best health indicators in the Latin American region. However, the Popular Front dissolved into Cold War politics and Peronist-style populism, and ultimately failed as a political model.

Similarly, the Christian Democratic "Revolution in Liberty" of the 1960s constituted such a structural political shock that it permanently wiped the old Liberal and Conservative parties off the Chilean political map. Under the first administration of President Frei (1964–1970) social and educational reform was promoted aggressively, and a more progressive taxation system was introduced that increased tax levels from 12.8 percent of GNP in 1964 to 21.2 percent in 1970, while public expenditure increased from 35.7 percent of GNP in 1965 to 46.9 percent in 1970 (the difference financed with profits from government firms). Frei also instituted a major agrarian reform that opened the way for a radical modernization, which ultimately laid a foundation for the development of the dynamic agricultural export sector that Chile boasts today.

At the time this political experiment was hailed around the world as the "Chilean model" for containing communism. However, the political aspects of the Christian Democratic interventions in the countryside failed, such as its flirtation with Yugoslav-style cooperatives based on agrarian Christian communes (Ahumada 1958; Ffrench-Davis 1973; Meller 1996).[5]

Even more radical was the experiment of Salvador Allende's Unidad Popular government that actually attempted to construct a path toward collectivist socialism through democratic means in the 1970s, with an idealist president who, to the very end, thought he could stare down military adventurers and fascist plotters. To this day, the main cleavages of Chilean politics (including the student protests of 2011) are born out of the events surrounding the victory, agony, and demise of the Unidad Popular.[6] However, it is also true that we owe a great deal to the Allende government, which completed the nationalization of the copper industry that to this day is one of the most important sources of fiscal revenues, and has allowed the Chilean state to benefit from the recent commodity boom and reconstruct its fiscal position and its welfare state.[7]

Political experiments of this kind, however, were not just a result of the flights of fancy of democratic leaders. A similarly profound level of utopian experiment was carried out under the dictatorship of Augusto Pinochet. The neoliberal revolution implemented in the 1980s by the Chicago Boys under the auspices of the dictatorship is universally considered to have been one of the earliest, most drastic, and most comprehensive applications of radical neoliberal thinking to an economy (Harvey 2007).[8] The legacy of economic growth, record levels of inequality, and political sclerosis still persist today. It is interesting to note that most of the growth that is attributed to the dictatorship actually happened during the transition to democracy, making it impossible to disentangle how much was due to the pro-market reforms and how much to the actual political transition that pulled the country out of its pariah status and allowed it to benefit from the early stages of economic and financial globalization. In all fairness, it is very likely that both the neoliberal reforms and the democratic transition ultimately contributed to growth. On the other hand, inequality is clearly a result of the neoliberal reform policies, peaking at its record level with a Gini of over 0.6 in the mid-1980s (Ffrench-Davis 2010; Larrañaga 2001; Ruiz-Tagle 1999; Vega 2007). Moreover, in the best of cases, the neoliberal reforms took a very long time to deliver net positive results in terms of growth. For example, the volatile process of reforms and the counterreforms were so intense that in 1985 Chile had the same total GDP in US dollars as in 1973, and the crisis in the mid-1980s was so deep that GDP only recovered its 1981 level by 1991. Ffrench-Davis (2008) has pointed out that this later year should be considered as the starting point of Chile's recovery from the debt crisis.

There were even more cases that would serve as examples of this twentieth-century Chilean propensity toward radical and utopian policy experiments. However, the important point for the purpose of this chapter's argument is that all of these experiments left their mark on the Chilean political process. These marks were frequently structural, but frequently also psychological: the volatility, uncertainty, and fear that these policy experiments induced among both the Chilean electorate and the political establishment made both groups highly risk averse and extremely reluctant to engage in any further economic experiments. Figure 8.1 illustrates the evolution of Chilean growth rates since independence. It shows the economic volatility Chile experienced during its history, how it increased during the political

Figure 8.1 Chilean Growth Rates Since Independence, 1811–2012 (annual variations in GDP per capita)

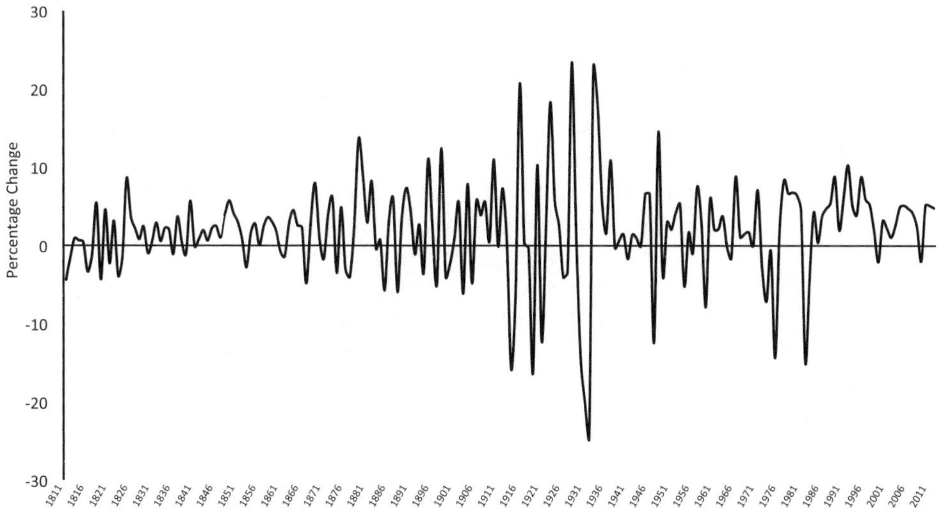

Sources: Díaz et al. (1998) and Banco Central de Chile data.

conflicts of the late twentieth century, and how it was smoothed away in the transition to the twenty-first century.

By the time the dictatorship was finally unwinding, Chileans were simply exhausted from a whole century of radical economic experiments. The working class in particular had been hurt by the continued economic volatility and uncertainty, as well as by the high social cost of the neoliberal experiment. Any politician promoting radical new ideas for development during the early 1990s would have been branded as a demagogue or populist. Conscious of the public mood, the negotiators of the transition to democracy focused on one guiding principle for their policies going forward: political and economic stability. In fact, as subsequent chapters in this volume will argue, the primary goal of stability even outweighed the urgent need for social palliatives generated by the neoliberal experiment. It is therefore no coincidence that the name decided on for the coalition that would drive the transition process was *Concertación*. This term explicitly conveyed the coalition's intention to foster political consensus and agreement among the ruling political parties, and hence to generate political and economic stability. To this day, the name of the coalition irritates left-wing sectors that disagree with the stability imperative.

The centrality of stability was justified, in the minds that led the transition, as profoundly redistributive because of the consequences of economic uncertainty and volatility among poorer households. On one hand, the leaders of the transition saw themselves as "risk redistributers." On the other hand, political uncertainty in particular was also an adverse force among a business community that had bet the whole of the economic future of the country to the capital-intensive and relatively innovation-free exploitation of commodities and natural resources. Given that the original appropriation process had already been conducted through the violence of the dictatorship, there was no need for much innovation and risk, just stability to invest, produce, export, and profit. The outlook of political uncertainty was, at that point, from the perspective of the business community, a much more disturbing possibility than any specific negotiation that led to the concession of any policy points. Hence, the transition to democracy was accompanied by a substantial tax reform that financed a significant increase in civil servant and teacher wages; this was the price that the business elite paid for stability. The price that the civil society and the Left paid was the postponement of a big part of their policy agenda. It's important to point out that the stability imperative we are arguing for as a central focal point of the Concertación's strategy is different from the usual "fear of authoritarian regression" argument that many have used to explain the policy slowness of these years. We do not deny that this fear had a role in incentivizing a stability-oriented policy. We do feel, however, that the stability objective had a policy base related to a particular way of understanding the Chilean development process. It was not only fear, it was also policy.

Hence, the political and policy deal that underpinned the transition to democracy was based on stability as the guiding principle that held the parties of the Center-Left coalition together and formatted their relationship with the business elite. Stability was seen as central to every aspect of Chile's future development, and underpinned the application of extremely Keynesian, radically anticyclical macroeconomic policies and very conservative financial regulations during most of the years of the coalition's administrations.[9] We are aware that most external spectators of Chilean policy history believe that the two decades of Concertación administrations continued with the neoliberal model of the dictatorship just because it continued to have economic growth as a central final policy objective, but this misses an important nuance: the central intermediate objective during the dictatorship was investment; during the Concertación administrations it was stability. For the Chicago Boys it was investment that brought growth no matter how much creative destruction and volatility were involved; for the Concertación it was, in reality, stability that brought progress. In the eyes of the Concertación this concern about volatility reflected a key political difference with the Chilean Right: the understanding that risk, fear, and uncertainty played an important role in generating inequality, poverty, and vulnerability.

Despite the ideology of stability that underpinned the political strategy of the transition to democracy, and in spite of the level of the agreement among conservative, Christian Democratic, Social Democratic, and Liberal elites that had negotiated the transition, the twenty years of the Concertación government always contained a core of progressives that tried to push for reforms from within the coalition.[10] These progressives had many names in their different incarnations. At the beginning, almost the entire Socialist Party pushed against the constraints imposed by the stability imperative; later the group expanded to include members from other parties in the coalition and became known as the "progressives," then as the "self-fla-gellators" (*autoflagelantes*), and finally as the "fractious" (*díscolos*). The story of these rebellious progressives always followed a pattern of chal-lenging the rule of the stability imperative, achieving some success in im-plementing a progressive agenda, and finally being absorbed (one could even say subsumed) into the stability consensus in exchange for having achieved their progressive agenda. Under the next Concertación govern-ment, the cycle would begin again with a new group of challengers who would contest the pact for stability. In this way, the stability imperative, in fact, was combined with a process of reconstruction of the social welfare system, which was the price paid to these rebellious factions in exchange for their allegiance to the stability pact. In hindsight one could say that this constitutes their main political achievement. Moreover, the final defeat of the Concertación shows the coalition's inability to continue this self-rein-venting process and inability to prevent the exodus of the latest generations of challengers.

The dynamic of the factions' challenges and their adoption is, of course, related to different policies in different moments of the two decades of Concertación history. The most important challenge was staged during the Frei administration by the so-called *autoflagelantes* during the late 1990s. The main issue, at that point, was the relative absence of a welfare system reconstruction policy and the inexistence of a progressive develop-ment policy (industrial policy, labor reforms, etc.). The debate was a seri-ous public controversy that was muted by the Asian crisis of 1998 but ulti-mately set the political situation for Ricardo Lagos's victory in the Concertación primaries of 1999 and the introduction of a social policy agenda during his administration and also Bachelet's. Although the slow speed of expansion of social policy was clearly not ideal from any progres-sive perspective, it was much more than was previously observed.

Until the moment of the Concertación's electoral defeat in 2010 this process of progressive reform from within seemed to be the perfect status quo to the coalition's elite. After all, what could be more consistent with a gentle third way policy of "risk redistribution" than to complement macro-economic Keynesianism with the slow reconstruction of a welfare state?

What better way to slowly push a progressive agenda than to administer a tension with these "fractious" internal progressive sectors by incorporating them at a price?

It is very revealing that the Concertación never used the term "welfare state" to refer to what they were establishing. A radical agenda of rapid reconstruction of a Scandinavian-style welfare state would not have been consistent with the stability imperative, as it would have involved substantial tax reform as well as structural labor reforms. Moreover, it would have implied that there was a policy of radically transforming the economic and social model. This would have disrupted the consensus. However, a slow, agonizing process by which the centrist governing elite used the reconstruction of the welfare state as the political currency that kept both the progressives and the business elite in line with the established consensus was the "perfect" compromise. Thus, the system of social policies that the Concertación established over time became known as the "social protection system."

Finally, it is interesting to observe that the exhaustion of the "stability imperative" coincides with the adoption by conservatives of this same policy and political framework. The political narrative presented by Sebastian Piñera in his presidential bid promised the same sort of equilibrium. This was an extremely clever strategy since, in effect, it diluted the reason that a big section of moderate voters had for supporting the Concertación.

The Politics of the Chilean Development Model

The political constraints under which the Concertación had to operate have been discussed extensively throughout this book. These constraints consisted both of the authoritarian enclaves that the democratic governments inherited from the dictatorship, as well as of the divisions within the Concertación itself that shaped policymaking debates. Within the coalition there were, and still are, also conservative forces trying to stop its "leftward drift" (*izquierdización*), as they call it. Most of this pressure was maintained by liberal elites operating from policy think tanks, but there were also somewhat more inarticulate expressions of this pressure.[11]

Many observers of the Chilean political process during the Concertación years hail it as one of the purest applications of what is commonly known as the Washington Consensus. We disagree; the Concertación did not deliberately follow this set of policies. Moreover, if you talk to the policymakers during those twenty years they will clearly tell you that they were in disagreement with the Washington Consensus because they considered it to be relatively primitive and, if applied with no corrections, conducive to instability and uncertainty, which was exactly what successive administrations were trying to avoid.

Instead, they operated within what could be considered a third way consensus, which is similar to what liberal Democrats in the United States or New Labour in Great Britain attempted or advocated in recent decades. Even though some observers, particularly those with a critical perspective toward economics as a discipline, consider the difference between the neoclassical Washington Consensus and New Keynesian third way stability-oriented policies to be a minor one, this chapter argues that there is a big difference between the two that is generally overlooked by many critics.

For example, it is noteworthy that Chile has not had a single bank failure since the mid-1980s—not what one would expect from a winner-take-all Darwinian system. It turns out that this is a result of very conservative banking regulation implanted as a result of the financial debacle of the 1980s and of a highly active Chilean Central Bank. This approach has little in common with the truly neoclassical hands-off approach of the European Central Bank or with neoconservative US Republican policymakers that corresponds with the deregulation of financial markets—one of the main precepts of the Washington Consensus. Similarly, few countries have applied policies even remotely comparable to the Chilean anticyclical, structural fiscal budgets. The classical Washington Consensus approach includes the avoidance of fiscal deficits. Chilean fiscal policy encouraged deficits during recessions as an anticyclical measure so long as the country was not in structural deficit, meaning in deficit on average along the economic cycle. Moreover, the slow but sustained reconstruction of the welfare state has very little to do with the Washington Consensus, especially the explosive increase of direct distributive subsidies and entitlements that has been continued by the Piñera administration. Most Chilean neoclassical economists also believed it was not a small difference. During the twenty years of Concertación governments, the neoclassical critique of Concertación policies was clearly directed at the importance they placed on stability, social protection, and constant growth of entitlements as opposed to growth and investment. Neoclassical economists regularly pointed out that the combination of the stability imperative and the social protection agenda was behind the falling growth rates of the Chilean economy.

However, there were three political economy restrictions for the Concertación that did not allow policymakers to deviate even more from the Washington Consensus and that made the self-reinventing political process of the coalition harder and, thus, the adoption of a social protection agenda slower than it would have been otherwise. One of these restrictions was the penetration of the coalition by anglophile liberal technocrats and quasi-conservative Christian Democrat sectors that were very close in ideology and policy convictions to the business elite and the neoliberal consensus of the Right. (To be fair, the core of the Christian

Democratic party is actually Social Christian and there are many liberal progressives in the Concertación.) The second restriction was the actual delivery of a plausible stabilization of policy and economics combined with a political economy (electoral and quorum rules included) that delivered victories for conservative rent-seeking business lobbyers rather than innovation-oriented actors. The third restriction was the network of institutional restraints under which the Concertación had to operate (discussed in the first half of this book as authoritarian enclaves). These three constraints on the political economy of the Concertación generated the struggle of progressive forces that slowly imposed the stability imperative, with the social protection imperative only coming to predominate in the very late years of the transition.

Hence, our main point is that Chile's economic model (particularly its macroeconomic model) was, toward the end of the Concertación administrations, something quite different from what is commonly understood to be the neoclassical Darwinian creative destruction-oriented Washington Consensus model. However, the transition from one to the other was slow as a result of the political economy and institutional constraints faced by the transition governments.

Several causative factors of Chile's economic success during the 1990s can be identified, but we must always remember that they are traceable to the peculiar political equilibrium that dominated the transition to democracy. First, the political, social, institutional, and economic stability established by Chile's transition to democracy generated a very attractive environment for foreign investors. This stability occurred just in time (in fact, slightly ahead of time) for a global boom in foreign direct investment flows toward all emerging markets. Second, an aggressive strategy of public investment in infrastructure, led by the state but sometimes also outsourced, combined with a strong public investment in institution building, clearly contributed to the attractiveness of this investment environment. This was very different from the Chilean dictatorship that left public infrastructure to decay and was another classical Keynesian feature of Concertación policies. Third, an equally important strategy of public investment in social policies succeeded in appeasing the demands of a population that had suffered a significant increase in poverty rates and inequality levels during the dictatorship, and also allowed the governing coalition to, agonizingly but effectively, process the dissent from its internal progressive critiques. The social investments undertaken by the Concertación also bought the democratic administrations time to stabilize the economy, bring down inflation, and sustain economic growth rates, which in turn would contribute to improving the socioeconomic situation of the population.

A Map of the Chilean
Macroeconomic Development Model

Even the most critical observers of the Concertación's development model have to admit that (with some exceptions that confirm the rule) its macroeconomic management during the last twenty years was very close to exemplary. However, while the next section will discuss the weaknesses of the Chilean development model, even a discussion of its strengths has to distinguish between the relative success of the model during the 1990s (until the Asian crisis of 1998–1999) and the more complicated post-crisis period during the 2000s. These two periods are clearly different both in institutional and policy choices as well as in economic performance.

One can see a clear process of stabilization of the internal volatilities and uncertainties of the economy and high growth rates during the first period, followed by a period with much lower growth rates and a reappearance of volatility, this time imported from an ever more unstable international economy. One could argue that Chile merely benefited from the global economic and financial stabilization known as the "Great Moderation" that stretched from the mid-1980s to the Asian crisis. And then Chile had to absorb the costs of the "Great Agitation," as the period that followed could be termed, due to its ever more violent and frequent financial crises that percolated into the economy. These crises occurred via the increasing fluctuations and unpredictability of trade flows, commodity prices, international asset prices, and liquidity in global money markets. However, one could also argue that Chile was able to negotiate both phases with relative success when compared to other Latin American or developing countries.

Although a proper counterfactual is extremely difficult to construct, the experience of historical crises during the twentieth century suggests that it is probably fair to assume that an economy as small and open as Chile's, without the stability imperative described above, would have actually amplified the fluctuations of the international economy as is usually the case among other Latin American countries. Hence, the achievement of relative stability when compared to the rest of the world is a clear Keynesian success.

Inflation Stabilization

As discussed by Angell in the Foreword, the Concertación inherited an economy in 1990 that was overheated: inflation rates were in the 20–25 percent range, the economy had just overcome a dramatic boom-bust cycle, but unemployment rates were still high at rates around 10 percent. Figure 8.2 summarizes inflation rates since 1990.

Figure 8.2 Chilean Year on Year Inflation Rates, 1990–2012

Source: Compiled by author from data from the Instituto Nacional de Estadisticas, Chile (INE, Chilean National Statistical Institute), www.ine.cl.

The first task of the newly elected Concertación government was there-fore to bring down inflation and stabilize the economy. In contrast to other Latin American countries, which have passed through contemporaneous in-flation stabilization processes (for example, Argentina and Brazil during the 1990s), Chile achieved this in a very gradual way, which in turn contained the social and economic costs of this process, particularly in terms of em-ployment levels.[12] Deflation in most Latin American countries was a quick process implemented through shock policies using fixed exchange rates and sharp fiscal policy contractions, quite similar to what had been done in Chile during the late 1970s and early 1980s by the dictatorship. These de-flations usually incurred high social costs and produced complicated after-maths. In Chile during the 1990s, it was a gradual policy, conducted through moderate fiscal restraint (but no real fiscal contraction) and a grad-ual "leaning against the wind" by the Central Bank that reduced inflation by a couple of percentage points each year for almost a decade. The main benefit of Chile's gradual process of deflation was that it was compatible with employment generation. As an example, during the early 1990s when Chile started its deflation process, its inflation rate was between 20 and 25 percent; ten years later, at the conclusion of this process, the inflation rate was at 3 percent. This means that on average inflation declined by 2 percent per annum, a process that occurred along with the generation of a relatively tight labor market, if the latter is to be defined by a declining unemployment rate. This contrasts very positively with other deflation processes in emerging economies, which generally have been much more abrupt and traumatic.

At the end of this deflation process (which lasted throughout the 1990s), international macroeconomic analysts widely agreed that the Chilean Central Bank had acted in an exemplary way, through a relatively unorthodox, slow, anti-inflation convergence, anticyclical, stabilization-oriented monetary policy. On the eve of the Asian crisis, this policy had very little internal opposition. Moreover, the opposition came from conservatives and monetarists who wanted a faster and more radical approach to deflation.

Unfortunately, this process of stabilizing and anticyclical monetary policy was interrupted during the Asian crisis of 1998–1999 during which the Central Bank faced the prospect of a balance of payment crisis. As the international crisis evolved, Chile faced a deteriorating current account as its exports declined and internal demand sustained import levels. At one point the current account was close to scoring a deficit of 7 percent of GDP, which is usually considered the trigger level for speculative currency attacks in international markets. This was a dangerous prospect since there were increasing signs that an important proportion of the country's largest firms were facing a severe currency mismatch in their balance sheets (assets in pesos, debt in dollars).[13] A sharp devaluation of the currency would drive them into insolvency and have potentially devastating effects on the local stock exchange and, due to the pension system's dependence on the local stock market, on the private pension system. This situation started to break up the political peace that had surrounded the Central Bank since some experts were skeptical of the dangers involved in the devaluation. Despite the doubts, when it seemed that the country would suffer a speculative attack, the Central Bank panicked and abruptly raised interest rates to stave off the looming crisis. We will never know what would have happened if they had called the bluff of the markets. However, we do know two things: First, the monetary management of the Asian crisis wiped out a generation of micro and small firms, producing almost a decade of high unemployment rates. Second, the Central Bank at that point lost much of its political constituency within the Left. One of the consequences of this is that from then on, the Central Bank has regularly had to confront offensives from progressive policymakers trying to reform its charter to include employment as a policy objective.

Fortunately for the Central Bank, inflation had almost converged to its steady-state level by the onslaught of the Asian crisis. Inflation was then in the 5–6 percent range and the international recession that was on its way would push inflation down even more. Hence the Central Bank was able to shift easily from its "inflation convergence" policy to a steady-state management of internal demand to try to get inflation within a target range. What we have seen since then is that the Central Bank continues to stabilize around its targets but the range of variation of inflation around these targets is becoming larger as the international economy and its prices become more and more volatile.

Fiscal Stabilization and Regulation

Once the immediate consequences of the Asian crisis had been dealt with, the second half of the Concertación period focused on institutionalizing an anticyclical fiscal policy regime that would protect Chile from the cyclical effects of international crises in the future, known as the "structural fiscal accounting system." This type of fiscal mechanism is quite unique; fiscal policy in every other Latin American country has continued to be extremely pro-cyclical and subject to fluctuations in international commodity prices. The system is even more unique if you consider that it has repeatedly been tried in many developed countries, namely, the European Union, only to be defeated by the complex political economy surrounding it. However, Chile was able to sustain it for a decade. Unfortunately, the Piñera administration has severely weakened this mechanism, although its framework remains and may be taken up by future administrations.

Fiscal policy in Chile during the Concertación era was oriented toward two principal objectives: first, macroeconomic stabilization, and second, the strengthening of the state's solvency. This second objective was also central to the Concertación's political strategy. The fiscal management of the dictatorship was characterized by an extremely high level of underinvestment and decapitalization of the state, mainly as a result of the classical shock doctrine privatizations, which had systematically given away public assets and companies to close associates of the regime. Furthermore, the state had suffered additional financial losses when it bailed out the banks involved in the 1982 banking crisis. At the beginning of the Concertación's administration, therefore, the state was poor, indebted, and, hence, immobilized. Even radical progressives within the coalition recognized that the rejuvenation of the financial health of the state was a necessary prerequisite for any welfare state reconstruction program to be conceivable. The long Latin American experience of ephemeral, unsustainable, and unfunded social policies was an important historical precedent that forced Concertación administrations to harness the political discipline necessary for the financial reconstruction of the state.

During the first decade of Concertación governments, this was expressed as a commitment to an average 1 percent fiscal surplus per annum. This allowed the Chilean state to pay down almost its entire external fiscal debt and then start saving in sovereign funds, finally transforming itself into a net international creditor. During the 2000s, this approach was replaced by the structural fiscal accounting approach, which was oriented toward making fiscal expenditures compatible with long-term fiscal revenues rather than short-term fluctuations. This allowed fiscal policy to become extremely anticyclical and run, for example, significant but "structurally consistent" deficits during the subprime crisis. At the beginning, this was constructed around the same fiscal objectives that characterized the first decade (i.e., an average 1 percent surplus). However, this objective evolved during the 2000s toward a balanced structural budget approach (the Piñera administration, on the other hand, has targeted structural deficits for its duration). This change coincided with the commodity boom, which allowed the Chilean state to become a significant investor in international markets given that the constraints of the structural fiscal rules actually produced significant fiscal surpluses for a couple of years (8–10 percent of GDP).[14]

But even in its approach to the management of sovereign funds, the stability imperative was ingrained. Chile established three types of sovereign wealth funds. The first fund is oriented toward financing the fiscal transition involved in pension policies, resulting from the demographic shifts from the old state-run system to the new privatized system, which requires significant fiscal subsidies in the form of guaranteed basic pensions for a large proportion of the population. The second sovereign wealth fund is oriented toward the stabilization of social spending over the economic cycle. As an example, this fund allowed Chile to engineer the fourth most aggressive fiscal response to the subprime crisis in the world, and still come out of the crisis with substantial sovereign funds. The third fund is oriented toward current fiscal spending, and is considered part of general fiscal policy. Hence, even in the management of the sovereign funds, the basic principles of stabilization and sustainability of social spending have been pursued (Contreras et al. 2008; Rodriguez, Tokman, and Vega 2007; Santiso 2008).

During the subprime crisis the Chilean government spent the equivalent of 10 percent of GDP from the sovereign wealth funds on a combination of policies that both sustained existing social expenditure levels and stimulated the economy, thus insulating fiscal spending from the fall in tax revenues. It is important to remember in this context that because Chile is such an open economy, international economic developments (in particular any kind of economic crisis) can produce an amplified ricochet effect. Accumulating sovereign funds for stabilization purposes therefore is extremely important to avoid the increasingly volatile economic cycles that the world economy is displaying.

Even the most radical sectors within the Chilean Left advocate the structural principle that permanent expenditures must be financed with permanent sources of income. Hence, they associate their demands for increased social spending with progressive tax reforms rather than deficit spending. This constitutes a clear difference between public policy discussions in Chile and those in other countries of the region (and even some major developed countries) where the spending and financing aspects of policy discussions seem to be very separate. In our view this is a major conceptual inheritance that the Concertación left to Chile's public policy debate.

An Open Economy

A factor that was crucial to Chile's development process during the Concertación period was the coalition's continued commitment to further opening of the economy through the negotiation of free trade agreements (FTAs). While tariffs during the Pinochet dictatorship had been lowered unilaterally, consistent with Washington Consensus prescription, the Concertación administrations changed this approach to the negotiation of bilateral FTAs.

The reason that the dictatorship did unilateral tariff reductions and did not negotiate bilateral agreements was twofold. First and foremost, the dictatorship was an infamous pariah regime in international politics, making it very unattractive for foreign governments to appear to support it through a trade agreement. Second, the neoliberal administrators of the dictatorship viewed trade opening as a fundamental pillar of their strategy that was best done as a shock therapy and not subjected to the prolonged timings and extensive negotiations of a free trade agreement.

Hence, the transition to democracy allowed Chile to transit to a more rational bilateral tariff policy. This coincided with the maturing of the World Trade Organization. Under this new approach Chile has successfully signed FTAs with almost all relevant markets. In many cases (such as the FTAs with Europe and China), Chile was the first country to achieve this status. Available evaluations of the impact of these FTAs on trade and labor conditions for Chilean workers are quite favorable.[15]

By 2010, Chile could be accurately described as one of the most open economies in the world. An important result of this trade policy is that the country's economy is extremely well diversified in terms of market access. Chile exports roughly one-third of its products to the United States, one-third to Europe, and the remaining third to Asia (although lately, given the economic woes of Europe and the United States, Asia's proportion has increased). A shortcoming that we will discuss in the next section is that it has not been able to successfully diversify its export portfolio. A second shortcoming is that Chile has, in a sense, developed a dependence on the "stability imperative" since its openness exposes it more to international volatility.

Exchange Rate Management

A very important element in the macroeconomic management of the Concertación administrations is their transition from a pegged or managed exchange rate regime toward a fully flexible one. Again, this process was undertaken in a gradual manner, which marks an important difference with the more abrupt transitions that can be observed in most Latin American countries and, actually, also in Chile during most of the twentieth century. It is very important to consider that from the balance of payments crisis of the mid-1980s to the independence of the Central Bank that occurred at the same time as the transition to democracy, the country had a pegged exchange rate (administrated) that was clearly oriented toward export promotion. This policy was very successful and clearly one of the main elements that allowed Chile to climb out of its crisis, but was wearing itself out toward the late 1980s and early 1990s as the development of the financial market started to generate important speculative pressures that made the peg increasingly hard to sustain. This also had the defect of exposing the Central Bank, further down the road, to another potentially destabilizing exchange rate crisis. However, a big part of stability-oriented policy of these years was generating a smooth transition toward flexible rates.

The current consensus within the macroeconomic policy community in Chile is that exchange rates should usually be flexible but that policymakers should be open to potential interventions in extreme cases, specifically when the exchange rate is perceived to be significantly deviated from its equilibrium path as a result of speculative overreactions of the market in one direction or the other. Exporter lobby complaints (sellers abroad with costs in pesos) should be expected when the exchange rate appreciates and financial sector lobby complaints (users of foreign credit that lend in pesos) should be expected when the exchange rate depreciates, but interventions should only be used when the price is significantly out of balance. One should add that assessing when this is happening is a difficult call to make, which creates much room for creative political economy analysis and spin (Edwards 1996; Ffrench-Davis 2010; Morandé and Tapia 2002; Velasco 2000; Williamson 2000).

Among the Left, the belief in exchange rate policy as a tool of development policy has slowly dissipated and been replaced by the belief in the need for more substantive industrial policy. It has become increasingly clear to most progressives that all-out exchange rate policy—while generating a competitive edge for new exporters—provides a significant subsidy to big multinational firms that dominate Chile's current commodity-based export patterns. The cost of this sort of implicit subsidy is an increasingly expensive consumer basket for Chilean workers, who, in a primary resource–specialized country such as Chile, import a big part of their consumption basket. This is why at present, the view that active exchange rate policy is a blunt weapon predominates, which helps some marginal exporters but mainly subsidizes companies that do not need it at substantial social cost to the state. On the other hand, designed and targeted industrial policy, while more difficult to implement and very demanding in terms of incentive design, can be much more effective in promoting the development of new products for export, and will eventually be much cheaper from a cost perspective. And, those who do not believe in industrial policy still believe that the best exchange rate system is a flexible one, but advocate deregulation of labor markets, flexibility of environmental codes, and tax cuts as an alternative approach. Hence, it is unlikely that Chile will return to active and permanent exchange rate policies.

Financial Regulation

Another factor in Chile's economic development success is that since the mid-1980s it has maintained a conservative approach to financial regulation. This approach was not brought about by the Concertación administrations but rather was a direct result of the significant disruptions and profound trauma generated by the banking crises of the mid-1980s. Since then, Chilean banking law has been extremely restrictive, strictly overseeing intermediary financial balance sheets, and with strong firewalls between different types of financial products (Brock 2000; Budnevich and Le Fort 1997; Cowan and De Gregorio 2007; Gallego and Loayza 2004; Larraín 1995). As a result, Chile has not experienced a single banking failure since the 1980s crisis, which is quite remarkable. In this area, the Concertación basically continued the policy stance it inherited from the final part of the dictatorship, which was substantially more oriented toward tough financial regulation than the original Chicago Boys' laissez-faire approach to capital markets of the 1970s and early 1980s. Its principal merit is to have resisted an increasingly strong financial sector lobby that has pressured governments for more substantial deregulation.[16]

In addition, the Concertación's approach to the regulation of capital flows has been extremely cautious. Most deregulation has been undertaken very carefully and in targeted areas.[17] For example, during the Concertación years there has been substantial innovation in pension fund regulation.

International financial flows, however, have been handled in a slightly less straightforward manner. During the last twenty years Chile started the transition to democracy with a very clear policy bias in favor of foreign direct investment (FDI) flows and against short-term capital investment and speculative flows. The expression of this bias had two elements. The first had been established by the dictatorship in the 1970s as part of a campaign to recover the country's standing among the international financial community. This consisted of a mechanism (known as the DL600) that gave large-scale and long-term investors indemnity from tax reform for as long as they stayed. The Concertación kept this mechanism, which has become a problem now that FDI flows to the country are anything but scarce. The second expression of the bias against short-term flows was a capital control based on a tax (*encaje*) that was designed to tax short-term speculative investments at a higher rate than long-term investments.

The *encaje* was active from 1991 to 1998. It was eliminated in the midst of the Asian crisis when the country faced the possibility of a severe credit crunch. Available evaluations show that the *encaje* affected the composition and timing of flows and hence reduced exchange rate volatility (Edwards and Rigobón 2009). On the other hand, eight years of capital controls in Chile taught policymakers that the establishment of these sorts of schemes is not a static policy. Once a tax like this is set up speculative capital flows are reduced for a while, but they usually find a way around the block. Hence, regulators have to play a cat-and-mouse game of continually chasing and closing loopholes. Inevitably, speculators invent mechanisms to circumvent the rules, which substantially reduce their effectiveness. The lesson that the Concertación learned from this experience is that these types of capital controls cannot be used as a permanent policy mechanism, but rather only as a transitory intervention. The *encaje* and similar mechanisms regularly reappear in monetary debates every time exchange rate volatility or accelerated appreciation causes concern.

Prestige and Hysteresis

Two additional characteristics of Chilean macroeconomic processes are worth highlighting. First, the Concertación was able to establish Chile as one of the best managed economies in the world. Many international rankings, such as the World Competitiveness Reports or the Economic Freedom Index, rate Chile very highly, above many developed countries. Chile has also earned praise from many prestigious international experts and observers.[18] One must concede this has generated a self-reinforcing and also self-perpetuating rhetorical circle between investors and policymakers, which maintained the momentum of economic growth despite the short dips of the Asian and subprime crises.[19] Second, high-quality macroeconomic policy has served as an organizing principle, and continues to do so, within the Left in Chile just as we start to observe a clear shift of conservative policies away from fiscal responsibility during the Piñera administration (which may parallel US politics). This has become one of the distinguishing characteristics of the Chilean Left within the continent and the subject of praise as well as criticism.

The Weaknesses of the Chilean Model

Much can be said to praise the stability-oriented macroeconomic policy of the Concertación. The Chilean model has certainly produced relatively high economic growth rates considering Chile's level of development (albeit declining in recent years) and has performed well on average in the context of a region that is still highly unstable. In particular, the model directed some of the extra resources that economic growth generated toward the gradual construction of a social protection system. However, from the perspective of a coherent development strategy it is clear that there are some evident shortcomings and pending challenges that the Concertación did not address. These include, for example, the need for substantial improvements in income distribution (see, in this volume, Chapters 10 and 11), in the labor market (Chapter 12), diversification of the country's export portfolio, significant increases in spending on research and development and innovation policies (Chapter 9), and substantial improvements in productivity, vocational training, and educational performance (Chapter 13). Unfortunately, these shortcomings are actually expressed in Chilean growth rates, which are shown in Figure 8.3.

Although as we have stated, Chilean growth has been quite good when compared to the region, it is less impressive when compared to a broader category of emerging markets. The International Monetary Fund's (IMF's) calculation of GDP per capita in purchasing power parity (PPP) shows that Chile's GDP was 23 percent of that in the United States in 1960, is currently around 32 percent, and is projected to be around 38 percent in 2020. This means that in the four decades after 1980, Chile will have shortened the distance between its own GDP and that of the United States by 15–20 percent, which is the same order of magnitude as countries like Thailand, Turkey, Malaysia, and Poland. However, countries like Slovenia, the Slovak and Czech Republics, and Russia will have shortened their distance by 50–60 percent over the same time period; Korea by 30 percent; and Singapore, whose PPP was 50 percent of that of the United States in 1980, will have caught up with the PPP GDP of the United States. The point is that when we start to compare Chile with non–Latin American standards, the trajectory still looks good but is nowhere near as outstanding.

The main problem with the Chilean development strategy is a lack of change in its productive structure. Chile export products continue to lack diversification. Most of the country's exports are concentrated in no more than a dozen products. Moreover, a high proportion of these products are exactly the same ones that Chile exported twenty, thirty, or even forty years ago (Agosin and Bravo-Ortega 2007; Prieto, Sáez, and Goswami 2011). The overwhelming majority of Chilean exports are outright commodities or commodities with a small manufacturing component, produced with capital-

Figure 8.3 Chilean Growth Rates, 1988–2012

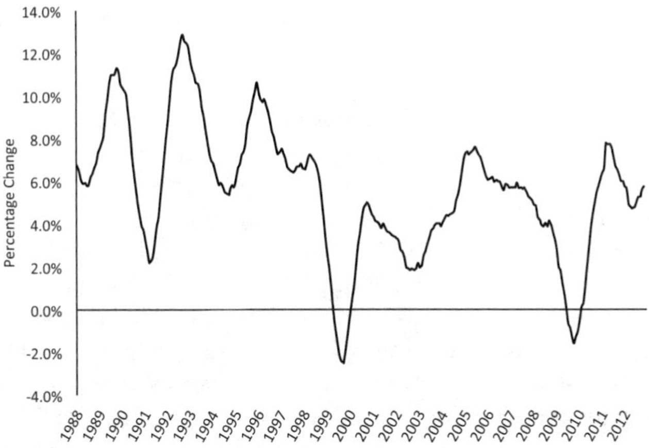

Source: Compiled by author from data from the Instituto Nacional de Estadisticas, Chile (INE, Chilean National Statistical Institute), www.ine.cl.

intensive technologies. Chile's private sector has little interest in innovation. Most of the investment in innovation is made by the state, which has a hard time resisting the pressures of academic interest groups that divert these investments away from innovation-oriented applied research toward more academic-oriented research. The country has one of the most privatized and expensive education systems in the world, based on the longest running and most comprehensive experiment with a neoliberal voucher system that has produced very little improvement in the quality of education and therefore negatively affects innovation.

Chile furthermore has antiquated labor legislation that was designed to avoid conflict rather than to foster negotiation. This has generated a dual labor market: half of it is completely flexible bordering on the informal, while the other half is subject to byzantine rules. Neither innovation, nor education or labor has played an important role in Chile's development strategy over the last four decades. Moreover, Chile has a tax system that is clearly biased toward investment in fixed or financial capital and against human capital and education. People who study or train themselves as well as innovators and new entrepreneurs are usually those who pay the highest tax rates; large business heirs are the ones who pay the least.

The main forces behind the Chilean model have consequently been the "property" of capital and natural resources. What workers have been asked to provide is cheap labor to compensate for low productivity. The stability imperative has been essential to this property-biased productive model that neglected policy discussions about structural or fundamental reforms in education and training policies, productive development, and labor regulation, and has instead sustained the appalling patterns of income distribution for which Chile has now become so well known. However, it is important to acknowledge that in recent years we have observed improvement in income distribution resulting from the social transfer policies of the last three administrations, especially Bachelet's universal minimum pension reform. The evolution of the Gini coefficient is depicted in Figure 8.4.

Other countries that have overcome the middle-income trap have developed new industries and sectors that have underpinned not only their economic growth but also their demand for a more qualified work force, a more innovation-oriented entrepreneurial sector, and more dialogue and negotiation within their industrial relations. These are the central changes that have improved income distribution in all of these countries during the final phase of their convergence to developed country status. The productive structure of countries that have closed the development gap changes radically during this process. This does not mean that in the process of developing they discarded their comparative advantages. Nor does it mean that they embarked on a voluntaristic crusade to set up industries for which they had no skills or qualifications. It simply means that part of the process of overcoming the middle-income trap is the development of an institutional design that promotes the emergence of new sectors through private innovation so that the availability of subsidies, support, infrastructure, capital, and funding is directed toward those who make innovative and qualified-labor-intensive entrepreneurial efforts and not to the traditional sectors and rent-intensive natural resources.

These policy gaps are the main failings of the "Chilean model." It is a major weakness that has the potential to bog down the process of development in economic sclerosis, social stagnation, and political indignation. The social uprising of 2011, known as the Chilean Winter of Discontent, seemed closely related to the shortcomings of Chilean development policy. One of the main concerns that drove student protesters to the streets was that they were being subjected to an expensive and ineffective education system that had no relation to the human capital requirements of the economy. In essence, they were being educated for an economy that did not exist, for which there were no policies in place to create it, and that was expected to "endogenously" appear around them. As larger and larger cohorts of new university students found that this did not happen and that the possibility of repaying student loans was consequently becoming harder than expected, the indignation increased and so did the force of social protest.

In my view, protests happened neither by chance nor due to the technical or ideological failings of the Chilean elite. I do not believe the objective of economic transformation has been left aside for so long because

Figure 8.4 Gini Coefficient for Chile, 1957–2011

Source: Compiled by author from data from the Instituto Nacional de Estadisticas, Chile (INE, Chilean National Statistical Institute), www.ine.cl.

of technical misconceptions, or that there is an error—an ideology-driven mistake—made by neoliberals within the Concertación who were obscured by the narrative of market-led development.

I believe that obnubilation may have been part of the political strategy that the consensus deployed among lower political ranks; but the choice against structural economic and social transformation as a development policy was a conscious political choice made by the governing elites of the transition to democracy. It seems much more plausible that this choice was made in support of the stability imperative. After all, each one of the policies I have described as stagnant (labor, education, tax, and industrial) is socially disruptive and both economically and politically threatening for dominating elites. So much so, that all of the successful developing countries that have managed to negotiate their way through this development phase have had to manufacture large-scale and comprehensive political deals to sustain a new consensus that includes these reforms. Each country has found its own way of doing so, appropriate to its own history and structure. Successful cases are few and formulas for this path are not replicable.

The practical political expression of this policy choice is that during the two decades of Concertación governments any advocate of these policies was gently ostracized and if necessary weeded out. A big part of the political crisis suffered by the Concertación in recent years has to do with the exponential growth of this point of view. As time passes, structural social, economic, and productive change remain stagnant. As the country continues to observe a slow deceleration of its trend and structural growth rates, it remains to be seen if this point of view will predominate in the next form that the Center-Left coalition takes.[20] The political battle that will deliver the result of this process is being fought as this volume is being written.

Notes

1. Piñera (2000).
2. "Juan Manuel Santos: Queremos copiar el modelo chileno," *El Mercurio*, August 12, 2011.
3. The Washington Consensus is a term originally coined by John Williamson to refer to the core beliefs on development held by policy analysts and advisers of the main multilateral institutions (International Monetary Fund [IMF], World Bank, the General Agreement on Tariffs and Trade [GATT]) as well as US government agencies (Department of Commerce, Federal Reserve, Securities and Exchange Commission [SEC], etc.). The "ten commandments" of the Washington Consensus were (1) fiscal discipline understood as avoidance of deficits; (2) redirection of public spending from subsidies and entitlements to productivity-enhancing public goods; (3) lowering of tax rates and increasing the tax base; (4) free-floating but competitive interest rates; (5) the same with exchange rates and increasing the tax base; (6) trade liberalization; (7) liberalization of inward foreign direct investment flows; (8) privatization of inward foreign direct investment flows; (9) deregulation; and (10) legal protection of property rights. It must be recognized that the term "Washington Consensus" has evolved in meaning from the original prescriptions to a more general concept of market fundamentalism.
4. The Popular Front was a coalition of Socialists, Communists, social democrats, and radical liberals.
5. For the political aspects see Gazmuri (2000); Molina (1977); and Moulián (2006).
6. For further critical views see Bardón (1993); Corvalán (2003); Garcés (1976); Garretón (1987a); Pinto and Moulián (2005); Salazar and Altamirano (2010), and Vial (2000).
7. To be fair, the nationalization of the copper industry had started during the previous two political administrations: slowly under the conservative Alessandri administration that used it as an appeasement policy for the Left, then accelerating during the Frei Montalva administration. It was radically completed during the Allende administration and was not reversed by the dictatorship that actually set up a scheme to use the proceeds of these nationalizations to finance the acquisition of weaponry for the Chilean armed forces. The reemergence of the private sector in the copper industry was a result of foreign direct investment flows coming in to develop new projects with the state systematically under investing and slowly losing its predominant position in this industry.
8. For further insight see Buchi (1993); Edwards and Cox-Edwards (1987); Ffrench-Davis (2010); Huneeus (2003); Larraín and Vergara (2000); and Meller (2005).
9. For further readings see Bosworth, Dornbusch, and R. Labán (1994); Contreras and Larrañaga (2010); Kalter (2004); Meller (2005); and Muñoz (2007).

10. The Concertación was originally a coalition of seventeen parties that opposed the military dictatorship, which coalesced into four political parties: the Christian Democratic Party, which in Chile is a Center-Left party, and three member parties of the Socialist International—the Socialist Party (mostly classical socialist and laborite), the Democratic Party (mainly social democratic, greens, and liberal democratic), and the Radical Party (social democratic). To this we must add a "shadow" liberal democratic elite that dominated the politics of the coalition for most of its history and was constituted by members of all parties, notorious public academics, and some very notorious independents. During all but two years of the coalition's twenty-year tenure in office, it faced an opposition congress and institutional restrictions that resulted from the imposed constitution and that made any policy initiative completely dependent on its capability to negotiate with the opposition and the business elite.

11. Only at the very end of the coalition's history did it suffer an exodus of political movements and leaders to the Left; during most of its history there was a continued diaspora of centrist movements of both liberal and Christian Democratic origins that left the coalition because they felt it had moved too much to the Left. The two most prominent examples are the Regional Independent Party (PRI) and the Chile First Movement (Ch1). The PRI was formed by a former senator and president of the Christian Democratic Party that was expelled from his party because of his "internal" opposition to both the Lagos and Bachelet administrations. The PRI was a moderately successful experiment. It currently has two members of parliament and some fifty or so city councilors. The Ch1 was formed by two major figures of the Concertación: a former senator and cabinet member of the Allende administration, and a former congressman and president of the Democratic Party. They both believed that the coalition had progressively abandoned its liberal pro-market policies and decided to form their own party, which does not have, to this date, any electoral successes to boast of. Both parties ended up supporting the Piñera presidential bid and the early stages of his administration (they have now abandoned his coalition).

12. For further reading describing the history of Chilean monetary policy since the independence of the Central Bank, see Boylan (2001); Corbo (2000, 2005); Lavezzolo (2006); Massad (2003); Mishkin and Savastano (2001); and Zahler (1998).

13. For further readings on the effects of the Asian crisis in Chile, follow the work of Calvo and Talvi (2008); Caporale, Cipollini, and Demetriades (2002); De Gregorio and Valdés (2001); ECLAC (1998); Ffrench-Davis (2010); and OECD (1999).

14. To study the evolution of fiscal rules and the accumulation of sovereign funds, follow Corbo (2011); Edwards (2010); Marcel et al. (2001); Rodriguez, Tokman, and Vega (2007); Tapia (2003); Velasco et al. (2010).

15. Chilean trade policy and its impact are analyzed by Agosin and Bravo-Ortega (2007); Álvarez (2004); Ffrench-Davis (2010); Ffrench-Davis, Leiva, and Madrid (1992); French-Davis, Agosin, and Uthoff (1995); Meller (1992); Monfort (2008); Saez (2005); and Schiff (2002).

16. Such a lobby was probably not faced by the economic authorities of the dictatorship during the late 1980s due to the fresh memories of the 1982 crisis, but became increasingly strong during the Concertación years.

17. For regulation of capital flows, see Budnevich and Le Fort (1997) for Chile, and for a complete survey of the literature, including Chile, see Ostry et al. (2010). For regulation on the pension system, see Arenas (2006); Arenas et al. (2008); and Krasnokutskaya, Ressner, and Todd (2010).

18. In the last report of the Global Competitiveness Index 2011–2012, Chile was ranked 31 out of 142 nations, beating developed countries like Spain (36) and Italy (43), and emerging economies like Brazil (53) and Mexico (58). Especially in the ranking of the Macroeconomic Environment Chile was 14 out of 142. For more details, see WEF (2011).

19. This point has been illustrated during the Piñera administration, which at the time of writing has significantly deviated from best macroeconomic practices, but still benefits from Chile's accumulated credibility.

20. Since 2010 there has been a reacceleration in growth rates resulting from a couple of transitory factors. First, the aftermath of the aggressive fiscal and monetary policies of 2008–2009; second, the acceleration in investment resulting from the reconstruction efforts following the 2010 mega earthquake; third, the continued commodity price boom; fourth, some entrepreneurial enthusiasm resulting from Piñera's victory.

9

Fiscal Policy: Promoting Faustian Growth

Ramón López

> *What lies beyond does not worry me.*
> —Dr. Faust, in Johann Wolfgang von Goethe,
> *Faust*, Part 1 (1808)

All over the world, tax policy systematically has the potential to cause more political tension than any other issue of public policy. Chile is no exception to this general rule, particularly as the issue of taxes is very closely related to the country's economic model. Broadly speaking, Chile's tax structures constitute a transitional enclave in the same way that its general economic model does, with the proviso that the Aylwin government took office with the stated priority of implementing a tax reform that would enable the government to increase social spending. A tax reform was thus negotiated in 1990, which boosted tax revenues by around 15 percent, and enabled the Aylwin government to increase fiscal spending on social policies from 9.9 percent to 11.7 percent of GDP. However, since then, the basic structure of fiscal revenues has not changed.

This chapter argues that two salient features have characterized Chile's economic development during the Concertación governments: first, economic growth has been highly unbalanced favoring the rapid growth of traditional natural resource and environment-degrading industries to the detriment of knowledge and human capital–intensive sectors. Second, while poverty has declined over the period, income inequality has remained appallingly high. Both of these issues in the long run will constitute a drag factor on Chilean growth, and arguably already do so.

The central hypothesis of this chapter is that fiscal policy has been in part responsible for the lack of progress toward developing an economy that is (1) based more on knowledge-intensive, environmentally clean industries; (2) less dependent on primary and related industries; and (3) less socially unjust. The chapter shows that tax policies have not only failed to provide the fiscal resources needed for promoting human capital expansion and to finance more effective and equitable social policies, but have instead exacerbated inequality and the economy's dependence on the production of raw materials and other primary commodities.

As other chapters in this volume have discussed, the emphasis of the Concertación's fiscal expenditures on the provision of public and social goods, including health, education, and social programs, has been exemplary compared to many other countries in the region. However, the key problem in Chile has been the reduced level of such spending due, in turn, to the incapacity of the tax system to generate enough fiscal revenues.[1] This has made government expenditures largely ineffective at promoting a decisive expansion of human capital, reducing inequality, and lowering the economy's overdependence on natural resource–intensive industries. Once again, and as noted repeatedly throughout this volume, political restraints and in particular the transitional enclaves have limited the scope and audacity of reforms, allowing the reproduction of fiscal policies that consistently reinforced inequality and promoted Faustian growth.

This chapter proceeds as follows: the next section presents an overview of the political reforms and debates that led to Chile's current tax structure. The third section then explains Chile's current tax system before going on to examine the linkages between the fiscal policies of the Concertación and the persistence of social inequality, on the one hand, and the overdependence of the economy on primary goods on the other. The chapter concludes by discussing the implications of fiscal policy for the long-term patterns of economic development.[2]

The Political Background of Tax Reform in Chile

The political impediments to structural reform in the area of fiscal policy are much the same as those discussed in other chapters of this volume. The straitjacket imposed by the authoritarian enclaves limited fiscal reform in the same way that it did many other structural reforms. However, in the area of fiscal policy there was one crucial difference. While in other social policy areas, reform had been limited by the Concertación's fear of military reprisals, in the area of fiscal policy it was the political Right that feared the social reactions to extreme and widespread poverty that could have burgeoned under democracy, and potentially could have threatened the stability of the economic model.

At the very beginning of its term in office, the Aylwin government therefore succeeded in negotiating a significant tax reform, which the Right conceded to in order to "assuage" the severe social debt the Concertación had inherited from the military dictatorship, and thus contain social unrest. This reform raised the corporate tax rate from 10 percent to 15 percent, and increased value-added tax (VAT) from 16 to 18 percent. In addition, during its term in office the Aylwin government introduced important reforms to reduce tax evasion. In exchange for these increases in the corporate tax rate, combined with reduced tax evasion, the Aylwin administration lowered maximum marginal personal income tax rates from 50 percent to 45 percent. This particular component of the reform made sense if it could help to lower tax evasion. These reforms were also very much in line with similar efforts across Latin America that occurred during transition periods from dictatorships to democracy.

However, this fiscal pact shaped long-term fiscal policy under the Concertación, and was considered untouchable by the right-wing opposition for many years. The neoliberal ideology that had shaped the dictatorship and its liberalizing reforms had been based on low tax rates. Raising fiscal resources for social expenditure produced severe ideological and political resistance beyond this basic pact, and thus silenced any further debate on tax reform for many years. This ideological foundation, however, also pervaded technocratic sectors of the Concertación, whose economists were almost equally reluctant to raise additional taxes.

It was not until the Lagos government in 2001 that fiscal reform again became a political objective of the Concertación. As described in Chapter 11, the administration's goal has been to raise taxes to finance a health reform that would constitute basic universal care for all people covered by the public health care system. This health care reform, additionally, was supposed to have included a shared financing mechanism between public and private health care insurance. In the end this component of the reform was not passed as private health care insurers lobbied heavily against this measure. However, the Lagos government did raise value-added tax by an additional percentage point and increased the corporate tax from 15 percent to 17 percent to finance this reform. It also further tightened loopholes to prevent tax evasion, even though bank secrecy legislation did not change significantly. In exchange, the Right pressured President Lagos to eliminate the capital gains tax and further lower the maximum marginal personal income tax rate from 45 percent to 40 percent.

Another reform that was enacted under the Lagos administration was the implementation of a small "royalty" tax of 5 percent, which in reality was a surcharge on copper extraction profits, which, as is explained below in this chapter, is even tax deductible. The struggles of the Lagos administration to implement even these minor reforms provide a good illustration of the resistance that Concertación governments faced on the issue of fiscal reform, principally from the right-wing opposition, but also from within its own ranks, especially from its own technocratic economists.

An opportunity to break out of this transitional enclave came during the early years of the Bachelet administration, which took office with a small majority in both houses of congress. However, this episode perhaps best illustrates the extent to which the original authoritarian enclaves had become transitional enclaves, and therefore constituted the Concertación's very own straitjacket. Taking advantage of the political situation, the Socialist Party at the time initiated an important internal debate that attempted to increase taxes. However, once again the technocratic forces within the Concertación itself became a major obstacle to implementing any important tax reform. Headed by the powerful finance minister, the right-wing technocratic forces within the coalition adamantly opposed and were able to block any tax increase. These groups were not only able to block tax increases, but they also led the government to implement important changes in the corporate tax code including a strengthening of the accelerated depreciation rules that reduced fiscal revenues by about US$600 million.

Why was the Concertación so unwilling to raise taxes despite the enormous unmet social needs and extremely unjust income distribution after the Aylwin administration? Seventeen years of military dictatorship shifted the political power forces radically in favor of a small elite that became immensely rich and powerful. This elite was able not only to persuade the military government to enforce highly conservative policies (including low taxes) but also to permeate all aspects of the social structure including full control of the media, think tanks, and universities. This created an ideology of the elites that became highly ingrained in the influential technocratic segments of society, particularly economists. This technocracy gave pseudoscientific legitimacy to the ideology of the elites that was based in the most extreme right-wing economic precepts.

The Concertación could not escape this ideology and also could not escape the dominance of the economist technocrats within its own ranks who shared the same ideology that had flourished during the military dictatorship. Thus, apart from the obvious external political factors that limited the policy scope of the Concertación, the main enemy to fiscal and other progressive reforms was within the coalition. The success of the Concertación technocrats in blocking these reforms was supported by the media, which was, in turn, totally dominated by the same ideology and made every effort to protect the pseudoscientific precepts held by the conservative economists both outside and within the Concertación.

In addition, the technocratic hegemony in economic policy was facilitated by a relatively dormant social environment. Civil society did not become reorganized and militant until the second half of the Bachelet government, especially through the student organizations. This awakening of civil society coincided with the development of the social media that to some extent made inroads into the ideological monopoly of the conventional media.

The emergence of important and truly independent or progressive electronic media that very quickly became highly popular has contributed in part to counterbalancing the right-wing conventional media. Social media and greatly improved social communications that facilitated the transfer of information and organization of civil society around important issues—such as the quality of education, environmental issues, and many others—have caused significant social upheaval and the diffusion of alternative views that have contributed to the questioning of the existing economic dogmas. This, in turn, is causing a gradual shift and renewal of the existing technocratic cadres toward a more progressive ideology.

Tax Policies and Structures

Low Tax Revenues and a High Reliance on Indirect Taxes

Chile has the lowest tax revenue per dollar of GDP among all OECD countries. In 2006, total tax receipts in Chile amounted to 20 percent of GDP compared to an average of 36.3 percent for all OECD countries. As shown in Figure 9.1, even within Latin America, Chile's tax revenues as a proportion of GDP are much lower than other countries in the region, including Brazil (34 percent), Argentina (23 percent), and Uruguay (25 percent). The database of the ECLAC (CEPALSTAT) finds that Chile is well below the

Figure 9.1 International Comparison of Tax Burden, 2006

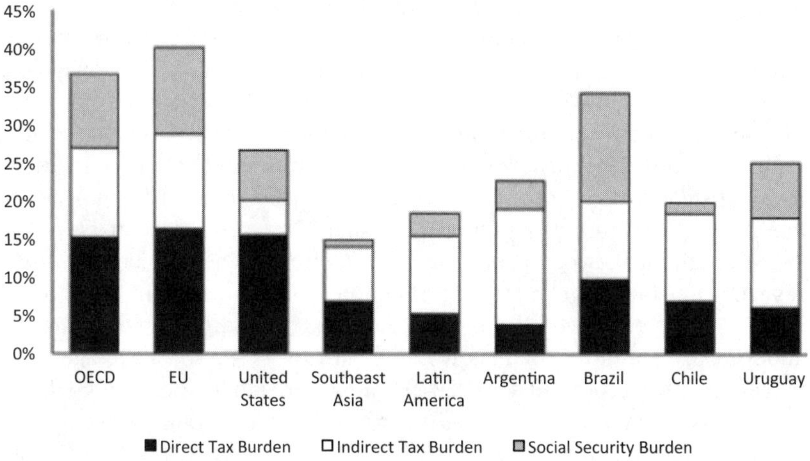

■ Direct Tax Burden   ▢ Indirect Tax Burden   ▨ Social Security Burden

Source: Gómez Sabaini and Martner (2010).

international tax revenue norm given its per capita income. These low levels of tax revenues impose a tight constraint on public expenditures.

By the early 1990s there was a consensus in Latin America that the tax systems that had originated during the authoritarian regimes of the 1980s were inadequate for raising the tax revenues needed to finance the more progressive social policies that democratic governments were required to implement in view of the prevailing high levels of poverty and income inequality. In most countries of the region, this led to tax reforms that succeeded in significantly increasing tax revenues.

While Chile did manage to increase tax revenues as well, its efforts in this respect were much more timorous than in most other countries in the region. In fact, the evolution of tax revenues in Chile over the 1990–2006 period shows only a slight increase of about 19 percent, from 16.5 percent of GDP in 1990 to 19.7 percent in 2006 (see Table 9.1). According to Jorratt (2009) the average tax burden during 1987–1990—corresponding to the last four years of the military dictatorship—was 17 percent of GDP while the average tax burden during 2006–2009—the last four years of the Concertación governments—was slightly more than 19 percent (ECLAC 2010).

This development contrasts with the evolution in most other countries in Latin America where tax revenues have increased much more rapidly. The average tax revenues as a proportion of GDP for the group of nineteen Latin American countries increased by 47 percent over the period, and among the high per capita income countries in the region (Brazil, Chile, Uruguay, Argentina, and Costa Rica) the average tax revenues increased by more than 30 percent. Chile therefore not only has one of the lowest tax burdens among the countries with comparable per capita incomes in Latin America, but also has been one of the most conservative countries in terms of reforming its tax system to generate more fiscal revenues.

Chile's tax structure continues to be heavily reliant on indirect taxes while income taxes provide a much smaller fraction of all revenues and constitute a very low proportion of GDP. In 2006 almost 60 percent of the total tax revenues came from indirect taxes (Jorratt 2009). As can be seen in Figure 9.1, this dependence on indirect taxation is extremely high by international standards: average dependence on indirect taxes in Latin America and the OECD countries was 54 percent and 32 percent, respectively.[3]

Over the last two decades the participation of indirect taxes in total revenues in Chile has declined significantly. Concomitantly the share of direct taxes in total tax revenues has steadily increased, from an average of about 21 percent of the total tax revenues in 1990–1993 to an average of 32 percent in 2004– 2006 (ECLAC 2010). However, at 6.9 percent of GDP, the share of direct taxes in Chile is still very low by international standards.

Corporate income tax rates have also remained very low over the period 2004–2006 at 3.2 percent of GDP, which is higher than the 2 percent

Table 9.1 Tax Revenues of the Central Government, 1990–2006 (as percentage of GDP)

	1990	2000	2006	Average, 1990–2006
Group 1	19.7	22.7	25.7	22.3
Brazil	26.4	30.4	34.2	28.5
Uruguay	22.4	23.6	25.6	23.8
Argentina[a]	16.1	21.5	27.4	21.7
Chile[a]	16.5	19.2	19.7	18.9
Costa Rica[a]	16.9	18.9	21.4	18.9
Group 2	11.6	15.9	19.9	15.6
Honduras[a, b]	15.3	17.0	19.3	16.8
Colombia	10.9	16.8	20.7	16.6
Nicaragua	9.0	17.5	21.3	15.9
Panama	14.7	16.0	15.9	15.7
Peru	11.6	13.9	16.4	14.6
Bolivia	8.2	14.0	25.7	14.0
Group 3	7.9	10.4	12.5	10.0
El Salvador	8.9	13.0	15.0	12.6
Mexico	12.6	12.1	11.0	12.3
Dominican Republic	8.2	12.7	14.1	11.9
Paraguay	9.9	12.0	13.5	11.8
Ecuador	10.1	11.6	14.2	11.2
Guatemala	7.6	10.9	12.1	10.3
Venezuela	4.4	9.4	12.6	9.3
Haiti	7.3	7.9	10.0	7.4
Simple Latin American Average	12.5	15.7	18.4	15.4

Source: Gómez Sabaini and Martner (2010).
Notes: a. Tax revenues correspond to the general government.
b. Data corresponding to 2005.

share observed during the early 1990s but still implies a very low effective tax rate for corporations (Jorratt 2009). Using the well-accepted lower bound estimate for the share of profits in GDP of 50 percent (used consistently by the World Bank) this would yield an effective tax rate on profits equal to about 6.4 percent, well below the legal corporate rate of 17 percent.

Legal Loopholes and Tax Evasion

According to a 2006 study by the Chilean tax authorities (Servicios de Impuestos Internos [SII] 2006), tax expenditures were extremely high, reaching 4 percent of GDP and more than 20 percent of all tax revenues in 2004.

According to the study about 80 percent of the tax loopholes consisted of a variety of income tax exemptions and another 18 percent affected the VAT. These large tax loopholes not only reduced the tax revenues of the state but are also greatly regressive. The above study found that more than 80 percent of the income tax loopholes benefit the wealthiest 5 percent of the population and 60 percent benefit the richest 1 percent of the population. That is, the wealthiest 1 percent of the people receives an annual transfer equivalent to 2 percent of GDP via tax expenditures. With respect to the VAT tax expenditures, the study shows that it is also quite regressive, albeit to a lesser extent than the income tax loopholes. About 70 percent of the VAT loopholes benefit the richest quintile of the population.

Of all income tax loopholes, tax deferments especially directed to create incentives for investment in capital equipment and similar categories of expenses are one of the most important components. Tax deferments are established mainly through exemptions to retained profits. However, it appears that part of the retained profits are never distributed because they correspond to "profits" generated by paper firms created for the specific purpose of avoiding the high personal income marginal tax rate, which reaches 40 percent for high incomes. These paper firms then become owners of durable consumption goods that are in fact used by the individuals.

Tax evasion rates in Chile are disparate depending on the type of taxes; they are low for indirect taxes, especially for VAT, but are high for income taxes. In fact, the tax evasion rate for VAT, estimated at about 11 percent, is the lowest in Latin America (Gómez Sabaini 2010) and is among the lowest in the OECD countries. By contrast, the rate of income tax evasion is quite high at almost 50 percent (Jorratt 2009), and according to Gómez Sabaini (2010) is comparable to several countries in Latin America including Argentina (50 percent), Mexico (46 percent), Peru (51 percent), and El Salvador (51 percent).

In 2005, the effective income tax revenues in Chile were about 5.9 percent of GDP. An evasion rate of 49.7 percent as estimated by Gómez Sabaini (2010) would imply a revenue loss of 5.8 percent of GDP.[4] Using somewhat more detailed data, Jorratt (2009) estimated a lower value for income tax evasion, of the order of 4 percent of GDP. In any case, even if we use the latter estimates we must conclude that income tax evasion is indeed quite widespread.

In Chile, like in most of Latin America, income taxes affect mainly the upper 10–15 percent of the population as the wages of lower income groups are tax exempt. Income taxes are automatically deducted from workers' wages but the richest segments of income tax payers obtain most of their income from nonwage sources, which gives them much greater scope for underdeclaring their incomes. This means that most tax evasion benefits the richest segments of the population that rely on nonwage revenues as their primary source of income. So we can expect that income tax evasion is at least as regressive as legal tax loopholes.

While it is in general easier to control evasion on indirect taxes such as the VAT than on income taxes, the gulf between evasion rates affecting the two types of tax in Chile is perplexing. In most countries in the region for which there are data for both VAT and income tax evasion, the ratio of VAT/income tax evasion is about one to two or three (Gómez Sabaini 2010). But for Chile this ratio is almost one to five. This suggests that Chilean governments made a conscious decision to place less emphasis on collecting income taxes than on value-added taxes. A key question is how a system that is extremely efficient in enforcing tax collections in some areas can be so ineffective in others.

Two factors explain the high income tax evasion rates: first, the very large difference between the maximum personal income tax rate and the tax rate on profits. The maximum marginal personal income tax rate is 40 percent, much higher than the legal tax for retained profits, which has been around 17 percent during most of the period considered. In reality this difference is much greater because of the many investment allowances and other legal loopholes that allow firms to reduce their profit tax to levels closer to 10 percent. High-income individuals receiving nonwage income have created paper firms, allowing them to transform income into profits, thus eluding taxes. In addition, the tax office faces great restrictions in accessing bank account information, much greater than in other countries such as Argentina (Fairfield 2010). The study by Fairfield (2010) has also shown that this has drastically limited the ability of the tax office to control income tax evasion.

In summary, the combination of income tax evasion and legal tax loopholes may easily reach at least 8 percent of GDP or 40 percent of the total government tax revenues. Part of these tax benefits, especially the tax deferments and accelerated depreciation allowances, may create additional incentives to invest in physical capital, but another significant part constitutes mainly tax losses. These not only represent significant losses of financial resources for the government, but also are resources that are appropriated mainly by the very rich.

Untaxed Capital Gains and Ineffective Inheritance Tax

Most capital gains are tax exempt, including capital gains associated with the sale of most stocks, mutual funds, and real estate. Chile is one of only three countries in the OECD that taxes neither long-term nor short-term capital gains. In Latin America, most of the high-income countries do have capital gains taxation. Mexico has a 35 percent rate and Brazil a 15 percent rate for short-term and long-term capital gains. Among OECD countries, most impose tax rates between 30 to 40 percent on short-term capital gains and 20 to 30 percent on long-term capital gains (Dalsgaard 2001).

Allowing capital gains to be untaxed constitutes another large break for the wealthy and also provides yet another mechanism for them to evade income taxes by disguising part of their income as capital gains. The conventional justification for not taxing capital gains is that it would reduce the international competitiveness of the Chilean financial markets. However, the fact that most middle- and high-income countries in the world do impose capital gains taxes renders this argument quite implausible.

The inheritance tax rate theoretically can be as high as 35 percent, but tax revenues actually collected are extremely low, yielding an insignificant part of total tax revenues. In fact, the revenues collected by this tax have in recent years averaged about US$60 million per annum or just 0.2 percent of all tax revenues (Jorratt 2009).

This may suggest that the inheritance tax is poorly conceived and allows for high rates of evasion due to the existence of significant mechanisms for elusion and low enforcement. In principle a well-conceived and enforced inheritance tax can potentially be an important source of tax revenues and an effective vehicle to ameliorate economic inequality. An argument often used by those opposing inheritance or other wealth taxes is that they constitute double taxation, by taxing wealth that has already been taxed when it was generated. However, in view of our previous analysis regarding income taxes, this argument lacks validity. As we have shown, the rich have been able to accumulate large fortunes in part thanks to legal and illegal schemes that have allowed them to pay extremely low effective income tax rates over the years. An inheritance tax is often the last opportunity for society to recover part of the tax revenue losses an ineffective income tax system has engendered.

Taxing Natural Resources

A large fraction of Chile's GDP consists of profits from natural resources. Just the copper profits and those of its many valuable by-products (including silver, gold, and molybdenum) were estimated at about US$21 billion per annum over the period 2005–2009 (CENDA 2010).[5] This represents about 14 percent of the average annual GDP over the period, which was US$150 billion. Of these rents, approximately half were generated by the state copper company (CODELCO). Most of these profits were paid to the central government. The large private copper mines produced net annual incomes or profits for the remaining US$14 billion (and paid about US$2.6 billion in taxes). If one includes the other major industries using natural resources—including salmon, other fisheries, noncopper mining, hydroelectric, and forestry—the profits are likely to be significantly higher. There are no estimates of resource rents for the noncopper sectors so one cannot obtain a reliable estimate of the total rents.

However, using new estimates of wealth recently developed by the World Bank one can indirectly obtain an estimate of the volume of noncopper rents. The World Bank estimated that the total value of tangible wealth for Chile, which includes produced physical capital and natural capital, is equivalent to 6.3 times the annual GDP (World Bank 2011a). Natural wealth comprises 60 percent of this estimate and the remaining 40 percent corresponds to produced capital. That is, using as a reference the annual estimate for GDP over 2005–2009 of US$150 billion, the total tangible wealth of Chile is about US$950 billion, of which US$560 billion is natural wealth and US$390 billion is produced capital.

If we use a benchmark annual rate of return of only 6 percent for natural capital, the total annual return to natural wealth is US$34 billion or 23 percent of GDP.[6] Given that the total annual copper rents amounted to US$21 billion, the rents for the noncopper resource sectors would amount to US$13 billion. That is, noncopper rents would equal slightly less than 9 percent of GDP. About 62 percent of the total resource rents of the country are generated by the copper sector and 38 percent by all the remaining resource-based sectors including fisheries, forestry, noncopper mining, hydroelectric power, and other sectors that rely heavily on natural resources.

Natural resources are a patrimony that belongs to all Chileans and yet the government has given rights of exploitation of such resources, for free, to large foreign and domestic corporations. One may expect that the corporations that exploit such resources be required to pay a royalty for them over and above the normal taxation. That is, the resource rents should be captured by the ultimate owner of the natural resources, the citizens of the country through the state. Since these rents are returns accruing to corporations that are allowed to exploit them over and above the normal returns to their capital, taxing these rents in principle would entail no economic distortions and would not discourage investments as long as the firms are still allowed to obtain normal or above-normal rates of return to their investments. In practice, however, it is difficult to ascertain what the "normal" returns to produced capital are, so it is often necessary to be cautious in setting levels of taxation that would allow corporations to retain part of the resource rents.

Most advanced resource-rich countries have established a variety of mechanisms to obtain a significant part of the resource rents while still allowing some margin to prevent the fall of returns to produced capital below a normal rate, which could discourage investment and cause deadweight losses. Countries such as Norway and Australia are able to share a much greater part of the resource rents than Chile. In fact, Australia uses special taxes on the rents of mining firms that imply an effective net income tax equivalent to more than twice the rate paid in Chile by the very same mining firms (CENDA 2010).

Other countries combine special exploration and exploitation rights with actual royalties applied to sales values. As shown in Table 9.2, Norway charges a 10 percent royalty on the total value of sales in addition to significant exploitation and exploration rights, as well as a 10 percent surcharge on profits (Figueroa 1998).

In Chile, however, copper firms are charged a modest 5 percent on declared profits as the only attempt to share part of the resource rents.[7] With this charge the effective corporate income tax rate for copper firms reaches 18.5 percent, which is less than half of the rate that the Australian government charges some of the same mining firms working in Chile.

The Chilean government does not apply any royalty or special tax surcharge to any of the other natural resources the country produces, despite the fact that a vast amount of land, water, and other resource rights have been arbitrarily allocated to selected private firms for exploitation without charge, often in perpetuity.

Chile is missing an opportunity to dramatically increase tax revenues (or reduce the rather exorbitant value-added tax currently at 19 percent) by using taxes that generate no deadweight losses. Taxing natural resource rents is likely to generate financial resources to increase investment in human capital and other assets that would come to replace resource income in the future as natural resources are depleted, and contribute to improved social equity. Chile could increase tax revenues significantly, even if it adopted a very cautious approach, by letting the resource firms retain a significant part of the resource rents.

Based on our estimate that natural resource rents constitute about 23 percent of GDP, if the government allowed resource firms to retain 75 percent of the rents instead of almost 100 percent as occurs now, tax revenues would increase dramatically. A surcharge equivalent to 25 percent of the net rents could increase tax revenues by as much as 3.5 percent of GDP (some US$5 billion) or by almost 30 percent of the current total tax revenues.[8] Using the average copper price of 2005–2009 as the "normal" reference price, the net pretax earnings of private copper firms are US$14 billion per annum. These firms paid taxes for US$2.6 billion per year over this period, meaning that US$11.4 billion of the rents were untaxed. So a 25 percent tax on the net rents would yield some US$3 billion per annum in extra tax revenues.

With the new tax surcharge, private mining firms would still pay much lower taxes as a proportion of their revenues than CODELCO. In fact, if the surcharge on private mines was equivalent to the one applied to CODELCO it would amount to about US$8 billion instead of US$3 billion. This should

Table 9.2 Natural Resources Policies in Chile and Norway

	Norway	Chile
Rights of exploration	Substantial	Very low mining patent
Rights of exploitation	Substantial	Very low mining patent
Royalty over sales	10 percent base, which goes up with the price	0 percent
Tax surcharge over profits	10 percent base, which goes up with the price	5 percent
Reserve to be exploited by the state company	Half	One-third
State quotas of production depending on the demand?	Yes	No

Source: Figueroa (1998).

be a guarantee that the tax proposed is not excessive given that, notwithstanding the fact that CODELCO's production costs are likely to be much higher than those of private firms, the state corporation has remained highly prosperous.

As indicated earlier the noncopper resource sectors generate rents equivalent to 9 percent of GDP. However, some of these rents are difficult to tax in part because some of them are produced by small and often poor producers. We assume that only two-thirds of these rents (or about 6 percent of GDP) can be realistically subjected to the tax surcharge. We assume that the taxable resource sectors pay the average effective income tax rate of 6 percent that applies to the country as a whole, yielding a base for the tax surcharge equal to 5.6 percent of GDP. Hence, a 25 percent royalty on these rents would yield 1.4 percent of GDP or US$2.1 billion per year.

The total additional tax revenues yielded by taxing private copper and noncopper rents would be above US$5 billion, from about US$30 billion per annum to US$35 billion, or more than 17 percent. All this can be achieved by using well-designed mechanisms already successfully implemented by developed countries.

An even more effective alternative mechanism could be to follow the Norwegian model and simply set a 10 percent royalty on the sales of natural resource products. Since an overwhelming portion of the sales of primary products are exported, this could be achieved by a 10 percent export tax on copper and other primary exports. The average annual exports of primary products amounted to US$48 billion over the 2005–2009 period, of which CODELCO exported about US$7 billion. Since the state company already pays a higher tax rate, the export tax would apply only to the remaining primary exports by private firms. Thus, for our reference 2005–2009 period, the 10 percent export royalty would apply to US$41 billion of primary exports and would have yielded about US$4 billion in extra tax revenues. In addition, a similar 10 percent royalty on the value of domestic sales for resource corporations such as electric utilities and others that produce mainly for the domestic markets may complement the above revenues to yield extra tax revenues similar to those generated by the profit tax surcharges discussed earlier.

Spending on Poverty but Not on Inequality

The share of total public spending in GDP has been consistently below 22 percent over the twenty years of Concertación governments (see Table 9.3). This is one of the lowest spending ratios among middle-income countries in Latin America and among the OECD countries and is a result of very low tax revenues. While the total volume of public spending in Chile has been low, the vast majority of this spending has targeted social expenditures. In fact, about 66 percent of total government expenditures have consisted of social expenditures. Moreover, about 75 percent of all government expenditures have been directed to either social goods or pure public goods including public order and safety and infrastructure.

Thus, the spending policies of the Concertación governments have emphasized the provision of goods that are complementary to, rather than substitutes for, private spending. As López and Galinato (2007) have shown, this is precisely the role of government spending: to mitigate the effects of market failures or imperfections that lead the private sector to underinvest in social goods (including education, health, and welfare), research and de-

Table 9.3 Government Expenditure by Function, 1987–2009 (as percentage of GDP)

	1987–1989	1990–1997	1998–2005	2006–2009
Government and public services	3.0	2.0	1.4	1.2
Defense and economic affairs	5.7	4.3	4.2	4.3
Public order and safety	1.0	1.0	1.3	1.4
Social expenditure[a]	14.5	12.7	14.4	13.8
Total	24.2	20.0	21.3	20.7

Source: Author's elaboration with Dipres data DIPRES (2011).
Note: a. Includes expenditures on education, health, housing, social protection, recreation and culture, and environmental protection.

velopment, the environment, and pure public goods by directing most government spending toward those areas. Thus, expenditure on social goods as a proportion of total government expenditure in Chile is much higher than that in most other Latin American countries. According to the World Bank's data, this fraction is higher only in Uruguay. For Latin America as a whole, this share is about 48 percent—well below that of 66 percent in Chile.

However, the picture radically changes when we consider social expenditures as a proportion of GDP instead of as a fraction of total government expenditure. Table 9.4 compares social spending as a share of GDP, the average spending in Latin America as a whole, and the average for OECD countries for the period 2005–2007. Total social spending in Chile at 12.4 percent of GDP was below the average for Latin America (14 percent) and well below levels prevailing in countries such as Argentina (21.5 percent), Brazil (23.7 percent), and Uruguay (20.7 percent). It was also much lower than the average for OECD countries.[9] The discordance between social spending as a share of total public spending and as a share of GDP is of course the result of the fact that Chile's total government expenditures as a proportion of GDP are much lower than most other countries of similar levels of development.

Table 9.4 also shows that the government expenditures in education and health as a percentage of GDP are well below the levels prevailing in most middle- and high-income countries in the world. The Chilean government spent only 3.3 percent of GDP on education, compared to 4.6 percent spent by OECD countries and countries with similar levels of development in Latin America including Argentina (5.1 percent), Brazil (4.9 percent), Mexico (3.9 percent), and Uruguay (3.7 percent).

Table 9.4 Comparison of Social Public Expenditures, 2005–2007 (as percentage of GDP)

	Total	Education	Health
Argentina	21.5	5.1	4.8
Brazil	23.7	4.9	4.5
Chile	12.4	3.3	2.8
Mexico	10.9	3.9	2.7
Uruguay	20.7	3.7	3.6
Latin America	14.0	4.6	3.1
OECD	19.5	4.6	5.8

Sources: OECD online dataset and CEPALSTAT online dataset, http://stats.oecd.org and http://estadisticas.cepal.org/cepalstat/WEB_CEPALSTAT/Portada.asp.

The gulf between Chile and comparable countries in public expenditures on health is even deeper than that of education. Public spending on health was only 2.8 percent of GDP in Chile, while the OECD average was more than twice that level at 5.8 percent. Moreover, Chile was well below the average of public health spending in Latin America, which was 3.1 percent of GDP, and also below all comparable countries in Latin America with the exception of Mexico.

The patterns of fiscal expenditure discussed in this chapter explain to a great extent the high levels of multidimensional inequality that characterize Chile today, and that are discussed in almost all chapters in this volume. Using household survey data (CASEN) for 2003, López and Miller (2008) conclude that inequality is as deep now as it was during the last years of the military dictatorship, and that most of this inequality occurs between the richest 10 percent of households and everyone else.

In fact, inequality among the bottom 90 percent of households is rather small. Solimano and Torche (2008) estimate a Gini of 0.38 for the bottom 90 percent of the population, which is much lower than the 0.55 of the country overall (CASEN 2009). Moreover, as is well known, household surveys greatly underestimate the true incomes of the rich as they are simply not represented in most surveys (Aguiar and Bils 2009; Attanasio and Szekely 1999). What this means is that the real gap between the richest 10 percent and everyone else is even greater than the CASEN-based data show.

Most analyses that estimate the rich's share of total income use income tax data rather than household survey data, although income tax data also tend to underestimate the income of the rich due to tax evasion, among other reasons (Brandolini and Smeeding 2008). Unfortunately, there are no analyses of income distribution using tax data in Chile.

The after-tax income distribution in Chile is more unequal than the pretax one. This sets Chile apart from most OECD countries and even from several middle-income Latin American countries. In fact, in most countries in the OECD, the after-tax income Gini coefficient is up to 15 percent lower than the pretax Gini coefficient (see Figure 9.2). By contrast, in Chile the opposite happens: the after-tax income Gini is higher than the pretax one (Gómez Sabaini 2010). In several countries in Latin America, taxes do contribute to reducing social inequality. In Argentina and Uruguay, for example, the after-tax income Gini coefficient is significantly lower than the pretax one while in Mexico and Colombia it is neutral. Among the large countries in Latin America, only in Brazil and Chile is the after-tax income distribution worse than the pretax one (Gómez Sabaini 2010). Of course, the fact that taxes in Chile exacerbate inequality should not be a surprise in view of previous analyses that have shown the significant pro-rich biases of the tax system.

Figure 9.2 Gini Coefficients Before and After Taxes in OECD Countries, 2008–2010

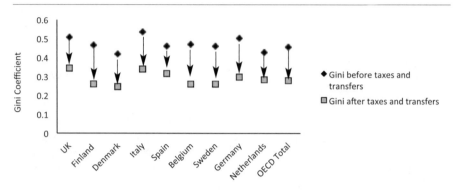

Source: Author elaboration based on http://stats.oecd.org.

Conclusion

As shown in the previous section, government spending on education and health has been very low compared to countries of similar levels of development. Moreover, the fact that Chile is much more unequal than most other middle-income and developed countries implies that a much larger fraction of its population must rely on the state as its only source of education, health care, and other social services.[10] That is, countries of similarly unequal per capita income levels need to spend much more on the provision of public education and health services than countries that have a more egalitarian income distribution where a higher fraction of the population has the financial means to buy them from the private sector. Thus, the case of Chile is doubly dramatic: not only does it spend less on public education and health services than countries of comparable levels of income, but also its level of inequality means it has much greater needs than other comparable countries.

Most taxes cause some deadweight losses and Chile's tax system is no exception. However, as shown earlier, Chile has missed an opportunity to reduce efficiency losses significantly by failing to tax natural resource rents. More generally, a key problem with the tax system is its highly unbalanced nature. The tax system tends to rely on extremes: it is highly dependent on high value-added taxes while it applies very low effective rates to corporations and exempts capital gains almost completely.[11]

Value-added taxes have often been advocated as "efficient" presuming that they would cause fewer distortions than income and profit taxes. However, in highly unequal countries such as Chile, a large portion of the population faces severe liquidity constraints as a consequence of their low incomes and of the existence of credit market imperfections.[12] Liquidity constraints become a binding factor limiting investments by the poor and the middle classes (say the bottom 80 percent or even 90 percent of the population) in both physical and especially human capital, despite the fact that these investments may have high rates of return. This creates underinvestment in human capital and consequently efficiency losses, which a tax system based on indirect taxes will only make worse by reducing the disposable income of already liquidity-constrained households. Forcing those that are most affected by liquidity constraints (i.e., the poor and most middle-income groups) to pay value-added taxes as high as 19 percent only worsens such constraints and further impairs their capacity to self-finance socially profitable investments, thus exacerbating economic inefficiency.[13]

Value-added taxes are often justified by appealing to the most naïve textbook models of perfect markets. Value-added taxes in the more realistic second-best scenario, where taxes coexist with capital market imperfections, also cause deadweight losses. These deadweight losses may be larger than those caused by equivalent income, profit, or capital gains taxes that exempt middle- and low-income groups, which are the ones most likely to be affected by liquidity constraints. The implication then is that a tax system that strives to minimize deadweight losses should strike a better balance among income, profit, rents, capital gains, and value-added taxes instead of relying on the latter for almost two-thirds of the tax revenue, as in the case of Chile.

The poor quality of education for the vast majority of students in Chile implies that the development of new productive skills, the process of adaptation, and creation of new scientific and technological knowledge become more difficult. However, the tax system, which provides for low taxes on corporate profits, generous investment allowances, and exemptions, offers significant incentives for investments in physical capital—especially for corporations that exploit natural resources and for other traditional industries. The combination of insufficient expenditures in human capital and generous tax policies that promote investment in physical capital has significant implications for the evolution of factor endowments. Factor endowments become increasingly more biased toward physical capital and against human capital. That is, the physical capital to human capital ratio of the economy tends to become artificially high.

In a small open economy such as Chile's there is a direct correlation between the structure of factor endowments and the patterns of specialization in production. Countries that fail to develop human skills and to adopt new technologies at the same rate as others are left behind and must increasingly specialize in physical capital–intensive or unskilled-intensive industries. In the case of countries as rich in natural resources as Chile, they end up specializing in natural resource–intensive industries as well.

In fact, certain technological and skill rankings place Chile quite low among comparable countries. For example, an index developed by Archibugi and Coco (2003) using indicators such as patents, scientific articles, telecommunications, engineering enrollments, and others, ranked Chile 41 among 120 countries considered. Chile's positioning was below countries of comparable or lower levels of per capita income such as Argentina, Belarus, Latvia, Cyprus, Slovenia, and others. Poor human capital has most likely been one of the key constraints for the development of new knowledge-intensive sectors in the economy.

Increasing Specialization in Resource-Intensive and Physical Capital–Intensive Sectors

The systematic biases of the tax system in favor of traditional industries demonstrated in the previous sections have meant that these traditional industries have been able to enjoy an unfair advantage over emerging sectors in attracting scarcely available qualified human resources. Because environmentally dirty and resource-dependent sectors do not pay for environmental damages and for the natural resources that they extract, and given that they tend to capture most of the large tax breaks available, these sectors have an unfair advantage that is reflected in the markets for the scarcest factors of production—high skills. While traditional industries are resource and physical capital–intensive they also use high skills, including scientists, engineers, and highly qualified operators. The artificial incentives that traditional industries enjoy imply that the marginal values of high-skilled workers employed in these industries are magnified, allowing the firms to pay higher wages than what infant high-tech industries can afford. This makes it more difficult for new knowledge-intensive sectors to emerge.

This same process is in part responsible for the retardation of the development of the most skill-intensive of all sectors: the academic and scientific research institutions (the knowledge-generating sectors) that produce new knowledge using almost as their sole input scientific and technological skills. This sector has faced not only the same shortage of highly trained personnel that the rest of the economy has suffered, but also serious difficulties in competing with traditional productive sectors to retain the top scientists and engineers needed to develop and disseminate new scientific knowledge that ultimately leads to practical innovations. To make matters worse, the public academic and research centers producing most of the scientific learning and dissemination have been subjected to chronic budgetary insufficiencies as part of the overall restrictions faced by the public education system.[14] These conditions may explain Chile's relatively poor rankings in terms of development of new scientific patents and publications as shown by various international comparisons (Archibugi and Coco 2003).

Thus, the traditional sectors are able to soak up most of the supply of technological and scientific skills available in the country, leaving both the knowledge-intensive and knowledge-generating sectors in disadvantaged positions. This lack of highly skilled human resources is one factor that explains the highly unbalanced patterns of Chilean economic growth that have translated into disproportionately physical capital– and natural resource–intensive sectors as well as underdeveloped knowledge- and technology-intensive sectors.

Unbalanced Growth and Economic Development

Chile's unbalanced structure of production forces the economy to be ever more dependent on resource extraction and environmental degradation. Physical capital accumulation in these sectors is ultimately affected by diminishing marginal productivity as the scope for economies of scale is smaller than in knowledge-intensive industries. Moreover, the traditional sectors often cause negative intertemporal resource spillovers (i.e., more intensive resource extraction leads to resource depletion, affecting future production) and negative environmental externalities.

Government fiscal policy has contributed to smothering the development of knowledge-based and knowledge-generating sectors. Unlike traditional resource and environment-dependent sectors, these underdeveloped knowledge sectors produce positive spillovers on the rest of the economy and are often characterized by increasing returns to scale (Feldman 1999; Fritsch and Franke 2004). That is, the country foregoes the development of sectors that have the greatest potential for productivity growth and innovation and that are often considered the prime engines of economic development. The underdevelopment of the knowledge-generation sectors perpetuates the undersupply of scientific and technological skills and hence causes a vicious circle leading to a model of development that is ever more dependent on traditional resource-intensive industries.

It is no accident that these types of fiscal policies persevered throughout the period of Concertación governments. Once again, and as repeatedly noted throughout this volume, the transitional model of politics and its twin "economic model" were well suited and satisfied veto players throughout the democratic transition. However, at the same time, fiscal policy reinforced the very inequality that produced the high level of political dissatisfaction that led to the end of the Concertación.

It is in this sense that the Concertación's tax policies were Faustian. Clearly, the Concertación, mostly due to the dominance of technocratic forces within it, chose a development and fiscal policy path that gave it significant political and economic dividends in the short run, at the expense of welfare gains for the majority of the population over the long run. This short-sighted pattern of economic growth also led to significant environmental and natural resource losses, the consequences of which are today beginning to emerge with potentially dramatic consequences for the future of the Chilean economy. The Concertación sold its political soul by betraying ingrained principles of social justice for the sake of short-run political gains that allowed them to remain in power. A Faustian bargain, indeed.

Notes

The author acknowledges Amparo Palacios's research assistance for this chapter.

1. In recent years international copper and other commodity prices have been unusually high and, in great part thanks to the jump of revenues from the state copper enterprise, the government has experienced large fiscal surpluses that were mostly saved rather than spent. The existence of unspent revenues during these years does not, however, mean that government expenditures are not constrained by tax revenues. The government rightly chose to save most of the extra resources with the understanding that they do not correspond to permanent or normal revenues.

2. This chapter uses international comparisons to assess Chile's fiscal policies. To make these comparisons rigorous we consistently use, to the extent possible, the same higher income countries in Latin America as well as OECD countries in all our analyses. We use the four richest countries in Latin America (Argentina, Brazil, Mexico, and Uruguay) because Chile's income is clearly among the top five economies in Latin America over the whole period of analysis. At times we also use poorer Latin American countries to emphasize the fact that in certain respects Chile's indicators are closer to those of lower-income countries than to the other four middle-income Latin American countries. In addition, we use the poorer OECD countries as comparative cases because Chile is a member of the OECD. An exception is in the analysis of royalties where we consider advanced resource-rich countries such as Australia and Norway as examples of policies that Chile could implement.

3. Indirect taxes include principally value-added taxes, as well as specific taxes on things such as financial and other transactions, and the additional surcharges on alcohol, tobacco, and gasoline.

4. Using a different approach to estimate tax evasion, we arrive at numbers very similar to Jorratt's. A recent study showed that legal corporate tax loopholes amounted to about 3.2 percent of GDP (SII 2006). Given that the corporate tax rate is 17 percent, the theoretical effective corporate tax rate should be about 13.8 percent once legal loophole deductions are considered. Thus, the effective corporate taxes paid are about one-half of the theoretical after-tax legal deductions, suggesting a tax evasion of about 50 percent, which is consistent with the estimated 49.7 percent income tax evasion rates reported by Jorratt (2009). The combination of legal loopholes and evasion subtracts 63 percent from the theoretical corporate income tax revenues.

5. The 2005–2009 period is representative because it includes years of both exceptionally high and low international copper prices. The rents are defined as the total revenues of copper and by-products less the total cost of production including interest and all other capital costs.

6. A long-term capital rate of return of 6 percent has often been used by economists in the context of climate change (Nordhaus 2007). The implicit rate of return to natural capital obtained by copper mines in Chile has been estimated at levels many times higher than 6 percent (Riesco 2008).

7. After the 2010 earthquake the tax surcharge has been increased to about 8 percent of declared profits.

8. This assumes that resource firms are allowed to deduct the tax surcharge from their net income on which the regular income tax is assessed, and we have excluded the profits of CODELCO, which already pays much higher tax surcharges.

9. However, apart from Mexico there are other countries in the OECD such as Turkey that spend even a smaller fraction of GDP on social services.

10. In fact, more than 90 percent of the primary and secondary student population in Chile is enrolled in public schools despite their much inferior quality of education compared to private schools (Missoni and Solimano 2010), more than 70 percent of the population must use the public health system despite the often long waiting lists for many pathologies, and 10 percent of the population simply has no access to any health care (Hoffmeister 2010).

11. It is as if those who designed the tax system suddenly forgot a maxim of marginal economic analysis: corner solutions are rarely optimal due to the increasing marginal costs that each tax may cause.

12. In fact, recent empirical literature has shown that credit market failure and liquidity constraints are pervasive and affect a large portion of households in both poor countries (Haque and Montiel 1989) and rich ones (Attanasio, Goldberg, and Kyriazidou 2008; Jappelli 1990).

13. The VAT triggers an income and a substitution effect. In fact, the exorbitant 19 percent value-added tax may reduce the disposable income of the poor and middle-income classes by at least 10 percent (Engel, Galetovic, and Raddatz 1999). A substitution effect in favor of savings or investment arises from the fact that the VAT tax targets mostly consumption expenditures. The literature has shown that the most important determinant of savings is disposable income. The income effect is likely to dominate the substitution effect especially in a context where credit markets are mostly inaccessible to low- and middle-income households.

14. A common complaint of academic administrators in Chile is their inability to retain top scientists who, after a few years in academia, tend to migrate to better paying jobs in the private sector. Some scientists stay in academia but spend a large part of their time as consultants with the private sector, leaving them very little time to do real research.

10

Reducing Poverty: Real or Rhetorical Success?

Silvia Borzutzky, Claudia Sanhueza Riveros, and Kirsten Sehnbruch

During the Concertación's period in office, official poverty rates decreased from 38.6 percent to 15.1 percent. In almost all of the literature on the Concertación, whether it is academic, institutional, or political, this fact is highlighted as one of the coalition's most important achievements (ECLAC 2011a). We can even go as far as to say that Chile has acquired a significant part of its reputation as a successful development model based on this fact.

When the Concertación took office in 1990, the poverty rate of 38.6 percent it inherited from the Pinochet dictatorship was one of the principal challenges the coalition faced. Reducing this extremely high level of poverty was an objective that fit into the Concertación's general mission of reducing the overwhelming "social debt" that was the legacy of the dictatorship and that can be defined as the combined underinvestment in all areas of social policy that accumulated during the military regime (see also Chapter 11 for a further discussion of this problem; Meller et al. 1993).

However, as has been discussed in many of the other chapters in this volume, this objective required striking a balance between the need to improve the country's dismal social conditions and the constraints imposed by a neoliberal economic model that has privatized many of the functions of the state, including social security, health care, education, infrastructure, and water rights, as well as the building of new roads and the construction of new hospitals. As López shows in Chapter 9, the model also called for a low tax base, which was deemed necessary for attracting both national and foreign investors. Moreover, as the political Right could obstruct many budgetary and policy decisions, funding for major social programs was often severely limited. With these constraints in mind, policymakers were forced to design social programs that were supposed to achieve far-reaching objectives without the necessary resources. The end result has been an economic model that has generated relatively high levels of growth (driven by the expansion of natural resource exports), a strengthening of the private sector, and a set of highly targeted benefits that merely palliate the problems of the extremely poor. Due to the same limitations, the Concertación also never contemplated constructing a system of universal benefits that would have been a more far-reaching solution to the problem of poverty in Chile.

This chapter examines more closely the frequently repeated assertion that poverty reduction was one of the most important achievements of the Concertación. We first discuss the development of absolute poverty rates from a methodological perspective, and argue that the definition used is both outdated and flattering to the statistics. Second, we argue that the use of an absolute poverty rate has led to an almost total neglect of income distribution issues. When the development of Chile's poverty rate is analyzed from a relative perspective, such as the one applied by member countries of the Organization for Economic Cooperation and Development (OECD), which now includes Chile, we observe only a minimal decrease of poverty levels since 1990. Given Chile's ambitions to become a developed country within the next decade, it is important to ask whether Chile's social development is par for its economic course.

Beyond absolute and relative poverty measures, this chapter also discusses the importance of examining poverty from a multidimensional approach, which provides a much more comprehensive perspective of the problem. Such an analysis presents us with more detailed results that allow us to differentiate between those areas of social policy in which the Concertación has been successful, and those in which it has been less so.

This chapter also discusses to what extent poverty reduction in Chile has been due to economic growth and to what extent it has been the result of economic redistribution. We conclude that poverty reduction has mainly been the result of economic growth.

To illustrate how the Concertación approached the subject of poverty from a policy perspective, this chapter analyzes one of its flagship social programs, Chile Solidario, whose stated purpose was to eradicate extreme poverty in Chile.

Although the Concertación continuously reiterated its political commitment to the reduction of poverty, the improvement of equity, and finally also to the creation of a system of social protection, we find that this commitment was not backed by the necessary fiscal resources, especially after 2000, which brings us back to the problem that the Concertación could not raise sufficient revenues from taxes. This chapter highlights the discrepancies between the official public discourse of Concertación politicians, who presented their social policies as universal, and the actual policies, which were limited and conditional.

Evolution of the Official Poverty Rate

Poverty measurement in Chile began in 1987 with the first application of the national household survey, the Encuesta de Caracterización Socioeconómica Nacional (CASEN). There are almost no data on poverty that precede this date, so it is difficult to make comparisons between absolute poverty levels during the Concertación period and the dictatorship that preceded it.

When the Concertación took office in 1990 the poverty measurements followed the methodology commonly used in Latin America at the time, which has been developed with technical assistance from the United Nations Economic Commission for Latin America and the Caribbean (CEPAL). This methodology comprised the establishment of absolute measures of poverty and extreme poverty based on the definition of a basic food basket and a set of additional goods considered essential for covering the basic needs of a population. Specifically, the basic food basket is constructed by identifying and estimating the cost of the amount of food required for a human being to survive for one month. The food included in the basket is supposed to be specific to that consumed in the country of study. The value of this basic food basket is then established as the line of "extreme poverty." This amount is then multiplied by the "Oarshansky coefficient," which is calculated by estimating the proportion of the total household income that is spent on food. When this methodology was developed for Chile during the late 1980s, it was estimated that households spent approximately 50 percent of their income on food. Thus, the value of the basic food basket was multiplied by 2 to establish the monetary value of the poverty line.[1] Every time poverty is measured, the values of the food and nonfood baskets have to be updated to account for inflation. Additionally, the Oarshansky method assumes that the components of food baskets are revised periodically, generally every ten years, to keep them up to date with consumption patterns (Haughton and Khandker 2009; Feres and Mancero 2001).

During the last twenty years in Chile, however, neither the content of the basic food basket nor the estimate of how much money a household proportionately spends on food has been updated. Poverty lines have only been updated according to inflation. An Oarshansky coefficient of 2 is low by today's standards. Updated coefficient estimates from Larraín (2008), the Fundación Nacional para la Superación de la Pobreza (2009), and CEPAL (2009) range from 2.5 to 3.3.

Although this is consistent with the methodology applied by the United Nations to other Latin American countries, it is not really the best method for measuring poverty in a country that aspires to close the development gap. As a result, current definitions of the poverty line are increasingly being questioned. This process began during the administration of President Lagos, and discussions have continued under the Piñera administration, which instituted a commission to establish the best way forward.

The problems with poverty level definitions exploded in the political debate that followed the release of the 2009 poverty statistics, which showed an increase in poverty for the first time since 1990. This increase was due to food price inflation, which raised the price of the basic food basket and in turn the overall poverty line. An intense political debate followed as members of the new Piñera government and experts from the Concertación argued over whether appropriate definitions were being used to define poverty. The Piñera government clumsily argued that all the social policies of the Concertación had failed while Eduardo Engel, one of Chile's most respected economists, showed that if poverty levels were adjusted for food price inflation the actual level of poverty would have decreased to 10.8 percent.[2]

Most European countries, on the other hand, use a relative poverty indicator to measure income poverty. In this case, the poverty line is defined as equal to the value of 60 percent of the median income. It is worth noting that this indicator is based not on basic but on relative needs, which in turn depend on the level of a society's overall development. Accordingly, when using this approach it does not matter how rich the country is because it will always have a certain level of relative poverty. In the international literature this situation is referred to as "low-income families" rather than poor families (Feres and Mancero 2001). In addition, such an indicator assumes that poverty is a relative condition, which varies according to different socioeconomic settings. For example, being poor at the beginning of the nineteenth century is not the same as in the twenty-first century. Similarly, being poor in England is not the same as being poor in Bolivia. Thus, developed societies where the whole population attains basic needs could still have relative poverty or low-income families.

To account for the differences between absolute and relative poverty, Table 10.1 shows the evolution of both rates in Chile since the 1990s. The table illustrates that relative poverty declined significantly less than absolute poverty during the Concertación administrations. Yet it is interesting to note that between 1990 and 1992 absolute poverty levels were higher than relative poverty levels, which means that during this period Chile was still such a poor country that the cost of two basic food baskets amounted to more than 60 percent of the median income. After 1994, however, absolute poverty rates declined much faster than relative poverty levels. This means

Table 10.1 Poverty Rates and Income Distribution, 1990–2009 (percentages)

	Poverty Rate	Extreme Poverty Rate	Poverty Rate Without Fiscal Subsidies	Extreme Poverty Rate Without Fiscal Subsidies	Social Expenditure (as percent of GDP)	Poverty Rate Based on 60% of Median Income	Gini Coefficient
1990	38.6	13.0	39.4	14.2	11.9	27.9	0.57
1992	32.9	9.0	33.8	10.2	12.2	27.9	0.56
1994	27.6	7.6	28.5	8.7	12.5	28.5	0.57
1996	23.2	5.8	24.8	7.1	12.8	28.7	0.57
1998	21.7	5.6	23.5	7.1	13.7	28.6	0.58
2000	20.2	5.6	21.8	6.6	15.0	28.9	0.58
2003	18.7	4.7	20.6	6.1	14.4	27.7	0.57
2006	13.7	3.2	15.8	4.5	12.1	26.4	0.54
2009	15.1	3.7	19.3	6.3	16.5	25.4	0.55

Source: Poverty rates are authors' calculations using CASEN data and OECD definitions. Percentage of social expenditure as a percent of GDP is based on CEPAL data.

that while Chile was still a low-income country, the absolute poverty method was a better tool of measurement. However, once the country had achieved a certain level of development, policymakers should have at least started to track both absolute and relative poverty levels. Alternatively, if the Oarshansky coefficient had been updated appropriately, the differences between the absolute and relative poverty rates would not have been so great.

If we look at relative poverty as is done in developed countries, and as Chile must do going forward since it is now a member of the OECD, the much vaunted achievement of reducing poverty looks less significant. In fact, poverty levels in Chile by this score look remarkably similar to those in Mexico, the other Latin American OECD member country, which were at 25.3 percent in 2008.

Table 10.1 also leads to two important additional conclusions: first, despite all the political and rhetorical commitment of the Concertación to social policies, the fiscal subsidies made only a minimal difference to the overall poverty rate. Between 1990 and 2006, fiscal expenditure decreased poverty and extreme poverty levels by an average of 1.5 percent and 1.2 percent, respectively. Only during 2009 did increased fiscal expenditure create a bigger difference of 4.2 percent and 2.6 percent, respectively. It is further interesting to note that the impact of fiscal expenditure on extreme poverty was even lower than on overall poverty levels. We can therefore conclude that the impact of fiscal subsidies on poor households in Chile was extremely limited.

A second important conclusion that we can draw from these data is that, again despite official rhetoric, social expenditure as a percentage of GDP did not increase greatly during the Concertación period. Average social expenditure fluctuated by approximately 1 percent around the 1990 level except during periods of economic crisis (1998–2003 and 2009).[3] This confirms the conclusion of other chapters in this volume that argue that the Concertación's fiscal policies were anticyclical, but it does not confirm a sustained commitment to expanding social policies.

In part these conclusions can be explained by the Concertación's focus on its successful reduction of absolute poverty rates, as there are several important political consequences of viewing poverty solely from an absolute perspective. First, the reduction of absolute poverty to relatively low levels in a very short period of time (especially compared to Chile's Latin American peers) generated evidence for policymakers that led them to believe they were on the right track. Targeted social policies and high economic growth appeared to be the right approach to reducing poverty levels. This meant that an increasing amount of institutional effort was directed at improving targeting mechanisms and making sure fiscal resources were spent in the most efficient way possible. However, as we will see below in the section of this chapter that analyzes the Chile Solidario program, one of the inevitable consequences of the inadequate methodology for measuring poverty levels is that the policies based on them will also be deficient.

Second, the improved poverty statistics constituted a powerful tool of political rhetoric that allowed governments to justify their social policy approach. The undoubtedly impressive achievement of reducing poverty levels faster than any other country in Latin America gave governments a sense of confidence in this approach while simultaneously creating a significant amount of institutional complacency and inertia. This meant that while those ministries responsible for social policy were asking for additional resources, the Ministry of Finance could always argue that such additional resources would distort the behavior of individuals and of the labor market, which would be undesirable. Furthermore, it was relatively easy to argue that additional resources were unnecessary.

Third, and perhaps most importantly, this combination of statistical success with policy self-confidence led to policies focused only on absolute poverty levels rather than on relative poverty. Consequently, no policies were instituted that would have improved the distribution of income as the latter issue did not figure prominently on the political radar while absolute poverty rates were declining. In fact, as we can see from the table above, Chile's Gini coefficient remained almost constant between 1990 and 2003, and only declined minimally after 2006. Policymakers simply assumed that economic growth and higher levels of education would improve income distribution over time. By the time the Bachelet administration finally had to recognize that income distribution simply was not improving as expected, the Concertación was already in its last government, and it was too late and politically unfeasible to come up with a significant policy initiative aimed at income distribution.

However, two debates did emerge during the past twenty years that questioned the standard analysis of poverty in Chile. The first was the consequence of data analysis that showed the extent to which poverty is a dynamic phenomenon, and the second was the result of increasing awareness at both the local and international levels of the multidimensional nature of poverty. The results of the multidimensional analysis of poverty are presented in the following section.

In regard to the dynamic nature of poverty, the results of a national panel survey undertaken in 2001 indicate that poverty was not a static phenomenon, but rather a dynamic one (Neilson et al. 2008). Panel data led to two important conclusions: over a period of ten years, only 3 percent of the population was in a permanent condition of poverty while 30 percent of the population fell under the poverty line at least once. In addition, this dynamic analysis of poverty demonstrated that the risk of falling below the poverty line extended to all income deciles with the only exception of the top 10 percent. This means that even relatively wealthy households in the ninth decile faced a degree of probability of falling into poverty if they encountered adverse circumstances, such as loss of employment, sickness, or other problems (Neilson et al. 2008; Denis, Prieto, and Zubizarreta 2007).

These results constituted a landmark in poverty analysis in Chile and changed the way policymakers viewed the problem. The results highlighted the limits of strict targeting and showed that highly focused social policies would not be effective in eliminating poverty. Instead, policies had to focus on a new group of people, who could be defined as facing a significant risk of falling below the poverty line (i.e., the socially vulnerable). In their analysis, Denis, Prieto, and Zubizarreta (2007) calculate that the bottom 60 percent of the income distribution was at risk of falling into poverty.

The consequence of this new awareness of the limitations of both targeting and the limited meaningfulness of existing poverty statistics, however, became more evident in the area of social protection policies under the governments of Presidents Lagos and Bachelet rather than in the social benefit programs themselves. As Chapter 12 discusses, both health and pension policy reforms began to establish universal benefits that covered 80 percent of the population in the case of the former and 60 percent of the population in the case of the latter. Benefits, however, remained highly targeted, as we will see in the final section of this chapter.

The Role of Growth, Social Expenditure, and Redistribution

One of the obvious questions that poverty statistics in Chile raise is to what extent the improvement in the official statistics is due to economic growth, social expenditure, or income redistribution. We can answer this question using the Datt-Ravallion disaggregation methodology (Datt and Ravallion 1992).

Table 10.2 sums up the results of a Datt-Ravallion desegregation of Chilean poverty levels and shows that poverty mainly decreased as a result of economic growth. For example, between 1990 and 1992 the desegregation shows that income growth reduced poverty by 6.7 percent, while redistribution increased poverty by 1 percent. Thus, overall, poverty decreased by 5.7 percent. Between 1992 and 1994, both the growth component and the redistribution component pushed poverty to decrease; however, the growth component was more important. Between 1994 and 1998, however, growth was again the driver of the decrease of poverty, while the redistribution component again increased poverty levels. Meanwhile, between 1998 and 2000 both growth and redistribution pushed poverty lower. The period 2000–2003, on the other hand, shows a growth component that increased poverty very slightly. This is the only period that shows such an effect, which is probably attributable to the economic crisis and high unemployment rates during those years. Between 2003 and 2006, poverty again decreased by 5 percent and the disaggregated values show that both components are relevant to explaining this drop. Finally, in the last period, 2006–2009, poverty increased by 1.4 percent: while the growth component decreased poverty, the redistribution component increased it.

These data lead to the conclusion that although the Concertación's social policies without doubt improved the capabilities and capacities of individuals to participate in economic growth (through the labor market), social policies were evidently not enough to change the distribution of income in Chile, which in turn is reflected by the limited impact that income redistribution had in the reduction of poverty rates. This conclusion should not be surprising since social policies during the Concertación period were not focused on improving income inequality and did not involve significant cash transfers such as in Brazil and Mexico, as we will see in the section on Chile Solidario later in this chapter, but on improving socioeconomic conditions in the long run by investing in health, education, and housing.

The following section of this chapter will examine the Concertación's success in this area as it is important to consider that the link between education, health, and housing and inequality is not trivial. As regards education, for example, the impact depends on the relative price of the educational level. Chile presents convex returns to schooling, as do many other Latin

Table 10.2 Datt-Ravallion Disaggregation of Chilean Poverty Levels, 1990–2009

Year 1 vs. Year 2	Year 1 (percentage of population in poverty)	Year 2 (percentage of population in poverty)	Change in Poverty due to Growth Component (percentage)	Change in Poverty due to Redistribution Component (percentage)	Overall Change in Poverty (percentage)
1990 vs. 1992	38.6	32.9	-6.7	1.0	-5.7
1992 vs. 1994	32.9	27.6	-3.5	-1.7	-5.2
1994 vs. 1996	27.6	23.3	-4.7	0.3	-4.4
1996 vs. 1998	23.3	21.7	-2.4	0.8	-1.6
1998 vs. 2000	21.7	20.2	-1.1	-0.4	-1.4
2000 vs. 2003	20.2	18.7	0.2	-1.7	-1.6
2003 vs. 2006	18.7	13.7	-2.0	-3.0	-5.0
2006 vs. 2009	13.7	15.1	-3.2	4.6	1.4

Source: Author calculations based on CASEN survey.

American countries. Thus, having a university degree increases income levels by almost 25 percent with respect to secondary schooling.

Multidimensional Poverty and the Entitlement Approach

In 2009, the Bachelet government commissioned a report on multidimensional poverty. Although this report came too late to change pro-poor policies during the Concertación period in office, its results have nevertheless been influential, and produced an interesting new perspective of poverty in Chile that complements the analysis presented so far in this chapter.

The Chilean Ministry of Planning (MIDEPLAN) had long been aware of the need to improve the methodology used to measure poverty. They had also been thinking about the need for incorporating criteria into this methodology that went beyond the simple measurement of income levels. Specifically, they had been considering the implications of the capability approach for their social policies.

Amartya Sen's extensive work on this issue is based on the idea that development should increase the capabilities and freedoms of people so that they can lead meaningful and fulfilled lives. He considers, for example, that a person may be wealthy, but may otherwise be denied access to activities that he or she may find fulfilling, such as study or work. This is the case of many women in the world. Similarly, at a macro level, a country may enjoy a high level of GDP per capita, but fail to ensure equal access to education and health services, which then severely limits the opportunities and capabilities of its citizens.

When the philosophical and theoretical work of Sen produced a new international research agenda that proposed the measurement of poverty from a multidimensional perspective that would capture the most relevant capabilities individuals would want to develop, Chile became the second Latin American country, after Mexico, to apply this approach (Alkire and Foster 2007).

One of the key issues in the construction of a multidimensional measure of poverty is the identification of the relevant dimensions to be incorporated in the definition of welfare.[4] In the Chilean case, Denis, Gallegos, and Sanhueza (2010) selected their poverty dimensions by following the measurement developed by the National Evaluation of Social Development Policy (CONEVAL) of Mexico. This measure intercepts the traditional measurement of income poverty with a social rights approach. It separately identifies two axes: the axis of welfare, measured by income, and the axis of social rights, which includes education, health, social security, food, housing, and services. As a result, the population is divided into four groups:

1. The multidimensional poor: people with an income level below the value of the minimum income level who are deprived in at least one dimension (quadrant I).
2. The vulnerable: people who are deprived in one or more dimensions, but whose income is above the minimum level (quadrant II).
3. The nonpoor: people who are not deprived in any dimension and whose income levels are above the minimum level (quadrant III).
4. The vulnerable income poor: people who are not deprived in any dimension, but whose income levels are below the minimum level (quadrant IV).

In addition, a fifth group of people is defined as extremely poor on a multidimensional scale if they suffer three or more deprivations and have income levels below the subsistence level, which corresponds to the value needed to buy essential food for good nutrition.

The dimensions used for the analysis are education, health, employment, housing, and income. The thresholds for each dimension are summarized in Table 10.3. Each dimension has an indicator of access and quality, subject to the availability of data. Access is considered a minimum level of attainment in general in very poor countries; however, once access has been attained, the quality of the access is considered. For example, the methodology asks not only whether a person has access to education in general, but also what the quality of this education is.

The results of this methodology are presented in Table 10.4, which presents privations in each dimension other than income, including education, employment, health, and housing (Denis, Gallegos, and Sanhueza 2010).[5] The level of privation in each dimension is significant, ranging from 15.6 percent in education to 33.8 percent in employment. We can see

Table 10.3 Dimensions Used for the Analysis of Poverty

Dimension	Threshold
Education	Failure to meet the years of education required by law; failure to acquire a literacy level (read and write)
Health	Not having access to health services; suffering a deteriorated health condition (being sick)
Employment	Not having (but wanting or looking for) a job; having a job without access to social security; employment in informal conditions
Housing	Not having access to a house; not having basic sanitation and electricity
Income	Not having an income that meets minimum needs

Table 10.4 Multidimensional Poverty Using CONEVAL Methodology, 1990–2009 (percent of population)

Year	Education	Health	Employment	Housing	Multi-dimensional Poverty	Extreme Multi-dimensional Poverty	Not Multi-dimensional Poor	Income Vulnerability	Vulnerability by Social Needs
1990	20.3	34.7	28.3	51.1	31.0	2.8	19.3	4.2	45.5
1992	20.4	31.2	28.4	48.5	25.4	1.7	22.5	4.2	47.8
1994	19.1	23.3	29.4	43.0	21.2	1.4	29.1	3.3	46.4
1996	18.2	23.3	26.8	40.2	17.5	1.2	32.8	3.1	46.7
1998	17.3	26.9	30.4	36.7	16.6	1.3	32.7	2.6	48.1
2000	16.0	19.5	31.0	31.9	15.5	1.1	37.3	3.0	44.3
2003	14.9	16.8	31.7	28.7	13.5	0.7	38.7	3.3	44.5
2006	15.9	18.8	33.2	25.4	9.9	0.5	39.0	2.3	48.7
2009	15.6	16.0	33.8	22.2	10.6	0.4	39.5	3.4	46.4

Source: Denis, Gallegos, and Sanhueza (2010).

that there is a permanent positive evolution in all dimensions except in employment, where conditions deteriorated. The dimensions of housing and health improved the most, followed by improvements in education, but to a much lesser degree.

Similar trends can be observed from the indicators of multidimensional poverty. We can observe a positive development in almost all categories: the data show that the percentage of the population of working age that is multidimensionally deprived has declined from 31 to 10.6 percent. The decline in income vulnerability, despite starting from a much lower level, also shows improvement although to a less significant extent. We observe a similar trend in extreme multidimensional poverty. Not surprisingly, the table also shows an increase of the population that is not multidimensionally poor from 19.3 to 39.5 percent. According to these measures, only the proportion of people considered vulnerable by their social needs has not improved. In fact, their number has increased slightly.

The data discussed in this section illustrate how important it is to look at poverty levels from a multidimensional perspective. While the analysis of poverty based on growth versus redistribution presented in the previous sections leads to decidedly mixed conclusions, and even questions the Concertación's famed success in reducing poverty levels, a multidimensional analysis leads to more nuanced conclusions: overall, while both multidimensional and extreme poverty have decreased in all dimensions except employment, the proportion of the population that must be considered vulnerable remains remarkably constant. This is an important analytical result that supports the conclusions reached by a dynamic analysis of poverty levels: there is little point in focusing social policy on a small group of the population that is income poor at a particular point in time. It makes much more sense to redirect quality policy attention toward the much larger group of people who are socially vulnerable. However, the almost exclusive focus and sincere belief of Concertación governments in their success in reducing absolute poverty levels has led to a neglect of the socially vulnerable, as the following sections of this chapter will illustrate.

Social Welfare Benefits and Programs

The Concertación governments have put much political effort into the design and implementation of social welfare benefits and programs as these have played an important role in the coalition's efforts to deal with the social debt it inherited. Chileans have the right to a broad range of social benefits and programs that can include everything from food baskets, minimal direct cash transfers, and subsidies for utility bills and housing to microcredit and vocational training programs designed to help members of vulnerable households generate income. Under the Bachelet administration these diverse social benefits were organized to form the Red Protege, a term that serves as an umbrella concept to describe Chile's incipient social protection system (Hardy 2010).[6]

Social welfare benefits and programs in Chile are administered through local municipal offices, which send social workers to the household applying for a particular benefit. This social worker then undertakes a survey of the household, which is processed by the Ministry of Social Development.[7] These social surveys, traditionally known as the Ficha Cas, used to focus on the material circumstances of a household: the condition of a family's housing, whether they have a refrigerator, a television, income levels, and so on. To obtain higher scores and thus more benefits, families in poor neighborhoods had learned how to take advantage of this system, in particular by maintaining the poor condition of their housing, or by hiding their material assets, especially electronic equipment. In recognition of the fact that this system functioned poorly, the Ministry of Planning established a new survey system in 2008, called the Ficha de Protección Social (FPS). This new survey constituted a significant shift as it focused on the capabilities of households to generate income rather than on their current material possessions. Thus, new criteria such as the composition of households, the educational levels of its members, the number of people employed, their income levels, or how many small children lived there became important.

Although this new system of resource allocation constituted an improvement on the old Ficha Cas system, it has not worked perfectly either. Social workers joke that families used to hide their TVs. Now they hide their husbands. Apart from the ability of families to game the system, experts also voice concerns about the ability of politicians to manipulate the system by exerting pressure on the Ministry of Social Development to change the allocation criteria for social policies.

In theory, the separation of the administrative tasks between the municipal officers and the ministry's central planning capability limits the potential for politicians to use social benefits for clientelistic purposes. Although this system is not perfect, it works significantly better than in other Latin American countries.[8]

Welfare benefits are assigned on the basis of the household needs revealed by these surveys, but are ultimately also subject to waiting lists as every municipality receives a limited amount of resources for a particular program or service. If these resources are insufficient to cover demand, which they generally are, potential recipients simply have to wait.

After 1990, each government instituted a flagship social program that constituted its main effort in the area of welfare policy. President Aylwin instituted a program called Chile Joven, which was designed to help poor young people with low levels of education join the labor force. Under President Frei a program called Chile Barrio began to operate, which specifically intended to eradicate shantytowns and improve living conditions in them with the participation of the community. President Lagos in turn established Chile Solidario, a type of conditional cash transfer program designed to eradicate extreme poverty by connecting vulnerable families to the existing network of social services, and helping them become part of the labor force. Finally, President Bachelet established Chile Crece Contigo, a program that focuses on supporting mothers from vulnerable families and their young children through the early years, from pregnancy to age five.

All of these social programs generated high expectations as to their potential success and effectiveness in addressing the problems of poor families. They have been innovative in their design, well focused on low-income households, relatively free of the political clientelism that characterizes such programs in other Latin American countries, and held up by international development institutions (especially the Inter-American Development Bank and the World Bank) as examples of effective pro-poor policies to other countries in the region (Fiszbein et al. 2009).

However, despite their innovative design and careful implementation, the relative success of these programs has been mixed. In the case of Chile Joven and Chile Barrio, a systematic evaluation of their impact is difficult as these programs were not designed with rigorous evaluation criteria in mind. Both programs were ultimately discontinued, and replaced by other social policies. In the case of Chile Solidario, a more systematic evaluation has been undertaken that will be discussed below (Larrañaga, Contreras, and Ruiz-Tagle 2012). These studies conclude that the program has been effective and appreciated by its participants in terms of the attention that is focused on connecting families with existing social services. Unfortunately, those components of the program that were intended to increase household incomes by helping people join the labor force were less successful.

The design of Chile Crece Contigo, the first social policy designed after the dynamic nature of poverty had been fully absorbed by the policy-making community, for the first time extends the coverage of a social program to all children born in the public health insurance system. This means that of all social policies, its design is the most universal, as less than 20 percent of Chileans have private insurance. Chile Crece Contigo exemplifies the important shift that took place in the thinking of the Bachelet administration concerning welfare policies: it constitutes the first social program that establishes a legal entitlement rather than merely focusing on the lower income deciles. It is too soon to tell how effective this program has been, as the first generation of children that it covers is only just about to graduate from the program. However, early research suggests that the program is suffering from the same lack of resources that characterized previous social policies and is thus unlikely to have a significant impact (Robles 2011; Bedregal 2010).

Chile Solidario

This section describes the origins and nature of the Chile Solidario program and provides an assessment of its impact as this has been by far the most emblematic, extensive, and researched social policy of the Concertación.[9] In addition, Chile Solidario constitutes an excellent example of everything good and bad in Chilean social policymaking.[10]

The original expectations raised by Chile Solidario were high. The program was supposed to help poor households overcome poverty by improving their own capabilities (Santibáñez 2005). On paper, Chile Solidario looked like the perfect social policy that incorporated state of the art wisdom about how best to target scarce resources to extremely poor families (by selecting them through the Ficha de Protección Social), raise their level of functioning by helping them overcome social exclusion and insert themselves into the labor market, and avoid perverse incentives through excessive cash handouts that would reduce their desire for generating their own resources through employment.

The program's aim was to incorporate indigent families into the state's social protection system, which, in turn, was going to give families participating in the program privileged access to its benefits and services that the poor were already entitled to, but did not know how to access. Thus, its objectives were to coordinate monetary benefits, subsidies, services, and programs already available, and to facilitate access to those programs. Social workers, known as *apoyos familiares,* provided them with information, helped them obtain identification cards if they did not already have them, ensured children attended school and received primary health care, and facilitated access to education for illiterate adults. They could also help families obtain preferential access to services that dealt with alcoholism, intrafamily violence, and substance abuse. Once minimal objectives had been achieved, families could apply for a small grant that would provide them with the startup capital necessary to set up a small microbusiness, such as selling produce or homemade food.

Chile Solidario was considered to have fulfilled its mission when the family was able to overcome its indigence and could sustain a set of fifty-three preestablished conditions that include basic living conditions (possessing sheets, blankets, pillows, one bed per person, etc.), health checkups, educational attendance, as well as more complex objectives such as functioning family dynamics, employment, and the generation of income.

It is important to note that the cash benefits provided specifically by Chile Solidario were very minimal and ranged from about US$19.50 a month during the first six months to US$6. Receiving the cash transfer, however, was conditional upon the fulfillment of minimal health and educational criteria. If all the subsidies are added together, a poor family in Chile received on average about US$40 monthly in cash transfers, and up to about $275 through the life of the program, which amounts to approximately 2 percent of the median income of the participating households (Agostini and Brown 2007). These benefits appear extremely minimal if compared with benefits that equal 25 percent of the median income in Nicaragua and Honduras and 22 percent for the families enrolled in the Progresa Program in Mexico, even when the percentage of indigents in these countries is larger than in Chile (Galasso 2006). Officials from the Ministry of Planning have always been adamant that Chile Solidario was never designed to be a conditional cash transfer program, and that its purpose is simply to connect beneficiaries with existing social services (Galasso 2006). However, even though the cash amounts that the program pays are minimal, they are conditional. Documents of the World Bank classify Chile Solidario as a conditional cash transfer program, and as such compare it to these other programs. The cost of the program amounts to only 0.08 percent of GDP in 2005 (World Bank 2011b).

The quantitative evaluations of the Chile Solidario program confirm the policy's low impact: while beneficiaries appreciated the program, its effects on social objectives such as increasing health and education levels were relatively minimal as most Chileans are already covered by these services. Therefore, there was little point to the conditionality of the program. Its effects on employment and income levels were insignificant, partly because cash benefits were so minimal, and partly because the program's efforts to increase labor market participation failed (Galasso 2006; Larrañaga, Contreras, and Ruiz-Tagle 2012; Gaete and Ruiz-Tagle 2011).

In the end, Chile Solidario failed to produce the hoped-for results due to a combination of financial constraints and institutional limitations. It is clear that the program was underfunded in a significant way: social workers were not necessarily qualified or experienced; they were hired only on a part-time basis and could not dedicate enough time to families. Monetary cash transfers were too minimal to make a difference in household consumption patterns or to provide resources that would allow people to participate in their market. Alcoholism, drug abuse, and intrafamily violence proved to be significant factors that interfered with the program's objectives for households, and were not adequately dealt with by the program. Extremely low levels of human capital of participating families required levels of education and vocational training that the policy simply did not contemplate. Attempts to insert beneficiaries into the labor market were therefore condemned to failure. Support mechanisms for potential microentrepreneurs were not included in the program. Municipalities were not equipped to deal with the implementation of the program, in terms of their fiscal or human resources, while waiting lists for social services had to incorporate the program's beneficiary families without receiving additional resources for them. The time frame of the program was too short. And finally, the program failed to eliminate extreme poverty, not only because of its limited cash transfers, but also because its design did not allow for the dynamic nature of poverty (Raczynski 2008).

Although poverty eradication presents a challenge to policymakers all over the world, it is nevertheless fair to say that Chilean governments could have dealt much more successfully with these problems if they had allocated a sufficient amount of resources to the program. The important lesson to be learned from Chile Solidario is that governments need to spend money in order to help poor people make money. Until basic household needs are satisfied by a stable flow of income, adults in extremely vulnerable households cannot be expected to seek vocational training or successfully establish a microenterprise.

Conclusion

The analysis of absolute, relative, dynamic, and multidimensional poverty rates in this chapter shows that the story of poverty under the Concertación is not the unqualified success story that political rhetoric would like to have us believe: while the reduction of absolute poverty levels was impressive, the methodology that measures it is questionable. By contrast, relative poverty levels show little significant improvement. Both the negligible impact of fiscal subsidies on absolute poverty levels and the relatively stable level of social expenditure belie the frequently cited commitment of the Concertación to overcoming poverty and improving inequality. In addition, the analysis of dynamic poverty suggests that strictly targeted social policies are not the best method for the long-term eradication of poverty, a point that is confirmed by the discussion of the Concertación's flagship poverty program, Chile Solidario.

On a more positive note, the analysis of multidimensional poverty shows significant improvements in the nonincome dimensions of poverty. However, indicators of social vulnerability remain stubbornly high and illustrate that social policies should cover a much larger proportion of the population than was originally thought. As Chapter 12 will explain, this finding began to influence social policymaking during the Lagos government and became a leitmotif of the Bachelet administration.

Perhaps the most important overall conclusion of this chapter is that although the Concertación governments were successful in reducing absolute poverty levels, ideological and political constraints prevented the dedication of an appropriate level of resources to social policies. Although Concertación governments dedicated a significant amount of effort and resources toward creating the institutional capacity for dealing with poverty, which involved the creation of basic social services and the administrative capacity for managing social programs targeted at specific issues, we can argue that the coalition's success in reducing absolute poverty levels is less a political than an economic achievement. We should therefore give the Concertación more credit for its sound economic policies than for its social policies.

Overall we can conclude, as does Chapter 12 of this volume, that although Chileans have access to a broad range of social welfare benefits and programs, and although these are administered well compared to other countries in the region (in particular through their focus on lower income deciles, which is slightly redistributive), their impact is still relatively limited, mainly due to the fact that their funding and coverage is insufficient to constitute a basic foundation for a welfare state.

The failure of Chile Solidario to live up to the expectations it had generated illustrates three of the principal problems with the Concertación's social programs: first, following recommendations of strict targeting criteria that partly responded to Chile's fiscal constraints during the 1990s—but also responded to efficiency concerns embedded in the development literature of the time, in particular the Washington Consensus—they were highly focused on only the poorest households. As discussed above, targeting considered poverty, and in particular extreme poverty, as a relatively static phenomenon. This meant that programs such as Chile Solidario never managed to eradicate extreme poverty as they, unwittingly, were shooting at a moving target.

A second characteristic that the Concertación's social programs have in common is that they were all designed from a fiscal position that reasoned a poor country has insufficient funds for direct social transfers. In part, this was due to the fact that it was generally the Ministry of Finance that obliged the Ministry of Planning to design these programs with a view to making them as efficient as possible with minimal resources. During the twenty years of Concertación government, it has always been the Ministry of Finance that has had both the technical expertise and the political clout to determine the final shape of social policy. In part though, it would also have been politically difficult to establish more universal and more generous benefits during the first sixteen years of the Concertación period. Technical experts from all sides of the political spectrum worried that benefits would create perverse incentives, and would negatively affect patterns of labor market participation, even if these benefits only consisted of absolutely minimal amounts. Therefore, when enough resources became available during the administration of President Bachelet, her finance minister, Andrés Velasco, managed these with extreme caution. Ultimately, this resource limitation negatively affected the potential impact of the social programs as policymakers had not yet assimilated the research findings that demonstrate the need to spend money to help people make money (Barnerjee and Duflo 2011).

Third, the problems experienced with Chile Solidario illustrate the lack of linkages between social programs and social insurance, employment, and vocational training programs. The expectation that people from households with extremely low levels of education would be able to learn a skill in a matter of weeks or months, or set up their own business with a small grant or microcredit, was unrealistic. In most cases, the attempt to help people join the labor force beyond their original ability to do so failed. Historically social programs in Chile have operated separately from emergency employment programs, which have constituted the main type of policy that has attempted to insert poor people into the labor market. During the last twenty years, those social programs that have incorporated some form of vocational training were poorly funded and poorly structured.

Put together, both the data and analysis of the Concertación's social programs make up a convincing argument that although Chile did a good job compared to other Latin American countries with regard to reducing its absolute poverty levels, this success is questionable in relative terms, especially given that social expenditure over the period did not increase significantly. We can certainly conclude that the Concertación's rhetorical commitment to paying down the social debt it inherited from the military dictatorship was not matched by a political and fiscal commitment.

Notes

1. In the case of the rural poverty line, the indigence line is multiplied by 1.75 as it is assumed that the cost of living in rural areas is lower than in urban ones (Metodología de Estimación de la Pobreza y la Indigencia [MIDEPLAN] n.d.).

2. See www.concerta2.com/centro-de-documentacion/analisis-de-la-encuesta -casen-elaborado-por-eduardo-engel/.

3. Total social expenditure is not the best measure of social spending as many other budget items such as housing, education, health, or employment policies may be directed at the poor. However, it does give us a general idea of the direction of budget allocation. The following section on multidimensional poverty will demonstrate that other dimensions of poverty have also improved.

4. Denis, Gallegos, and Sanhueza (2010) followed the recommendations of the United Nations Development Programme (UNDP), especially its 2000 Human Development Report; work done in Mexico, the first Latin American country to adopt

a multidimensional measure of poverty, in December 2009; work done by the Fundación Nacional para la Superación de la Pobreza (National Foundation for Overcoming Poverty) in *Umbrales Sociales para Chile* (Social Thresholds for Chile); and finally, a human rights approach focused on the constitution of Chile.

5. In this chapter, we present the results for the working-age population. Denis, Gallegos, and Sanhueza (2010) also present an analysis of multidimensional poverty for children and the elderly.

6. Red Protege is not a social program or an institution. It is simply the name given to the social protection system that is formed by the various different social programs. In particular, it refers to those social programs (for example, pre- and postnatal care, free nurseries and kindergartens, educational scholarships, and housing subsidies) or legal entitlements (such as guaranteed health care services for children or the right to a basic pension) that protect Chileans throughout the life cycle.

7. As of 2012 the Ministry of Planning became the Ministry of Social Development, which has greater powers and resources to coordinate the different agencies that provide social services.

8. The authors thank Osvaldo Larrañaga for pointing this out. For a system such as this to work properly, the criteria used to evaluate household surveys need to remain unknown to everyone beyond a small group of technical experts. If evaluation criteria are leaked and become public, then politicians, social workers, and individuals will be tempted to game the system.

9. The program is operating in 332 municipalities, and by the end of 2005 it incorporated 225,000 families (MIDEPLAN n.d., presentation by Yasna Provoste, minister of planning).

10. Chile Solidario in fact consists of four separate social policies: the Programa Puente, Calle, Vínculos, and Abriendo Caminos. This section is about the Programa Puente, which is by far the largest and best known component of Chile Solidario. In fact, the Puente Program became synonymous with Chile Solidario in the policymaking jargon as the other programs were negligible by comparison. We therefore use the term Chile Solidario to refer to the Programa Puente.

11

Social Policies: From Social Debt to Welfare State?

Dante Contreras and Kirsten Sehnbruch

> *Our purpose has been to construct the basis of a social*
> *democratic state that moves from social assistance*
> *to policies focused on individual entitlements.*[1]
> —Michelle Bachelet

When the Concertación took office in 1990, one of its clearest political objectives was to alleviate what had become known as the "social debt" inherited from the dictatorship (Hardy 1997; Meller 1999; Raczynski 1998).[2] This social debt can be defined as the combined underinvestment in social services—in particular health, education, and housing—and the provision of welfare benefits accumulated during the dictatorship (Meller et al. 1993). Its clearest and most obvious manifestation was the high poverty rate of 38 percent, but also the high levels of income inequality discussed in Chapter 11 of this book.

However, even if the payment of the accumulated social debt was a unifying theme for the Concertación on which broad consensus could be achieved within the coalition, tensions emerged around the questions how, to what extent, and over what period of time this social debt was to be paid. As discussed in Chapter 8, the stability pact underlying Concertación policymaking proved to be a significant restraint in this debate.

Considerations of both economic and political feasibility shaped this debate and limited the social policy interventions that the Concertación could undertake at the time. The main economic restriction was simply that in 1990, Chile was still a relatively poor country with a per capita income of US$2,427 according to IMF data.[3] This low level of income therefore also limited the amount of resources that could initially be spent on social policy interventions.

However, the main factor that shaped social policy during the last twenty years was political: as has been discussed in previous chapters, the principal task of the Aylwin and Frei governments was to ensure a smooth transition to democracy. During the 1990s, the Chilean population and political establishment valued the protection of this renascent democracy more than the instant repayment of the social debt, a fact reflected by the low levels of social demands and demonstrations during the 1990s (Ottone 1999).[4] Social adjustment was considered an important long-term objective that had to be reached gradually, without immediate structural changes to the development model that would have been fiercely resisted by the Right, and that potentially might have destabilized the democratic transition.

Yet, this attitude of caution persisted even under President Lagos. As the first Socialist president since Salvador Allende, Lagos was subjected to particular scrutiny, as the opposition argued that a Socialist would not be able to govern successfully, while even the Christian Democrats of his own coalition were skeptical of the potential success of a Socialist president. Thus President Lagos and his minister of finance, Nicolás Eyzaguirre, had to be particularly careful to demonstrate fiscal responsibility and restraint in the area of social policy, and had to act in the most conciliatory fashion toward their political opposition and the business sector.[5] It was therefore not until the Bachelet administration that a president established an explicit and concerted social development emphasis for the policy agenda. However, by then the limitations imposed by the transition had turned into the transitional enclaves discussed throughout this volume. Political and fiscal caution thus became permanent features of the social policy agenda.

Yet despite the fact that the Concertación's social policies were limited both by tensions arising within the coalition and between the Concertación and the opposition (and its designated senators), they also constitute one of the most important components of its legacy. Beginning with President Lagos, but particularly during the Bachelet government, the Concertación began to move away from its initial objective of highly targeted, low expenditure social programs to policies that at least established near universal entitlements in the areas of health insurance and pensions, even if this shift did not go so far as to incorporate elements of risk socialization or redistribution within the social legislation. Perhaps the coalition's greatest achievement is that its social policy objectives have been continued by the Piñera government that took office in 2010.

This chapter will examine the social policies of the Concertación from the perspective of welfare state theory. The next section will focus on the key question of whether Concertación governments really have laid the *foundations* for something that could develop into a liberal welfare state such as can be found in Anglo-Saxon countries. We present six initial arguments, which show that, overall, and despite its many achievements in the area of social policy, the Concertación governments did not succeed in undertaking the necessary structural reforms that such an objective would require. The chapter will go on to examine this question by looking at the pension, health, and unemployment insurance systems, as well as at the benefit structures the Concertación created. Many of the arguments presented in this chapter are also applicable to the education sector, and are covered by Elacqua and González in Chapter 13 of this volume. The chapter concludes by questioning whether Chile's social systems are sustainable in the long term.

A Social Protection System or a Welfare State?

In their more contemplative moments during their period in office, Concertación politicians have paused to consider toward which direction Chile should develop: should the country abandon its European roots in favor of a North American–style economic and social model? Or have the country's European roots and original intentions for the establishment of the welfare state during the middle decades of the twentieth century created indelible expectations among the population for universal and equitable social services provided by a strong state?

Although we might well argue that these questions have never been appropriately discussed or fully resolved by the political establishment, we can answer them by analyzing how Chilean social policies fit into existing models of welfare state analysis, particularly as the political objective of the Concertación, and most especially of President Bachelet, was to construct a burgeoning welfare state with basic universal entitlements that extend to and fully cover at least the lower 60 percent of the income scale, just as the opening quotation to this chapter suggests.

Given the privatized social security systems the Concertación governments inherited from the dictatorship, it would be unrealistic to expect that these could be transformed into a continental European or Scandinavian welfare state model as the latter are too far removed from Chilean reality. However, it is not unrealistic to expect that over time Chilean welfare structures can develop into something that resembles an Anglo-Saxon or liberal welfare state (Esping-Andersen 1990, 1996, 1999).

The key question for analysis in the course of this chapter, however, is whether the Concertación governments have really laid the foundations for such a liberal welfare state. While the following section will examine in more detail how the Concertación's policy initiatives were stymied by its own internal divisions and by the right-wing opposition, this section will present six initial arguments, which show that despite its many achievements in the area of social policy, the Concertación governments did not succeed in undertaking the necessary structural reforms that such an objective would require.

First, we have to consider that even the liberal welfare state models in developed countries contain significant components of redistribution and of risk socialization *within* their social insurance systems. In Anglo-Saxon countries, private insurance plans are generally used to supplement social security and health services provided by the state. Even the United States has now implemented a health insurance system that, although it is still mainly based on private insurance plans, provides universal guarantees to all citizens.[6] However, all Anglo-Saxon social protection systems provide basic insurance that is financed either through fiscal revenues or universal contributions to a centralized system.

Even though Concertación governments established some universal entitlements in the areas of pension and health insurance, which are financed from fiscal revenues, they did not construct a tax base that generates sufficient fiscal resources to compensate for the above-mentioned lack of distribution within social insurance systems. As López has shown in this volume, Chilean fiscal revenues amounted to approximately 20 percent of GDP in 2010 compared to the OECD average of 36 percent. So the universal entitlements the Concertación did establish therefore remain very basic, are limited in their coverage (especially in the area of health insurance where not all medical treatments are covered equally), and do not compensate for the inherent inequalities of the existing social insurance systems. This constitutes a second argument as to why the social policies that the Concertación undertook do not lay a solid foundation for a welfare state.

Third, as a result of these inherent inequalities, the quality of services and benefit levels received by beneficiaries of Chile's social insurance systems are distributed very unequally depending on whether an individual has contacted a private or public provider. It is therefore difficult to imagine that Chileans will receive in the near future the kind of uniform entitlements, particularly in the area of health insurance, that populations in developed countries take for granted, and that populations in developing countries aspire to. We should therefore not only ask whether the social security system structures are redistributive in terms of income levels, but also whether in the medium term they can begin to provide a similar quality of service for rich and poor.

A fourth reason why the Chilean social security systems are structurally deficient is that the private social insurance systems would be largely dysfunctional without significant fiscal subsidies.

In Esping-Andersen's 1996 volume that discusses emerging welfare state models in Latin America, Asia, and Eastern Europe, the contributing authors explore the different adaptations of welfare state models that have been made in these regions. At the time, one of the central questions raised by Huber was whether the Chilean model of privatized welfare systems based on individual contributions for individual benefits could serve as a model for other Latin American and developing countries (Esping-Andersen 1996). Several criticisms of the Chilean system were already noted at the time, in particular that individual retirement accounts required significant public subsidies, which de facto constituted a subsidization of private insurance, and that operating costs appeared to be high, while genuine coverage was modest. Huber concluded that "the new private schemes are essentially inoperable for the large mass of low paid, marginalized, or unemployed workers. In other words, privatization in Chile has largely meant a replication of many of the same faults that characterize public insurance. The principal advantage of the new system is that it is financially solvent, and that its huge savings help capital markets" (Huber in Esping-Andersen 1996).

Fifteen years later, we can only agree with this assertion as public subsidies to the system have had to be increased to compensate for the inherent regressiveness of social policy structures (especially in the areas of health and pension provision), and for the social segmentation that is their result.[7]

A fifth consideration that we need to take into account in this context is that the development of employment conditions during the period of Concertación government has undermined the functioning and long-term viability of existing social security structures. This point was not yet apparent when Esping-Andersen's book about different welfare state models and developing countries was written. As Sehnbruch discusses in Chapter 12 of this volume, the historical data on employment conditions are sketchy, making it extremely difficult to tell whether they were always precarious or whether they have in fact deteriorated during recent decades. Survey data gathered after 1996 show a significant decline in the proportion of formal, open-ended, and stable employment contracts. The growing proportion of short-term jobs, the continuous rotation of workers between them with interrupting periods of unemployment or informal employment, and the persistently high proportion of informal jobs (both in the salaried and self-employed labor force) were not factors that had been contemplated at the time when Chile's social insurance systems were privatized. In fact, as this chapter discusses below, even in 2001 the Chilean government had no data on the characteristics of the jobs held by workers before becoming unemployed. When the administrative data from the unemployment insurance system then began to show extraordinarily high levels of job rotation and of short-term contracts, government officials were shocked into reforming the system only a few years after its initial implementation (Sehnbruch 2006).[8]

This example of lack of data brings us to our final point in our argument regarding the deficiencies of Chile's welfare state foundations: since before Concertación governments took office, there has been insufficient analysis of the original assumptions that underlie Chilean social security structures, which time has proven erroneous. When Chile's modern social security systems were designed during the 1980s, nobody would have thought that unemployment rates would remain relatively high while participation rates would remain relatively low, that an increasing proportion of workers would be hired on a short-term basis, and that levels of informality would remain high.

However, the Chilean labor market is not the only thing that has not developed according to the plan of the original architects of Chile's social security policy. Apart from the unexpectedly weak employment conditions, other assumptions that shaped both health care and pension insurance structures have also failed to live up to original expectations. In the case of the pension system, the returns on the funds invested by individual contributors have been far below original estimates. In addition, and related to labor market developments, workers have achieved neither the overall coverage nor the consistency of contributions that were originally expected by the system. Thus, a pension system that was expected to deliver replacement rates of at least 90 percent has ended up producing pensions that replace only 23 percent of wages in the case of women, and 43 percent in the case of men (Margozzini 1988).[9]

In the case of health care, poor employment conditions have led to extremely low rates of coverage by private health insurers, who, due to lack of regulation after the inception of the private insurance system, acquired a very poor reputation for ensuring only low-risk contributors, or increasing the cost of plans for higher-risk contributors. Furthermore, the cost of private insurance is much too high for average wages: only the earners from the top two income deciles can afford it. Thus the proportion of the population actually covered by private health care insurance has declined rather than expanded after its inception, a process that coincides with the consolidation of the insurance business into a group of a few providers, which parallels the consolidation that occurred in the pension fund industry. This consolidation has effectively created health and pension insurance oligopolies, and limits competition between firms in each sector. Again, this is an unintended consequence of the original insurance design, which had aimed to generate competitive industries.

Overall, it is difficult to gain an in-depth understanding of the exact expectations that originally motivated the design of social insurance systems in Chile. During the dictatorship, policy debates were extremely limited and not discussed publicly. That the military government did not see eye to eye with the Chicago Boy technocrats on these matters is best expressed by their refusal to privatize their own health and pension insurance systems.

Together the structural weaknesses of Chile's social policy structures discussed in this section amount to a critical assessment of the Concertación's argument that it established the foundation of a welfare state in Chile. Although we definitely agree that the coalition undertook significant and successful improvements in the area of social policy, particularly by instituting universal rights in some areas, the sum of this progress does not amount to the *foundation* of a welfare state, and is, of course, still extremely far removed from a welfare state itself.

This is particularly true when social policy structures, such as pension, health, or unemployment insurance systems, are tied to employment conditions; these systems require high levels of formal employment, adequate wages, and job stability to function satisfactorily for the majority of the population. If, however, employment conditions are poor from the outset or deteriorate, social policy structures require increasing levels of public resources, to extend both coverage and benefit levels, which subsidize those workers and their dependents whose employment conditions are informal or unstable.

Yet, even in developed countries with redistributive tax systems, direct welfare benefits can rarely make up for deficiencies in insurance payouts if the employment conditions that generated these payouts were precarious. In developing countries, where levels of fiscal revenues are low as a percentage of GDP, direct social transfers do not even come close to compensating for precarious employment conditions and their effects on the results of privatized insurance systems. Individual capabilities may be severely limited by low levels of employment and poor working conditions (Sehnbruch 2006).[10]

Our criticisms of the Concertación's social policies, however, beg the question how a coalition that intended to overcome the social debt it inherited from the dictatorship could have failed to make structural progress even while it was succeeding in improving the social insurance systems it inherited. As mentioned above, two main factors stand out that limited the Concertación's success in this area: the first was the systematic, steadfast, and often virulent opposition of the Right to any social reform that involved raising taxes or a structural redistribution of any kind once the initial reforms of the Aylwin government had been undertaken.[11]

The second factor was the division of opinions within the Concertación itself. While progressive sectors of the Concertación consistently favored the expansion of social entitlements, especially during the Lagos and Bachelet governments, more conservative sectors continually resisted these demands. Ideological differences largely explain divisions both within the Concertación and between its governments and the opposition.

For example, one of the issues that caused particular tension in the political debate about social policy after 1990 was whether the government should undertake social policies based simply on welfare benefits, or whether it should endeavor to create appropriate incentive structures. In this debate, welfare benefits were derogatorily referred to as *asistencialismo*. If they were to be established at all, they had to be strictly targeted to the poorest 5 to 20 percent of the population in the most minimal amounts possible to avoid all forms of moral hazard.[12] As Chile's income per capita grew during the 1990s, the debate about *asistencialismo* split not only the Concertación, but also the right-wing opposition.

Only during the Lagos administration did policymakers begin to question the underlying principles of the insurance systems they inherited, and instituted health care reform with universal guarantees as well as incipient unemployment insurance, without, however, changing the fundamental structures of the systems. This process was continued and intensified during the government of President Bachelet. Two parallel processes led to a significant shift in social policy thinking that began to consider individuals as subjects with rights rather than mere needs: increased levels of education had produced a more informed and aware citizenry that knew its rights and demanded access to them.[13] Simultaneously, public policy experts became increasingly aware of the limits of targeting, which shifted their discourse from the objective of overcoming poverty to one of guaranteeing equal opportunities.

However, despite these shifts, the tension about *asistencialismo* was still clearly evident during the work of the commission on employment and equity during the Bachelet government. Even though there was an explicit appreciation of the elevated levels of inequality of income and opportunities in Chile, experts were simultaneously reticent in advocating direct income transfers to the poor. Arguments against these transfers were related to the targeting of public resources solely to the poorest households to avoid the filtration toward the "middle classes," to fears about reducing the incentive for personal effort, and to the discrediting of European welfare states.[14]

These arguments demonstrate the extent to which debates about public policy are dominated by economic arguments, and indeed by economists. In fact, in all of the presidential commissions appointed by President Bachelet, the majority of members were economists.[15] Overall, in the process of Concertación policymaking, there has been little active or serious participation by nongovernmental organizations (NGOs), representatives of civil society, labor organizations, or other social actors. Few opinion makers in the area of public policy are noneconomists or representatives of civil society. Although the latter participated in policy debates, the Ministry of Finance together with economist technocrats dominated the decisionmaking process.[16]

It is partly for this reason that concerns about moral hazard and economic efficiency penetrated the political establishment so deeply and by far outweighed any real preoccupation with social cohesion.

These reasons partly explain why it has taken so many years for the experts of the Concertación to appreciate the full extent of the weaknesses of the social security systems they inherited. During the 1990s, it was still impossible to undertake a systematic criticism of the existing structures, in part because data and information on labor market and social security developments were still extremely rudimentary, and in part because undertaking structural reform was inconceivable given political constraints and the ideological force of the neoliberal reforms (Arellano 1986).[17] In addition, we must bear in mind that these reforms were thought of as a development "model," as discussed in several other chapters in this volume. Questioning the structures of Chile's social security systems during the 1990s was therefore analytically premature (due to lack of data), ideologically difficult, and politically complicated.

Beyond the Concertación's own limitations and internal divisions, however, the opposition of the right-wing parties to structural social reforms led to self-censorship measures within the Concertación as they did not even contemplate policy reforms they knew would be rejected by the Right. In addition, right-wing opposition led to the many watered-down reforms the Concertación undertook in which key aspects, such as risk socialization in the health insurance system (discussed below), had to be scratched from the initial reform proposal so as not to jeopardize the whole reform.

In the following sections we will examine how these political restrictions shaped policy outcomes in the areas of health, pension, and unemployment insurance.

Health Insurance Reforms Under the Concertación

In 1990, the Concertación inherited a dual health care system from the military government, which had attempted to create privatized health care through the institution of private insurers called ISAPRES. From 1983 onward, Chilean wage earners contributed 7 percent of their earnings to either a public or private provider of health insurance services. For a high-income earner, a 7 percent contribution was usually enough to buy a health insurance plan with a private provider for the worker and his or her dependents. However, in the case of low- or middle-income earners, their 7 percent contribution was generally insufficient to purchase private care, and would therefore be paid to the National Health Service (FONASA). Workers who contribute neither to private nor to public health care, such as the self-employed, the elderly, the unemployed, or the informally employed, are cared for by FONASA under emergency provisions, and only in state-run hospitals. This system instituted a dual health care system, in which the quality of health care services received is essentially dependent on the resources of beneficiaries.[18]

After 1990, the primary task of the Concertación health care policy was to recover the infrastructure and general functioning of the public health care system, which during the seventeen years of military regime had become severely underfinanced (Infante and Paraje 2010). The second task was to improve the system's regulation. Therefore, for the first ten years, the Concertación's health care policy consisted mainly of increasing resources to the public system.

However, the main health care reform undertaken by the Concertación was the Plan AUGE in 2000.[19] This reform was important not only in the context of health care, but also in the context of the Concertación's social policies in general. Its most important characteristic was that it established universal citizenship rights and service guarantees for the users of the national health care system, and as such was the first reform to institute universal rights.

The basic premise of AUGE is that it establishes a system of guaranteed treatments and services for the most commonly suffered pathologies that affect the Chilean population. These guarantees are universal and are paid for by a specific proportion of health insurance contributions. The original fifty-six pathologies covered by AUGE were selected so that they would cover approximately 65 percent of all medical situations in Chile (Vargas and Poblete 2008). The long-term objective of AUGE is to cover all essential medical services provided by FONASA.

For the medical situations it covers, AUGE thus eliminates the system of *cupos* that previously characterized health care (and other social services) in Chile by fixing a maximum number of treatments (or services) that a particular social service could finance in any given period of time. In addition, AUGE limits the proportion of copayments that the insured have to make.[20]

The problem with AUGE is that it does not yet cover all medical situations, thus discriminating between different pathologies of the same type. For example, patients suffering one type of cancer are covered by it, while other types are not. During the Bachelet government, the main health care policy priority was to expand the number of pathologies covered by AUGE from fifty-six to a total of eighty, which covers approximately 80 percent of medical procedures.

During the initial political discussions about health care reform, the Lagos government had to confront two major issues: first, the medical establishment had to be convinced of the need to focus health care on only the most common medical conditions while simultaneously accepting that these conditions had to be treated under fixed cost regimens. Second, any reform that intended to establish universal health care, even in its most minimal form, had to confront the question of how this reform was to be financed. When the Lagos government attempted to raise the taxes necessary for such a reform, it ran into stiff opposition from the Right.

As regards the financing of the health reform, a compromise had to be reached with the Right that minimally increased value-added taxes on all consumption. An increase in VAT is, of course, not a progressive financing mechanism, although it has the advantage of being easy to collect. However, when we add up the net cost of AUGE for the different income deciles, we find that the higher amount of taxes higher income deciles pay covers a significant proportion of the cost of AUGE for poorer people.

Still, Chile's health care system continues to be marked by extremely high inequalities with the wealthy having access to first-class health care services that fall little short of the care delivered in developed countries, while the poor have access to services of a much lower quality.

Despite these inequalities, AUGE represents a structural shift in the health care system and the data show that it is one of the few social policies the Concertación instituted that actually had a significant and immediate impact that could be perceived by the population.

Chile's Pension System

In 1981, Chile replaced its system of public pensions that was based on shared contributions with a new privatized system based on individual savings accounts. The reasons for this change were an increasingly high level of underfinancing in the old system combined with a high level of inefficiency in the structure and administration of the old system.[21] The new system that was instituted requires all wage earners to contribute 12 percent of their wages to an individual savings account, which is then administered by one of the licensed investment management firms, known as the Administradoras de Fondos de Pensiones (AFP), according to regulated investment criteria. For many years the Chilean pension system was considered to be a model for other developing countries as it eliminated inefficiencies that characterized traditional systems (Arenas et al. 2006).

The basic operating principle of the pension system is based on the idea that each worker receives a final pension commensurate with his or her earnings during his or her working life. The pension system itself makes no provision for socializing risk among the different contributors to the system. It also does not oblige informal workers and the self-employed to contribute. However, the system did provide for two types of minimum pension: a basic pension for senior citizens who had never contributed to the pension system, and a minimum pension for senior citizens who had contributed to the pension system for a minimum of twenty years, but who had not accumulated enough savings during this period of time to ensure a minimal level of income.[22] According to 2006 data, 60 percent of current pensioners are receiving pensions from the old system, while 30 percent receive their pensions from the new one.

After twenty years of the pension system's operation, it became clear that the system was inadequate in several ways. Despite the fact that it constitutes a significant improvement relative to the old pension system, three principal problems stood out: first, the overall coverage of the system was relatively low as a large proportion of workers in the Chilean labor market continue to work informally or independently. Second, the replacement ratio of the system (i.e., the pensions received relative to the average wages of workers) was extremely low by international standards.[23] Third, workers, in particular female workers, were not accumulating sufficient funds in their individual accounts due to frequent and lengthy periods in which they did not contribute to the system. As discussed above, the Chilean labor market and the employment conditions of individual workers have become much more fragmented and precarious than the original design of the system had contemplated. The high levels of income inequality discussed throughout this book that have not improved during the last twenty years further compound the inequalities inherent in the system's design.

In response to these problems, the government of Michelle Bachelet introduced one of the most important reforms of Chile's recent social policy history: a committee of experts on pension reform proposed changes to the system, which became law. The reform established a basic pension (Pensión Básica Solidaria) for all senior and handicapped citizens regardless of their level of contribution to the pension system. This basic pension has been designed to cover the elderly living in the poorest 60 percent of households.[24]

A social policy that accords people living in the lower 60 percent of the income distribution scale a universal right to a public benefit constitutes a significant shift in the structure of Chile's social security system. Some experts have even argued that the reform constitutes a first step toward a welfare state such as those in developed social democratic countries as it conceives of individual citizens as having individual rights as opposed to relating entitlements to the family unit (Arenas 2010).

The principal difference between this reform and the social security structures of developed countries, however, is that it is financed by general fiscal revenue, rather than through any risk-sharing component incorporated into the pension system.

Unemployment Insurance

In 2002, following the Asian crisis of 1998–1999, the Lagos government instituted an unemployment insurance system that was supposed to protect workers, especially the most vulnerable segment of the labor market, from economic shocks. The institution of the insurance reflected a shift in the thinking of policymakers: they now publicly accepted that labor market flexibility was simply a fact of life. High levels of job rotation therefore left workers and their families extremely vulnerable in periods of unemployment between jobs. Hence the task of social policy was to protect workers as much as possible when they became unemployed.

The political debate about the need for an unemployment insurance system had been going on for many years. However, there was much disagreement on how such a system should be structured. There was a broad consensus across political coalitions that Chile had neither the fiscal resources nor the administrative capacity required to manage a traditional unemployment insurance system successfully. Along with many other middle-income developing countries across the world, Chile therefore ended up instituting an unemployment insurance that relied on individual savings accounts. Employers and workers contributed a small proportion of each employee's gross wage to an individual savings account, from which contributions could be withdrawn in the event of unemployment. In Chile, experts considered that the country's long-standing experience of managing individual savings accounts in the pension system would make it easy to manage insurance contributions. Institutionally, the unemployment insurance could also piggyback off existing institutions and administrative capacity.

The individual savings accounts were further complemented by the establishment of a solidarity fund from which workers could withdraw funds—under certain conditions, of course—if their own savings were insufficient to constitute an adequate replacement rate.

However, this insurance system treats workers differently according to their contractual status. Only workers with open-ended contracts, who have contributed to the insurance for at least twelve of the previous twenty-four months, were entitled to funds from the solidarity fund. Workers with short-term contracts of any type were only entitled to withdraw their own savings out of the system in a single payment worth approximately one-third of their monthly wage. In addition, workers without formal written contracts, the self-employed and domestic employees (who have their own unemployment insurance), are excluded from the system.

As discussed above, when the insurance was established, it was unclear that employment conditions, in particular the types of contracts and their duration, had deteriorated so significantly. The Chilean government had no official data on the characteristics of the jobs that workers had held before becoming unemployed. Once the system became operational, government officials were shocked to find such high levels of fixed-term contracts and job rotation among contributors to the system. Even workers with open-ended contracts suffered frequent job rotation. It therefore did not take long for experts to criticize the system for its deficiencies, in particular its low replacement rates and limited coverage.

The system was reformed only seven years after it became operational. The reform concentrated on making access to the solidarity fund easier for workers with both short-term and open-ended contracts, while extending periods of coverage to a maximum of seven months in the case of workers with open-ended contracts and three months for workers of fixed-term contracts. Replacement rates, though, remained significantly lower for the latter group of unemployed. Furthermore, the restriction that workers can only withdraw funds from the system twice within a five-year period severely limits its coverage for contributors whose average employment duration is one year according to the statistics of the insurance system's administrative data.

However, particularly if we consider the characteristics of the jobs that the unemployed held prior to becoming unemployed, we find that the insurance system is still inadequate, even after the reform. Approximately half of the unemployed never had a formal written contract prior to becoming unemployed. Their exclusion from the system means that its real coverage is extremely low. Even those workers who did have formal written contracts, either fixed or open ended, often cannot receive benefits from the system as the high levels of job rotation prevent them from accumulating sufficient savings in between periods of unemployment (Landerretche and Sehnbruch 2011).

In their endeavor to circumvent issues of moral hazard associated with traditional unemployment insurance systems, Concertación governments have ended up designing a savings scheme for the unemployed with a very low insurance component. Although many developing countries have adopted unemployment insurance based on individual savings accounts, the job rotation levels of the Chilean labor market mean that such a system is unlikely to provide the unemployed with a real sense of protection when they lose their job. However, the insurance system does constitute progress if compared with the extremely limited benefits that existed for unemployed workers in Chile prior to its introduction.

Chile's unemployment insurance system, like its pension and health insurance systems, is an example of how deteriorated employment conditions will limit the extent of social security coverage if the latter is conditional upon a stable and formal job with a reasonable level of income. Rather than protecting vulnerable workers during times of economic crisis, it is more likely to replicate the existing inequalities of the labor market.

Conclusion

From the analysis presented in this chapter, it is clear that the Concertación during its twenty years in office made significant progress in assuaging the social debt it inherited from the dictatorship. We can also conclude that the Concertación administrations undertook a significant expansion of social policies beyond this debt. By 2010, for the majority of the population, Chile's social protection systems were functioning better than at any other point in the country's history. To understand how far these efforts have gone, we need to come back to the question of whether the Concertación has actually laid the foundations for a social protection system that could develop into a welfare state.

The positive answer to this question is that the Concertación took two important steps in this direction: first, it shifted its policy objective from covering only the most basic needs of poor people (targeting) to one of expanding both the range of services and their coverage to at least 60 percent (and in some cases 80 percent) of the population. Second, this shift has been accompanied by a corresponding change of emphasis that views citizens as having rights rather than just needs. A rights-based approach together with the expansion of services constitutes the theoretical foundation of welfare states based on universal entitlements. Both of these important principles of progress have been achieved despite persistent right-wing opposition during the twenty years of Concertación government.

As mentioned in the introduction, perhaps the Concertación's greatest achievement in the area of social policy is the fact that the Piñera government that succeeded it has continued to expand social policies according to the same principles established by the coalition. The right-wing government's expansion of social benefits and rights in 2011, as exemplified by the extension of maternity benefits, the establishment of minimum family income levels, and the elimination of health insurance contributions for pensioners, marks not only a step in the same direction, but also the abandonment of the right-wing's traditional discourse about the negative effects of *assitentialism*.[25] In fact, it could even be interpreted as an effort—albeit a minimal one—to expand Chile's incipient welfare state.

However, we must also recognize the limitations of the welfare state that was constructed under the Concertación. The central criticism that stands out in the analysis of the Chilean social protection system is the combination of the six factors described above: (1) the lack of risk socialization and redistribution within social insurance systems; (2) the absence of a redistributive tax system that can compensate for this failure to share risk; (3) the poor distribution of the quality of services as a result of the separation between public and private providers; (4) the need for fiscal subsidies so the private systems can function; (5) the unforeseen deterioration of employment conditions to which private insurance systems are linked;

and (6) the fact that the original assumptions on which social security systems are based have been proven erroneous.

Among these six issues, perhaps the one that was least considered by the Concertación is the fact that Chile's labor market development has undermined its social development. Concertación governments have focused on social policy objectives without considering employment conditions because improving access to social benefits was ideologically less complicated than strengthening the rights of labor, effectively enforcing labor legislation, or in any way counteracting the dogma of labor market flexibility.

This has generated the following dilemma: if policymakers accept that labor markets have to operate with maximum levels of flexibility regardless of the effects on workers, then they should institute social security systems that establish guaranteed universal rights and entitlements, regardless of employment conditions. If, however, policymakers continue to operate social security systems that are tied to employment conditions, then significantly more political effort should go into formalizing and improving these employment conditions. Failing that, we are allowing the foundations of our social security systems to become undermined. The central problem with the Concertación's social policy is that it allowed employment conditions to become extremely flexible and precarious, while it attempted to improve social security systems that are structurally tied to these same precarious conditions, which in turn undermine progress toward the foundation of a welfare state.

Given that the reality of the labor market is very different from what was originally assumed by the architects of Chile's social security systems, the Concertación should probably have raised the political question of whether it makes sense to maintain their basic structures. In particular, the lack of risk socialization within each social insurance system makes it difficult for the model to move toward the much praised "flexicurity" that later Concertación governments theoretically aspired to (Jørgensen 2010).

Perhaps this argument is most evident in the health insurance sector: when the system was originally designed, the expectation was that it would cover approximately 50 percent of the population through private insurance. However, the high cost of private insurance plans relative to incomes combined with the poor reputation of the insurance companies for cherry picking only high-income and low-risk clients has meant that they have ended up covering less than 20 percent of the population. As public health services have improved, people have moved toward public health insurance (and, if they can afford it, have complemented this with supplementary private insurance). Thus, the proportion of the population covered by the private health insurers has declined and may decline further during coming years.

In the same way, we have to ask whether the existing pension system will be able to provide pensions commensurate with people's expectations in the future. Given the low replacement rates that the private system is producing, structural reforms to the system are necessary. And if contributions to the system have to be increased to improve replacement rates, it would make sense to implement simultaneous policies of redistribution within the system so as to ensure the existence of a permanent and structural mechanism that would finance minimum pensions for low-income earners.[26]

Yet in this debate of the Concertación's limitations and achievements, we should also highlight that the coalition successfully built the social policy institutions necessary for administering a basic welfare state with universal entitlements. As many development experts have argued, the bottleneck to providing universal social benefits in developing countries is institutional and political, not fiscal, due to the fact that the cost of instituting social benefits is broadly speaking proportional to per capita incomes. The success of the Concertación in building institutions that are developed enough to administer a greater extent of social benefits without falling prey to clientelistic political practices as in other countries in the region must therefore be highlighted as a particularly important achievement.

In a region where social security and tax systems fail to redistribute (see Wehr 2011), the Concertación did better than average. But Chile, like other Latin American countries, is still a long way from instituting anything that could be considered the foundation for a liberal welfare state.

Notes

The authors would like to thank Osvaldo Larrañaga for sharing his encyclopedic knowledge of social policies in Chile with us. This chapter in part draws on materials from the book *Las Nuevas Políticas de Protección Social en Chile* by Dante Contreras and Osvaldo Larrañaga (2010).

1. State of the Union speech, May 21, 2008.

2. By the early 1990s the term "social debt" was being used in many Latin American countries to refer to the social consequences of structural adjustment policies, which in Chile had brought about particular social hardship as they were carried out by a dictatorship.

3. GDP per capita based on 1980 US dollars.

4. The Central Workers Union (CUT), in particular, had made a deal with the early Concertación governments to restrain its social demands so as not to jeopardize the transition to democracy.

5. "We were under a lot of pressure during our government. There were many, who thought from the outset that we would be incapable of governing and maintaining fiscal responsibility. We were under constant scrutiny as the first socialist

government since the democratic transition." Interview with Nicolás Eyzaguirre, August 2011.

6. However, as has been widely discussed during health care reform debates in the United States, its health insurance system is one of the most expensive in the world and produces the worst results if compared to the standards of developed countries. For basic details on health outcomes, see UNDP Human Development Indicators (http://hdr.undp.org/en/). For spending on health care, see OECD (www.oecd.org). Within the United States, the most effective and cost-efficient insurance is the Veterans Health Administration, which is not only a state-run and -financed system, but also shares medical risk among a broad and diverse population.

7. See, for example, the Lagos health reform of 2005 and the Bachelet pension reform of 2008, discussed below.

8. Author interviews with cabinet-level officials at the Ministry of Labor and with the cabinet adviser in charge of designing and implementing the unemployment insurance system during 2002 and 2003 recorded the surprise, shock, and consternation that characterized discussions of the unemployment insurance data at the time.

9. For the original estimates on which the pension system was based see Margozzini (1988: 259, 268). Margozzini estimates a replacement rate of approximately 80–90 percent, using a rate of real return on the pension funds of 5 percent, a fixed commission, and average contribution gaps of 15 percent. However, he also estimated that if workers contributed an extra 5 percent of their wages to their pension funds during their working life, then this would give them replacement rates of around 130 percent.

10. The key working conditions that must be considered in this context are a worker's type of contract, the resultant entitlements to social insurance systems (health, pension, unemployment, and disability), the duration of employment or job stability, and wage levels.

11. Chapter 9 in this volume by López discusses how the Aylwin government undertook a tax reform in 1990 that raised some additional revenue that was used toward increasing the education budget.

12. A good example of this type of policy is the Chile Solidario social program, which was established by the Lagos government and, unlike its peers in Latin America, provided only the most minimal cash transfers. See the discussion below.

13. The student demonstrations and the strikes of subcontracted workers of 2006 and 2007 were an initial sign of a more active and organized citizenry that had put the democratic transition behind it, was no longer afraid of destabilizing democracy, and was therefore more willing to demonstrate its dissatisfaction.

14. Only recent evidence that shows a significant fluctuation of income levels even among the "middle class" has facilitated public policy designs that have abandoned the more traditional criteria of fiscal targeting.

15. In the context of these arguments it is relevant to mention that one of the authors of this chpater, Dante Contreras, was a member of both the Education Commission and the Employment and Equity Commission appointed by President Bachelet.

16. A good example of how the Ministry of Finance ended up calling the shots was the dilution of the earned income tax credit proposed by the commission into a subsidy for young people from low-income households who found it difficult to participate in the labor market. The subsidy that was implemented in the end only constituted a fraction of the policy that was proposed by the commission.

17. Arellano was the first to criticize the pension system during the dictatorship.

18. Other health care insurance systems also exist but cover only a relatively small proportion of the population. In particular, as mentioned above, members of the armed forces were excluded from the privatization of social security systems and therefore have their own public health insurance systems, which provide significantly better services than the general public health insurance, FONASA.

19. AUGE stands for Acceso Universal con Garantías Explícitas.

20. FONASA A and B: no copayments; FONASA C: 10 percent copayment; and FONASA D: 20 percent copayment.

21. Chile's previous pension system was based on a multitude of public providers, which each administered the pension contributions of a different group of the population according to different investment and payout criteria.

22. The basic pension, known as the Pensión Asistencia (Pasis), in 2008 amounted to approximately US$100 per person, and was dependent on availability (*cupos*). The minimum pension in 2008 amounted to between US$200 and US$240, depending on the age of the pensioner.

23. Given the ratios of contribution density, the replacement rate for men is 43 percent and 23 percent for women versus an OECD average of 72 percent (OECD 2011d).

24. Note that the basic pension is not contingent upon the total income of the household in which a senior citizen lives, but is based on his or her individual resources. The income threshold that gives individuals the right to receive a basic pension moves in relation to Chile's overall income levels.

25. In fact, the main pillar of Piñera's social policy has been a basic income program known as the Ingreso Ético Familiar. The legislation is based on a proposal originally made by the Commission on Equity and Employment instituted by President Bachelet in 2008.

26. Of course, any structural pension reform of the future would also have to consider regulatory reform of the system to improve its performance and ensure that providers compete with each other.

12

A Precarious
Labor Market

Kirsten Sehnbruch

In her 2005 election manifesto, Michelle Bachelet captures the essence of the Concertación's labor policy during the past decades:

> The main source of employment generation is economic growth. There is no public policy, government subsidy or labor reform that can compete with the capacity of a healthy economy to generate growth. There is no substitute for sustained growth; it is the best insurance against unemployment. This is why macroeconomic growth and stability have been a priority of the Concertación.[1]

If labor market developments are essentially considered the fallout from other macroeconomic policies, and if, as is discussed by Landerretche in Chapter 8 in this volume, the economy is generally developing successfully, then there is no real need to interfere with the labor market. This, therefore, also means that there is no urgent need for labor reform or employment policies beyond basic measures to protect workers in situations of unemployment (such as unemployment insurance and emergency employment programs), or to establish appropriate institutions that help the labor market run more smoothly (such as employment placement services or vocational training programs). In short, this means that during its twenty years in office, the Concertación never really prioritized or even paid much attention to the development of its labor market, basically because it believed that things were on the right track. Too many other urgent public policy issues competed for the coalition's attention.

Ideologically, this view also fits nicely into the prevailing consensus established by the transitional enclaves discussed throughout this volume. Like tax reform, labor reform has the potential to be deeply contentious and politically divisive as it pitches the interests of employers against those of organized labor, individual workers, and potentially the common good (if lack of investment in human capital stymies the country's development process, as is argued in previous chapters).

This chapter will show that the overall development of Chile's labor market has not been as successful as the simple focus on employment and unemployment rates implied by the quotation above suggests. In fact, it will argue that labor policy under the Concertación was a neglected policy area due, in part, to the coalition's confidence that macroeconomic growth would resolve the problems of its workforce, and in part to the transitional enclaves that characterized the Concertación's period in office. Consequently, the progress of labor reform under the Concertación was limited while the performance of employment variables has been somewhat mixed. Although basic indicators such as employment rates and wages increased (but not as much as in other developing countries that are considered success stories), employment conditions deteriorated as the proportion of "precarious" jobs increased. Furthermore, the rates of high income inequality discussed in the previous chapter translate into a permanently depressed "feel-good" factor even when the economy improves and the unemployment rate goes down. Employment therefore consistently figures among the top concerns of Chileans in public opinion surveys.[2]

Meanwhile, progress on labor reform has been limited to initiatives on which agreement could be reached, such as the institution of an unemployment insurance system or the institution of employment subsidies. Labor reforms that would have potentially strengthened the position of unions were stymied, mostly due to fierce opposition from the Right, but also due to lack of agreement within the Concertación. Chile has ended up with labor legislation, a union movement, and also with employment characteristics that are not conducive to the country's future development, let alone to making the leap into the league of developed countries.[3]

This chapter will proceed by briefly examining the development of labor legislation under the Concertación before reviewing some basic data on the Chilean labor market to demonstrate how these developments came about.

Labor Reform and the Position of Unions

Over the last two decades the debate over labor reform has been shaped by the same factors that have shaped other policy debates discussed in this volume, such as education and social policy. Deep ideological divides pitch proponents of labor regulation against those who oppose it. Although the social actors involved in labor debates have achieved some degree of consensus, policy decisions are still discussed from a perspective that supposes a trade-off between labor rights and employment generation. This means that policymakers and employers assume that improved employment conditions will result in lower levels of competitiveness for the economy while less regulation is perceived as preferable. Conversely, there is little discussion of win-win policy strategies for all social actors.

The coming together of political coalitions in the political Center has made it easier to achieve consensus on some aspects of labor policy, such as unemployment insurance, vocational training, or employment subsidies. However, beneath these reforms lies the tension of unresolved issues and deeply rooted antagonisms. The political conflict between employers, who generally backed the dictatorship, and unions meant that employers and workers were separated by profound political differences that included the memory of brutal violence and repression. There is therefore a far higher level of antagonism and a lower level of trust between Chilean employers and their workers than in some other Latin American countries (Armstrong and Águila 2000).

This situation is compounded by the fact that Chilean union legislation continues to rank among the most restrictive in the world, prohibiting collective bargaining at the sector level and allowing for the replacement of striking workers.

When the Concertación took office in 1990, labor reform was one of the most delicate and important political negotiations it faced. As discussed in Chapters 10 and 11 of this volume, the Concertación inherited a level of "social debt" with Chile's workers and low-income families that became one of the guiding principles of Concertación policy, especially during the Aylwin and Frei governments. The combined effects of two economic crises and Chile's structural adjustment process had left a high unemployment rate and wages below precrisis levels. Furthermore, the dictatorship had systematically persecuted unions and their leaders, while simultaneously pursuing labor reform that weakened their political power.

Despite this, the union movement played a fundamental role in paving the way for a return to democracy through the mass demonstrations it organized from 1982 onward (Huneeus 2007). Union leaders therefore hoped that a return to democracy would restore their political influence and predictatorship labor rights.

The Aylwin government approached these combined social and political deficits with a double strategy: establishing a social dialogue on labor issues and legislative reform. The four tripartite agreements (Acuerdos Marco) that were established during the years of the Aylwin government were an expression of this approach. The first such agreement, signed in April 1990, expressed a "joint vision" regarding the challenges facing the country under the new democratic regime and agreed on substantial increases of minimum wages and basic minimum pensions (Cortázar 1993).

These agreements were more significant in terms of their symbolic value than their content, which did not include the subject of labor reform. Their most important characteristic was perhaps that they established a dialogue between the social actors, but they also set the limitations of this dialogue in terms of the range of matters that were dealt with, as well as their depth, by steering clear of the more controversial issues.

The reforms that were implemented by the Aylwin administration are the most important that were undertaken during the Concertación governments. They took the legislation inherited from the dictatorship and, through changes that had only a minor impact in practice but a significant symbolic importance, generated the basis for labor legislation under democracy.

The reforms concentrated on the two main issues of regulating the termination of contracts and union rights. Perhaps their most important element was that employers were again obliged to justify dismissals. On paper this meant that they could no longer hire and fire at will as the 1979 labor reform had stipulated. But in practice, this clause had little impact as employers could still make workers redundant for economic reasons without complex bureaucratic or legal procedures.

The 1990 reform also raised the ceiling on severance payments in cases of redundancies from five to eleven months, thus increasing dismissal cost for employers. As will be discussed in the following section, practicalities limit the impact of this reform as few wage earners in Chile today have formal contracts with such levels of tenure.

The reform further marginally strengthened the position of the unions: intercompany collective negotiation was permitted provided all parties concerned agreed to it (in practice this almost never happens). It was made easier for unions to be founded, particularly in smaller companies; the sixty-day limit on strikes was abolished so that the duration of strikes could again be unlimited (but with the provision that employers could hire replacement workers) (Mizala and Romaguera 1996; González 1996); and other aspects such as the financing and negotiation rights of the unions were strengthened. Again, most of these provisions were symbolic concessions to the unions that had little or no practical impact on how they would function in practice (Frank 2002, 2004; Haagh 2002).[4]

As discussed above, the reforms introduced by the Aylwin administration were effectively a compromise between union and employer demands, typical of the transition period. However, as a compromise, the reforms did not entirely satisfy anyone, especially not the unions, which viewed the administration's labor relations as authoritarian rather than participative and fought for a return to the rights they enjoyed prior to the dictatorship. For their part, employers were still seeking measures that would allow them more flexible use of labor. In particular, they resisted having to provide eleven months of severance pay.

President Eduardo Frei proposed a new set of reforms in 1995 that intended to resolve these issues, but was ultimately unsuccessful. Critics of the attempted reform have asserted that it came at a time when no new consensus on labor issues had been achieved. The reform ultimately foundered as a result of opposition from the right-wing parties and a failure to reach consensus within the Concertación. Although briefly resurrected as a political maneuver to call the opposition's bluff during the 1999 election campaign, this initiative also failed due to the persistent lack of consensus (Angell and Pollack 2000).

In the end, the Frei government made only marginal progress in the area of labor policy. It reformed the law of professional training, increased the capacity of the Labor Office (Dirección del Trabajo) to enforce legislation, instituted a minimum of one free Sunday a month for every worker, and prohibited pregnancy tests before employing a female worker. At the end of the Frei administration, however, labor relations were considerably tenser than they had been when President Frei assumed office.

By the inauguration of the Lagos government, voters were concerned with losing their jobs as the unemployment crisis hit Chile in the run-up to the elections in 1999.[5] Nevertheless, Lagos promised that a new labor reform would be among his government's first priorities, together with legislation for an unemployment insurance system. However, even before the president's inauguration, employers announced that they would oppose any reform that included sector-level collective bargaining and the prohibition of replacing striking workers.

The new labor market reform package—essentially containing the same issues as previous packages—was proposed very soon after the new administration took over. Yet, the Concertación still lacked the necessary majority in both houses to pass it (Frías 2002).

The reform that was finally passed in September 2001 included none of the principal measures that Lagos had originally intended to pass. Instead, it instituted a number of policies, such as new legislation against discrimination at work, against sexual harassment, and to establish equal opportunities for workers.[6] The change that had the most practical effect was the reduction of the working week from 48 to 45 hours as of 2005. It is interesting to note that the decision to reduce the working week (which was partly a measure to reduce unemployment) was the only point of the reform on which all parties could agree (Frías 2002).

The Lagos government made more progress in the institution of compulsory unemployment insurance for salaried workers.[7] This had already been attempted by both the Aylwin and Frei governments, but the project had been stalled for twelve years because the social actors could not agree on its structure and financing. However, the insurance is mainly based on individual savings accounts and pays out these savings in case of redundancy. As discussed in Chapter 11, the real insurance component of the system that pays out benefits from a "solidarity fund" in cases where individual savings fall below certain minimums is extremely limited. The system the government presented as unemployment insurance is, in reality, a compulsory savings scheme, not an unemployment insurance system, as it only covers a very small percentage of the unemployed effectively.

During the presidential election campaign of President Bachelet, labor reform again moved to the top of the political agenda as the Lagos government, with the intention of calling the opposition's bluff, repeated the maneuver of the Frei government and proposed new legislation that would regulate subcontracting in Chile. This time the legislation was not approved during the campaign (as it predictably did not receive the backing of the right-wing opposition), but was one of the first pieces of legislation that the new Bachelet government, with its newly acquired majority in congress (see Chapter 6), approved.[8]

The new legislation has theoretically put an end to the ability of companies to outsource responsibility for their workers. Companies are now ultimately responsible for *all* their workers, whether they are subcontracted or not. However, the new legislation does not resolve the issue of unequal pay or of employment conditions that are otherwise unequal. This means that one year after this legislation was passed, many subcontracted workers still noted the inequality of their employment conditions. Widespread discontent first erupted in the forestry sector in the south of Chile, where subcontracted workers from the paper and pulp manufacturer Grupo Arauco successfully organized, struck, and thus forced their employer to bargain collectively with them.

This strike by the Arauco workers is perhaps the most successful such industrial action in Chile in many years. Its success rests not only on the fact that the company eventually had to give in to the demands of the workers. More importantly, other companies in the sector immediately sat down and negotiated favorable deals with their workers to avoid a similar debacle. This success clearly empowered the Chilean union movement as a whole and has led to further industrial action in other economic sectors.

In particular, the Arauco strike was followed by industrial action by workers from the state-owned copper company CODELCO. When the government's Labor Office (Dirección del Trabajo) ordered the company to reinstate 5,000 outsourced workers, thus enforcing the newly passed subcontracting legislation, the company refused, arguing that this would increase its labor costs by too much. Workers immediately organized a strike, which dragged on between June and October of 2007. It was during this period that the Central Workers Union (CUT) organized a strike in support of the increased worker mobilizations that were being seen all over the country, using minimum wage demands as a trigger.

In the midst of these developments, Archbishop Goic, president of Chile's Episcopal conference, made a statement that called for the institution of an ethical wage of 250,000 pesos per month (approximately US$500), a 40 percent increase relative to Chile's current minimum wage. This statement led to a political storm and a vigorous debate.[9]

The government took these events to heart. Soon after the CUT demonstration, President Bachelet instituted a commission to examine issues of employment and equity. Like the other commissions instituted by her government, this one also brought together experts in the field with representatives from all three social actors and politicians from all segments of the political spectrum. The commission's work was divided into four principal policy areas: equity, labor market institutions, labor market policies, and small companies.[10]

The commission presented its final report with policy suggestions in March 2008. It proposed measures that included the improvement of the existing unemployment insurance system (however, without fundamentally changing its structure), an earned income tax credit scheme for workers with low income levels, improvements in labor intermediation, and vocational training services. However, the commission was unable to reach agreement on the two key issues that labor reform in Chile has been stuck on since the Aylwin reforms: severance pay and union legislation, in particular strike and collective bargaining regulation. The fact that unions were unable to negotiate their demands successfully again illustrates their limited power, which did not recover despite the increased mobilizations of 2007.

This account of labor reform in Chile over the last two decades neatly illustrates Cook's argument that "labor laws often hold symbolic value, serving as a reminder of a time when workers' organizations were more powerful" (Cook 2007; Sehnbruch 2006). The symbolic value of legislation, however, is important not only for workers, but also for employers and the associations that represent them politically. In the Chilean case, while workers look back on the Allende period as the status quo that they would like to recover in terms of their power to organize and influence politics, employers remember the period of the dictatorship for its few restrictions on firing workers and limited union activity.

Two fundamental trends can be distinguished from the processes of labor reform described above. First of all, it is clear that the Chilean labor movement, and in particular its national association, the CUT, never really regained the political power it lost under the military dictatorship. It lacks the numbers in terms of its membership as well as the resources (especially the financial resources) really to be able to insist on the changes that they would like to see introduced. In fact, in the course of all three labor reforms (or attempted reforms in the case of the Frei and Lagos administrations), the CUT has probably lost more influence as its principal demands have been consistently rejected. As a political lobby, the CUT faces a dilemma that is common in many countries ruled by governments of the Center-Left or the Left: politicians from these parties take the votes of the unions for granted as they are extremely unlikely to vote for right-wing parties. This means that the political bargaining power of the unions is reduced unless they can come up with a means of pressuring governments other than their votes. In the case of the CUT, it must also be pointed out that they never undertook a serious campaign to garner more extensive backing for their demands, which means that they have failed to build up a serious support base among both voters and politicians. Campero (2000) has described the CUT as a "political orphan" and it is clear that until it adopts a serious alternative strategy that incorporates the overwhelming logic of free markets, the CUT will remain in this position.[11]

What can now be regarded as the main success of the CUT is first that it managed to establish itself as a relatively unified voice of labor, and second that it managed to maintain the issues of labor reform on the political agenda of the Concertación for such a long time. But debates about reform and political discourse, not the content of legislation, are really the main manifestations of support that the CUT has received during the last three governments in Chile.

The second trend that can be discerned is that the position of the Chilean business sector really has not changed since the country's return to democracy. It remains essentially aligned with the political Right, continues to focus on achieving greater labor market flexibility and less regulation, and remains fundamentally opposed even to relatively minor changes that might strengthen the position of the unions. It may even have gained political power as it appears to have won over more members of the Concertación to its point of view that more regulation necessarily means fewer jobs.

The Performance of the Chilean Labor Market: The Quantity and Quality of Employment

The quotation from Michelle Bachelet's election manifesto cited and discussed in the introduction to this chapter captures the consensus that has formed around employment policy in Chile. It reflects the assumption that economic growth generates employment, which leads to a tighter labor market, and in turn to a lower unemployment rate, increased wages, higher labor market participation, and improved employment conditions. Although this consensus may not explicitly include the unions, their inability to articulate an alternative approach has implicitly made them part of it. The consensus view that economic growth leads to more and better jobs is so firmly entrenched in the consciousness of Chilean policymakers that most experts do not even analyze the characteristics of employment.[12] This is partly due to a lack of data on employment conditions, but also because most analysts agree that a modern labor market has to be flexible, especially in a country like Chile, which is export driven, is highly integrated into the globalized economy, and has to compete with other countries that have much cheaper labor costs.

The data discussed in this section illustrate that the empirical evidence for this premise in Chile is mixed: while some employment variables have improved, these gains are offset by the consistent deterioration of employment conditions, in particular the contractual status and tenure of workers. Growth, therefore, has generated more jobs, but not necessarily better jobs.

This section briefly examines the performance of standard labor market indicators that refer to the "quantity" of employment (i.e., variables related to the number of jobs generated and their associated salaries). It will then go on to discuss employment conditions related to the "quality" of employment in Chile.

On the surface, the general evidence on the Chilean labor market looks relatively good compared to its Latin American peers. In a region of high average unemployment rates, Chile's strong economic growth rates during the 1990s led to a consistent decline in the country's official unemployment rate, reaching a low of 5.3 percent in 1997. Although the economic crisis that affected Latin America in 1999 and 2000 brought about a dramatic increase in unemployment to 9.8 percent, this rate was still below the Latin American average of 10.5 percent at the time. Unfortunately, unemployment has been slow to decrease since then, spiked again—although not as dramatically in 2009—and finally began to drop again to below 7 percent in 2011.

On a more positive note, between 1990 and 2005, average wages in Chile increased by 53 percent, a rate surpassed only by Costa Rica over the same period of time (76 percent). Minimum wages almost doubled (95.4 percent), the third highest increase in Latin America after Argentina and Bolivia (ILO 2007). Furthermore, on a continent where almost half of the labor force works informally (according to the ILO's definition), the proportion of informal workers in Chile constitutes only about a third of the labor force. Perhaps Chile's weakest indicator is its participation rate, which since 1990 has consistently remained below the Latin American average (of around 70 percent) at roughly 60 percent, mainly due to the low participation rates of Chilean women.

As Figure 12.1 indicates, another positive indicator is that the proportion of salaried workers participating in the labor market has increased, although not significantly. These are the main employment indicators, which are published by Chile's official source of labor statistics, the Instituto Na-

Figure 12.1 Percentage of Wage Growth and Economically Active Population, 1990–2010

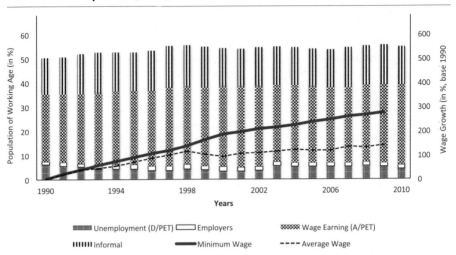

Source: Compiled by author from data from the Instituto Nacional de Estadísticas, Chile (INE, Chilean National Statistical Institute), www.ine.cl.

cional de Estadísticas, and by international sources such as the International Labour Organization (ILO). However, a discussion of Chile's labor market focused on these basic indicators would be extremely simplistic and would give us no explanation as to why Chileans on average cite employment issues as one of the two main problems the country faces.[13] Thus, it is important to look at other indicators to obtain a fuller and more accurate picture of the employment situation.

Latin American labor codes and the statutes governing the associated social security systems make a clear distinction between the salaried or dependent work force and the self-employed or independent work force. Then within the category of dependent workers, a further distinction is made between different types of contracts. The variable "contract or occupational status" must be considered as fundamental to the concept of quality of employment as it determines not only the potential duration of a job but also forms the legal basis of employees' rights and entitlements (e.g., to pension, health, and unemployment insurance) (Sehnbruch 2004, 2006).[14]

Table 12.1 shows the distribution of the different types of contracts and occupational positions in the total labor force. In 2006, only 43.5 percent of the total labor force still had a traditional open-ended contract.

Table 12.1 Development of Occupational Status, 1996–2006

Status	1996	1998	2000	2003	2006
Open-ended contracts	46.4	46.4	46.8	44.2	43.5
Atypical contracts	9.7	9.1	9.7	11.2	12.9
No contracts	20.0	20.5	19.4	20.2	18.9
Employers	3.7	4.1	4.3	4.0	3.1
Professional self-employed	2.0	2.6	2.6	2.9	3.2
Self-employed	18.3	17.4	17.2	17.6	17.4
Total	100.0	100.0	100.0	100.0	100.0

Source: Author's calculations based on CASEN data. The 2009 survey data have been excluded from this series due to changes in the relevant survey questions, which distort the series.

The remaining wage earners were distributed between atypical forms of contracts (12.9 percent) and workers without written contracts (18.9 percent). In the independent sector, the proportions of self-employed, professional self-employed, and employers were roughly stable at around 24 percent.

An analysis of other employment characteristics based on this basic breakdown of the labor force shows that the most precarious category of employment in terms of a worker's employment conditions is the wage earner without a formal written contract (Sehnbruch 2006; Ruiz Tagle and Sehnbruch 2010). They are the workers with the lowest wages; they do not pay social security contributions; they generally receive no vocational training whatsoever; they have the shortest tenures and rotate frequently between low-quality jobs; they cannot unionize; they can obviously be hired and fired at will; and they are not entitled to severance pay or unemployment insurance.[15] Any analysis of labor market data that does not specifically look at the employment conditions of workers without formal written contracts is thus ignoring one of the most important problems of the Chilean labor market.

Another issue that is extremely important in this context is subcontracting, especially because it is not only a component of the quality of employment, but also because it makes collective action very difficult. Unfortunately, the available data on subcontracting are scarce and unreliable. As a result, the variable is rarely used in labor market analysis.

Table 12.2 shows the percentages of Chilean companies that subcontract. The Labor Office estimates that 30 percent of companies in Chile subcontract out part of their production. This represents an increase of approximately 50 percent since 1998. While medium-sized companies tend to use subcontractors less (44 percent), larger companies do so more extensively

Table 12.2 Subcontracting in Chile (percentage of companies)

Company Characteristics	1998	2008
Companies that subcontract	20.0	30.5
Companies that do not subcontract	80.0	69.5
Companies by size		
Medium-sized firms		44.2
Large firms		58.7

Source: Data from Encla survey database, www.dt.gob.cl/documentacion/1612/w3-article -98995.html.

(just under 60 percent). As discussed above, subcontracting is one of the typical employment mechanisms used in Chile to make a company's labor force more flexible. In practice, subcontracting has led to very different employment conditions among workers who ultimately work for the same employer and perform the same tasks, even though on paper they are hired by two (or more) separate companies. Subcontracted workers often not only have different contractual relationships (e.g., atypical contracts versus open-ended contracts), but can earn less and work under conditions that are less safe or otherwise inferior to conditions of workers hired directly (Echeverría 2010; Echeverría and Uribe 1998; López 2007a, 2007b; Sehnbruch 2011).

Overall, within the companies that employ subcontracted workers, the average proportion of workers who have been subcontracted is only 12 percent. Although this figure does not appear very high, we have to remember that subcontracting is a widespread method in some industries in particular. In the mining sector, for example, 38 percent of workers are subcontracted, while construction subcontracts 22 percent.

Prior to the new legislation, companies could not only reduce the number of their work force by outsourcing production (a smaller work force requires compliance with fewer and less rigorous legislative requirements), but could also use this mechanism to prevent workers from organizing strong unions. Although subcontracted workers are allowed to unionize, they are only allowed to form a union within the company that employs them directly. A good example of this is the department store chain Almacenes Paris, which has fifty stores all over Chile, but only employs 153 workers directly. All others are subcontracted (Echeverría 2010). There is therefore no single union for all workers who work in the company. And since Chilean labor legislation prevents workers from negotiating on a sector-wide basis or beyond the confines of their immediate employer, unless the employer agrees to supra-union collective bargaining, there is no firm-wide collective bargaining either.

Another important source of information on the Chilean labor market is the administrative data produced by the unemployment insurance system that was instituted in 2002. These data are not representative of the entire labor market because they exclude salaried workers without contracts, the self-employed, as well as workers whose contracts predate 2002, the year of the system's inception. Nevertheless, the database has by now captured the employment history of the majority of Chilean workers who are formally employed. It is therefore a good indicator of both job rotation and the types of contracts prevalent among those workers covered by the insurance.

Table 12.3 shows that 58.4 percent of the insured have been in their present jobs for three months or less. Perhaps the most astonishing result of the data is that only 17.4 percent of those covered by the insurance have held their jobs for longer than three years. Put differently, Table 12.3 shows that only 3.2 percent of those workers who joined the system in 2002 are still in the same job seven years later. We should also note that almost 56 percent of open-ended contracts have lasted fewer than two years, which leads to the conclusion that high job rotation is not limited to short-term contracts.[16] (See Table 12.4.)

We should note that the information provided by the unemployment insurance system is based on the contracts signed by workers. The rotation is high because employers often rotate their workers between different subsidiaries, with different tax identification numbers, of the same holding company.[17] This kind of rotation exploits a legal loophole, which allows firms to avoid labor legislation, in particular severance pay rights. However, the extent of this phenomenon is impossible to estimate.

The information presented in this section indicates that the Chilean labor market has become more flexible during the Concertación governments, both in terms of the hiring conditions of individual workers as well as through subcontracting arrangements. The different sources of data present a coherent picture in terms of the overall increasing trend toward flexible hiring conditions, although they differ on the extent of this flexibility.

Furthermore, the data illustrate that employment conditions have deteriorated under the Concertación despite the relatively stable regulatory environment described above, in which no substantive changes were made to the basic structure of labor legislation. Employers have circumvented those aspects of labor legislation they oppose—severance pay and union regulation—by increasing the proportion of short-term contracts, rotating workers between different subsidiary companies within a holding group, and subcontracting more workers. These mechanisms specifically reduce the ability of unions to organize effectively and prevent workers from accumulating severance pay entitlements.

Table 12.3 Contributors to the Unemployment Insurance System by Type and Duration of Contract, 2010 (as percentage of total contributors)

	0–3 months	3 months– 2 years	+2–3 years	+3–4 years	+4–5 years	+5–6 years	+6–7 years	Total
Open-ended contracts	19.8	10.0	7.5	5.4	4.2	3.4	3.0	53.3
Atypical contracts	38.6	5.1	1.7	0.6	0.3	0.2	0.1	46.7
Total labor force	58.4	15.1	9.2	6.1	4.5	3.6	3.2	100.0

Source: Superintendencia de AFP, www.sapf.cl.

Table 12.4 Contributors to the Unemployment Insurance System by Type of Contract, 2002–2010 (as percentage of total contributors)

	2002	2003	2004	2005	2006	2007	2008	2009	2010
Open-ended contracts	21.6	37.0	46.4	51.4	55.6	58.4	61.2	64.1	62.4
Atypical contracts	78.4	63.0	53.6	48.6	44.4	41.6	38.8	35.9	37.6
Total contracts	100.0	100.0	100.0	100.0	100.0	100.0	100.0	100.0	100.0

Source: Author's calculations with data from unemployment insurance system database.
Note: All data refer to year-end statistics, except 2010, which corresponds to September.

First, only 43.5 percent of the labor force works under contractual relationships that are covered by traditional labor legislation of the kind that presumes continuous employment with the same employer (i.e., an open-ended contract). The proportion of workers who are likely to unionize is therefore declining.

Second, if we consider the relatively short job durations found even among workers with open-ended contracts, add to this those workers with atypical contracts or without any contracts and the low-income self-employed, we can estimate that approximately two-thirds of the Chilean labor force works under employment conditions that are either short-term or precarious in some way, and therefore unlikely to unionize.

If we add the very high proportion of subcontracted workers to this equation, it becomes obvious why the proportion of Chilean workers who would be able to unionize or be interested in unionizing is low and declining.

The combination of these factors can be summarized as a declining quality of employment for workers, who are facing increasing job instability and find themselves excluded from social security entitlements. In addition, we have to consider that the institutional structures related to the labor market in Chile do not function well: the unemployment insurance system covers only a very small proportion of the unemployed, the vocational training system is ineffective for those workers who most need to upgrade their skills, job placement services are almost nonexistent, and the enforcement of labor regulation is weak (both in terms of compliance and legal prosecution).

Conclusion

Perhaps the most important conclusion the data lead to is that despite consistently high economic growth, employment conditions have not improved in Chile. Although the Chilean labor market looks relatively good by regional standards, this is not an appropriate comparative perspective for a country that hopes to join the ranks of "developed" countries sooner rather than later. Chile's informal sector has not decreased, while atypical forms of work and precariousness have increased. In addition, the positive effects of wage growth are wiped out in the public consciousness by the high levels of inequality that cause the widespread perception that no matter how hard the poor or even the not so poor work, most of the country's wealth accrues to the rich (Huneeus 2003a). Dissatisfaction about overall working conditions is clearly compounded by fears concerning job security, fears that were shown to be justified by the last economic downturn, which caused unemployment rates to double within a year. If we add to this the general perception that Chilean unions are powerless and weak, that workers are afraid of organizing unions because they think their employers will fire them if they do, and that collective bargaining is almost becoming extinct, we can begin to understand why Chileans rarely respond positively when asked about their employment situations.

This chapter presents data that show that employers in Chile have influenced labor market outcomes more as economic rather than as social actors, although as the previous section argued, they have acted politically too. This means that in practice, despite unchanged regulation, the structure of the Chilean labor market has changed, which in turn has further weakened unions. It is this weakening of unions through the contractual conditions of formal employment relationships that has been overlooked by the academic literature as well as by Chilean unions themselves, as they have never included hiring conditions in their political agenda for labor reform.

The Concertación governments, despite having a Center-Left orientation, have acted as an effective regulator of labor relations, leaving free market forces to shape them instead. The consequence of this approach, apart from having a negative effect on equity and economic productivity, is that Chile's unions have been unable to find political purchase.

Notes

1. "La principal fuente de generación de empleo es el crecimiento. No hay programa público, subsidio gubernamental o reforma laboral que pueda competir con la capacidad de una economía sana para generar empleos. El crecimiento sostenido no tiene sustitutos, es el mejor seguro contra el desempleo. Por eso el crecimiento y la estabilidad macroeconómica han sido una prioridad para los gobiernos de la Concertación." Michelle Bachelet, *Election Manifesto*, 2005; author's translation.

2. National opinion polls that investigate questions of well-being and economic expectations are notoriously subjective. Nevertheless, the level of discontent that Chilean workers display with regard to employment issues is consistent and persistent since the early 1990s. That is to say that even when the general economic situation is perceived to be improving, even when unemployment rates are low, Chilean workers complain about their employment situation. See, for example, opinion poll surveys run by the Centro de Estudios Públicos (CEP), the Centro de Estudios de la Realidad Contemporanea (CERC), and the Instituto de Ciencias Sociales (Universidad Diego Portales).

3. Many countries have witnessed a decline in their union movement and activities since the 1980s. However, the Chilean union movement has been particularly weakened in comparative terms by the systematic attempts of the military dictatorship to reduce its numbers, intimidate members through human rights violations, and establish extremely restrictive legislation on union and collective bargaining rights.

4. This chapter really does not do the complexities of the Chilean union movement justice and touches only briefly on the issues of union regulations as they are not central to the task of this book. Since union coverage is so low in Chile, the impact of unions at the national level is more political rather than practical.

5. See the CERC surveys (1999) and the UNDP (1999, 2000). The unemployment crisis is widely recognized as having been an important factor in eroding support for the government, thus turning an election that should have had a foregone conclusion into a very close race indeed.

6. One rather amusing example of these alterations is that workers can now no longer be dismissed for swearing at each other (only if they insult their employer!), nor for their behavior outside of the workplace.

7. In all his speeches, President Lagos puts the unemployment insurance at the top of his list when it comes to enumerating the achievements of his administration, especially when he is talking about issues of social policy. See, for example, the presidential addresses held on May 21 each year (Presidencia de la República 2000–2005).

8. The final legislation was only enacted in January 2007. See Law No. 20.123, "Trabajo en Régimen de Subcontratación y Empresas de Servicios Transitorios."

9. "The idea is to put myself into the situation of the neediest and to ask myself if I could live with my wife and child on 120,000 pesos (US$240). I'm not saying that we're all going to be equal, because that would be utopian . . . but there can be no doubt that there are large companies that earn a lot of money. How can they not allow their workers to participate more in these earnings? They are the ones who help generate the wealth of this country." Author's translation from *El Mercurio* August 3, 2007.

10. The commission is composed of forty-eight experts in total and is presided over by one of Chile's most well-known economists, Patricio Meller. The subcommissions were headed by Andrea Repetto (labor market and policies), Dante Contreras (equity), Humberto Vega (labor market institutions), and Mario Astorga (small companies). For details on the commissions and a dedicated website, see www .trabajoyequidad.cl.

11. Campero further argues that the weakness of the unions is compounded by their internal divisions that prevent them from developing an alternative strategy.

12. An important exception to this general situation is the work of the ILO, which focuses on decent work. We should also note that in 2010 the National Institute of Statistics for the first time began releasing data on contractual and other employment conditions. This is likely to include employment condition variables in future research.

13. The other issues of major national concern are delinquency and public security.

14. This method of classifying workers was developed in Sehnbruch (2004, 2006). I have argued extensively elsewhere that other forms of analyzing the Chilean labor force miss the legal entitlements that form the basis of an employment relationship. This method of analysis was adopted by the government in 2009 (see Ruiz-Tagle and Sehnbruch 2010).

15. Although Chilean labor law recognizes the existence of a working relationship even if a contract did not exist, obtaining this recognition (and therefore the associated entitlements) requires the worker to take legal action, which is time consuming and costly, and therefore not an option available to most workers in Chile. In practice, therefore, not having a contract is equivalent to not having any legal protection at all.

16. This is consistent with data gathered by the Encla surveys. According to the 2008 Encla, half of the open-ended contracts last no longer than three years, while one in five ends within one year after being signed.

17. The data from the unemployment insurance system contradict survey data as workers generally indicate how many years they have worked at the same company, without distinguishing the number of times they have had to sign new contracts from subsidiaries of the same holding company.

13

Education: Freedom of Choice or Enterprise?

Gregory Elacqua and Pablo González Soto

Chile's secondary school graduation rates have increased: almost 90 percent of twenty-five- to thirty-four-year-olds hold high school degrees versus less than 40 percent of fifty-five- to sixty-four-year-olds. Access to higher education has expanded fourfold over the last twenty years. More than 1 million students are enrolled today in institutions of higher education (compared to less than 250,000 in 1990). Today, seven out of ten Chileans attending university are the first generation in their families to do so. At the same time, national and international tests point to significant improvements in the quality of Chile's primary and secondary schools while the socioeconomic achievement gap has also narrowed.

So why did students organize the most important social movement of the Concertación period? And perhaps even more importantly, how is it that as soon as the Concertación left office, protests over education exploded and formed probably the most far-reaching social movement in Chile's recent democratic history?

The simple answer to these questions is that while coverage of schooling has expanded, the quality of education is perceived to be lacking by students, parents, and the Chilean population as a whole. Equally problematic is the high cost of education in Chile, which takes up a higher proportion of the income of recently graduated students than in other OECD countries. In addition, public anger has been aggravated by the lack of regulation of Chile's education system. Both at the school and university level educational institutions are perceived to be raking in large profits funded by unreasonable price increases and taxpayers' money: the sector is seen as being ruled by freedom of enterprise rather than the freedom of choice that the system's originators promised. But perhaps the most significant problem is the inequality that characterizes Chile's education system on all levels: the gap between public and private education is one of the widest in the world.

One important question the student movement has generated is whether the Piñera government of 2011 is paying the price for poorly conceived Concertación educational policies, or whether it is reaping the fruits of having obstructed educational reform over the last twenty years. As we will see in this chapter, both the Concertación and the right-wing opposition were trapped in the transitional enclaves that were born out of the Pinochet legacy. However, the Right was definitely more comfortable in these enclaves than the Concertación.

In fact, education policy is one of the public policy issues that most clearly illustrates the authoritarian and transitional enclaves that were the legacy of the military dictatorship: three days prior to handing over government to the Concertación, the military regime enshrined the education reforms it had implemented during its period in office into the constitution by enacting the Organic Constitutional Law of Education (Ley Orgánica Constitucional de Enseñanza, LOCE). This constitutional reform meant that future governments could only change education legislation with a two-thirds majority in the Senate, a condition that, as we know from previous chapters in this volume, was impossible to achieve under the constitution that Pinochet had forced on the country.

From the perspective of history, it seems incredible that a democratic government would feel bound by legislation instituted by a dictatorship three days before giving up power. However, as in the many other policy areas discussed in this volume, the delicate balance of transition politics at the time shaped both the pace and depth of education reform during the Concertación period, and thus transformed the authoritarian enclaves into transitional enclaves. In the area of education reform, however, the authoritarian enclaves were more permanent and explicit due to this constitutional restriction.

So although education policy figured highly among the Concertación's priorities during its twenty years in office, the coalition never attempted to undertake any structural reforms of the education system it inherited and maintained its free market orientation. However, it did attempt to improve the system on a continuous basis and struggled with the position of the right-wing opposition that was steeped in free market ideology. In particular, the Right refused to contemplate any legislation that would favor public schools over private schools, even if public schools were most in need of support. In fact, they pushed for a shared financing system discussed below, which especially favored private schools. As a result of this combination of authoritarian legacy, constitutional constraints, and right-wing opposition, Chile is one of the very few countries in the world where schools subsidized by public funds had the right to select students at preschool age (forbidden up to sixth grade only in 2009), expel students who underperform, and make a profit.

This chapter explores the politics of education reform during the Concertación period. It traces the different emphases of each president: from the Aylwin government's focus on inputs into education and appeasing the teachers' union, the Frei government's top priority on education and its institution of important reforms such as the increase of the school day from a half day to a full day, the Lagos administration's emphasis on improving the educational system's equity, and finally the Bachelet government's forced decision to prioritize education after the student movement of 2006 and final success in bringing down Pinochet's organic constitutional law of education (González 1998; Mizala 2007).[1] Although this reform was not as structural as many educators had hoped, it was still important to shrug off this legacy of the dictatorship.

The Legacy of the Dictatorship

All social sectors in Chile underwent important transformations during the dictatorship, consisting of a simplistic (but revolutionary) application of neoliberal principles inspired by Milton Friedman (Friedman 1962; Fischer, González, and Serra 2006; González 2000).[2] However, probably no other sector experienced such a deep and controversial transformation as education. Prior to the Pinochet education reforms, Chile had a centralized public schooling system with almost 80 percent of students in public schools managed by the Ministry of Education; 15 percent of schools were private and received some limited public subsidies, and the rest were elite private schools that did not receive government funding.

In 1981, the military government enacted a sweeping reform program. First, the administration and ownership of state schools were gradually transferred from the central government to individual municipalities between 1981 and 1987.[3] In this process, teachers lost their status as civil servants, meaning they could then be easily hired or fired. Second, a voucher system was introduced for all public and privately subsidized schools: anyone could set up a subsidized school provided they had a high school diploma. The requirements for receiving the voucher were extremely lax and demanded only basic infrastructure and staff.[4]

The goal of the national voucher program was to induce competition between private and municipal schools and help middle-class and low-income students obtain a better education. The Chicago Boys technocrats in the Ministry of Finance maintained that the lack of incentives explained the low performance of public schools. Competition was expected to generate new schools that would compete in a free market, which in turn would produce a higher quality of education, preferably at the same cost. The ideological principle of *libertad de enseñanza* (freedom of teaching) became preeminent and was used as a justification for giving subsidized schools the right to expel students more easily. While at the time there was no empirical evidence to support this theory, the technocrats used this argument to convince the military government of the need to introduce such a sweeping reform, which was conceived, designed, and implemented in less than eighteen months (Guari 1998).[5]

Subsidized schools at this time received a voucher from the state and were allowed to make a profit. Although they could theoretically charge top-up fees, these would then have been deducted from the voucher, and therefore did not constitute a financing mechanism that made much economic sense. Top-up fees were therefore rarely ever charged.

The Pinochet education reform also had a strong political motivation. During the early 1980s the national teachers' union maintained very active opposition to the military regime despite the repression that was directed against it. The military government hoped that the reforms would reduce the strength of the union by breaking up the centralized bureaucracy of the public school system (González 1998). However, the military regime's reasons and justifications for education reforms are for the most part speculative given that the authoritarian regime precluded a public discussion of the many trade-offs of school choice and educational vouchers that have been an important part of education policy debates in other countries (Godwin and Kemerer 2002; Henig 2008). The explicit expectation was that the quality of the schooling system would improve even though the state had not established its own authority to regulate the quality of education services. Furthermore, no mechanism was established to evaluate progress. The first national test of educational performance was established in 1982, but was undertaken for internal information purposes only and did not produce comparable data over time. At the time, Chile had already been doing well in comparative terms on issues such as enrollment and dropout rates with a pace of improvement similar to South Korea's. After the reform, however, this rate of improvement diminished (Bellei and González 2003).

In addition, fiscal constraints during the 1980s, especially as a result of the profound crisis of 1982–1983, led to a significant underinvestment in the education sector as a whole. After the reform, the real value of the voucher declined by 25 percent and teacher salaries were reduced by 40 percent in real terms, which, combined with deteriorated working conditions and infrastructure, undermined the morale and prestige of the education sector. Far from achieving its promise of improving the quality of education, the legacy of the dictatorship was a deterioration of standards at all levels, which brought with it significant consequences for the future as students with high academic achievement were discouraged from becoming teachers.

The Educational Reforms of President Aylwin:
Improving the Inputs into the Education System

One of the historical legacies the first Concertación government inherited was a conflict between the traditional educational establishment (which consisted of teachers, their unions, and their representatives in government) and the proponents of the voucher system instituted by the dictatorship (who were mostly economists). While the former preferred traditional public education and wanted to improve it through better regulation, the latter believed that free market mechanisms in the education sector would suffice to improve its quality and coverage.

During the Aylwin administration (1990–1994), the Ministry of Education was dominated by the traditional establishment. Educational policy therefore attempted to circumvent the representatives of the reforms instituted by the military dictatorship, principally the legal entities responsible for running schools, the *sostenedores,* which were either municipalities with mayors appointed by the dictatorship or private entities. This meant policies targeted individual schools directly with additional resources and disregarded (and at times interfered with) market mechanisms. The aim of this strategy was to restore a deteriorated public school system in a political context where legislative initiatives required negotiating with the right-wing opposition.[6]

The government's stated education policy objective shifted from "access and quality" in the 1980s to "quality and equity," although equity was not a particularly important component in education policies instituted during the Aylwin administration, with the exception of the 900 Schools Program (Programa 900 Escuelas) that provided resources and technical support to low-performing and disadvantaged schools (García-Huidobro 1994) but accounted for a negligible proportion of the total education budget (González, Mizala, and Romaguera 2000).

An example of the authorities' disregard for market mechanisms was the teacher labor statute enacted in 1991 (Estatuto Docente), which was a special concession to the teachers' union (González 1998).[7] Its original version was the most rigid piece of labor legislation ever enacted in the country and it applied mostly to municipal schools. The statute established a single pay structure of wages tied mainly to years of experience and thereby de facto centralized bargaining.[8] The objective of introducing a national pay scale was to reduce the differences between teachers with similar experience and responsibilities and to eliminate employers' discretion in wage setting.[9] The teacher labor statute also made it virtually impossible to fire a public school teacher even after the official age of retirement, and reduced the authority of municipalities to reassign teachers to schools within the same municipality.

Three Christian Democrats in the cabinet at the time (Minister of Finance Alejandro Foxley, Secretary General of the President Edgardo Boeninger, and Minister of Labor and Social Security René Cortázar) attempted to convince the president of the negative consequences of the teacher labor statute. The president supported the minister of education, Ricardo Lagos, leader of the left-wing bloc (PS-PPD) of the ruling coalition. However, the divide was not so much between parties of the coalition but rather constituted the first important confrontation between economists and educators within the Concertación. Educators dominated the Ministry of Education and included historically well-respected leaders of the union such as Alfonso Bravo, a Christian Democrat. The public *sostenedores* opposed the teacher labor statute. However, since many of them were appointed by the military government, they had little political influence at the time.[10]

It is interesting to note that several opposition lawmakers also supported the teacher labor statute because it protected school principals, many of whom were appointed during the dictatorship, from being fired. The opposition anticipated a poor electoral result in the municipal elections—which were to be held one year after the enactment of the new teacher labor statute—and therefore hoped that satisfying school principals would help mobilize votes in their schools and municipalities. The conservative opposition's position on this issue contradicted their ideological public discourse on labor flexibility and modern management (and their economists' opinions). Despite this, they blocked any legislation that would require principals to participate in a competitive and transparent hiring process until 2005.

The teacher labor statute that established a single pay structure of wages and made it difficult to dismiss teachers, combined with the national voucher program that tied school budgets to a subsidy based on student enrollment and attendance, produced large financial deficits in most municipalities. The government set up a temporary fund for municipalities to defray the costs of maintaining higher teacher salaries. Many mayors complained that municipalities were still underfunded. In response, the government designed different short-term mechanisms to help alleviate the municipal financial crisis (Baytelman et al. 1999).[11]

In addition to the teacher labor statute, the educators in the Ministry of Education advocated for more targeted programs. During the Aylwin administration, the ministry introduced policies intended to improve graduation rates and the quality of education in the most disadvantaged schools (García-Huidobro 1999; Cox and González 1997).[12] Although it is generally not possible to evaluate the impact of these programs on test scores, one such program, the P-900 (which worked with the 900 lowest performing primary schools in the country), did produce positive results (García-Huidobro 1994; Chay, McEwan, and Urquiola 2003).[13] The problem with these educational programs, however, was that once schools graduated from the program, their results deteriorated again, especially as parents had the option of moving their children to nearby schools with better results (González, Mizala, and Romaguera 2000).

All of these programs were designed to circumvent the public *sostenedores* that the decentralization of the education system had instituted during the dictatorship, and dealt directly with school principals and teachers. At the time, most municipalities lacked the administrative capacity and resources to provide technical assistance to their schools that decentralization required. The Ministry of Education supervisors therefore had to fill this hole and assume a more pedagogical role at the school level.[14] This division of responsibilities tended to further blur the lines of accountability for public school performance and reduced the effectiveness of the incentives the voucher was supposed to create.

As discussed in Chapter 8, the government of President Aylwin undertook an important tax reform in 1993, which was designed to palliate the social debt the Concertación had inherited on all levels from the dictatorship. A significant proportion of the money raised by this reform was used to improve educational standards in Chile. During the negotiations for the reform, the right-wing opposition conditioned their support on the inclusion of two bills: tax breaks for school donations and the establishment of a shared financing mechanism for schools (*financiamiento compartido*). The school donation legislation enacted in 1993 provided tax incentives to private companies that donated money or equipment to schools, but it had little impact because companies feared increased scrutiny from tax authorities if they made use of this mechanism. The shared financing law, enacted in 1993, allowed schools to charge fees that would top-up their voucher.[15] Once top-up fees were introduced, they became compulsory for all parents sending their children to the school regardless of their socioeconomic status.

The justification for the shared financing program was that it would inject more private resources into education and increase parental choice. The program's design was attractive for the Ministry of Finance—which negotiated the agreement with the opposition—because discounts were to be applied to the voucher progressively, based on the fees charged, which meant more private resources flowed into the school system. However, the reform reduced the discount rate compared to the existing system.

Some critics have argued that both measures increased the potential for inequality and segregation in the system (González 1998; Elacqua 2006), as these resources are correlated with families' socioeconomic status. How-

ever, the progressive deduction of the value of the voucher contributed to
the targeting of public resources while private resources in the voucher system contributed to narrowing the gap with private nonvoucher schools
(González, Mizala, and Romaguera 2000).

An All-Encompassing Reform, 1994–2000

The second period of the coalition was marked by a deep conviction by
many high ranking officials, including the president, regarding the importance of improving the quality and equity of schooling. The 1994 National
Education Commission was key to creating the momentum for the next
wave of reforms. Chaired by the prominent education scholar, José Joaquín
Brunner, its mandate was to recommend short- and long-term policies for
boosting achievement and narrowing the learning gaps. The technical report
was followed by a political analysis, highlighting the limits of a possible
consensus on many of the issues under discussion. For instance, the commission called for a profound revision of the teacher labor statute, which
was rejected by the teachers' union and several representatives on the Left.
The education reform path in Chile continued to be defined by the tensions
between the two souls of the Concertación reformers within the Ministry of
Education (the educators and the economists) and the conservative opposition, which continued to defend the unregulated national voucher program.

During the first two years of the Frei administration, the government
emphasized financing and governance. One of the first bills sent to congress was an increase in the real value of the voucher (González 1998). The
legislative initiative also introduced modifications to the teacher labor
statute. This was partly a response to pressure from a new and powerful political constituency: the newly elected mayors, many of whom were members of Concertación parties, were so disgruntled by the combination of
lack of funding and responsibilities as school administrators that they
threatened to "give schools back to the central government." The legislation
passed by Frei also allowed mayors to reallocate teachers among schools
and to dismiss teachers when a municipality experienced declines in enrollments (and a corresponding reduction in their budgets). Although these
changes might be considered slight, the original version of the Teacher
Statute had not even contemplated this minimal level of flexibility. Rural
schools were also provided with some incentives to merge. All of these
measures were designed to correct for differences of costs between different types of schools and to strengthen the management and fiscal capabilities of municipalities.

The 1994 negotiation between the government and the teachers' union
resulted in important changes to the wage structure of teachers. However,

the outcome of this negotiation weakened the position of Concertación union leaders who accepted these changes. Since then the Communist Party has been in control of the teachers' union. Part of the wage readjustment was channeled through a new supply-side incentive scheme, the National Evaluation System of Publicly Funded Schools (Sistema Nacional de Evaluación de Desempeño de Establecimientos Subvencionados [SNED]), which was implemented in 1996. The system provided a monetary incentive to teachers who worked in the highest performing schools—the top 25 percent after adjusting for student demographics. To start challenging the popular notion—espoused by the teachers' union—that teachers were underpaid, the government introduced a minimum wage bill applicable to all teachers working in publicly funded (municipal or private voucher) schools.[16] The government also made public the starting and average teacher wage levels based on a workload of forty-four hours per week instead of the thirty hours per week previously reported.

Union leaders and their advisers tend to justify their calls for high wage increases on the basis of a historical deterioration of teacher salaries that occurred during the dictatorship. However, teacher wages are not low if compared to workers with similar years of education (Mizala and Romaguera 2005), and they are similar to OECD averages in relation to the GDP per capita. A problem that has not been resolved is the low quality of the institutions providing teacher education, as the state lacks any channel of command or other tools to affect the behavior of these institutions—and aside from the competitive funds, it has seldom used incentives to induce higher quality.

In 1995, the secretary general of the president met separately with the ministers of the social sectors to invite them to propose social policies that could become the legacy of the Frei administration. The internal debate that ensued within the Ministry of Education is a good example of how educators and economists within the Concertación were unable to agree on many of the fundamental education reform issues.[17] However, a compromise was reached and the government decided to advocate for an extended school day. This was a significant reform in a country where most public schools in urban areas normally had a morning and an afternoon shift for two separate cohorts of students. Advocates argued that extending the school day would have a positive effect on learning achievements as well as on other externalities such increased female labor participation, a decline in risky behavior among adolescents, and more cohesive local communities.

President Frei favored the proposal made by the Ministry of Education and announced the extended school day reform in his 1996 equivalent of the State of the Union speech. Schools would be required to increase the length of the school day to total forty-two hours per week and would receive a higher per pupil voucher to finance the increased costs of having longer school days. The reform was implemented gradually as it required abolishing school shifts, which in turn required substantial investment in new infrastructure.[18] Rural schools, which already had single shifts and did not require additional infrastructure, implemented the extended day reform before most urban schools. The costs of this reform were significant (US$2 billion in capital expenditure and more than a 30 percent increase in recurrent expenditures in the long run), and it was not implemented with adequate procedures for evaluating its impact in mind. However, a quasi-experimental evaluation showed modest improvements in tests scores (Bellei 2009).

The government also introduced a new curriculum from preschool to high school, which was implemented gradually and combined with teacher training programs. Prior to this reform, Chile had an out-of-date national curriculum and schools had a lot of flexibility on the minimum contents they were required to teach. In 1995, the government also began to publish school-level test scores. The average test scores were made available to parents, teachers, and administrators.[19]

The Concertación members of the education committee in both chambers of congress were concerned that the voucher system was exacerbating school segregation. To address these concerns, in 1997 the government introduced a compulsory scholarship program for voucher schools. The objective of this measure was to provide schools with incentives to enroll disadvantaged students who were unable to pay school fees. In addition, recognizing that parents usually expect a long-term relationship with the school they choose for their children, voucher schools were required to inform parents at the end of the school year of the maximum increase in the average school fee over the following three years.

Accountability and Equity, 2000–2006

Since the return to democracy in Chile in 1990, following the advice of educators, the core of education reforms focused on improving quality and equity through curricular reform, targeted programs, and longer school days. However, the economists in the Frei administration also made some modifications to the teacher labor statute and introduced pay incentives for teachers based on merit. Overall, the Aylwin and Frei administrations adopted a pragmatic and gradual process of change. They did not try to restructure the organizational and funding components introduced by the military government. They concentrated on promoting quality and equity in education within the framework inherited by the military regime. In 2000, however, there was a general consensus among most reformers on the Left and some on the Right that some of the regulations under which the education system operated fostered inequities and were an obstacle to achieving the overriding goals of boosting student achievement and narrowing learning gaps. For example, Chile had an unrestricted flat per-pupil voucher that could be topped up by parents. This provided few incentives for schools to locate in poor neighborhoods and enroll disadvantaged children from low-income families. Private voucher schools were also permitted to select students based on independent criteria (interviews, tests, etc.), which also likely induced self-selection of low-income parents out of high-quality private voucher schools and exacerbated school segregation. The government also provided parents with little information on school quality, and schools and teachers were not held accountable for schooling outcomes.

The Lagos administration set out to introduce changes in some of these aspects of Chile's education system. The government also continued to develop compensatory programs to equalize the distribution of learning opportunities.

Finance

An adjusted voucher law figured foremost in this strategy. The Preferential Subsidy Act (Subvención Escolar Preferencial [SEP]), which was designed and sent to congress by the Lagos administration late in his term, was passed by the Bachelet administration in 2007. The SEP law recognizes that it is more costly to educate disadvantaged students with an extra per-pupil subsidy (50 percent over the base voucher) for students classified as priority in the Ministry of Education's socioeconomic status classification system and with additional increases for schools depending on the concentration of priority students.[20] The SEP law is also designed to increase the incentives of high-quality private voucher schools to enroll disadvantaged students and locate in poor neighborhoods underserved by local public schools. The SEP's aim was to enable schools to devote more resources to children from disadvantaged home environments, to boost their achievement, and narrow the persistent learning gaps in Chile.

This is perhaps the most aggressive educational policy to reduce achievement gaps ever launched by any country in the world. It favored 40 percent of total enrollments. Previously, the Netherlands increased their voucher amounts for immigrants and eventually for all economically disadvantaged students (between 2.1 and 1.8 times the regular voucher) but this affected a smaller proportion of the population. South Africa instituted a distribution rule awarding schools that were in the lowest quintile seven times more resources than schools in the top quintiles, but this rule included recurrent expenditures other than teacher salaries.

It is still too early to evaluate the impact of the SEP, as the program was fully implemented only in 2010, and schools are still learning how to take advantage of these extra resources.

Regulations and School Accountability

The Lagos administration also introduced several changes to the rules and regulations under which the voucher system operates. The legislative reforms regulated school selection procedures. The SEP law forbids participating schools from using parental interviews and admissions tests to select and expel students. In addition, participating schools cannot charge tuition to priority students. During the school year school administrators can no longer suspend or expel students because they cannot pay tuition. Prior to the SEP, schools were allowed to select students and could expel pupils that fell behind on tuition payments.

In 2005, the government also established low-income student quotas (affirmative action) to foster school integration and expand the schooling options of disadvantaged families. Schools that received government funding—public and private voucher schools—were required to enroll at least 15 percent of "vulnerable" students, unless the school could demonstrate that it had not received enough applications to fill this quota.[21] This was more of a declaration of concern as this law (contrary to the SEP law, which conditioned extra funding) had no enforcement mechanisms, which were frowned upon by the right-wing opposition.

The government also changed the rules that must be adhered to by schools that receive public funding. SEP ties the additional per-student voucher to an increased role of the Ministry of Education in monitoring and classifying schools based on student performance and holding them accountable for their outcomes. SEP classifies schools in three categories (autonomous, emerging, and in recovery) based on student performance over time and holding them accountable for their outcomes. The classification affects the degree of autonomy schools have in spending additional resources.[22] The SEP law requires the ministry to publish the school classification on its website and schools are required to explain to parents the consequences of their classification.

Teacher Accountability

The Aylwin and Frei administrations followed a three-pronged strategy to professionalize teaching and to attract higher achieving high school graduates into the profession. First, they introduced a teacher labor statute that established centralized bargaining, which made it virtually impossible to fire a public school teacher who is not performing adequately. The law also introduced a single pay structure of wages and dramatically increased public teachers' salaries. Second, they introduced a merit pay incentive based on a qualitative and quantitative assessment of teacher performance and a team (school) incentive named SNED. The authorities also created an incentive for teachers who worked in disadvantaged schools. Finally, they invested copious resources in professional development for existing teachers. This included several measures announced in the 1996 presidential address such as competitive funds to improve the quality of initial teacher training institutions, short-term internships in prestigious institutions abroad for teachers, an annual prize for the best teacher in each province, and so on. The ministry also had teacher training programs, and the installment of the new curriculum was accompanied by significant training in its content. The Teacher Statute also contained a pay increase linked to the number of hours spent on teacher training courses certified by the ministry. All of these programs and incentives likely affected the quality of applicants (Arellano 2000; Vegas and Umansky 2005).[23]

Despite improvements in salaries and labor conditions, the quality of the teacher force was still inadequate. For example, according to the TIMSS results in 1999, only 24 percent of Chilean teachers were confident in the mastery of the skills of the subject they taught, whereas the average in other countries was 63 percent (TIMSS 2000). Moreover, only 55 percent of teachers felt confident in their teaching skills, compared to 84 percent of their peers in other countries.

The Lagos administration adopted two measures to confront this policy challenge. First, the government instituted a compulsory system of teacher evaluations in public schools. In 2004, Minister Bitar succeeded in implementing the public school evaluation established by the original version of the Teacher Statute—successfully opposed by the union for the previous thirteen years. This comprehensive assessment consisted of a self-evaluation, an interview with the evaluator, a principal and assistant principal evaluation, a peer assessment conducted by a teacher from a different school in the same municipality, and a video of classroom performance. Teachers were classified into four categories of performance. Teachers who received a negative evaluation over two consecutive years were required to leave the classroom and participate in an intensive teacher training program for one year. The evaluation allowed municipalities to dismiss teachers who received a negative evaluation three years in a row, while providing a generous severance package.

The second measure taken to improve teacher quality was to increase the transparency in the hiring of new public school principals. The theory behind this measure was that competent principals would be more likely to attract and retain high quality teachers, especially in the most disadvantaged public schools, and would be more effective leaders. The Public

School Principal Act, enacted in March 2005, required municipalities to make all principals go through a competitive hiring process. The law started with the principals that had more than twenty years of experience (those appointed during the dictatorship). This legislation was opposed by several right-wing lawmakers because many of the public school principals appointed by the military government continued to run public schools.

High School Graduation Rates

Although high school enrollment rates had improved, Chile continued to face high school dropout rates in the poorest schools.[24] The Lagos administration introduced two measures to confront the problem. First, in 2000, it launched the High School for All Students Program (Liceo para Todos), a targeted program that supported disadvantaged high schools, including pro-retention scholarships granted to students at risk of dropping out.[25] The program also provided a subsidy for schools in exchange for their commitment to reduce dropouts. The second strategy used to reduce the number of dropouts was to extend compulsory education to twelve years. The Twelve Years Education Act, enacted in 2003, guaranteed students access to free secondary education (in the municipal sector).

Student Protests and Change, 2006–2010

The education reforms of the first three Concertación administrations were politically popular because they provided politicians with resources to distribute to constituencies (e.g., jobs in construction and teacher training programs; children in school more hours a day, which helps reduce child care expenses). They also imposed fewer costs and provided more benefits (jobs, job stability, improved working conditions, and wages) for teachers, administrators, and bureaucrats. The conservative political opposition was also receptive to the reforms because they did not challenge the voucher program and the decentralization of public schools.

Most experts at the time agreed that these investments increased coverage especially for low-income children in high school[26] and preschool,[27] improved the quality of school facilities, provided many children with the opportunity to spend more hours a day at school (Bellei 2010), and increased teachers' salaries, the quality of applicants, and school construction.[28] Parents also reported high levels of satisfaction with the quality of their children's schools (Fundación Futuro 2004).[29] Despite these positive outcomes, and a fourfold increase in spending in inflation-adjusted terms between 1990 and 2006, as summarized in the introduction to this chapter, there had not been significant improvement in the average quality of learning up to that point. Student achievement in Chile was among the highest in Latin America, but still lagged significantly behind a number of emerging countries in Asia and Eastern Europe, as demonstrated by the poor results achieved on the Trends in International Mathematics and Science Study (TIMSS), the Program for International Student Assessment (PISA), and the International Civic Education Study (CIVIC). National test scores were also stagnant between 1997 and 2006, and large test score gaps persisted between socioeconomic groups. Schools were also stratified by socioeconomic status. Students attending private schools, on average, came from families that had much higher incomes and were headed by parents with substantially more schooling than students enrolled in public schools.

These factors converged to motivate one of the largest protests in Chilean history that is widely known as "the march of the penguins"—in reference to the protesters' school uniforms. The protests began in July 2006, less than three months after President Michelle Bachelet took office. The first Bachelet minister of education, a Christian Democrat, was functional to the student movement, as he publicly criticized the fact that public education was handed over to the municipalities (and without having designed an alternative), perhaps reflecting for the first time in public the dissent between economists and educators within the Concertación. More than 600,000 high school students walked out of class and occupied hundreds of schools all over Chile. The student movement had widespread popular support among university students, the teachers' union, the workers' central unions, and average citizens.[30]

The student demands included more teachers and improved school construction, the elimination of fees for the national college entrance exam, free student public transportation fares, and most importantly, the repeal of the LOCE (Ley Orgánica Constitucional de Enseñanza).[31]

President Bachelet responded to the students' demands by creating a Presidential Commission of Education of eighty-one members, including representatives of students (secondary and university), parents, municipalities, rectors, the private sector, teachers, lawmakers, indigenous people, and experts. Following the recommendations of the majority of the members of the commission, the government introduced three education reform proposals along with additional resources.[32] First, her administration proposed to repeal the LOCE to create a new General Law of Education (LGE), which would redefine the balance between school and teacher autonomy and students' rights to receive a high-quality education. The key points of the legislative initiative dealt with increasing public and private voucher school regulation, reducing discrimination and selection in private voucher schools, introducing grade-level reforms, facilitating lateral teacher entry, and allowing the creation of a system-wide accountability program (quality assurance system). President Bachelet also introduced a bill that created the education quality assurance system, including the creation of two agencies that would be responsible for school supervision and accountability: the Education Quality Agency and the Superintendence of Education. Finally, the Bachelet administration introduced a separate bill that would reform the institutional framework for publicly managed education and provide additional funding and technical pedagogical support to public schools.

The Chilean legislature enacted the LGE in 2008. The LGE had bipartisan support and was passed by a majority. The other Quality Assurance System was not approved until August 2011, well after the end of Bachelet's term. The public school reform initiative is still under congressional debate.[33]

Conflicts and Compromises

Even though the divergent approaches (teacher labor statute, schooling inputs, program incentives, accountability) defined the contours of the education reform debate in Chile between 1990 and 2010, its core consisted of widely shared goals. The central goals of improving student outcomes and narrowing the gaps were well established. Chilean policymakers have judged schools first and foremost in terms of outcomes (mainly achievement, but also completion rates). But the reform consensus that produced real traction in the national debate and in classrooms began to unravel over the design and implementation of the Ley SEP and the LGE. Educators were concerned that these legislative initiatives were too "market oriented," while some right-wing members of congress criticized their heavy-handedness and the fact that some measures curtailed the autonomy for schools.

The LGE that passed congress was rejected by students, the national teachers' union, and a few Concertación lawmakers, who demanded the overhaul of the national voucher program. One of their main objections was that for-profit schools were still allowed to compete with nonprofit and public schools for students.[34] Some lawmakers and Concertación reformers (educators) also opposed the SEP and the Quality Assurance System because they claimed that they would legitimize Chile's voucher system.

The main criticism from the conservative opposition and the private voucher school guild was that school accountability and no school selection would stifle innovation and restrict the diversity of private school supply and parents' freedom to pursue their own educational preferences. They also claimed that these initiatives restricted school autonomy, which violated the "freedom to educate" principle enshrined in the constitution.

Other issues that have proven to be difficult to handle due to the set of rules governing the educational system include the admission process of schools (many schools put three- to five-year-olds under heavy pressure to take entrance exams), expulsion policies, sexual education policies, and civic education. UNDP (2010) gives an account of the difficulties in implementing sexual education policies due to the high transaction costs that result partially from the lack of a line of command from the ministry to the schools and the low visibility of the problem in the educational arena. A similar problem of lack of mechanisms to improve the supply of initial teacher training institutions or control of the number and quality of new teachers is part of the problem of low-quality teaching (OECD 2004). Other illustrations of the coordination problems arising from the unregulated market and the incentives in place are the decline in the aggregate pupil teacher ratio and the continuous increase in the number of private schools while the number of students is falling.

Contentious as the education debate seemed, it still continued to be defined by a consensus about the broader goals of quality and equity. This shared vision allowed for a political agreement between Ministry of Education officials and technical advisers of the right-wing opposition that was endorsed by political parties, which was key for coordinating the congressional consensus needed for the passage of the Quality Assurance System, which was enacted during the Piñera administration after four years under congressional review.

Conclusion: Did the Concertación Deliver on Its Promise to Improve Quality and Equity?

Pending issues include the expansion and quality improvement of preschool education for three- to five-year-olds, the quality of teachers, and the quality of teacher training institutions. While the first requires mostly the allocation of more resources, the last two have mostly relied on market mechanisms and small-scale competitive funds that have not delivered adequate results. Policy innovations on all three fronts should be expected in the near future.

In summary, there has been a tension within the Concertación that still persists. The Concertación's economists have attempted to regulate the education market created by the dictatorship while the Concertación educators have emphasized inputs and have so far lacked the force to reverse market reforms. The first decade was mostly dominated by educators, with programs that supplied inputs and attempted to guide process improvement within schools. While these initiatives were the prerogative of the executive branch, the conservative opposition did not oppose them—and approved their financing in the budget law—because they did not alter the status quo, the national voucher program, and the principle "freedom of choice" (or more precisely, in its Chilean version, "freedom of enterprise"). While they often complained to the minister or undersecretary of finance when middle-ranking officials in the Ministry of Education diverted some inputs from private voucher schools, they usually supported most measures because they did not alter the structure of the school system. Moreover, most policies introduced during the first decade of democratic rule benefited private *sostenedores* in the form of higher subsidies, without any obligations except for the teacher minimum wage. While the right-wing opposition publicly criticized the teacher labor statute, it is partly responsible for the rigidity that protects its public school teacher and principal constituency appointed during the dictatorship.

Some reforms might be considered advances in strengthening market mechanisms: increases in the value of the per student subsidy not linked to wages and the introduction of an adjusted voucher and greater school accountability (Ley SEP), all within the framework of educational vouchers and parental choice. These structural reforms were often rejected by Concertación educator reformers because they believed such reforms would strengthen the market and private schools would have incentives to compete with public schools in poor neighborhoods for the most vulnerable students.

The supply-side incentive SNED was approved as part of a wage readjustment when the mood was favorable for initiatives that would modernize the public sector and link wages to productivity. Individual evaluation of teachers was made possible when mayors gained political influence and politicians started to lose confidence in supply-side programs to narrow the learning gaps. However, these evaluations are expensive and unlikely to be cost effective if they are only used for contract termination.

The right-wing opposition resisted market regulation during most of the Concertación period. Unlike right-wing parties in most developed nations, including US Republicans, they have defended for-profit schooling and the right of schools to shape their pool of students over parents' right to choose the best school for their children. The secondary school student protests in 2006 and the demand of a higher quality public education system were key to the right-wing parties' acceptance of a new regulatory framework. The deliberation process, first in the National Education Commission, followed by a technical and political agreement between the two major blocs, yielded the Quality Assurance System, which passed in April 2011. However, in 2011 secondary and university student protesters demanded a new deal for public universities, the return of municipal schools to the state, and that for-profit institutions in primary, secondary, and tertiary institutions be ineligible for public funding.

The fact that the current school architecture in Chile (municipal schools, private voucher schools, and school choice) was conceived, designed, and implemented during the dictatorship is still an important political issue for many in the Concertación two decades after the return to democracy. The unregulated market has exacerbated the decline of public school enrollments from 60 percent in 1990 to 40 percent today, and increased school segregation, and thus, according to some, discredited the entire system.

As this chapter demonstrates, the discussion of educational reform in Chile is deeply rooted in opposing ideological doctrines and is therefore extremely contentious. It is this ideological divide that converted an authoritarian enclave (the LOCE) into a transitional enclave, which ensured that educational reforms, even when their objective was to improve equity of access and quality, would use market mechanisms to achieve their goals without ever making a significant attempt to strengthen public education for its own sake. It was the student movements of 2006 and especially 2011—not the Concertación—that questioned the overall market-driven logic and structure of Chile's education system. While parts of the coalition may have felt uncomfortable with the structure of the educational system, the logic of the transitional enclaves nevertheless contained this discomfort even once new legislation (the LEGE) put a formal end to the authoritarian LOCE and at least theoretically made structural reforms possible.

Student protesters often refer to Pablo Neruda and Gabriela Mistral, Chile's two Nobel laureate poets, originally from blue-collar families who studied in a free education system at all levels and taught in Chilean public schools, as a romantic tribute to public education. The future is uncertain regarding structural reforms, which have not been undertaken since 1981. Rather, the objective of education reform over the last two decades has been to fine-tune the system, but fine-tuning has more to do with the rationality of political elites in a political system that by design requires compromise rather than the sweeping change demanded by many of its citizens.

Notes

Pablo González would like to acknowledge support from the Project Implementación e Instrumentación de Políticas Públicas en su Dimensión Regional y Local, SOC-08, 2o Concurso Anillos de Investigación en Ciencias Sociales, Innovación de Políticas Públicas, CONICYT, and CONICYT-PIA Project CIE-05.

1. Previous efforts in the same spirit include González (1998) and Mizala (2007).

2. Fischer et al. (2006) provide a comprehensive account of these transformations in the pension, health, and education systems and González (2000) describes the key issues of the higher education reforms.

3. One exception was the transfer of seventy-two vocational high schools to a group of business guilds on a five-year contractual basis (without a bidding process). They were granted bloc subsidies—that were not tied to student enrollments—to run the schools.

4. While private *sostenedores* were allowed to open a school with the infrastructure and staff for the first grade of attendance alone, municipalities were required to have a building for a complete school. Municipalities were also required to go through a rigorous project evaluation process, which was often difficult for rural and poor municipalities. Both elements contributed to explain a response that was often too slow to accommodate population flows produced by changes in social housing policies.

5. The empirical evidence in Chile today on the effects of greater school competition on efficiency is mixed. See, for example, Hsieh and Urquiola (2006) and Gallego (2002).

6. As explained elsewhere in this book, this situation prevailed during the democratic period. The Concertación's majority of nearly 60 percent of the votes was not reflected in the distribution of congressional seats given that some members were still appointed by the military government in the initial period and that representatives and senators were elected through the binomial system.

7. The teachers' union initially opposed the legislation. They demanded that the government return the public schools to the state (González 1998).

8. Since the national pay scale was established, the teachers' union negotiates annual pay increases directly with the Ministry of Education. In addition, the teachers' union participates in the annual negotiation of public sector wages.

9. Anecdotal evidence suggests that mayors appointed by the military government would often pay higher salaries to political employees or relatives, which at the time cast doubt on the transparency of the hiring and firing process and the wage structures of public school teachers.

10. Local elections were not held in Chile until 1992.

11. By 1995, on average, 85 percent of municipalities' education budget financed by the per pupil voucher was allocated to teacher salaries (Baytelman et al. 1999). Fifty out of a total of 341 municipalities allocated over 100 percent of their income from vouchers to teacher salaries, while only 37 spent less than 70 percent on wages.

12. These programs included the P-900, then the MECE Básica (K1–K8) and the MECE Media program (see Cox and González 1997; Garcia-Huidobro 1999).

13. Chay, McEwan, and Urquiola (2003) showed that this could be only partly attributed to mean reversion and therefore the P-900 had a statistically significant positive effect. A similar evaluation of the impact of the other programs is not possible as they affected the whole subsidized education system at the same time (or at least no good record of entrance to the program was kept).

14. Many supervisors considered that the municipal schools were their responsibility, and, given that the municipalities' role was mainly administrative, they often endeavored to exert "pedagogical leadership" over the public schools.

15. While private voucher school owners could choose whether to charge school fees, municipalities were only permitted to levy fees in their high schools if the majority of parents voted in favor of the initiative, and therefore fees have been used by only a handful of elite municipal schools.

16. The purpose of this measure was to improve initial wages without increasing all of the other wage components of the national pay scale.

17. The technocrats' (mostly economists) agenda for strengthening the functioning of the market included the repeal of the Estatuto Docente, means-tested vouchers, fines to schools selecting and expelling students (both practices still common in the country), and an increase in the value of the voucher conditional on later improvements in tests scores, which was rejected by the educators.

18. The Ministry of Education created a special fund for infrastructure that was awarded on a competitive basis, giving priority to the most disadvantaged schools.

19. The equating methodology, implemented by SIMCE (System of Measurement of the Quality of Education) in 1998, allowed for comparability of test scores over time.

20. This system determines whether a student is "priority" based on individual and household surveys collected by the Chilean government.

21. This system determines whether a student is "vulnerable" based on individual and household surveys collected by the government nutrition agency JUNAEB (National Scholarship and School Aid Board).

22. In cases where schools meet minimum standards and show adequate progress over the previous four years, they are classified as "autonomous" and have flexibility in the way they choose to spend the additional SEP resources. In cases where schools show some progress, they are classified as "emerging" and they must present a plan to the Ministry of Education for how they would use the additional resources. If a low-performing school does not show adequate improvement over four years, it is classified as "in recovery," and is reconstituted or shut down.

23. For example, between 1990 and 2000, school of education applicants increased 39 percent, and the average university entrance exam score of applicants increased by 16 percent (Vegas and Umansky 2005).

24. The fraction of the lower quintile of the age group twenty-five to thirty-four years old having completed secondary education was 33.6 percent in 2000 compared to 94.9 percent in the top quintile (CASEN 2000). In 1998, only 45 percent of twenty-year-old students from the lowest quartile had completed secondary education, compared to 91 percent in the top quartile. Nevertheless, international comparisons suggest that high school graduation rate gaps were narrower in Chile than in some of the most developed Latin American countries. For example, in Uruguay the gap was 15 percent (first quintile) and 65 percent (fifth quintile) and in Argentina 26 percent (first quintile) and 81 percent (fifth quintile).

25. This program included a conditional cash transfer similar to Progresa or Oportunidades in Mexico and Bolsa Escola in Brasil. This was the only part of the program evaluated with a quasi-experimental design as part of the impact evaluation program of the Ministry of Finance (see www.dipres.cl). Although these evaluations have the problem of defining ex-post an adequate control group (in the case in question a regression discontinuity approach might have been more appropriate) and building a baseline subject to recall bias, it was not possible to identify a statistically significant effect. Partly this was explained by cultural factors, as the program required teachers to identify students at risk and award them the conditional cash transference. As this replicated the methodology of a long-lasting merit scholarship awarded to the best students, teachers resisted to give a similar "incentive" to students at risk, often those with the lowest marks and more disciplinary problems.

26. Between 1990 and 2006 the percentage of twenty- to twenty-four-year-old adults from the lowest income quintile who had completed high school increased from 26 to 62 percent.

27. While there have also been significant advances in preschool coverage across socioeconomic groups, Chile is still lagging behind most industrialized and some developing countries. Michelle Bachelet made this issue a cornerstone of her campaign platform.

28. Since 1997, over 75 percent of primary schools have adopted a full-day school program. See Bellei (2010) for an analysis of whether lengthening the school day had an impact on student achievement.

29. For example, Fundación Futuro (2004) reports that over 75 percent of parents surveyed report high levels of satisfaction with their children's schools and teachers.

30. Public support for the protests was nearly universal with almost 90 percent of Chileans polled stating they supported the student movement (*El Mercurio* 2006).

31. With prices of copper—Chile's chief export—at record highs at the time, and government reserves with several years of budget surpluses, the students maintained that the government could afford to invest more in education. A common slogan on student banners read, "Copper sky high and education in the gutter" (Rohter 2006).

32. This did not include most of the student representatives and the teachers' union, grouped in the so-called social movement, which presented an alternative proposal to reverse Pinochet's reforms by returning the public schools to the Ministry of Education.

33. Congress also enacted the adjusted voucher act (Ley de Subvención Preferencial or SEP) in 2007, which was introduced by the Lagos administration in 2006. The SEP law differentiated the voucher by the student's socioeconomic status and introduced measures of school accountability.

34. The president of the students' union asserted in *La Tercera* that "profit is the cancer that is killing education in Chile" (2008). The three senators from the ruling coalition who voted against the law expressed similar views in their floor speeches.

Part 3

Conclusion

14

The Future of the
Rainbow Coalition

Kirsten Sehnbruch and Peter M. Siavelis

The chapters in this volume have unveiled the complexity of evaluating the global performance of the Concertación coalition. Simplistic arguments related to whether the coalition was a success or a failure ring empty when one considers the richness and nuances revealed here. In this sense, we feel the chapters speak for themselves. Therefore in this conclusion, rather than attempting to provide such a global evaluation of the Concertación, we seek rather to outline what the chapters tell us about what went right and what went wrong with the Concertación and what this means for the future. To do so we revisit in depth the arguments set out in the introduction and develop them more fully in light of the insights provided by the chapters.

A central organizing assumption of the volume is that behaviors, norms, and formal and informal institutions left over from the transition—or what we have termed transitional enclaves—have deeply conditioned post-authoritarian Chilean politics. Each of the chapters has pointed to how these enclaves have played out with respect to its respective issue area. By way of conclusion, we consider two policymaking tendencies that have resulted from the interaction of these enclaves: the overwhelming power of and domination by political elites and a pattern of consensus politics that bordered on an ideology, preventing deeper and much-needed reforms to the political, economic, and social systems.

First, we argue that the Concertación continued to rely on a model of elite politics developed during the democratic transition, which, while initially successful, became counterproductive with the passage of time. Second, the transitional enclaves analyzed here have pushed elites into a situation where consensus-making has approached the status of a religion. While we certainly do not contend that consensus making is a bad thing, and do recognize that it was key to underwriting the stability of the transition, it also exacted a cost. We also recognize that in most countries politics are necessarily and by definition dominated by elites. What sets post-authoritarian Chile apart is the depth, entrenchment, and perseverance of these tendencies, and the difficulty in engaging in reform even for elites who themselves recognize these very problems. The combination of elite politics and consensus deal-making, though necessary to sustain the democratic transition and maintain the Concertación coalition, undermined democratic responsiveness, accountability, and legitimacy. Governability was certainly maintained, but at the expense of these other equally essential elements of democracy.

Furthermore, in this conclusion we take this argument a step further to contend that while the elite pattern of politics has remained unchanged, Chile and Chilean society have not. We argue that Chile has undergone a process of political normalization typical in post-transitional societies. We consider normalization to mean the absence of the special constraining features of the democratic transition, and a pattern of competition and elections characteristic of more established democracies. This contention may seem to contradict the point made above with respect to the entrenched model of elite politics. However, our point is precisely that normalization has taken place at the level of the citizenry, and is incongruent with an elite still operating under the mechanisms of transitional politics. While elites negotiate consensus politics with little citizen participation, the Chilean public vocally demands practical changes and solutions to everyday problems, in particular to Chile's glaring inequalities. Through widespread protests of government policies on education, labor issues, and public transport, as well as through regular opinion polls, Chileans have expressed discontent with "politics as usual." Furthermore, many of the structural conditions that necessitated this model of politics no longer exist (i.e., the veto power of the military, a nondemocratic Right, and the authoritarian enclaves), which in turn means that the rationale for this model of politics has diminished.

We consider it important to examine this post-transition political normalization in detail because it is unlikely that this process will be reversed. Future governments of whichever coalition, even under strong leadership, will have to contend with this lack of congruity. Thus, it would be a mistake to consider the current travails of Chilean politics as a by-product of a particular government without considering the new contextual and structural realities, which are likely to persevere. This section deals with each of the policymaking elements and then turns to an analysis of the normalization of politics.

Elite-Dominated Politics

First, with respect to structure, we underscore the centrality of elite politics in managing the transition. The success of the Concertación coalition was based on a complex elite power sharing arrangement, but it is one that increasingly brings charges of elite domination and politics by quota. While it was certainly a stabilizing phenomenon in the context of a delicate transition with a still-powerful military, it also sidelined congress and the public. Hence, most Chileans now chafe at the same elitism—whether on the Left or Right of the political spectrum—that made the transition possible.

Elite politics were at the core of Chile's successful democratic transition, as evidenced in three areas: the decisionmaking power of elites, the negotiation of elaborate power sharing arrangements in the executive branch (for example, the distribution of cabinet positions according to party politics, a practice referred to somewhat derisively as the *cuoteo*), and elite domination of the candidate selection process. Ordinary Chileans continue to have few tools with which to shape the political agenda or to hold leaders accountable (as will be more fully noted below in the discussion of the electoral system). Again, we do recognize that elite politics are very much a part of most political systems around the world, and they certainly characterized pre-authoritarian Chile. However, once again it is a matter of how entrenched and difficult to reform they have become, even when elites recognize the problem. In addition, it is the combination of elite politics with other elements of the policymaking process (i.e., extra-institutional deals among social actors and few avenues for citizen input) that makes this brand of politics stand apart in relative perspective.

In terms of decisionmaking power, in Chapter 2 Siavelis underscores the centrality and domination of party elites, which we have termed an enclave of the transition. He notes that party elites are central to decisionmaking and controlling the legislative agenda. In addition, party elites were the central actors in negotiating the extra-institutional agreements that underwrote the success of the transition. He argues that internal party democracy is limited. With few exceptions, the presidents and what have become known as party "barons" of individual parties are the determinative decisionmakers in the Chilean political system. Indeed, in the Socialist Party, the majority of both electoral and congressional votes are controlled by a handful of party leaders: Camilo Escalona, Marcelo Schilling, Ricardo Nuñez, and Ricardo Solari. In an interview with a member of the PS following the December 2007 cabinet reshuffle, the reasons given for the removal of Clarisa Hardy from the cabinet were that Solari had not yet been awarded with a ministerial position under the Bachelet administration and that it was therefore time to replace Hardy (who has recognized expertise in social policy) with somebody close to Solari. This power is further exemplified by the behavior of the Partido Por la Democracia (Party for Democracy [PPD]) during the municipal elections of 2008. Rather than running as part of the Concertación, the PPD's president Pepe Auth decided to run on a separate party ticket.

The second mechanism mentioned above that has historically enshrined elite politics in Chile is the negotiated sharing of executive power, commonly referred to as the *cuoteo*. Siavelis analyzes this arrangement in detail in Chapter 2. During the transition, this arrangement, which amounted to something of a pacted democracy, underwrote the maintenance of coalition unity and prevented the potential divisiveness that might have led to renewed military intervention. However, the mechanism means that key government positions are not necessarily awarded based on political talent, experience, or technical expertise but rather according to the exigencies of party politics. While many coalition governments in other countries rely on similar types of appointment norms, Chile stood out for its bolder use of explicitly political criteria for cabinet appointments, and the visibility of *cuoteo* politics at all levels of government.

This additional form of elite politics was also problematic because of its direct ties to political campaigns. In particular, ministerial posts were often awarded to reward individuals, party factions, or whole parties for their efforts and support during the preceding presidential campaign. Indeed, even those candidates who were willing to compete in especially close congressional races were rewarded with positions in government for taking this risk (Carey and Siavelis 2005). The complexities of the *cuoteo* mechanism are equally clear during cabinet reshuffles: decisions on incoming and outgoing ministers can either preserve the balance of power within the cabinet, reward (or punish) parties or party factions for their support (or lack of support) of the government, or act as the president's statements of support for a particular political leader.[1] This also means that ministers who underperform are not always removed when they should be and that ministers who are technically competent or perform well, as discussed above with reference to Clarisa Hardy, are sometimes removed from their positions to make way for political appointees. In addition, coalition making in the executive branch was in large part driven by the exigencies of maintaining the alliance to compete as a single coalition in legislative elections (a dynamic dictated by the very structure of the election system, as will be stressed more fully later). At first the *cuoteo* functioned well and was well regarded by a public who understood the need for consensus building and power sharing during the transition. However, with the passage of time the effects of the *cuoteo* caused it to reek of cronyism and clientelism in a post-transition Chile where expectations of meritocracy were gradually increasing.

It was partly due to the negative perception of the *cuoteo* that President Bachelet attempted a new formula, that of gender parity and new faces. Yet the essential rules and nature of the *cuoteo* did not change. The combination of *cuoteo* rules and these two new conditions, however, made the selection of cabinet members very difficult.[2] As Navia (2007b) points out, gender parity complicated this appointment process at two levels: not only did the overall number of ministers have to be equally distributed between men and women, but also ministers from individual parties had to be distributed at least relatively equally between men and women. Bachelet also refused to negotiate cabinet positions with the political parties in the same way previous presidents had done in an additional attempt to establish her own style of government and to distance herself from typical party pressures. Although she asked the parties for ministerial nominations, she did not negotiate these with party leaders and simply announced her choices. The result was that President Bachelet appointed a cabinet that theoretically respected *cuoteo* rules but did not contain the people that the party presidents would have liked.[3] This later translated into more difficulties and open conflict among the coalition when it came to governing.

Another problem with *cuoteo* politics is that they often oblige presidents to appoint cabinet ministers favored by a particular party leader but whom the president does not really trust. Each president since 1990 has instituted his or her own mechanism for dealing with this problem. President Aylwin appointed a very strong political team (Enrique Correa and Edgardo Boeninger); President Frei instituted his *círculo de hierro* (iron circle), which included a select group of ministers whom he trusted and with whom policy decisions were made; and President Lagos appointed a team of very competent and trusted personal advisers that served as a kind of supercabinet, known as the *segundo piso* or "second floor," named after the location of their offices in the presidential palace. These advisers directed policy and made sure that cabinet ministers were doing their jobs according to the president's instructions.

Because such mechanisms circumvent formal executive decisionmaking structures and reek of cronyism, President Bachelet vowed that there would be no visible second floor during her term in office.[4] However, the lack of a strong team of political advisers combined with the inexperience of her ministers caused President Bachelet's administration to lurch from one political crisis to another during its first two years in office.[5] Only three months after taking office, the president had to make her first cabinet changes. Several more were to follow. In particular, the political team within the cabinet (the ministers of interior, government, and the presidency) was unstable and weak. With each reshuffle, the cabinet that once was populated with new faces began to look increasingly like traditional Concertación cabinets as party elites pushed to insert their nominees into the cabinet and it proved too politically risky to move away from tried and tested political formulas.

The third mechanism of elite politics mentioned above is the selection of legislative candidates through a complex pattern of closed-door negotiations. As Siavelis notes in Chapter 2, citizens have very little input with regard to who gets on the ballot, and once in office, candidates are extraordinarily difficult to remove. The almost complete domination of the process by elites further distances the Chilean public from its representatives and likely has contributed to growing disgust with the current political model.

While the candidate selection process has the potential to allow for more citizen input in choosing representatives, the dynamics of the electoral system when considered alongside the exigencies of coalition maintenance prevented any significant democratization of this process. Because the binomial system provides only two electoral slates for each coalition, and the Concertación is composed of four parties, the number of candidacies that each party in each coalition receives is subject to arduous negotiations before the elections. The complexity and political horse-trading involved in placing candidacies on individual lists leaves candidate selection completely in the hands of party elites and works at cross purposes with any efforts to democratize the legislative candidate selection process. Legislative candidates for the Chamber of Deputies are moved from district to district in negotiations, often with little consideration for representative ties to that district, and at times Senate candidacies have been traded away for a number of Chamber candidacies. Elites across the spectrum agree that party elites have absolute say over the final placement of legislative candidates (Siavelis 2002c).

Even where efforts to introduce primaries have been undertaken, party elites have often overridden the decisions of their own parties. Especially in the case of the Partido Demócrata Cristiano (Christian Democratic Party [PDC]), party elites have actively tried to dissuade certain candidates from running in primaries. Some candidates who managed to garner positions on the ballot found their seats traded away to smaller parties in the interests of coalition maintenance. Even more serious, in a few cases party central committees simply overruled the results of primaries. Navia cites the case of a 2001 Chamber of Deputy race in District Twenty-Four where the PDC National Committee designated Tomás Jocelyn-Holt as the candidate despite his defeat in an open primary (Navia 2008: 106–107). Most egregiously, during an interview conducted by one of the authors of this chapter with a high-level party official in Chile, who asked not to be quoted, this leader charged with assembling his party's list for legislative slates removed a candidate the party had agreed upon from the list on the way into coalition negotiations because he "could not stand her"![6]

Since 1990, Concertación presidential candidates and presidents consistently had a significant say in the selection of legislative candidates. Aylwin and Frei actively participated in the negotiations regarding legislative candidacies, and Frei openly urged PDC elites to cede seats to smaller coalition partners in 1993 and 1997 (Navia 2008: 106–107). This constitutes one of the informal mechanisms through which presidents have exercised their influence over parties and the legislature. However, it is also clearly a mechanism that perpetuates the power of the elite. The extent to which the public perception of this mechanism has changed was illustrated in 2008 by the reactions to a declaration made by President Lagos, who at the time was considering becoming a presidential candidate in the 2009 elections. He wrote, "It is incomprehensible to me that whoever leads the ruling coalition would not have a word to say about the coalition's candidates who are to be chosen in a concurrent election." That is to say that to President Lagos, it was essential and obvious that he should be able to exercise his influence over the candidate selection process. In a very critical column about the Lagos declaration, Navia wrote, "Lagos seems to think that he can impose conditions on the Concertación. . . . Now he also thinks he can become the great decider in defining who the Concertación's parliamentary candidates will be."[7] While the opinions of the press do not necessarily represent the opinions of the electorate at large, it is nevertheless indicative that the Lagos declaration should have generated such objections even though he was merely stating what had long constituted standard practice, and constituted a mechanism the former president clearly deemed fundamental to the functioning of Concertación politics. This reaction could also be interpreted as an increasing level of public intolerance with elitist institutions and mechanisms of policymaking.

Presidential candidate selection within the Concertación was also completely dominated by elites, despite repeatedly stated intentions to democratize the process. In 1989, Patricio Aylwin was chosen in negotiations among elites. In 1993, party militants and adherents did participate in a primary process, but the candidates put on the ballot, Eduardo Frei and Ricardo Lagos, were simply designated by the elite members of their own parties. For the 1999 election, because the PDC candidate had been named the standard-bearer for two elections in a row, it was widely understood and accepted that it was Lagos's turn, and he was simply confirmed in a primary that was a foregone conclusion. Though a primary in the Concertación was planned for 2005, PDC candidate Soledad Alvear trailed so far in the polls that she dropped out of the primary before it took place, effectively handing the race to Michelle Bachelet. What is more, it was widely acknowledged that Lagos had tagged Bachelet as his successor (Altman 2008). For the 2009 race a single regional primary between candidates chosen by the elites of their respective parties took place on April 5, 2009, in the Maule and O'Higgins regions between former president Eduardo Frei and José Antonio Gómez from the Social Democrat Radical Party. Frei beat Gómez by a wide margin (65 percent versus 35 percent). Had the margin between candidates been less than 20 percent, other primaries would have continued in other regions, but the magnitude of Frei's victory prevented additional popular input. Therefore, the process of popular inclusion or influence in determining the outcome of presidential primaries was minimal throughout all of the Concertación governments.

Chileans were more likely to accept these relatively unresponsive, elite-centered arrangements when the democratic transition was perceived as delicate, and the threat of military intervention real. However, with the secure installation of democracy, criticism of the model increased. More and more Chileans made reference to the *cuoteo político* (a long-standing negative reference in Chilean politics referring to the distribution of partisan spoils), decisions made *a puertas cerradas* (behind closed doors), and an increasing tendency toward *partidocracia*. Public opinion survey data suggest that citizens perceive and object to elite dominance and the lack of turnover. When asked whether members of congress are concerned about the problems of average people, only 14 percent of the population answered in the affirmative.[8] When asked to name the two principal defects of political parties, the top three responses were "they are not transparent" (36 percent); "they are always the same . . . there is no turnover" (33 percent); and "they pass out government positions among themselves" (31 percent).[9] While it is impossible to tie demands for electoral reform directly to these responses, it is notable that when asked about reforms to the binomial system, 46 percent said it should be changed completely; 42 percent said it should be maintained; and 12 percent did not know or did not answer.

The "Ideology" of Consensus Politics

The second policymaking pattern that grew from the enclaves of the transition was a near ideology of consensus. Consensus building is generally understood as a positive process that can contribute to the success of democratic transitions. However, consensus building can also be dangerous if elites hijack the democratic process to reach that consensus without sufficient input from the electorate in general and if that consensus results in delaying decisions on issues deemed important by the public. While a policy process based on a model of consensus was central to the success of the transition, it has less of a place in, and is indeed counterproductive to, the consolidation of a fully representative democracy in Chile. The first postauthoritarian president, Patricio Aylwin, recognized early in the democratic transition that the economy was the Achilles' heel of the new government. To maintain the transition, presidents avoided going beyond simple tinkering with the Pinochet economic model. Aylwin publicly acknowledged that the private sector was the primary "motor" of economic growth in the country. Similarly, in 1999 the Right and the business community openly suggested that should Ricardo Lagos, whom they labeled as socialist, be elected president, it would represent a return to the chaotic economic policies of the Salvador Allende government. The Concertación's decision to adopt a hands-off policy on the economy left its presidents hamstrung when it came to economic policymaking. To avoid confrontation, they concentrated on the political transition, only tackling economic problems that did not fundamentally alter Pinochet's economic legacy. This is not to say there were no reforms; the chapters demonstrate there were. We refer to the lack of deep reforms that challenge the structural manifestations of the deeply ingrained ideology of market economics and a minimal role for the state that the Concertación inherited. This dynamic played out again and again in the economic and social policies dealt with throughout this volume, with reforms that were rarely audacious or risky and that rarely touched the reality of an unequal two-tiered system. This was the case in social security, health care, education, and policies regarding inequality, with the haves and the have nots living distinct lives in two fundamentally different Chiles.

As we have underscored throughout this volume, the overriding concern with maintaining consensus limited the playing field for reform. In Chapter 7 on human rights, Collins, though pointing to some limited success in dealing with the human rights questions, also demonstrates how the transition limited the extent of deeper reforms. Haas and Blofield make a very similar argument in Chapter 6 concerning gender because the democratic transition provided exaggerated veto power to precisely the economic and political actors most opposed to progressive gender policies.

The exigency of maintaining consensus also spilled over into the policymaking process. Elites structured patterns of political deal making that sidelined key democratic actors and democratic processes. The post-transitional political model involved a series of deals between party elites both within the Concertación and between the Concertación and potential veto players on the Right.

It should be noted that, to a large extent, this mechanism of policymaking was driven by the constitution that the Concertación inherited from the dictatorship. As noted in Chapter 4 by Claudio Fuentes, until the constitutional reforms of 2005, the institution of nonelected senators ensured that the right-wing opposition held a Senate majority. In addition, many legislative changes to the so-called constitutional laws required more than a simple majority, which was impossible to achieve given the effective veto power the Right held in the Senate until 2005. Even since then, the Concertación has only temporarily held a simple majority in both houses of congress, which has not allowed it to reform any of these constitutional laws.[10] It has therefore been impossible for the coalition to pass legislation that was not prenegotiated with the opposition. Needless to say, this proved to be a significant political handicap for the Concertación and accounts for its timid reforms since 1990. These constitutional arrangements also led to a pattern of negotiations behind closed doors and the putting forward of prenegotiated legislative proposals that required very little debate or revision in congress. Furthermore, with respect to the constitution itself, despite limited reforms, Chile fundamentally still operates under Pinochet's constitution, and the ideology of consensus has consistently kept the issue of a new constitution and a potential constitutional convention off the table.

However, beyond the constraints of the constitution, there was also an ethos of extra-institutional consensus building. In terms of the Concertación's relationships with veto players on the Right, the bargain included a tacit agreement that the president should negotiate with powerful economic actors and leaders on the Right to arrive at consensus solutions for the most controversial legislation. Concertación governments negotiated directly with the opposition and with powerful players on the Right, like business associations and producer groups, to craft agreements before legislation is introduced in congress. This model of *democracia de los acuerdos* (democracy by agreement), analyzed in Chapter 2, was used in reforming the tax code, expanding social welfare and anticorruption legislation, and in the comprehensive constitutional reforms of 2005. These major policy deals involved very little popular or congressional involvement (Silva 1992; Boylan 1996).

Negotiated agreements outside congress have also often been the norm between the Concertación and its allies such as trade unions. While aimed at securing the democratic transition by avoiding potentially destabilizing demands, this model has also minimized the role of the citizenry and congress in government policymaking. Two good examples of this kind of policymaking are labor reform and educational reform. In both of these examples, the Chilean population and electorate would probably benefit from potential reforms, but the power of the respective union organizations prevents this.

In the case of labor reform, as Sehnbruch notes in Chapter 12, unions have blocked any attempt to reform the relatively high levels of severance pay that employers in Chile are required to provide when they dismiss workers without just cause. Although most analysts agree that severance pay, at least theoretically, introduces rigidities into the labor market and stymies employment growth, unions view the legislation as an acquired right and block any reform. Thus Concertación governments did not use severance pay as a bargaining chip to negotiate other much-needed labor reforms with the opposition, even though such reforms would probably benefit the labor force much more than severance pay does (Sehnbruch 2006).[11]

This elite-centered consensus model of political and economic development has limited both the content of political debates and policymaking itself, resulting in widespread dissatisfaction with politics and political parties among the electorate as the population's demands for greater equity and more equal opportunities are not being addressed by either coalition.

Nowhere is this point more evident than in Chile's socioeconomic development. As Landerretche argues in Chapter 8, the political consensus was vital in producing a pact on economic stability, which in turn was pivotal to Chile's economic development. At the same time, the rigidity of the stability pact stifled the need for innovation and imaginative creation, thus leading to an export economy that differed very little in 2010 from the one inherited in 1990. These arguments are backed by López, who demonstrates in Chapter 9 to what extent fiscal policies have failed to redirect resources toward higher added value activities. All of the chapters on social and economic policy have underscored a politics of "reform around the edges" and the temerity of the coalition in tackling inequality at its core. Fearful of offending powerful interests, the coalition did little to counteract unequal access to social benefits, education, and maldistribution of income in a country that is routinely ranked among the least equal in the world.

A good example of the coalition's unwillingness to greatly upset the status quo is the health reform implemented by the Lagos government, analyzed by Contreras and Sehnbruch in Chapter 11: the reform initially proposed a Solidarity Fund and differential value-added taxes that would have paid for a broad range of minimum services for all Chileans, regardless of their incomes or insurance status. The opposition, however, vetoed both financing proposals, leaving the government with a much-watered-down reform and more limited health service guarantees.[12] Ironically though, during the 2005 election campaign, the health reform was presented as an "achievement" of the Lagos administration, and the opposition's role in blocking its most essential components was not mentioned.

In the area of social policy, the double-edged sword of the elite-centered consensus politics has perhaps provoked simultaneously the greatest successes and failures of the Concertación. Chapter 11 by Contreras and Sehnbruch explains how fundamental reforms in the areas of health, pension, and unemployment insurance did not occur as consensus could not be achieved on how they should be structured. Particularly in the areas of health and pension policy, Chile is still running the same systems it inherited from the dictatorship with the only difference that higher levels of minimum services have been established together with the service guarantees. However, the segmentation between public and private provision of services remains, producing predictably unequal outcomes.

Educational policy is similar. Student protests under President Piñera have gone from being about education to being about much more. They really grow from much deeper frustrations, and the roots of the protests have to do with social justice. In another example of an incongruity between elites and masses, the protesters object to the policies pursued by elites who have ensured that the fruits of Chile's economic success continue to be funneled to the top. Furthermore, there is a widespread perception that the educational system is rigged to underwrite the continuing power of economic elites. The private educational system with its elite schools is central to how the system is rigged to perpetuate this inequality (see Chapter 13 by Elacqua and González). The more than forty protests in Chile during 2011 are in many ways like the political protests that erupted elsewhere around the world, including in other Latin American capitals. They have to do with justice and fairness, with protestors' widening their demands from basic educational reforms to demands for inclusion, equality of opportunity, reform of the political system, and deeper labor and tax reforms.

Perhaps one of the most important dilemmas that this book reveals is the question of whether the Concertación was genuinely successful in reducing poverty rates given that this has been touted as one of its principal achievements by almost anyone who knows anything about Chile. The reexamination of poverty data by Borzutzky, Sanhueza, and Sehnbruch in Chapter 10 shows that while absolute poverty rates have certainly declined in Chile during the last two decades, in relative terms this success looks very questionable. Based on relative rates, Chile looks similar to Mexico, and worlds away from the standards that should prevail in a country looking to escape the middle-income trap. In addition, the chapter shows that social expenditure has done very little to reduce even absolute poverty rates in Chile. If we bear in mind the crucial role that paying the social debt played in the establishment of the Concertación's policy consensus, and if we consider that social policy has been the leitmotif of the Center-Left coalition, then these results are disappointing indeed and lead us to question the official rhetoric that portrays the Concertación's record on poverty as an unqualified success.

One of the most important reasons for questioning this rhetoric of success is that since 1990, and as a result of the consensus model of politics, Chile's two main coalitions have increasingly converged in terms of their political agenda.[13] Consequently, Chilean politics are extremely nonconfrontational, at least as far as substantive policy discussion goes. Furthermore, the absence of in-depth discussion allowed the Alianza to hijack the Concertación's political agenda from 1999 onward, claiming that it is the coalition that will overcome poverty and inequality. The nonconfrontational nature of Chilean election campaigns, in particular the almost complete lack of discussion of the past voting records of both candidates and political coalitions, means that the electorate is unaware of the hypocrisy of such a statement given that the Alianza has consistently blocked legislative proposals that would institute greater equity or shift power from business interests to workers.[14]

One might have expected Bachelet's model of involving citizens in policymaking (*gobierno ciudadano*) to have brought an end to policymaking by negotiated consensus. However, under President Bachelet, the process of consensus politics in fact took on an even more formalized shape. Bachelet established extracongressional commissions to prepare major reforms and to respond to popular demands for reform. Although the members of these commissions were supposed to represent a broad range of social interests, in their majority they were nevertheless composed of members of the same elite charged with governing.[15] When their makeup was more varied, members of congress and powerful actors in the executive branch often simply ignored their findings. The success of these commissions differed: while the pension commission put together the basis of a successful reform, the educational commission produced legislation that is widely regarded as not resolving the main problems it set out to address.[16] Similarly, the commission on employment and equity resulted in some new legislative proposals (most notably reform of the unemployment insurance system), but none of these commissions translated into any legislation on the issues that have historically divided Chile.

Despite the fact that the main emphasis of the Bachelet government has been on social policy, as with previous Concertación governments (and as Borzutzky, Sanhueza, and Sehnbruch and Contreras and Sehnbruch note in Chapters 10 and 11, respectively) legislation has focused on the allocation of additional funding to social policies rather than on any structural changes to the existing social security systems. For example, expenditure on minimal pensions has been increased, but there is still no social risk-sharing component within the pension system that can redistribute funds from the higher to the lower end of the income scale. The problem with fiscal rather than structural solutions to social issues, of course, is that once fiscal resources become scarce, or if there is a change in government, the increased spending can very easily be cut back, especially if the opposition coalition holds a firm belief in the value of tax cuts in a country that already has a very low level of fiscal revenue from taxation relative to its level of GDP per capita. However, moving forward more aggressively to attack the structural roots of the problem would have upset the tacit post-authoritarian political deal.

In sum, the politics of consensus underwrote a very successful transition but they also limited the political room for maneuver, the range and audacity of reforms, and the extent of popular participation in politics. Furthermore, the politics of consensus also sowed the seeds of a policymaking process that became informally institutionalized and difficult to dislodge. Attempts to change the process were sabotaged both by the correlation of political forces in congress and through the erosion of support for the Concertación—ironically because of its very unwillingness to confront the social and economic legacies of the authoritarian regime. Political consensus can limit the substance of public debate, and it is precisely due to this lack of debate that the electorate generally does not appreciate the extent to which the Concertación's policies were limited by the actions of the opposition. In the end, then, widespread dissatisfaction with public policies and unequal opportunities negatively affected Chileans' view of both the Concertación and the opposition alliance, especially as the population at large did not understand how and why the Concertación stuck to consensus politics. This proved an infertile environment for the consolidation of citizen government connections, as policy was brokered between veto players and imposed from the top down with an eye to maintaining a consensus that would not disturb the post-authoritarian status quo and to allowing the Concertación to function within this limitation. As politics have become normalized with the fading of the threat of military incursion, this policymaking process appears more and more anachronistic.

The Normalization of Politics

Concertación elites continued to operate according to the logic and structures of transition politics in the realm of party politics. However, at the same time we argue that the contextual political environment is one characterized by what we can consider normal politics, yet the electorate has moved on to establish and expect a pattern of post-transitional politics that in other countries would be considered "normal." The normalization of politics in Chile is multidimensional—essentially several phenomena having to do with both the institutional or structural context and the attitudes and orientation of the electorate.

First, as Weeks underscores in Chapter 5, veto players are less important, both in terms of the military's role in politics and in terms of the non-military Right. In political terms, though Concertación governments skillfully managed civil-military conflict and in hindsight it appears that the restoration of civilian authority over the military was a foregone conclusion, it is crucial to remember that for many years there was a great deal of uncertainty given the continuing veto power of the military. Unlike Argentina, the defeat of the authoritarian regime in Chile was only partial, and the Chilean military consistently sought to protect itself. While in many countries former dictators fled the country in disgrace, Augusto Pinochet simply moved across the Alameda (Santiago's main avenue) to the armed forces building, literally overviewing the presidential palace. During the initial phases of the transition the establishment and maintenance of democracy was very much in doubt and the military retained de facto veto authority—

functionally, and indeed, constitutionally. Angell notes that during this time "there seemed to be two parallel systems of power in Chile, one democratic" and "another a carryover from the authoritarian past posing a veiled threat to the civilian authorities—in Pinochet's words, a sleeping lion" (Angell 2007: 147).

However, as Weeks also notes, civil-military relations transformed from a situation where the military as an institution posed a real threat to the maintenance and stability of democracy to one where the military is firmly ensconced in the barracks. This is a remarkable transformation for a military that was a relatively short time ago responsible for vicious human rights abuses and a wavering commitment to democracy. The idea that the military could return to politics is as unthinkable among the electoral Right as it is within the ranks of the Concertación.

As Navia and Godoy also argue in Chapter 3, the nature and orientation of the Right has also changed, underscoring an additional element of the normalization of politics. At the outset of the democratic transition many on the Right were convinced that Concertación governments would fail. These sectors, and particularly leaders of UDI, maintained their commitments to the authoritarian regime as a way to hedge their bets in case the military was to return to politics. Indeed, Garretón argues that the Chilean Right had an "atavistic" link to the military regime (2000: 66). This very atavistic link, however, would actually grow to hurt the Right as Concertación governments began to enjoy success and it became clear that the coalition was likely to remain in power for some time. As Navia and Godoy note, however, though not unified, the Right did gradually realize that democracy was the only game in town. It also became clear that the Right would need to work with the Concertación or it would be seen as a simple impediment to the establishment of full democracy (Pollack 1999). With the return of full democracy following the 2005 constitutional reforms, the Right has been able to return to its pre-authoritarian practice of using electoral politics and democratic institutions to advance its goals and protect its interests.

The rehabilitation of the Right also occurred as a result of its disappointing electoral performance at the outset of the transition. During the height of Concertación governments, it appeared that the Right was doomed to perpetual exile from government. As the years passed, the parties of the Right became increasingly frustrated with their inability to win the presidency, despite coming very close and the need to resort to a second round in the 1999–2000 and 2005–2006 elections. The Right experienced a process of political learning and came to realize that this lack of electability really lay with its association with the Pinochet regime. Once again, the return of an electorally competitive Right committed to competition within the bounds of democratic institutions represents an advance and an additional signal of the normalization of politics.

Another structural element of the "normalization" of politics is institutional. Fuentes underscores in Chapter 4 the power of the constitution in influencing the democratic transition as well as the functioning of democratic government. Unlike many transitional polities, Chilean elites inherited an institutional structure that they did not design and that was extraordinarily difficult to reform (Siavelis 2000; Barros 2002). The 1980 constitution was one of the legacies of the Pinochet government most fiercely defended by the parties of the Right, particularly by UDI. The constitution established a number of provisions that provided effective veto power for the Right. Concertación elites were consistently aware that the Right would be able to employ these institutional veto powers should it be perceived to step out of line. Therefore, it made sense that the Concertación would put together all of the conflict dampening and consensus cultivating devices that it did.

However, despite what has been characterized as temerity in proposing a completely new constitution, the days of constitutional veto power for the Right are over. Indeed, the Right supported the elimination of the most egregiously authoritarian aspects of the constitution when it was reformed during the Lagos administration in September 2005. As Fuentes notes, the reforms eliminated the positions of appointed senators and senators for life, reduced the powers of the National Security Council, returned to the president the authority to remove the commanders in chief of the armed forces, and reduced the presidential term from six to four years. These reforms prompted President Lagos to declare that the Chilean democratic transition was finally complete. Fuentes traces the Right's abandonment of its unyielding defense of Pinochet's constitution to a "forward-looking" strategy. However, it is undeniable that the Right also realized that the power of appointment of these authorities fell to Concertación governments over time and that these elements of the constitution had increasingly worked to the Center-Left's advantage.

Another aspect of the normalization of politics that we underscore, and that has been repeatedly analyzed in this volume, is at the level of the electorate. We see this in many ways. There is a process of disaffection with politics at the popular level that has produced a new, post-transition status quo with less concern for politics and less engagement with dissipating potential threats to democracy. This is not to suggest that "dissatisfaction" defines "normal" politics. Rather, political participation was high by Chile's historical standards during the transition period. There has been a gradual decline of popular participation in political processes, in the shape of lower voter registration, lower electoral turnout, and lower levels of political participation as well as in identification with political parties. For at least a decade now, analysts have commented on declining levels of participation in Chile's political parties and elections. In 2007, Angell analyzed popular affiliation with political parties and the behavior of the electorate and concluded that Chilean political parties were developing in line with expectations, given what has been observed in the international context (Angell 2007).

In Chile, young people in particular have disengaged from traditional formal electoral political activity. This process was probably compounded by the fact that for much of the transition period electoral registration in Chile was not automatic. While voting was compulsory for those who registered, registration was not.[17] Analysts lamented the fact that the vast majority of young voters in Chile have not bothered to register in recent years (Riquelme and Segovia 1999). Marta Lagos, however, argues that this is a normal process in mature democracies as people only start voting at a point in their lives when they have something to protect or to lose. Using comparative international data, she shows that voter participation tends to coincide with the stage of their lifecycle when young people establish families, have children, and establish careers.[18]

This process of reduced voter turnout rates goes hand in hand with the lower political participation and reduced levels of identification with political parties. At the elite level, the party system seems remarkably like that of the pre-authoritarian period, and numerous studies attest to the extent of continuity. Once again, this point underscores how little elite politics has changed. However, the fundamentally different nature of party-society relations has been less recognized and less analyzed and likely lies at the root of Chileans' dissatisfaction with the state of democracy in their country. Given the centrality of parties, one is tempted to argue that they still form the "backbone" of Chilean politics as once famously argued by Garretón (Garretón 1987b: 64). However, while they have been central to structuring elite politics and the democratic transition, the nature of society-party relations is very different than in the pre-authoritarian period.

When surveys began, immediately following the return of democracy in 1990, 62.5 percent of the Chilean public attested to identifying with a political party. By 1992, the number of Chileans self-identifying with political parties increased to 87 percent. From there this percentage has registered gradual declines, to the point that in 2008 only 43 percent of Chileans said they identified with a particular political party, and none of the parties registered a level of adherence above 10 percent.[19]

This low level of party identification is certainly a function of the low esteem in which Chileans hold political parties. When asked their opinion of a series of sixteen institutions in 2008, Chileans ranked political parties last. Only 6 percent expressed "some" or "much" confidence in political parties, trailing far behind the military (51 percent), the government (30 percent), newspapers (28 percent), and unions (26 percent). The courts and congress, which ranked fourteenth and fifteenth, respectively, had "some" or "much" confidence of 18 percent and 16 percent of the population, respectively (CEP 2008). Certainly, support for political parties is relatively low across Latin America. In terms of comparative referents, among the eighteen countries included in the Latinobarómetro survey, Chile ranks ninth with respect to the citizenry's expressing the least confidence in political parties (Latinobarómetro 2007: 94).While not at the bottom regionally with respect to the evaluation of parties, this position is remarkable given the strong historical connections between society and parties, and the scholarly work that lauds the quality and institutionalization of Chile's parties.

However, while formal political participation in Chile has declined, informal participation seems to have increased—another indication of a more normal pattern of politics not conditioned by the democratic transition. We argue that the Chilean public is less willing to excuse limited popular input and the lack of deeper reform as simply an inevitable result of the delicate politics that characterized a sensitive transition and that it is treading much less lightly.

For the first time since 1990, in 2006 the population mobilized against the Concertación on a massive scale, thus putting an end to an era in which mobilizations tended to be in support of the government and against the former authoritarian regime and its vestiges under democracy. This again is an additional testament to the normalization of politics at the mass level. Frustrated demands for social justice, particularly for more equal opportunities and income levels, have brought large numbers of citizens into the streets. These protests, however, are merely the expression of a much more general phenomenon: Chile now has a population that is willing to mobilize and protest against Concertación governments, and the population's willingness to do so is increased by the structural inequalities that characterize Chilean society as well as by the certainty that their protests will not destabilize democracy or bring back an authoritarian regime.

The most large-scale and successful of these demonstrations was undoubtedly the student protests of May 2006, which mobilized up to 1 million students nationwide and became known as the March of the Penguins (Revolución de los Pinguinos) after the school uniforms the protesters wore. The demonstrators initially demanded free bus fare and the waiving of the university admissions test fee. However, more substantive demands soon became part of their agenda as the protests increasingly focused on the quality of education and legislative changes. The mobilization became Chile's largest demonstration during the Concertación period. Its articulate leaders generated support and sympathy among the population at large, which considered their demands fair and valid. It was to become the first political crisis Bachelet had to confront, occurring only months after her administration took office.

The student protests were perhaps the best demonstration of the extent to which Chile has changed since 1990. Its leaders were articulate, organized, thoughtful, and no longer prepared to tolerate the significant inequality inherent in Chile's education system (Kubal 2010). However, leaders of other social movements have become equally or even more adept at organizing effective protests. In addition, environmental protesters were much more proactive under the Bachelet administration, no longer adhering to legal norms and initiating protests against projects from the outset rather than after their environmental impact studies had been published (Borzutzky 2008).

Similarly, workers became much more effective at protesting and striking over unequal working conditions and general levels of inequality, also ignoring legislation that theoretically prohibits such actions. In particular, several strikes by subcontracted workers—who organized sector-wide strikes, which are technically illegal—forced sector-wide collective bargaining agreements for the first time since 1973.[20] In fact, 2007 was a year of much increased union activity. In response to the protests, President Bachelet instituted a special commission on employment and equity to come up with policy proposals that would address the causes of the protests. She had initiated a similar response to the student protests.

The eruption of protests also points to normalization of politics in another way. During the transition the Concertación kept a tight rein over the internal components of its coalition, including social movements, to prevent them from embarrassing transitional governments. However, with a president of the Right these groups have been liberated from such restraints, and are quite willing to make their discontent known.

Finally, generational change also points to normalization. First, the memory and threat of an authoritarian regime, embodied by the figure of former dictator Pinochet, have declined gradually but steadily since 1990. Pinochet's arrest in London in 1998 and subsequent events marked the effective end of this threat. Furthermore, demographic changes mean that a young generation of Chileans, born after 1980, now participates in (or at least observes) politics that has no or very little memory of the dictatorship. Increased levels of education, especially of this younger generation, have led to the formulation of much more specific demands for social justice. These demands are also driven by the very visible economic growth that Chile has experienced during the last two decades, which has generated consumption patterns and desires that sit ill with the country's inequality of income and opportunities and which therefore also generates a more urgent desire for social justice and social mobility. One statistic that exemplifies this fact is that seven out of every ten college or university students are first-generation college students. So even though there are persistent and justified complaints about the quality of education in Chile, nobody can deny the expansion of its coverage, which in turn generates a more demanding set of social and professional expectations.

Thus, despite a political elite that continues to operate under a political model deeply embedded in the logic of the democratic transition, Chilean society and the political context of the post-transitional period have been fundamentally transformed. Chile can now be characterized as a fully functioning democracy, without the constraints and limits that characterized the transitional period. Chilean elites, both in the Concertación and the Alianza, must now adjust to this new reality.

Conclusion

This chapter has perhaps presented a very critical evaluation of Concertación governments. It is not our intention to be too negative. It is undeniable that the Concertación oversaw one of the most successful democratic transitions in Latin America, and indeed, the world. The Concertación guided Chile through an extremely tense and precarious transition with an array of veto players and potential pitfalls and dangers. Political leadership was extraordinary. In hindsight it appears that the durability of democracy was a given, but nothing could have been further from the truth in 1990, as has been noted repeatedly throughout this volume. Indeed, the first post-transitional president, Patricio Aylwin, expressed this very idea in interviews when his government was criticized by those who contended he lacked the audacity to take transformative measures that would make Chile a more fully democratic and equitable society.[21]

What is more, with respect to governing, despite allegations of corruption and missteps by various governments it is undeniable that the Concertación governed well. It oversaw periods of impressive economic growth, stability, and success in the diversification of exports as well as increased insertion in the global economy. The coalition's political model and policy success allowed it to win four consecutive presidential elections.

Despite this reality, the intention of this book is to look both back and ahead. We simultaneously sought to evaluate Concertación governments while providing suggestions and guidelines for how Chilean democracy can be improved. We offer the criticisms here in that spirit, with the recognition that a critical evaluation will ultimately contribute to a more responsive and effective democracy in the future.

Although the issues raised in this chapter could be interpreted as simple symptoms of fatigue in a coalition that governed for almost twenty years, they are also very much related to the lack of congruence between an elite tied to the model of the transition and a public operating with a different set of assumptions within a transformed political context free of the practical limits imposed by the transition. A conflict emerged between the political need to maintain the elite power structures that stabilized the Concertación and the transition during its first four governments and the imperative for a more inclusive form of politics characteristic of a well-functioning democracy. Virtually every country that has been through a period of profound political transformation, especially after an authoritarian regime, eventually stabilizes around a new status quo. However, while Chilean politics at the mass level is perhaps crystallizing around a new status quo, elites cling to what worked in the past, both out of habit and due to an institutional structure that reinforces elitist patterns. We also realize that this model is underwritten institutionally by an electoral system that obligates elites in many ways to act the way that they do.

Rather than being a result of general civic disillusionment with respect to a single leader or government, this conclusion and the chapters in this volume have shown that the often-lauded democratic transition and the elitist model inherited from it are, ironically, part of the cause. In particular, we have argued that the very model for transitional success planted the seeds of eventual decline in governing effectiveness. While elite politics were at the core of underwriting the success of the democratic transition, their perseverance has been damaging to the long-term consolidation of democracy because everyday Chileans perceived politics to be a game of questionably legitimate negotiation and deal making between elites. While strong parties provided the mechanisms to structure, broker, and enforce the interparty agreements that underwrote the transition, the party elite domination of significant policy and candidate selection decisions moved the mass public another step away from a meaningful representative connection. The consensus model of politics put off controversial decisions and avoided adverse reactions by veto players, but the negotiations to reach consensus again involved the few and the powerful.

Concrete policies under dispute in Chile today are also an outgrowth of this dynamic. While the political model limited participation and citizen input into reform, the interplay between this model, the ideology of consensus, and the existence of powerful economic veto players all conspired to constrain the audacity of potential reforms that could have ameliorated the nagging social and economic inequalities noted throughout this volume. Academics and analysts puzzle as protests spill onto the streets in Chile's "model" economy. However, as authors in this volume repeatedly note, many Chileans see the system as set up to reproduce social and economic inequality, entrenching this reproduction within the educational system, but also within each and every dual system of social provision that existed during the Pinochet dictatorship and continues to exist today.

Chapters in this volume have recounted reforms (some piecemeal, some significant), but the underlying schemas and organizational principles underwriting these systems have never been challenged. We are not advocating widespread state intervention into the area of social provision, but rather make the point that evening the playing field and promoting equality-enhancing reforms are the ultimate solution for the Concertación and for Chile. Chileans do not want to systematically dispense with an economy that has moved many into the middle class and provided one of the highest standards of living in Latin America. Rather, they want an economy that will more evenly distribute the fruits of Chile's much vaunted economic success to allow a more representative mix of Chileans to enjoy this standard of living.

Finally, while in the context of a very delicate transition where an authoritarian reversion was entirely possible, the model of politics employed by the Concertación was widely accepted by the public. However, with the normalization of politics, we argue, the logic and the structures of the democratic transition are not only outdated, they are potentially damaging, effectively preventing Chile's evolution from a successful transition toward a fully representative and successful democracy. We stress that we are not critical of the process of transition, nor do we dispute its successful nature. Rather, our point is that running a successful democratic transition is distinct from running a longer-term consolidated democracy.

This analysis has serious ramifications. It suggests that Chile is not just facing a crisis of a particular leader or government but rather faces a significant crisis of representation. Political parties and political leaders have to change the way of doing politics in Chile. Unfortunately, many of these elitist patterns of politics are underwritten by the incentives produced by the binomial election system. Therefore, a good place to start would be the introduction of some form of moderate, small-magnitude proportional representation that would provide greater competition and accountability and break the lock that parties have on nominations. A proportional representation system with district magnitude of four or five would allow each of the parties to field the candidates they would like, and, depending on the list system, allow voters to opt for their favored candidates either on their own party lists or from the various parties of the coalition.

Electoral system reform is not, however, a panacea. The representative capacity of the political system has been shaped in other ways by the persistence of the models inherited from the transition. The traditionally positive role of Chile's relatively effective and representative parties has been perhaps irreparably damaged. However, it is difficult to imagine substantive representation taking place any other way than via political parties. Indeed, it is ironic how effective parties were in the past, only to have their effectiveness diminished by the experience of authoritarian rule and further diminished through adherence to a less-than-representative transitional political model that served to maintain the transition but undermined deeper democratization. Chilean parties must regain some of the support and levels of identification they enjoyed historically by attempting to reconnect with the citizenry. However, improving the representative capacity of parties is a multidimensional task, and when—and if—electoral reform takes place, additional efforts to ameliorate the collateral damage produced by the transitional enclaves will also be necessary.

There is hope for change and the abandonment of these transitional enclaves beyond the realm of simple institutional and party reform. Perhaps most importantly there is an exhaustion of potential political models. As Concertación governments wound down, some had hoped that the Piñera government would bring a fundamental change to Chilean politics. What it brought by most accounts was a governmental process quite similar to that pursued by the Concertación itself, similarly seeped in the policymaking model produced by the transitional enclaves. The Right seems to have accepted the basic outline of this policy model. There is a sense in Chile that now that we have tried "both sides" there is little choice but to try something new.

As we have noted, even though this may be the case among the population, the problem lies with politics at the elite level. This is not an intractable problem and there are signs of change on the horizon. The country and society have experienced some real transformations in recent years and there is hope that elites are waking up to this new Chile. We have characterized social mobilization as part of the "normalization" of politics, but it has the potential to jar elites enough to realize the seriousness of the manifold crises facing Chilean democracy. While initially students were at the helm of these protests, during 2011 and 2012 mobilizations ramped up, including protests by environmentalists, Mapuche indigenous groups, and trade unions. It may finally be sinking in among elites that these protests emerge from a widespread dissatisfaction with the responsiveness of political institutions.

In addition, social transformation is clearly afoot. Long, and perhaps incorrectly, portrayed as a "traditional" society, Chile is undeniably quite different than it was at the outset of the transition when even divorce remained illegal. The spectacular growth of women's involvement in politics and the scope, activism, and the growing acceptance of the environmental and gay movements point to an increasingly progressive society. Chilean social movements are shaking off the notion that human rights are defined solely with reference to the activities of the military, and engaging issues of identity including ethnicity, gender, and sexual orientation.

Chile's loss of status as Latin America's economic superstar is equally jarring and potentially transformational for politics. For many years Chile was considered a unique and laudable model to copy in the region. Now Chilean elites watch as Brazil and Peru surge ahead, and Chile must ponder its economic future as a natural resource–dependent country in which these resources, apart from copper, are fast becoming depleted, where the energy supply is increasingly limited and expensive, and where labor is not only relatively expensive, but also relatively unproductive. What will Chile's economic model look like for the next decades? The realization that Chile no longer makes headlines as Latin America's economic tiger should prompt a thorough soul-searching regarding how the country can maintain the edge it so desperately worked to achieve, being the first South American country that proudly joined the OECD club.

Even despite what we have argued here about the lack of deep reform to formal institutions, there is also momentum for change on the institutional front. As this book goes to print, Chile has already seen the end of obligatory voting, for better or for worse, and the potential for reform to the binomial electoral system has never been higher. Political elites have realized that it is a real impediment to change in the political model of the transition. In addition, a serious debate has emerged concerning the possibility of a completely new constitution.

Thus, despite the critical, and one might argue pessimistic, tone of this chapter, potential change is on the horizon. New forms of connection between the citizenry and parties, more real power for legislators in the legislative process, enhanced levels of internal party democracy, more responsive political institutions, and a real debate on the future of Chile's economic model are all elements of a much-needed and new form of politics and policymaking in Chile. These changes have the potential to dislodge the enclaves of the transition and produce a political model that better underwrites democracy in all of its dimensions including representation, legitimacy, and accountability.

Notes

The authors thank Alan Angell, Kent Eaton, Carlos Huneeus, and Gregory Weeks for their comments on an earlier version of this chapter, portions of which were previously published as a UC Berkeley Center for Latin American Studies Working Paper.

1. After Adolfo Zaldívar left the Christian Democratic Party in 2007 following an intense process of open political conflict within the party during which the leadership of the party's president, Soledad Alvear, was widely criticized, President Bachelet demonstrated her support for Alvear by nominating Edmundo Pérez Yoma as her new minister of the interior. The previous appointment to this position, Belisario Velasco, had also been a concession to Soledad Alvear, even though the minister and the president could never establish a good working relationship.

2. The appointment of Alejandro Foxley to the Ministry of Foreign Affairs (an area in which he had no particular expertise) and of Andrés Zaldívar to the Ministry

of the Interior were the most obvious rewards that President Bachelet handed out to two old hands of the Concertación who had helped her refocus her election campaign during the second round.

3. For example, President Bachelet appointed seven ministers from the PDC. This was a relatively low proportion of ministers compared to previous cabinets and left the PDC feeling marginalized. Furthermore, she appointed no ministers who were recognized supporters of the PDC president, Adolfo Zaldívar. Although Zaldívar supported President Bachelet during her election campaign, he did not reap his share of executive power rewards. President Bachelet's PDC nominations instead favored Zaldívar's archrival, Soledad Alvear. The structure of Bachelet's cabinet nominations therefore did nothing for the unity of the PDC and in fact stoked its already pronounced internal conflicts, which culminated with the expulsion of Adolfo Zaldívar from the party in November 2007, depriving the Bachelet administration of its legislative majority in the Senate.

4. Despite this official policy, President Bachelet also had a hermetic circle of advisers. It included finance minister Andrés Velasco, her communications strategist Juan Carvajal, and one of her best friends, María Angélica Alvarez ("la Jupi").

5. Navia has referred to these political mistakes as *los errores no forzados*. *Revista Capital*, "Las Culpas de Juan Carvajal," August 10, 2007.

6. Off the record interview with Siavelis, August 2009, Santiago.

7. Navia, "La Carta de Lagos," *La Tercera*, November 13, 2008. The opinion of his column was widely echoed in the press at the time.

8. Centro de Estudios Públicos (CEP), "Estudio Nacional de Opinión Pública, No. 56," November–December 2007. Available at www.cepchile.cl/bannerscep /encuestascep/encuestas_cep.html.

9. Ibid.

10. This majority was gradually whittled down as over time the Concertación was able to designate its own senators and as both Presidents Aylwin and Frei became lifelong senators. Changing the organic laws requires a three-fifths or four-sevenths majority as instituted by the Chilean constitution. The 2005 constitutional reform did not change this requirement.

11. This example holds for all Concertación governments, including the Bachelet government. Severance pay probably induces employers to attempt to circumvent legislation by hiring workers on a short-term or informal basis. In practice, a very large proportion of severance pay is never actually paid out in full, so workers rarely benefit from the legislation, and a potential reform would have little real impact on the functioning of the labor market. It would make much more sense to replace severance pay with more generous unemployment insurance.

12. For a discussion of the health reform, see Iniciativa Chilena de Equidad en Salud (2005).

13. This process of convergence can mainly be attributed to the fact that the right-wing Alianza has moved toward the political Center to make itself more electable.

14. In Chile, of course, the candidates themselves often do not have a voting record: in the Concertación's case, all presidential candidates since 1990 were former ministers of government. As for the opposition, some candidates have been senators (e.g., Sebastián Piñera), while others were also ministers or other officials.

15. If we consider union leadership as part of the policymaking elite that operates behind closed doors, the only nonelite members of the commissions were four representatives of the student movement.

16. The main divisive issues in education revolved around the teachers' statute (Estatuto Docente), union and collective bargaining legislation, and severance pay. For a discussion of these commissions, see Sehnbruch (2010) and Kubal (2010).

17. Reforms approved under the Piñera administration now make registration automatic and voting voluntary.

18. Marta Lagos (2008) and TV Senado interview, August 2008.

19. These numbers are based on analysis of every political opinion survey undertaken by the Centro de Estudios Públicos (CEP) between 1990 and 2008 where this question was asked. A total of thirty-seven surveys were consulted, which can be found at www.cepchile.cl/dms/lang_1/home.html.

20. Subcontracted workers launched strikes against the state copper company CODELCO, Aguas Claras, Arauco, and the fruit sector in Coquimbo. For details see López (2007a); Sehnbruch (2009); and Ugarte (2008).

21. Patricio Aylwin interview with Siavelis, Santiago, August 20, 2009.

Acronyms

AFDD	Agrupación de Familiares de los Detenidos Desaparecidos (Relatives of the Disappeared)
AFP	Administradoras de Fondos de Pensiones (Pension Fund Administrators)
ANI	Agencia Nacional de Inteligencia (National Intelligence Agency)
AUGE	Acceso Universal con Garantías Explícitas (Universal Access with Explicit Guarantees)
CASEN	Encuesta de Caracterización Socioeconómica Nacional (Chile's National Household Survey)
CEPAL	Comisión Económica para Amérca Latina y el Caribe (United Nations Economic Commission for Latin America and the Caribbean)
Ch1	Movimiento Chile Primero (Chile First Movement)
CIVIC	International Civic Education Study
CNI	Centro Nacional de Inteligencia (National Intelligence Center)
CNRR	Corporación Nacional de Reparación y Reconciliación (National Corporation for Reparation and Reconciliation)
CNVR	Comisión Nacional de Verdad y Reconciliación (National Commission on Truth and Reconciliation)
CODELCO	Corporación Nacional del Cobre (Chile's State-owned Copper Company)
CONEVAL	Consejo Nacional de Evaluación de la Política de Desarrollo Social (National Evaluation of Social Development Policy)

CPC	Confederacin de Producción y Comercio (Employer Confederation for Commerce and Production)
CUT	Central Unitaria de Trabajadores (Central Workers' Union)
DINA	Dirección Nacional de Inteligencia (National Intelligence Directorate)
ECEC	Early Education and Care Policies
ECLAC	Economic Commission for Latin America and the Caribbean
FDI	Foreign Direct Investment
FONASA	Fondo Nacional de Salud (National Health Service)
FPMR	Frente Patriótico Manuel Rodríguez (Manuel Rodríguez Patriotic Front)
FPS	Ficha de Protección Social (Social Protection Survey)
FTA	Free Trade Agreement
GATT	General Agreement on Tariffs and Trade
GDP	gross domestic product
GDR	German Democratic Republic
ICSO	Instituto de Investigación en Ciencias Sociales UDP (Universidad Diego Portales, UDP's Social Science Research Institute)
IMF	International Monetary Fund
INDH	Instituto Nacional de Derechos Humanos (National Human Rights Institute)
JOCAS	Jornadas de Conversación sobre Afectividad y Sexualidad (Conversations About Sexuality and Affection)
JUNAEB	Junta Nacional de Auxilio Escolar y Becas (National Scholarship and School Grants Board)
LGE	Ley General de Educación (General Law of Education)
LOCE	Ley Orgánica Constitucional de Enseñanza (Organic Constitutional Law of Teaching)
MAS	Movimiento Amplio Social (Broad Social Movement)
MIDEPLAN	Ministerio de Planificación (Chilean Ministry of Planning)
MUN	Movimiento de Unión Nacional (National Union Movement)
NGO	nongovernmental organization
NSC	National Security Council
ODEPLAN	Oficina de Planificación Nacional (National Planning Office)
OECD	Organization for Economic Cooperation and Development
Pasis	Programa de Pensiones Asistenciales (Pension Relief Program)
PELA	Parliamentary Elites in Latin America
PDC	Partido Demócrata Cristiano (Christian Democratic Party)
PH	Partido Humanista (Humanist Party)
PISA	Program for International Student Assessment

PN	Partido Nacional (National Party)
PPD	Partido por la Democracia (Party for Democracy)
PPP	purchasing power parity
PR	Partido Radical (Radical Party)
PRI	Partido Regionalista Independiente (Independent Regionalist Party)
PRSD	Partido Radical Social Demócrata (Radical Social Democratic Party)
PS	Partido Socialista (Socialist Party)
PSD	Partido Social Demócrata (Social Democratic Party)
RN	Renovación Nacional (National Renewal Party)
SCCJL	Senate Commission on the Constitution, Justice, and Legislature
SEC	Securities and Exchange Commission
SEGPRES	Ministerio Secretaría General de la Presidencia (Ministry General Secretariat of the Presidency)
SEP	Subvención Escolar Preferencial (Preferential Voucher Act)
SIMCE	Sistema de Medición de la Calidad de la Educación (Education Quality Measurement System)
SNED	Sistema Nacional de Evaluación de Desempeño de Establecimientos Subvencionados (National Evaluation System of Publicly Funded Schools)
TIMSS	Trends in International Mathematics and Science Study
UDI	Unión Demócrata Independiente (Independent Democratic Union)
UNDP	United Nations Development Program
UNHCHR	United Nations High Commissioner for Human Rights
UP	Unidad Popular (Popular Unity; the political coalition of Salvador Allende)
VAT	value-added tax

References

Agosin, M., and C. Bravo-Ortega. 2007. "The Emergence of New Successful Export Activities in Latin America: The Case of Chile," Working Paper no. 236, Department of Economics, University of Chile, Santiago.

Agostini, C., and P. Brown. 2007. *Local Distributional Effects of Government Cash Transfers in Chile.*William Davidson Institute Working Paper no. 872. Ann Arbor, University of Michigan.

Agüero, F. 2006. "Democracia, Gobierno y Militares desde el Cambio del Siglo: Avances Hacia la Normalidad Democrática." In R. Funk (ed.), *El Gobierno de Ricardo Lagos: La Nueva Vía Chilena hacia el Socialismo.* Santiago: Universidad Diego Portales.

Aguiar, M., and M. Bils. 2009. "Has Consumption Inequality Mirrored Income Inequality?" University of Rochester, mimeo.

Ahumada, J. 1958. *En vez de la Miseria.* Santiago: Editorial del Pacífico.

Alan Guttmacher Institute. 1994. *Aborto clandestino: Una realidad latinoamericana.* New York: Alan Guttmacher Institute.

Alkire, S., and J. Foster. 2007. *Counting and Multidimensional Poverty Measurement.* OPHI Working Paper Series. Oxford: Oxford Poverty and Human Development Initiative.

Allamand, A. 1999. *La travesía del desierto.* Santiago: Aguilar.

———. 2007. *El desalojo. Por qué la Concertación debe irse el 2010.* Santiago: Aguilar.

Altman, D. 2008. "Political Recruitment and Candidate Selection in Chile, 1990–2006: The Executive Branch." In P. M. Siavelis and S. Morgenstern (eds.), *Pathways to Power: Political Recruitment and Candidate Selection in Latin America.* University Park: Pennsylvania State University Press.

Alvaredo, F. 2011. "A Note on the Relationship Between Top Income Shares and the Gini Coefficient." *Economics Letters* 110(3): 274–277.

Álvarez, R. 2004. "Desempeño exportador de las empresas chilenas: Algunos hechos estilizados." *Cepal Review* 83: 121–134.

Andrade, C. 1991. *Reforma de la Constitución Política de la República de Chile de 1980.* Santiago: Editorial Jurídica de Chile.

335

Angell, A. 2003. "Party Change in Chile in Comparative Perspective." *Revista de Ciencia Política* 23(2): 88–108.

———. 2004. *Party Change in Chile in Comparative Perspective.* Paper presented at the Meeting of the Latin American Studies Association, Las Vegas, NV.

———. 2007. *Democracy After Pinochet.* London: Institute for the Study of the Americas, University of London.

Angell, A., and B. Pollack. 1990. "The Chilean Elections of 1989 and the Politics of the Transitions to Democracy." *Bulletin of Latin American Research* 9: 1–23.

———. 2000. "The Chilean Presidential Elections of 1999–2000 and Democratic Consolidation." *Bulletin of Latin American Research* 19: 357–378.

Archibugi, D., and A. Coco. 2003. "A New Indicator of Technological Capabilities for Developed and Developing Countries." *World Development* 32: 629–654.

Arellano, J. P. 1986. "Una mirada crítica a la reforma previsional de 1981." In S. Baeza (ed.), *Análisis de la previsión en Chile.* Santiago: CEP.

———. 2000. *Reforma educacional: Prioridad que se consolida.* Santiago: Editorial Los Andes.

Arenas, A. 2006. "The Structural Pension Reform in Chile: Effects, Comparisons with Other Latin American Reforms, and Lessons." *Oxford Review of Economic Policy* 22(1): 149–167.

———. 2010. *Historia de la reforma previsional chilena: Una experiencia exitosa de política pública en democracia.* Santiago: ILO.

Arenas, A., D. Bravo, J. Behrman, O. Mitchell, and P. Todd. 2008. "The Chilean Pension Reform Turns 25: Lessons from the Social Protection Survey." In S. Kay and T. Sinha (eds.), *Lessons from Pension Reform in the Americas.* Oxford: Oxford University Press.

Armstrong, A., and R. Aguila 2000. "Las huelgas en empresas del sector privado en Chile: 1979–1999." *Abante* 3(2): 165–201.

Arriagada, E. 2005. *UDI: ¿Partido popular o partido populista?: Consideraciones sobre el éxito electoral del Partido Unión Demócrata Independiente (UDI) en los sectores populares.* Santiago: Colección de Ideas.

Arriagada, I., and C. Mathivet. 2007. *Los programas de alivio a la pobreza Puente y Oportunidades: Una mirada desde los actores.* Santiago: CEPAL, Divisi n de Desarrollo Social.

Atkinson, A. B., T. Piketty, and E. Saez. 2009. "Top Incomes in the Long Run of History." *Journal of Economic Literature* 49(1): 3–71.

Atria, R. 2002. "La relación civil-militar entre 1994 and 2000: bases para un vambio." In Ó. Muñoz and C. Stefoni (eds.), *El período del Presidente Frei Ruiz-Tagle.* Santiago: Editorial Universitaria.

Attanasio, O., P. K. Goldberg, and E. Kyriazidou. 2008. "Credit Constraints in the Market for Consumer Durables: Evidence from Micro Data on Car Loans." *International Economic Review* 49(2): 401–436.

Attanasio, O., and M. Szekely. 1999. *An Asset-Based Approach to the Analysis of Poverty in Latin America.* Washington: IDB-OCE Working Paper no. R-376. Available at http://ssrn.com/abstract=223582 or doi:10.2139/ssrn.223582.

Austen-Smith, D., and J. Banks. 1988. "Elections, Coalitions, and Legislative Outcomes." *American Political Science Review* 82(2): 405–418.

Aylwin, P. 1998. *El reencuentro de los democratas: del golpe al triunfo del no.* Santiago, Chile: Ediciones B.

———. 2010. *Mensaje Presidencial, 21 de Mayo de 2010.* Santiago: Ministerio Secretaría General de la Presidencia.

Bachelet, M. 2005. *Programa de Gobierno.* Santiago.

Baldez, L. 2001. "Coalition Politics and the Limits of State Feminism." *Women and Politics* 22(4): 1–28.

Baldez, L., and J. M. Carey. 1999. "Presidential Agenda Control and Spending Policy: Lessons from General Pinochet's Constitution." *American Journal of Political Science* 43(1): 29–55.

Banerjee, A., and E. Duflo. 2011. *Poor Economics: A Radical Rethinking of the Way to Fight Global Poverty*. New York: Public Affairs.

Bardón, M. 1993. *Una experiencia económica fallida: Crónicas económicas (1971–1973) sobre el gobierno de la Unidad Popular*. Santiago: Universidad Finis Terrae.

Barozet, E., and M. Aubry. 2005. "De las reformas internas a la candidatura presidencial autónoma: Los nuevos caminos institucionales de Renovación Nacional. Política." *Política* 45: 165–196.

Barros, R. 2002. *Constitutionalism and Dictatorship: Pinochet, the Junta, and the 1980 Constitution*. New York: Cambridge University Press.

Baytelman, Y., K. Cowan, J. de Gregorio, and P. González. 1999. "Chile." In E. Ganuza, A. León, and P. Sauma (eds.), *Public Expenditure in Social Services in Latina America and the Caribbean. Analysis from the 20/20 initiative*. Santiago: UNDP-ECLAC-UNICEF.

Bedregal, P. 2010. "Hacia la evaluación de Chile Crece Contigo: Resultados psicosociales del estudio piloto." *Revista Médica de Chile* 138(6): 791–793.

Bellei, C. 2009. "Does Lengthening the School Day Increase Students' Academic Achievement? Results from a Natural Experiment in Chile." *Economics of Education Review* 28(5): 629–640.

Bellei, C., and P. González. 2003. *Educación y competitividad en Chile*. Documento de Trabajo. Santiago de Chile: Facultad Latinoamericana de Ciencias Sociales.

Bernales, E. 2005. "Los caminos de la reforma constitucional en el Perú." *Anuario de derecho constitucional latinoamericano* 5: 1–17.

Blofield, M. 2006. *The Politics of Moral Sin: Abortion and Divorce in Spain, Chile, and Argentina*. New York: Routledge.

———. 2012. *Care Work and Class: Domestic Workers' Struggle for Equal Rights in Latin America*. University Park: Pennsylvania State University Press.

Blofield, M., and L. Haas. 2005. "Defining a Democracy: Reforming the Laws on Women's Rights in Chile, 1990–2002." *Latin American Politics and Society* 47(3): 35–68.

———. 2011. "Gender Equality Policies in Latin America." In M. Blofield (ed.), *The Great Gap: Inequality and the Politics of Redistribution in Latin America*. University Park: Pennsylvania State University Press.

Boeninger, E. 1989. Gestión de gobierno y proceso de decisiones púbicas. Santiago: unpublished memorandum.

———. 1997. *Democracia en Chile: Lecciones para la gobernabilidad*. Santiago: Editorial Andrés Bello.

Borzutzky, S. 2002. *Vital Connections: Politics, Social Security, and Inequality in Chile*. Notre Dame: Notre Dame University Press.

———. 2009. "Anti-Poverty Policies in Chile: A Preliminary Assessment of the Chile Solidario Program." *Poverty and Public Policy* 1(1): 6.

———. 2010. "Socioeconomic Policies: Taming the Market in a Globalized Economy." In S. Borzutzky and G. Weeks (eds.), *The Bachelet Government*. Miami: University Press of Florida.

Borzutzky, S., and G. Weeks (eds.). 2010. *The Bachelet Government*. Miami: University Press of Florida.

Bosworth, B., R. Dornbusch, and R. Labán. 1994. *The Chilean Economy: Policy Lessons and Challenges.* Washington: Brookings Institution Press.

Boylan, D. 1996. "Taxation and Transition: The Politics of the 1990 Chilean Tax Reform." *Latin American Research Review* 31(1): 7–31.

———. 2001. *Defusing Democracy: Central Bank Autonomy and the Transition from Authoritarian Rule.* Ann Arbor: University of Michigan Press.

Bradshaw, S., and A. Quir s Víquez. 2008. "Women Beneficiaries or Women Bearing the Cost? A Gendered Analysis of the *Red de Protecci n Social* in Nicaragua." *Development and Change* 39(5): 823–824.

Brandolini, A., and T. M. Smeeding. 2008. "Income Inequality in Richer and OECD Countries." In W. Salverda, N. Nolan, and T. M. Smeeding (eds.), *Oxford Handbook on Economic Inequality.* Oxford: Oxford University Press.

Brock, P. 2000. "Financial Safety Nets: Lessons from Chile." *The World Bank Research Observer* 15(1): 69–84.

Brunner, J. J. 1986. *Notas para la discusión.* Personal Archive: unpublished manuscript.

———. 1990. "Chile: Claves de una transición pactada." *Nueva Sociedad* 106: 6–12.

Buchi, H. 1993. *La transformación económica de Chile.* Bogotá: Editorial Norma.

Budnevich, C., and G. Le Fort. 1997. "Capital Account Regulations and Macroeconomic Policy: Two Latin American Experiences." In *International Monetary and Financial Issues for the 1990s,* vol. 8. New York and Geneva: UNCTAD.

Buquet, D., and D. Chasquetti. 2004. "La Democracia en Uruguay: Una partidocracia de consenso." *Política y Gobierno* 42: 221–247.

Calvo, G., and E. Talvi. 2008. "Sudden Stop, Financial Factors and Economic Collapse in Latin America: Learning from Argentina and Chile." In N. Serra and J. E. Stiglitz (eds.), *The Washington Consensus Reconsidered: Towards a New Global Governance.* Initiative for Policy Dialogue Series. New York: Oxford University Press.

Campero, G. 2000. "Union Organization and Labor Relations." In C. Toloza and E. Lahera (eds.), *Chile in the Nineties.* Stanford: Stanford University Press.

Caporale, G. M., A. Cipollini, and P. Demetriades. 2002. *Monetary Policy and the Exchange Rate During the Asian Crisis Identification Through Heteroscedasticity.* Discussion Papers in Economics 00/11, Department of Economics, University of Leicester.

Carey, J., and P. M. Siavelis. 2005. "Insurance for Good Losers and the Survival of Chile's Concertación." *Latin American Politics and Society* 47(2): 1–22.

Casas, L., N. Nuñez, and X. Zavala. 1998. *Aborto: Elementos para una discusión necesaria.* Santiago: Instituto de la Mujer.

CASEN. 1989–2010. *Resultados Encuesta de Caracterización Socioeconómica Nacional.* Santiago: Ministerio de Planificación. http://observatorio.ministerio desarrollosocial.gob.cl/casen_publicaciones.php.

Castiglioni, R. 2005. *The Politics of Social Policy Change in Chile and Uruguay: Retrenchment Versus Maintenance, 1973–1998.* New York: Routledge.

Cavallo, A. 1992. *Los hombres de la transición.* Santiago: Andrés Bello.

———. 1998. *Historia oculta de la transición.* Santiago: Grijalbo.

Cavallo, A., M. Salazar, and O. Sepúlveda. 2004. *La historia oculta del régimen militar, 1973–1988.* Santiago: Debolsillo Ediciones.

CENDA. 2010. *Royalty a la minería. Antecedentes para un debate.* www.cenda chile.cl.

Central Bank of Chile. 1989–2010. Statistics Database. Santiago: Banco Central. www.bcentral.cl.

CEP. 1989–2010. Public opinion surveys. Santiago: Centro de Estudios Públicos. www.cepchile.cl.

CEP, Cieplan, Libertad y Desarrollo, PNUD y Proyecto América. 2008. *Estudio nacional sobre partidos políticos y sistema electoral*. Santiago.

CEPAL. 2009. "Panorama social de América Latina." Santiago: CEPAL/ECLAC.

CERC. 1989–2010. Public opinion surveys. Santiago: Centro de Estudios de la Realidad Contemporánea. www.cerc.cl.

Chay, K. Y., P. J. McEwan, and M. Urquiola. 2003. "The Central Role of Noise in Evaluating Interventions That Use Test Scores to Rank Schools." NBER Working Papers 10118. National Bureau of Economic Research, Cambridge, MA.

Chioda, L. 2011. *Work and Family: Latin America and Caribbean Women in Search of New Balance*. Washington, DC: International Bank for Reconstruction and Development.

Collins, C. 2009. "Memorial Fragments, Monumental Silences and Reawakenings in 21st-Century Chile." *Millennium* 38(2): 379–400.

———. 2010a. *Post-Transitional Justice: Human Rights Prosecutions in Chile and El Salvador*. University Park: Pennsylvania State University Press.

———. 2010b. "Human Rights Trials in Chile During and After the 'Pinochet Years.'" *International Journal of Transitional Justice* 4(1): 67–86.

CONEVAL. 2012. *Metodologia de Medicion Multidimensional de la Pobreza en Mexico (CONEVAL)*. http://www.coneval.gob.mx/Paginas/principal.aspx.

Constable, P., and A. Valenzuela. 1991. *A Nation of Enemies: Chile Under Pinochet*. New York: Norton.

Contreras, A., J. Rodríguez, C. Tokman, and E. Vásquez. 2008. *Activos financieros del tesoro público chileno: Resultados y desafíos*. Santiago: Government of Chile, Ministry of Finance, Public Finance Studies.

Contreras, D., and O. Larrañaga. 2010. *Las nuevas políticas de protección social en Chile*. Santiago: Uqbar.

Cook, M. L. 2007. *Politics of Labor Reform in Latin America: Between Flexibility and Rights*. University Park: Pennsylvania State University Press.

Coppedge, M. 1994. *Strong Parties and Lame Ducks: Presidential Partyarchy and Factionalism in Venezuela*. Stanford: Stanford University Press.

Corbo, V. 2000. *Monetary Policy in Latin America in the 90s*. Santiago: Central Bank of Chile.

———. 2005. *Ochenta años de historia del Banco Central de Chile*. Working Document no. 345. Santiago: Central Bank of Chile.

———. 2011. *Propuestas para perfeccionar la Regla Fiscal*. Final Report. Comité Asesor para el Diseño de una Política Fiscal de Balance Estructural de Segunda Generación para Chile. Santiago: Ministry of Finance.

Corkill, D. R. 1976. "The Chilean Socialist Party and the Popular Front 1933–41." *Journal of Contemporary History* 11(2/3): 261–273.

Correa, J. 1999. "Cenicienta se queda en la fiesta: El poder judicial chileno en la década de los 90." In Paul Drake and Iván Jaksic (eds.), *El modelo chileno: Democracia y desarrollo en los noventa*. Santiago: LOM Ediciones.

———. 2001. *Historia del siglo XX chileno: Balance paradojal*. Santiago: Editorial Sudamericana.

Correa, S. 2005. *Con las riendas del poder. La derecha chilena en el siglo XX*. Santiago: Editorial Sudamericana.

Cortázar, R. 1993. *Política laboral en el Chile democrático: Avances y desafíos en los noventa*. Santiago: Dolmen Ediciones SA.

Corvalán, L. 2003. *El gobierno de Salvador Allende*. Santiago: LOM Ediciones.

Cowan, K., and J. De Gregorio. 2007. "International Borrowing, Capital Controls, and the Exchange Rate: Lessons from Chile." In S. Edwards (ed.), *Capital Controls and Capital Flows in Emerging Economies: Policies, Practices and Consequences.* Chicago: University of Chicago Press.

Cox, C., and P. González, 1997. "Education: From Improvement Programs to Reform." In René Cortázar and Joaquín Vial (eds.), *Building Options: Economic and Social Proposals for the Next Century,* 1997. Santiago: CIEPLAN-Dolmen.

Cox, G., and S. Morgenstern. 2001. "Latin America's Reactive Assemblies and Proactive Presidents." *Comparative Politics* 33(2): 171–189.

Cristi, R. 2000. *El pensamiento político de Jaime Guzmán. Autoridad y libertad.* Santiago: LOM Ediciones.

Dalsgaard, T. 2001. "The Tax System in New Zealand: An Appraisal and Options for Change." Economics Department Working Paper no. 281. Paris: OECD.

Datt, G., and M. Ravallion. 1992. "Growth and Redistribution Components of Changes in Poverty Measures." *Journal of Development Economics* 38: 275–295.

De Gregorio, J., and R. Valdés. 2001. "Crisis Transmission: Evidence from the Debt, Tequila, and Asian Flu Crises." *World Bank Economic Review* 15(2): 289–314.

Deheza, G. I. 1997. *Gobiernos de coalición en el sistema presidencial: América del Sur.* Unpublished manuscript.

Deininger, K., and L. Squire. 1996. *Measuring Income Inequality: A New Database.* World Bank Group. www.worldband.org/research/growth/absineq.htm.

Denis, A., F. Gallegos, and C. Sanhueza. 2010. *Pobreza multidimensional en Chile: 1990–2009.* Documento de Trabajo, ILADES-Universidad Alberto Hurtado, Santiago.

Denis, A., J. J. Prieto, and J. R. Zubizarreta. 2007. "Dinámica de la pobreza en Chile: Evidencias en los años 1996, 2001 y 2006." *Persona y Sociedad* 21(3): 9–30.

Díaz, J., R. Lüders, and G. Wagner. 1998. Economía Chilena, 1810–1995: Evolución Cuantitativa del Producto total y sectorial. Documento de Trabajo no. 186, Instituto de Economía de la Pontificia Universidad Católica de Chile, Santiago.

DIPRES. 2011. Estadísticas de Finanzas Públicas. www.dipres.cl.

Dirección del Trabajo. 2008. Encuesta Laboral (ENCLA). Biannual survey of the Dirección del Trabajo.

Drake, P., and I. Jaksic (eds.).1999. *El modelo chileno: Democracia y desarrollo en los noventa.* Santiago: LOM.

Durruty, A. V. 1999. *La derecha desatada.* Santiago: Planeta.

Echeverría, C., P. González, and P. Romaguera. 1995. "Chile: Reforming the Labour Market in a Liberalised Economy." In G. Márquez (ed.), *Regulación del mercado de trabajo en América Latina.* Baltimore and Washington: Johns Hopkins University Press and the Interamerican Development Bank.

Echeverría, M. 2010. *La historia inconclusa de la subcontratación.* Santiago: Dirección del Trabajo.

Echeverría, M., and V.Uribe.1998. *Condiciones de trabajo en sistemas de subcontratación.* Santiago: ILO.

ECLAC. 1998. *Impact of the Asian Crisis on Latin America.* Santiago.

———. 2011a. *Social Panorama of Latin America.* Santiago: ECLAC.

———. 2011b. "CEPALSTAT, Latin America and the Caribbean Statistics." Econstat database, online dataset. www.eclac.cl/estadisticas.

Edwards, S. 1996. "Exchange-Rate Anchors, Credibility, and Inertia: A Tale of Two Crises, Chile and Mexico." *American Economic Review* 86(2): 176–180.

Edwards, S., and A. Cox-Edwards. 1987. *Monetarism and Liberalization: The Chilean Experiment.* Cambridge, MA: Ballinger.

Edwards, S., and R. Rigobón. 2009. "Capital Controls on Inflows, Exchange Rate Volatility and External Vulnerability." *Journal of International Economics* 78(2): 256–267.

Elacqua, G. 2006. "Enrollment Practices in Response to Vouchers." Teachers College. National Center for the Study of Privatization in Education. Occasional Paper 125, London.

El Mercurio.com. 2009. "Presidenta Bachelet vuelve a marcar récord de apoyo a su gestión." September 4.

Engel, E., A. Galetovic, and C.-E. Raddatz. 1999. "Taxes and Income Distribution in Chile: Some Unpleasant Redistributive Arithmetic." *Journal of Development Economics* 59: 155–192.

Ensalaco, M. 1994. "In with the New, Out with the Old? The Democratising Impact of Constitutional Reform in Chile."*Journal of Latin American Studies* 26(2): 409–429.

———. 1999. *Chile Under Pinochet: Recovering the Truth.* University Park: Pennsylvania State University Press.

Esping-Andersen, G. 1990. *The Three Worlds of Welfare Capitalism.* Cambridge, UK: Polity Press.

———. 1996. *Welfare State in Transition: National Adaptations in Global Economies.* London: Sage.

———. 1999. *Social Foundations of Post-Industrial Economies.* Oxford: Oxford University Press.

Fairfield, T. 2010. "Business Power and Tax Reform: Taxing Income and Profits in Chile and Argentina." *Latin American Politics and Society* 52(2): 37–71.

Feldman, M.P. 1999. "The New Economics of Innovation, Spillovers and Agglomeration: A Review of Empirical Studies." *Economics of Innovation and New Technology* 8:5–25.

Feres, J. C., and X. Mancero. 2001. *Enfoques para la medición de la pobreza: Breve revisión de la literatura.* Estudios Estadísticos y Prospectivos. Santiago: CEPAL.

Ferraro, A. 2008. "Friends in High Places: Congressional Influence on the Bureaucracy in Chile." *Latin American Politics and Society* 50(2): 101–129.

Ffrench-Davis, R. 1973. *Políticas económicas en Chile, 1952–1970.* Santiago: Ediciones Nueva Universidad.

———. 1991. "Desarrollo económico y equidad en Chile: herencias y desafíos en el retorno a la democracia." *Colección Estudios Cieplan* no. 31. Santiago.

———. 2008. "La equidad social, un gran desafío para Chile." Working Paper SDT276, Department of Economics, University of Chile, Santiago.

———. 2010a. *Economic Reforms in Chile: From Dictatorship to Democracy.* London: Palgrave.

———. 2010b. "The Structural Fiscal Balance in Chile: Toward a Counter-Cyclical Macroeconomics." *Journal of Globalization and Development* 1(1): 1–19.

Ffrench-Davis, R., P. Leiva, and R. Madrid. 1992. *Trade Liberalization in Chile: Experiences and Prospects.* Santiago: United Nations.

Ffrench-Davis, R., and O. Múñoz. 1990. "Desarrollo Económico, Inestabilidad, y Desequilibrios Políticos en Chile." *Colección Estudios Cieplan* no. 28, Santiago.

Ffrench-Davis, R., M. R. Agosín, and A. Uthoff. 1995. "Capital Movements, Export Strategy, and Macroeconomic Stability in Chile." In R. Ffrench-Davis and S. Griffith-Jones (eds.), *Coping with Capital Surges: The Return of Finance to Latin America.* Boulder: Lynne Rienner.

Figueroa, E. 1998. "Economic Rents and Environmental Management and Natural Resource Sectors." Faculty of Business, Universidad de Alberta, Alberta, Canada.

Fischer, R., P. González, and P. Serra. 2006. "Does Competition in Privatized Social Services Work? The Chilean Experience." *World Development* 34(4): 647–664.

Fiszbein, A., N. R. Schady, and F. H. Ferreira. 2009. *Conditional Cash Transfers: Reducing Present and Future Poverty.* Washington, DC: World Bank Publications.

Fleet, M., and B. H. Smith. 1997. *The Catholic Church and Democracy in Chile and Peru.* Notre Dame: University of Notre Dame Press.

Forbes Magazine. Various years. "The World's Billionaires." www.forbes.com.

Franceschet, S. 2010. "Explaining Domestic Violence Policy Outcomes in Chile and Argentina." *Latin American Politics and Society* 52(2): 1–29.

Frank, V. 2002. *The Labour Movement in Democratic Chile, 1990–2000.* Working paper no. 298, Helen Kellogg Institute for International Studies, University of Notre Dame.

———. 2004. "Politics Without Policy: The Failure of Social Concertation in Democratic Chile, 1990–2000." In P. Winn (ed.), *Victims of the Chilean Miracle: Workers and Neoliberalism in the Pinochet Era, 1973–2002.* Durham, NC: Duke University Press.

Frías, P. 2002. *Desafíos del sindicalismo en los inicios del siglo XXI.* Buenos Aires: CLACSO.

Friedman, M. 1962. *Capitalism and Freedom.* Chicago, IL: University of Chicago Press.

Fritsch, M., and G. Franke. 2004. "Innovation, Regional Knowledge Spillovers and R&D Cooperation." *Research Policy* 33: 245–255.

Frohmann, A., and T. Valdés. 1993. "Democracy in the Country and in the Home: The Women's Movement in Chile." Santiago: Flacso.

Fuentes, C. 2006. *La Transición de los Militares.* Santiago: LOM.

Fuentes, C. (ed.). 2010. *En nombre del pueblo: Debate sobre el cambio constitucional en Chile.* Santiago: Universidad Diego Portales y Fundación Böll Cono Sur.

Fuentes, C. 2010–2011. "A Matter of the Few: Dynamics of Constitutional Change in Chile, 1990–2010." *Texas Law Review* 16(2): 1741–1776.

Fundación Futuro. 2004. *Estudio de opinión pública: informe de la comisión sobre prisión política y tortura.* www.fundacionfuturo.cl.

FUNASUPRO (Fundación para la Superación de la Pobreza). 2009. *Umbrales Sociales para Chile.*

Gaete, G., and J. Ruiz-Tagle. 2011. *Evaluación de impacto del Programa de Apoyo al Microemprendimiento (PAME) mediante datos administrativos.* Unpublished manuscript.

Galasso, E. 2006. *With Their Effort and One Opportunity: Alleviating Extreme Poverty in Chile.* Development Research Group. Washington, DC: World Bank.

Gallego, F. A. 2002. "Competencia y resultados educativos: teoría y evidencia para Chile." Working Paper 150, Central Bank of Chile, Santiago.

Gallego, F., and N. Loayza. 2004. "Financial Structure in Chile: Macroeconomic Developments and Microeconomic Effects." In A. Demirgüç-Kunt and R. Levine (eds.), *Financial Structure and Economic Growth: A Cross-Country Comparison of Banks, Markets, and Development.* Cambridge: MIT Press.

Garcés, J. E. 1976. *Allende y la experiencia chilena: las armas de la política.* Barcelona: Editorial Ariel.

García-Huidobro, J. E. 1994. "Positive Discrimination in Education: Its Justification and a Chilean Example." *International Review of Education.* 40(3–5): 209–221.

———. 1999. *The Chilean Education Reform.* Madrid: Editorial Popular.

Garretón, M.A. 1983. *El proceso político chileno.* Santiago: FLACSO.

———. 1987a. *La unidad popular y el conflicto político en Chile.* Santiago: Ediciones Minga.

———. 1987b. *Reconstruir la política: Transición y consolidación democrática en Chile.* Santiago: Editorial Andante.

———. 1989. "La oposición política partidaria en el régimen militar chileno: Un proceso de aprendizaje para la transición." In M. A. Garretón and M. Cavarozzi (eds.), *Muerte y resurrección: Los partidos políticos en el autoritarismo y las transiciones del cono sur.* Santiago: FLACSO.

———. 1993. *La redemocratización en Chile: Transición, inauguración y evolución.* Estudios Interdisciplinarios de América Latina y el Caribe (EIAL). www.tau.ac.il/eial/IV_1/garreton.htm.

———. 1996. "Human rights in Democratization Processes." In E. Jelin and E. Hershberg (eds.), *Constructing Democracy: Human Rights, Citizenship, and Society in Latin America.* Westview: Boulder.

———. 2000. "Atavism and Ambiguity in the Chilean Right: Conservative Parties, the Right and Democracy in Latin America". In K. J. Middlebrook (ed.), *Conservative Parties, the Right, and Democracy in Latin America.* Baltimore: Johns Hopkins University Press.

———. 2003. *Incomplete Democracy: Political Democratization in Chile and Latin America.* Chapel Hill: University of North Carolina Press.

Garretón, M. A., and R. Garretón. 2010. "La democracia incompleta en Chile." *Revista de Ciencia Política* 30(1): 115–148.

Gazmuri, C. 2000. *Eduardo Frei Montalva y su época.* Santiago: Editorial Aguilar.

Godwin, K., and F. Kemerer, 2002. *School Choice Tradeoffs: Liberty, Equity, and Diversity.* Austin: University of Texas Press.

Gómez-Sabaini, J. C. 2010. "Tributación, evasión y equidad en américa latina y el caribe." Presentation in Finanzas Publicas y evasión en América Latina, Antigua, Guatemala, August 25–26.

Gómez Sabaini, J. C., and R. Martner. 2010. "América Latina: Panorama global de su sistema tributario y principales temas de política." *Gobernanza democrática y fiscalidad.* Madrid: Editorial Tecnos.

González, P. 1996. "Normativa y política laboral en Chile." Colección Estudios, CIEPLAN 43, Santiago, September.

———. 1998. "Financiamiento de la educación en Chile." In PREAL-UNESCO (ed.), *Financiamiento de la educación en América Latina.* Santiago: UNESCO.

———. 2000. "Educación superior: ¿Asignatura pendiente?" *Revista Perspectivas en Economía, Política y Gestión* 4(1): 89–120.

González, P., A. Mizala, and P. Romaguera. 2000. "Recursos diferenciados para la educación subvencionada." Informe final. Santiago: MINEDUC.

Guari, V. 1998. *School Choice in Chile: Two Decades of Educational Reform.* Pittsburgh: University of Pittsburgh Press

Haagh, L. 2002. *Citizenship, Labor Markets and Democratization: Chile and the Modern Sequence.* Basingstoke: Palgrave Macmillan.

Haas, L. 2010. *Feminist Policymaking in Chile.* University Park: Pennsylvania State University Press.

————. 1999. "The Catholic Church in Chile: New Political Alliances." In C. Smith and J. Prokopy (eds.), *Latin American Religion in Motion*. New York: Routledge.

Haque, N. U., and P. J. Montiel. 1989. "Consumption in Developing Countries: Tests for Liquidity Constraints and Finite Horizons." *Review of Economics and Statistics* 71(3): 408–415.

Hardy, C. 1997. *La reforma social pendiente*. Santiago: Ediciones de Chile 21.

Hardy, C. 2010. *De la protección social a una sociedad que iguala oportunidades y derechos.*" Ideas para Chile: Aportes de la Centroizquierda. Santiago: Lom.

Harvey, D. 2007. *A Brief History of Neoliberalism*. Oxford: Oxford University Press.

Haughton, J., and S. R. Khandker. 2009. *Handbook on Poverty and Inequality*. Washington: World Bank.

Heiss, C., and P. Navia. 2007. "You Win Some, You Lose Some: Constitutional Reforms in Chile's Transition to Democracy." *Latin American Politics and Society* 49(3): 163–190.

Henig, J. 2008. *Spin Cycle: How Research Is Used in Policy Debates: The Case of Charter Schools*. New York: Russell Sage Foundation.

Henoch, P., R. Troncoso, and E. Valdivieso. 2010. "Evolución de la pobreza y focalización de los subsidios: ¿Por qué hay más pobres en chile?" *Libertad y Desarrollo, Informe Social* 130: 38.

Hilbink, L. 2007. *Judges Beyond Politics in Democracy and Dictatorship: Lessons from* Chile. New York: Cambridge University Press.

Hite, K., and C. Collins. 2009. "Memorial Fragments, Monumental Silences and Reawakenings in 21st-Century Chile." *Millennium* 38(2): 379–400.

Hoffmeister, L. 2010. "¿Quiénes están insatisfechos con su sistema provisional de salud?" Santiago: Ministerio de Salud.

Hsieh, C. T., and M. Urquiola. 2006. "The Effects of Generalized School Choice on Achievement and Stratification: Evidence from Chile's Voucher Program." *Journal of Public Economics* (90): 1477–1503.

Htun, M. N., and L. Weldon. 2010. "When Do Governments Promote Women's Rights? A Framework for the Comparative Analysis of Sex Equality Policy." *Perspectives on Politics* 8(1): 207–216.

Human Rights Watch. 2004. "Undue Process: Terrorism Trials, Military Courts and the Mapuche in Southern Chile," October 27. http://www.hrw.org/en/reports /2004/10/27/undue-process.

Huneeus, A. 2010. "Judging from a Guilty Conscience: The Chilean Judiciary's Human Rights Turn." *Law and Social Inquiry* 35(1): 99–135.

Huneeus, C. 1998. *Malestar y desencanto en Chile: Legados del autoritarismo y costos de la transición*. Working Paper no. 63, Corporación Tiempo.

————. 2001a. *El régimen de Pinochet*. Santiago: Sudamericana.

————. 2001b. *La derecha en el Chile después de Pinochet: El caso de la Unión Demócrata Independiente*. Working Paper, no. 285, Kellog Institute, Notre Dame.

————. 2003a. *Chile: un país dividido*. Santiago: Catalonia.

————. 2003b. "The Consequences of the Pinochet Case for Chilean Politics." In M. Davis (ed.), *The Pinochet Case: Origins, Progress and Implications*. London: Institute for Latin American Studies.

————. 2007. *The Pinochet Regime*. Boulder: Lynne Rienner.

————. 2011."La Iglesia en la encrucijada." *Revista Mensaje* (May): 134–139.

Huneeus, C., and S. Ibarra. Forthcoming. "The Memory of the Pinochet Regime in Public Opinion." In C. Collins, K. Hite, and A. Joignant (eds.), *The Politics of Memory in Chile: From Pinochet to Bachelet*. Boulder: Lynne Rienner.

Hunter, W. 1997. "Continuity or Change? Civil-Military Relations in Democratic Argentina, Chile, and Peru." *Political Science Quarterly* 112(3): 453–475.

ILO. 2007. "Panorama Laboral." Lima. www.ilo.org/americas/publicaciones/panorama-laboral/lan--es/index.htm.

Infante, R. (ed.) 1991. *Social Debt: The Challenge of Equity*. Santiago: PREALC.

Iniciativa Chilena de Equidad en Salud. 2005. "En la perspectiva de la equidad: determinantes sociales de la salud en Chile." Santiago.

Infante, A. and G. Paraje. 2010. "Reforma de salud: Garantías exigibles como derecho ciudadano." In D. Contreras, and O. Larrañaga (eds.), *Las nuevas políticas de protección social en Chile*. Santiago: PNUD and Uqbar Editores.

Instituto Nacional de Derechos Humanos (INDH). 2011. *Primera encuesta de derechos humanos 2011*. Santiago: INDH.

Insunza, A., and J. Ortega. 2005. *Michelle Bachelet: La historia no oficial*. Santiago: Debate, Random House Mondadori.

Izquierdo, J. M., and P. Navia. 2007. "Cambio y continuidad en la elección de Bachelet." *América Latina Hoy* 46: 75–96.

Jappelli, T. 1990. "Who Is Credit Constrained in the US Economy?" *Quarterly Journal of Economics* 105(1): 219–234.

Joignant, A., and P. Navia. 2003. "De la política de individuos a los hombres del partido: Socialización, competencia política, y penetración electoral de la UDI (1989-2001)." *Estudios Públicos* 89: 129–171.

Jørgensen, H. 2009. "The Danish 'Flexicurity' System and the Relevant Lessons for Latin America." In J. Weller (ed.), *Regulation, Worker Protection and Active Labour-Market Policies in Latin America*. Santiago: CEPAL.

Jorratt, M. 2009. "La tributación directa en Chile: Equidad y desafíos." Serie Macroeconomia para el Desarrollo 92. Santiago: Comisión Económica para América Latina y el Caribe (CEPAL).

Kalter, E. 2004. *Chile: Institutions and Policies Underpinning Stability and Growth*. Washington: International Monetary Fund.

Krasnokutskaya, E., L. Ressner, and P. Todd. 2010. "Choice of Product Under Government Regulation: The Case of Chile's Privatized Pension System.", Unpublished manuscript, http://www.bus.umich.edu/academics/departments/be/pdf/krasnokskaya%20chile1104_1.pdf.

Kubal, M. R. 2010. "Challenging the Consensus: The Politics of Protest and Policy Reform in Chile's Education System." In S. Borzutzky and G. Weeks (eds.), *The Bachelet Government*. Miami: University Press of Florida.

Lagos, M. 2008. "La Concertación de Partidos por la Democracia: Análisis de una Experiencia Exitosa y Proyecciones." Presentation given at the seminar Fundación Chile 21, Santiago.

Lagos, R. 2008. *Declaración*. November 12. Santiago: Fundación por la Democracia y el Desarrollo.

Lahera, E., and M. Ortúzar. 1998. "Military Expenditures and Development in Latin America." *CEPAL Review* no. 65 (August), Santiago.

Landerretche, O., and K. Sehnbruch. 2011. *The Quality of Employment in Different Economic Sectors*. Unpublished manuscript.

Larraín, C. 1995. "Internacionalización y supervisión de la banca en Chile." *Estudios Públicos* 60 (Spring): 118–142.

Larraín, F. 2008. "Cuatro millones de pobres en Chile: Actualizando la línea de pobreza." *Estudios Públicos* 109: 101–147.

Larraín, F., and R. Vergara. 2000. *La transformación económica de Chile*. Santiago: CEP.

Larrañaga, O. 2001. "Distribución de Ingresos en Chile: 1958–2001." In R. Ffrench-Davis and B. Stallings (eds.), *Reformas, crecimiento y políticas sociales en Chile desde 1973*. Santiago: CEPAL/LOM Ediciones.

Larrañaga, O., D. Contreras, and J. Ruiz-Tagle. 2012. "Impact Evaluation of Chile Solidario: Lessons and Policy Recommendations."*Journal of Latin American Studies* 44(2): 347–372.

Latinobarómetro. 2007. "Informe, Latinobarómetro 2007." www.latinobarometro.org.

Laver, M., and K. A. Shepsle.1990. "Coalitions and Cabinet Government." *American Political Science Review* 84(3): 873–890.

Lavezzolo, S. 2006. "Central Bank Independence in Developing Countries, a Signaling Mechanism?" Estudio/Working Paper 2006/229, Instituto Juan March de Estudios e Investigaciones, Madrid.

Lehmann, C. 2002. "¿Cuán religiosos son los chilenos? Mapa de la religiosidad en 31 países." *Estudios Públicos* 85: 21–40.

Linz, J. J., and A. Valenzuela (eds.). 1994. *The Failure of Presidential Democracy. Vol. 2: The Case of Latin America*. Baltimore: Johns Hopkins University Press.

Lira, E. 2006. "Human Rights in Chile: The Long Road to Truth, Justice, and Reparations." In S.Borzutzky and L. Hecht Oppenheim (eds.), *After Pinochet: The Chilean Road to Democracy and the Market*. Gainesville: University Press of Florida.

Londregan, J. B. 2000. *Legislative Institutions and Ideology in Chile*. New York: Cambridge University Press.

López, D. 2007a. "Subcontratación y Negociación Colectiva: Porqué Sí y Porqué No." Santiago, blog post. Accessed, January 20, 2008.

———. 2007b. Interview in La Segunda.

López, R., and G. Galinato, 2007. "Should Governments Stop Subsidies to Private Goods? Evidence from Rural Latin America." *Journal of Public Economics* 91: 1071–1094.

López, R., and S. Miller. 2008. "Chile: The Unbearable Burden of Inequality." *World Development* 36(12): 2679–2695.

Loveman, B. 1991."¿Misión cumplida? Civil Military Relations and the Chilean Political Transition." *Journal of Inter American Studies and World Affairs* 33(3): 35–74.

———. 1999. *For la Patria. Politics and the Armed Forces in Latin America*. Wilmington, DE: Scholarly Resources.

———. 2001. *Chile: The Legacy of Hispanic Capitalism*. New York: Oxford University Press.

———. 2005. "The Transition to Civilian Government in Chile, 1990–1994." In Paul W. Drake and Iván Jaksic (eds.), *The Struggle for Democracy in Chile*. Lincoln: University of Nebraska Press.

Loveman, B., and E. Lira. 2000. *Las ardientes cenizas del olvido*. Santiago: LOM Ediciones.

Luna, J. P. 2008. "Partidos políticos y sociedad en Chile: Trayectoria histórica y mutaciones recientes." In A. Fontaine (ed.), *Reforma de los partidos políticos en Chile*. Santiago: CIEPLAN.

Luna, J. P., and R. Mardones. 2010. "Chile: Are the Parties Over?" *Journal of Democracy* 21(3): 107–121.

Mainwaring, S. 1993. "Presidentialism, Multipartism, and Democracy." *Comparative Political Studies* 26(2): 198–228.

Mainwaring, S., and T. R. Scully (eds.). 1995. *Building Democratic Institutions: Party Systems in Latin America.* Stanford: Stanford University Press.

Marcel, M., M. Tokman, R. Valdés, and P. Benavides. 2001. "Balance estructural: La base de la nueva regla de política fiscal chilena." *Revista Economía* 4(3): 5–27.

Marcel, M., and C. Tokman. 2005. "Como se financia la educación en Chile?" *Estudios de Finanzas Publicas.* Santiago: Gobierno de Chile, Ministerio de Hacienda.

Marenghi, P., and M. García Montero. 2008. "The Conundrum of Representation." In M. Alcántara Sáez (ed.), *Politicians and Politics in Latin America.* Boulder: Lynne Rienner.

Margozzini, F. 1988. "Estimaciones de las pensiones de vejez que otorgará el actual sistema de pensiones." In S. Baeza and R. Manubens (eds.), *Sistema privado de pensiones en Chile.* Santiago: CEP 1988.

Massad, C. 2003. "Central Banking: The Chilean Experience from the 1990s." Washington, DC: Center for Strategic and International Studies (CSIS).

Meller, P. 1992. *Estrategia comercial chilena en la década del 90: Elementos para el debate.* Santiago: Ediciones CIEPLAN.

Meller, P., S. Lehman, and R. Cifuentes. 1993. "Los gobiernos de Aylwin y Pinochet: Comparación de indicadores económicos y sociales." Apuntes CIEPLAN no. 118. September.

———. 1996. *Un siglo de economía política chilena: 1890–1990.* Santiago: Editorial Andrés Bello.

Meller, P. 1999. "Pobreza y distribución de ingreso en Chile (Década de los noventa)." In P. Drake and I. Jaksic (eds.), *El Modelo Chileno: Democracia y Desarrollo en los Noventa.* Santiago: LOM Ediciones.

———(ed). 2005. *La paradoja aparente: Equidad y eficiencia, resolviendo el dilema.* Santiago: Taurus.

Mendelson, S., and T. Gerber. 2006. "Failing the Stalin Test." *Foreign Affairs* 85(1): 2–8.

MIDEPLAN. 2004. "Chile Solidario." Presentation by Yasna Provoste, minister of planning, October 26, Santiago.

Milos, P. 2008. *Frente Popular en Chile: Su configuración, 1935–1938.* Santiago: LOM Ediciones.

Mishkin, F., and M. A. Savastano. 2001. "Monetary Policy Strategies for Latin America." *Journal of Development Economics* 66(2): 415–444.

Missoni, E., and G. Solimano. 2010. *Towards Universal Health Coverage: The Chilean Experience.* Background Paper, Working Paper no. 4, Geneva, World Health Organization, Geneva.

Mizala, A., and P. Romaguera. 1996. *Estándares laborales y protección potencial: ¿Amenazas para Chile?* Documentos de Trabajo, Serie Económica, Centro de Economía Aplicada, Universidad de Chile, Santiago.

———. 2005. "Teacher's Salary Structure and Incentives in Chile." In Emilia Vegas (ed.), *Incentives to Improve Teaching: Lessons from Latin America.* Washington, DC: World Bank.

Mizala, A. 2007. "La economía política de la reforma educacional en Chile." *Serie Estudios Socioeconómicos* no. 36. Santiago: CIEPLAN.

Molina, S. 1977. *El proceso de cambio en Chile: la experiencia 1965–1970.* Santiago: Editorial Universitaria.

Molineaux, M. 2006. "Mothers at the Service of the New Poverty Agenda: Progresa/ Oportunidades, Mexico's Conditional Transfer Program." *Social Policy and Administration* 40(4): 437.

Monfort, B. 2008. *Chile: Trade Performance, Trade Liberalization, and Competitiveness* (EPub), Vol. 8–128 of IMF working paper.

Morales, M., and R. Bugueño. 2001. "La UDI como expresión de la nueva derecha en Chile." *Revista de Estudios Sociales* 107: 215–248.

Morales M. 2004. *Zorros y leones en la derecha política chilena: La coalición de partidos UDI-RN, 1989–2001.* Tesis para optar al grado de Maestro en Ciencias Sociales XIV Promoción, 2002–2004, FLACSO.

Morandé, F., and M. Tapia. 2002. "Exchange Rate Policy in Chile: From the Band to Floating and Beyond." Working Paper no. 152, Central Bank of Chile, Santiago.

Morgenstern, S., and B. Nacif (eds.). 2002. *Legislative Politics in Latin America.* Cambridge: Cambridge University Press.

Moulián, T. 2006. *Fracturas: de Pedro Aguirre Cerda a Salvador Allende: 1938–1973.* Santiago: LOM Ediciones.

Muñoz, O. 2007. *El modelo económico de la concertación 1990–2005: ¿Reformas o cambio?* Santiago: FLACSO.

Navia, P. 2000. "A Shrinking Electorate in Post-Pinochet Chile." Paper presented at the meeting of the Latin American Studies Association, Miami, FL.

———. 2005. "Transforming Votes into Seats: Electoral Laws in Chile, 1833–2004." *Politica y Gobierno* 12(2): 233–276.

———. 2007a. "Las culpas de Juan Carvajal." *Revista Capital,* August 10.

———. 2007b. "¿Qué le pasó a Bachelet?" *Nueva Sociedad* 212.

———. 2008. "Legislative Candidate Selection in Chile." In P. M. Siavelis and S. Morgenstern (eds.), *Pathways to Power: Political Recruitment and Candidate Selection in Latin America.* University Park: Pennsylvania State University Press.

Neilson, C., D. Contreras, R. Cooper, and J. Hermann. 2008. "The Dynamics of Poverty in Chile." *Journal of Latin American Studies* 40: 251–273.

Nordhaus, W. D. 2007. "The Stern Review on the Economics of Climate Change." *Journal of Economic Literature* 45: 686–702.

O'Donnell, G. 1994. "Delegative Democracy." *Journal of Democracy* 5(1): 55–69.

OECD. 1999. "Structural Aspects of the East Asian Crisis." Paris: OECD Publishing.

———. 2004. "Revisión de políticas nacionales de educación: Chile." Paris: OECD Publishing.

———. 2008. "Growing Unequal? Income Distribution and Poverty in OECD Countries." Paris: OECD Publishing.

———. 2011a. "Education at a Glance 2010: OECD Indicators." Paris: OECD Publishing.

———. 2011b. "Society at a Glance: OECD Social Indicators." Paris: OECD Publishing.

———. 2011c. OECD online database. www.oecd.org.

———. 2011d. "Pensions at a Glance: Retirement-Income Systems in OECD and G20 Countries." Paris: OECD Publishing.

Ostry, J., A. Ghosh, K. Habermeier, M. Chamon, M. S. Qureshi, and D.B.S. Reinhardt. 2010. "Capital Inflows: The Role of Controls." IMF Staff Position Note SPN/10/04.

Otano, R. 1995. *Crónica de la transición.* Santiago: Planeta.

Ottone, E. 1999. "La equidad en América Latina en el marco de la globalización: La apuesta educativa." Santiago: Cepal (Comision Economica para America Latina y el Caribe).

Pereira, A.W., and J. Zaverucha. 2005. "The Neglected Stepchild: Military Justice and Democratic Transition in Chile." *Social Forces* 32(2): 115.

Piñera, J. 2000. "Russia Does Not Need a Pinochet, but It Does Need the Chilean Economic Model." *Foreign Affairs* 79(5): 62–73.

Pinto, J., and T. Moulián. 2005. *Cuando hicimos historia: La experiencia de la Unidad Popular*. Santiago: LOM Ediciones.

Pion-Berlin, D. 2004. "The Pinochet Case and Human Rights Progress in Chile: Was Europe a Catalyst, Cause or Consequence?" *Journal of Latin American Studies* 36: 479–505.

Politzer, P. 1999. *El libro de Lagos*. Santiago: Ediciones B Grupo Zeta.

Pollack, M. 1999. *The New Right in Chile 1973–1997*. New York: St. Martin's Press.

Presidencia de la República, Presidential Speeches. 2000–2005. Santiago: Gobeirno de Chile, http://www.gob.cl/categoria/discursos/.

Pribble, J. 2013. *Political Parties and Welfare Politics in Latin America: Between Elites and the Masses*. Cambridge: Cambridge University Press.

Prieto, F., S. Sáez, and A. G. Goswami. 2011. "The Elusive Road to Service Export Diversification: The Case of Chile." In A. Grover Goswami, A. Mattoo, and S.Saez (eds.), *Exporting Services: A Developing Country Perspective*. Washington, DC: World Bank Publications.

Provoste, P. 1996. *Justicia y derechos en las relaciones familiares*. Santiago: Servicio Nacional de la Mujer.

Raczynski, D. 1998. "The Crisis of Old Models of Social Protection in Latin America: New Alternatives for Dealing with Poverty." In V. E. Tokman and G. O'Donnell (eds.), *Poverty and Inequality in Latin America. Issues and New Challenges*. Notre Dame, IN: Univ. Notre Dame Press.

_____. 2008. *Sistema Chile Solidario y la política de protección social de Chile: Lecciones del pasado y agenda para el futuro*. Santiago: CIEPLAN.

Rehren, A. 1992. *Organizing the Presidency for the Consolidation of Democracy in the Southern Cone*. Paper presented at the Meeting of the Latin American Studies Association, Los Angeles, CA.

Renovación Nacional. 2008. "Parlamentarios piden terminar con el cuoteo en el MINSAL," Renovación Nacional, November 3, 2008, http://rn.cl/2008/11/03/parlamentarios-piden-terminar-con-el-cuoteo-en-el-minsal/ .

Requena, M. (ed.). 1990. *El aborto inducido en Chile*. Santiago: Edición Sociedad Chilena de Salud Pública.

Riesco, M. 2008. *Acerca de rentas mineras y desarrollo social en chile*. Santiago: CENDA.

Riquelme Segovia, A. 1999. "La transition démocratique au Chili et la fin de la guerre froide." *Matériaux pour l'histoire de notre temps* 54(1): 22–25.

Riquelme Segovia, Alfredo. 1999. "¿Quiénes y por qué 'no están ni ahí? Marginación y/o automarginación en la democracia transicional. Chile, 1998–1997." In Paul Drake and Iván Jaksic (eds.), *El Modelo Chileno: democracia y desarrollo en los noventa*. Santiago: LOM.

Robles, C. 2011. *El sistema de protección social en Chile; una mirada desde la igualdad*. Santiago: CEPAL.

Rodrigo, P., and E. Silva. 2010. "Contesting Private Property Rights: The Environment and Indigenous Peoples." In Silvia Borzutzky and Gregory Weeks (eds.),

The Bachelet Government: Conflict and Consensus in Post-Pinochet Chile. Gainesville: University Press of Florida.

Rodriguez, J., C. Tokman, and A. Vega. 2007. *Structural Balance Policy in Chile.* Santiago: Government of Chile, Ministry of Finance, Public Finance Studies.

Roht-Arrizaz, N. 2005. *The Pinochet Effect: Transitional Justice in the Age of Human Rights.* Philadelphia: University of Pennsylvania Press.

Rohter, L. 2006. "Chileans Promised a New Deal: Now Striking Youth Demand It." *New York Times.* June 5, http://www.nytimes.com/2006/06/05/world/americas/05chile.html?_r=0.

Ruiz-Dana, A. 2007. *Commodity Revenue Management: The Case of Chile's Copper Boom.* Winnipeg: International Institute of Sustainable Development. www.iisd.org/pdf/2007/trade_price_case_copper.pdf.

Ruiz Rodríguez, L. M. 2006. "El sistema de partidos chileno: ¿Hacia una desestructuración ideológica?" In M. Alcántara and L. M. Ruiz Rodríguez (eds.), *Chile: Política y modernización democrática.* Barcelona: Ediciones Bellaterra.

Ruiz-Tagle, J. 1999. *Chile: 40 años de desigualdad de ingreso.* Working Paper, Department of Economics, University of Chile, Santiago.

Ruiz-Tagle, J., and K. Sehnbruch. 2010. *Elaboración de un indicador de la calidad del empleo.* Unpublished report. Santiago: UNDP.

Saez, S. 2005. *Implementing Trade Policy in Latin America: The Cases of Chile and Mexico.* International Commerce Series no. 54, ECLAC, Santiago.

Salazar, G. 2009. *Del poder constituyente de asalariados e intelectuales.* Santiago: LOM Ediciones.

Salazar, G., and C. Altamirano. 2010. *Conversaciones con Carlos Altamirano: memorias críticas.* Santiago: Debate.

Sanhueza, C., and R. Mayer. 2009. *Top Incomes in Chile 1957–2007: Evolution and Mobility.* Documentos de Trabajo 06, Universidad Diego Portales, Santiago.

Santibáñez, C. 2005. "The Informational Basis of Poverty Measurement: Using the Capability Approach to Improve the CAS Proxy Tool." *European Journal of Development Research* 17: 89–110.

Santiso, J. 2008. *Sovereign Development Funds: Key Financial Actors in the Shifting Wealth of Nations.* OECD Emerging Markets Network Working Paper. Paris: OECD.

Schiff, M. 2002. "Chile's Trade and Regional Integration Policy: An Assessment." *World Economy* 25(7): 973–990.

Schwindt-Bayer, L. 2006. "Still Supermadres? Gender and Policy Priorities of Latin American Legislators." *American Journal of Political Science* 50(3): 570–585.

Scully, T. R. 1992. *Rethinking the Center: Party Politics in Nineteenth and Twentieth Century Chile.* Stanford: Stanford University Press.

———. 1996. "Chile: The Political Underpinnings of Economic Liberalization." In J. Dominguez and A. Lowenthal (eds.), *Constructing Democratic Governance: South America in the 1990.* Baltimore: Johns Hopkins University Press.

Scully, T. R., and Valenzuela, S. 1997. "Electoral Choices and the Party System in Chile: Continuities and Changes at the Recovery of Democracy." *Comparative Politics* 29(4): 511–527.

Sehnbruch, K. 2004. "From the Quantity to the Quality of Employment: An Application of the Capability Approach to the Chilean Labour Market." CLAS Working Papers, UC Berkeley.

———. 2006. *The Chilean Labor Market: A Key to Understanding Latin American Labor Markets.* Basingstoke: Palgrave Macmillan.

———. 2007. "The Chilean Presidential Elections of 2006: More Continuity than Change." Working Paper no. 12, Center for Latin American Studies, University of California at Berkeley.

———. 2009. "A Record Number of Conflicts? Michelle Bachelet's Inheritance of Unresolved Employment Issues." Working Paper no. 27, Center for Latin American Studies, University of California at Berkeley.

———.2010. "Unresolved Conflict Within the Consensus: Bachelet's Inheritance of Labor and Employment Issues." In S. Borzutzky and G. Weeks (eds.), *The Bachelet Government*. Gainesville: University Press of Florida.

———. 2011. "Unable to Shape the Political Arena: The Impact of Poor Quality Employment on Unions in Post-transition Chile." DEV-OUT Working Paper Series no. 4, Santiago.

Servicios de Impuestos Internos (SII). 2006. "Informe de gasto tributario 2006: Presupuesto de gastos tributarios." www.sii.cl/aprenda_sobre_impuestos /estudios/gasto_tributario.htm.

Shugart, M. S., and J. Carey. 1992. *Presidents and Assemblies: Constitutional Design and Electoral Dynamics*. Cambridge: Cambridge University Press.

Siavelis, P. 1997. "Continuity and Change in the Chilean Party System: On the Transformational Effects of Electoral Reform." *Comparative Political Studies* 30(6): 651–674.

———. 2000. *The President and Congress in Post-Authoritarian Chile: Institutional Constraints to Democratic Consolidation*. University Park: Pennsylvania State University Press.

———. 2002a. "Exaggerated Presidentialism and Moderate Presidents: Executive-Legislative Relations in Chile." In S. Morgenstern and B. Nacif (eds.), *Legislative Politics in Latin America*. Cambridge: Cambridge University Press.

———. 2002b. "Coalitions, Voters and Party System Transformation in Post-Authoritarian Chile." *Government and Opposition* 37(1): 76–105.

———. 2002c. "The Hidden Logic of Candidate Selection for Chilean Parliamentary Elections." *Comparative Politics* 34(4): 419–438.

———. 2006. "Accommodating Informal Institutions and Democracy in Chile." In G. Helmke and S. Levitsky (eds.), *Informal Institutions and Democracy: Lessons from Latin America,* 33–55. Baltimore: Johns Hopkins University Press.

———. 2009. "Enclaves de la transición y democracia chilena." *Revista de Ciencia Política* 29(1): 3–21.

———. Forthcoming. "El poder ejecutivo y la Presidencia en Chile: Organización formal e informal." In J. Lanzaro (ed.), *El presidencialismo latinoamericano y el parlamentarismo europeo "cara a cara."* Madrid: Centro de Estudios Constitucionales de España.

Sieder, R., L. Schjolden, and A. Angell (eds.). 2005. *The Judicialization of Politics in Latin America*. London: Palgrave Macmillan.

Sierra, L., and L. Mac-Clure. 2012. *Frente a la mayoria: Leyes dupermayoritarias y Tribunal Constitucional en Chile*. Santiago: UNDP.

Silva, E. 1992. "Capitalist Regime Loyalties and Redemocratization in Chile." *Journal of Interamerican Studies and World Affairs* 34(4): 77–117.

Solimano, A., and A. Torche. 2008. *La distribución del ingreso en Chile 1987–2006: Análisis y consideraciones de Política*. Working Paper no. 480, Central Bank of Chile, Santiago.

Soto Gamboa, A. M. 2001. *La irrupción de la UDI en las poblaciones,1983–1987*. Meeting of the Latin American Studies Association,Washington, DC.

Staab, S., and R. Gerhard. 2010. "Childcare Service Expansion in Chile and Mexico: For Women or Children or Both?" Gender and Development Program Paper no. 10, UNResearch Institute for Social Development, Geneva.

Stevenson, J. R. 1970. *The Chilean Popular Front.* Michigan: Greenwood Press.

Tapia, H. 2003. *Balance estructural del gobierno central de Chile: Análisis y propuestas.* CEPAL, Serie Macroeconomía del Desarrollo, no. 25, Santiago.

TIMMS. 2000. "International Mathematics Report." International Association for the Evaluation of Educational Achievement, Boston.

Tironi, E., and F. Agüero. 1999. "¿Sobrevivirá el nuevo paisaje político chileno?" *Estudios Públicos* 74: 151–168.

Torcal, M., and S. Mainwaring. 2003. "The Political Recrafting of Social Bases of Party Competition: Chile, 1973–95." *British Journal of Political Science* 33: 55–84.

Ugarte, J. L. 2008. Inspección del trabajo en Chile: Vicisitudes y desafíos. *Revista Latinoamericana de Derecho Social* 6: 187–204.

UNDP. 1999, 2000. Human Development Reports. Santiago: United Nations Publications.

UNDP. 2010. Human Development Report 2010: *The Real Wealth of Nations, Pathways to Human Development.* New York: United Nations Publications.

Valdés, R. 1997. *Transmisión de la política monetaria en Chile.* Working Paper no. 16, Central Bank of Chile, Santiago.

Valdés, T. 2010. "El Chile de Michelle Bachelet: ¿Género en el poder?" *Latin American Research Review* 45: 248–273.

Valenzuela, A. 1994. "Party Politics and the Crisis of Presidentialism in Chile." In J. J. Linz and A. Valenzuela (eds.), *The Failure of Presidential Democracy,* vol. 2. Baltimore: John Hopkins University Press.

———. 1995. "The Military in Power: The Consolidation of One-Man Rule." In P. W. Drake and I. Jaksic (eds.), *The Struggle for Democracy in Chile.* Lincoln: University of Nebraska Press.

Valenzuela, S. 1995. "The Origins and Transformations of the Chilean Party System." Working Paper no. 215, Helen Kellogg Institute for International Studies at Notre Dame University, Notre Dame.

———. 1999. "Respuesta a Eugenio Tironi y Felipe Agüero. Reflexiones sobre el presente y futuro del paisaje político chileno a la luz de su pasado." *Estudios Públicos* 75: 273–290.

Valenzuela, S., and T. R. Scully. 1997. "Electoral Choices and the Party System in Chile: Continuities and Changes at the Recovery of Democracy." *Comparative Politics* 29 (4): 511–527.

Varas, A., C. Fuentes, and F. Agüero. 2008. *Instituciones cautivas: Opinión pública y fuerzas armadas en Chile.* Santiago: FLACSO-Chile y Catalonia Ediciones.

Vargas, V., and Poblete, S. 2008. "Health Prioritization: The Case of Chile." *Health Affairs* 27(3): 782–792.

Vega, H. 2007. *En vez de la injusticia: Un camino para el desarrollo de Chile en el siglo XXI.* Santiago: Debate.

Vegas, E., and I. Umansky, 2005. *Improving Teaching and Learning Through Effective Incentives: What Can We Learn from Education Reforms in Latin America?* Washington, DC: The World Bank.

Velasco, A. 2000. "Exchange-Rate Policies for Developing Countries: What Have We Learned? What Do We Still Not Know?" G-24 Discussion Paper Series, United Nations, New York.

Velasco, A., A. Arenas, J. Rodríguez, M. Jorratt, and C. Gamboni. 2010. *El enfoque de balance estructural en la política fiscal en Chile: resultados, metodología y aplicación al período 2006–2009*. Government of Chile, Ministry of Finance, Public Finance Studies, Santiago.

Veras Soares, R.,R. Perez Ribas, and R. Guerrero Os rio. 2010. "Evaluating the Impact of Brazil's Bolsa de Familia: Cash Transfer Programs in Comparative Perspective." *Latin American Research Review* 45(2): 179.

Vial, G. 2000. *Salvador Allende. El fracaso de una ilusión.* Santiago: Universidad Finis Terrae.

———. 2001. *Historia de Chile (1891–1973): De la República Socialista al Frente Popular (1931–1938)*, vol. 5. Santiago: Editorial Zig-Zag S.A.

Villela, L. 2011. "Gastos tributarios: Reduciendo abusos y mejorando la efectividad." Paper presented at the XXIII Seminario Internacional de Política Fiscal, División de Gestión Fiscal y Municipal, Santiago.

Walker, I. 1999. *El futuro de la democracia cristiana.* Santiago: Ediciones B.

———. 2003. "Chile: Three Stories of Informal Institutions in a Limited Democracy." Paper presented at the conference, Informal Institutions and Politics in Latin America, University of Notre Dame, Notre Dame.

Waylen, G. 2000. "Gender and Democratic Politics: A Comparative Analysis of Consolidation in Argentina and Chile." *Journal of Latin American Studies* 32: 765–793.

Weeks, G. 2000. "The Long Road to Civilian Supremacy over the Military: 1990–1998." *Studies in Comparative International Development* 35(2): 65–82.

———. 2003. *The Military and Politics in Postauthoritarian Chile.* Tuscaloosa: University of Alabama Press.

———. 2008. "A Preference for Deference: Reforming the Military's Intelligence Role in Argentina, Chile and Peru." *Third World Quarterly* 29(1): 45–61.

———. 2010. "The Transition Is Dead, Long Live the Transition: Civil-Military Relations and the Limits of Consensus." In S. Borzutzky and G. Weeks (eds.), *The Bachelet Government: Conflict and Consensus in Post-Pinochet Chile.* Gainesville: University Press of Florida.

Wehr, I. 2011. *Soziale Ungleichheiten in Lateinamerika: Neue Perspektiven auf Wirtschaft, Politik und Umwelt.* Nomos.

Weyland, K. 1997. "'Growth with Equity' in Chile's New Democracy?" *Latin American Research Review* 32(1): 37–67.

Wilde, A. 1999. "Irruptions of Memory: Expressive Politics in Chile's Transition to Democracy." *Journal of Latin American Studies* 31(2): 473–500.

Williamson, J. 2000. *Exchange Rate Regimes for Emerging Markets: Reviving the Intermediate Option.* Policy Analyses in International Economics 60. Washington, DC: Institute for International Economics.

Winn, Peter (ed.). 2004. *Victims of the Chilean Miracle: Workers and Neoliberalism in the Pinochet Era, 1973–2002.* Durham and London: Duke University Press.

World Bank. 2011a. "Composition of Total Wealth." www.worldbank.org.

———. 2011b. "World Development Indicators (WDI)." http://data.worldbank .org/data-catalog/world-development-indicators/wdi-2010.

World Economic Forum (WEF). 2011. "The Global Competitiveness Report 2011–2012." www.weforum.org.

World Values Surveys. First (1990), second (1995), third (2000), and fourth (2005) waves .www.worldvaluessurvey.org/wvs/articles/folder_published/article_base _11.

Zahler, R. 1998. "El Banco Central y la política macroeconómica de Chile en los años noventa." *Revista de la CEPAL* 64: 47–72.

The Contributors

Alan Angell joined the Latin American Centre at Oxford University in 1966 when he was appointed to a senior research fellowship jointly with the Institute of International Affairs in London. In 2008 he was made a Gran Oficial of the Order of Bernardo O'Higgins by the government of Chile. His first book on Chile was *Politics and the Labour Movement in Chile* (1972). He is the author of many articles and books on Chile, including *Democracy After Pinochet: Politics, Parties and Elections in Chile* (2007), and coeditor of *The Judicialization of Politics in Latin America* (2009).

Merike Blofield is associate professor in the Department of Political Science at the University of Miami. She is author of *Care Work and Class: Domestic Workers' Struggle for Equal Rights in Latin America* (2012) and *The Politics of Moral Sin: Abortion and Divorce in Spain, Chile and Argentina* (2006). She is also editor of *The Great Gap: Inequality and the Politics of Redistribution* (2011). Her articles have appeared in *Comparative Politics, Latin American Research Review,* and *Latin American Politics and Society.* She directed the Observatory on Inequality in Latin America (2007–2009), financed by the Ford Foundation.

Silvia Borzutzky is teaching professor of political science and international relations at Carnegie Mellon University. She is the author of more than forty articles on Chilean politics, social security, social assistance, and health policies, as well as Latin American politics and international relations, and is also the author of *Vital Connections: Politics, Social Security and Inequality in Chile* (2002) and coeditor of *After Pinochet: The Chilean Road to Capitalism and*

355

Democracy (2006). She also coedited *The Bachelet Government: Conflict and Consensus in Post-Pinochet Chile* (2010) with Gregory Weeks.

Cath Collins runs a database and bulletin project at the Universidad Diego Portales (UDP), Santiago, Chile, mapping human rights trials and related truth and memory initiatives in the Southern Cone of Latin America. She was recently (March 2013) appointed professor of transitional justice at the University of Ulster in the north of Ireland. Her relevant publications include, since 2010, the "Verdad, Justicia y Memorialización" chapter of UDP's Informe Anual sobre Derechos Humanos en Chile and the book *Post-Transitional Justice: Human Rights Trials in Chile and El Salvador* (2010). She is coeditor of the forthcoming volume *The Politics of Memory in Chile from Pinochet to Bachelet* (2013).

Dante Contreras is professor and director of the Department of Economics at the University of Chile. Between 2008 and 2010 he was one of the executive directors of the World Bank. He has also worked as a consultant for the UNDP and the Inter-American Development Bank. His research focuses on the determinants of poverty and inequality, the economics of education, and the impact evaluation of public policies.

Gregory Elacqua is the director of the Public Policy Institute at the School of Economics at the Universidad Diego Portales in Chile, as well as a member of the PISA-OECD Questionnaire Background Expert Group. He was an adviser to the minister of education in Chile between 2003 and 2006, and has also served as an adviser to a member of the Education Committee in the Chilean Senate. He was actively involved in the design of the education reforms signed into law in recent years and has consulted with the World Bank, the Inter-American Development Bank, UNESCO, and different national governments on education policy. He holds a PhD in Politics and Public Policy from Princeton University.

Claudio A. Fuentes is professor of political science and the director of the Social Science Research Institute (ICSO) at Universidad Diego Portales in Santiago, Chile. His dissertation received the American Political Science Association Award for Best Dissertation (Human Rights Section). In 2011 he held the Andronico Luksic Fellowship as Visiting Scholar at the David Rockefeller Center for Latin American Studies at Harvard University. He is the author of five books, five edited volumes, and more than thirty journal articles on issues concerning democratization, security, and international relations. His most recent book is *El Pacto* (2012).

Ricardo Godoy graduated as a political scientist from Universidad Diego Portales (UDP) and is currently pursuing a master's degree in public opinion at UDP. Since 2010, he has been an adviser to presidential candidate Marco Enriquez-Ominami. He is currently a vice president of the Progressive Party in Chile. He is also the executive director of the Desarrollo Igualitario Foundation.

Pablo González Soto is coordinator of the National Human Development Report for Chile at the UNDP (Santiago) and an adjunct professor in the Department of Industrial Engineering at the University of Chile. He served as the head of the Division of Planning and Budget at the Ministry of Education (1994–1999) and as an adviser to the minister of education. He has published extensively on development and social policies with a particular emphasis on education. His recent publications include various academic articles related to education, such as "Expanding the Possibilities of Deliberation: The Use of Data Mining for Strengthening Democracy with an Application to Education Reform," *Information Society* 26, no. 1 (2010): 1–16 (with Juan Velásquez).

Liesl Haas is professor of political science at California State University, Long Beach. She received her PhD from the University of North Carolina, Chapel Hill, in 2000. Her research interests focus on gender and politics, religion and politics, and nationalism. She has a forthcoming book, *Feminist Policymaking in Chile*, and is currently working on two projects, one that explores the impact of gender quotas on public policy in Costa Rica, and another exploring American national identity in comparative perspective.

Óscar Landerretche Moreno is the director of the School of Economics and Business of the University of Chile. He received his PhD in Economics from the Massachusetts Institute of Technology and has since focused his research on macroeconomics, labor, and political economy. He has served extensively as adviser and consultant to the Ministry of Finance, the Central Bank of Chile, and Wall Street. He was the executive secretary of the Commission on Equity and Employment (2007–2008) and served as chief economist of the presidential campaign of Eduardo Frei in 2010, and as programmatic coordinator of the Bachelet 2006 primary campaign. He is the author of numerous articles and forthcoming books on Chile's development history.

Ramón López is professor in the Department of Economics at Universidad de Chile and professor of economics in the Department of Agricultural and Resource Economics at the University of Maryland, College Park. He has been an invited scholar at several academic institutions including the University of Bonn (Germany) and the University of Gothenberg (Sweden), and has worked as an international consultant with the World Bank, Inter-American Development Bank, and FAO, among others, as well as for individual governments. He is also chair of the Publication Review Board at the International Food Policy Research Institute in Washington, DC, and cochair of the Environmental Task Force at the Initiative for Policy Dialogue, Columbia University. Professor López is the author of several books and of a large number of journal articles on economic development, poverty, and the environment. In 2002 he was awarded the prestigious Alexander Von Humboldt Prize.

Patricio Navia is adjunct assistant professor at the Center for Latin American and Caribbean Studies at New York University. He is also a researcher and associate professor at the Universidad Diego Portales in Chile. He has published many scholarly articles and book chapters on democratization, electoral rules, and democratic institutions in Latin America. As founding director of the Observatorio Electoral at the Universidad Diego Portales, he edited *El Genoma Electoral Chileno: Dibujando el Mapa Genético de las Preferencias Políticas en Chile* (with Mauricio Morales and Renato Briceño, 2009). He is also the author of several books on Chile and on Chilean politics, including *Las Grandes Alamedas: El Chile post Pinochet* (2004).

Claudia Sanhueza Riveros is associate professor of economics at ILADES/ Universidad Alberto Hurtado and professorial lecturer in economics at Georgetown University. Her research has focused on issues of labor economics, social policy, economics of education, and economics of the family. She has published several articles and book chapters on these subjects and edited a book on the Chilean labor market. She was also part of the Presidential Commission for Equity and Employment in Chile in 2007–2008.

Kirsten Sehnbruch is professor of public policy and director of the Center for New Development Thinking at the Department of Economics at the University of Chile in Santiago. She is also the executive director of the Center for Social Conflict and Cohesion there. Prior to this, she was lecturer and senior scholar at the University of California at Berkeley. Her research focuses on Latin American labor markets and social policy, development policy, and Chilean politics. She is author of *The Chilean Labor Market: A Key to Understanding Latin American Labor Markets* (2006) as well as numerous academic articles and papers. She holds a PhD in social and political sciences from Cambridge University.

Peter M. Siavelis is professor of political science at Wake Forest University and director of the Latin American and Latino Studies Program. He received his PhD from Georgetown University and has been a visiting professor at the

Catholic University of Chile and the Universitat Pompeu Fabra in Barcelona, Spain, and a visiting researcher at the University of Salamanca, Spain. He has published on Latin American electoral and legislative politics in numerous journal articles and book chapters. He is the author of *The President and Congress in Postauthoritarian Chile: Institutional Constraints to Democratic Consolidation* (2000). He is also the coeditor of *Getting Immigration Right: What Every American Needs to Know* (2009) with David Coates, and *Pathways to Power: Political Recruitment and Candidate Selection in Latin America* (2008) with Scott Morgenstern.

Gregory Weeks is professor and chair of the Department of Political Science and Public Administration at the University of North Carolina at Charlotte. His research focuses on Chilean politics, US–Latin American relations, and immigration. His books include *The Military and Politics in Postauthoritarian Chile* (2003), *US and Latin American Relations* (2008), *The Bachelet Government: Conflict and Consensus in Post-Pinochet Chile* (coedited with Silvia Borzutzky, 2010), and *Irresistible Forces: Latin American Migration to the United States and Its Effects on the South* (with John R. Weeks, 2010).

Index

361

About the Book

How was Chile transformed both politically and economically during the two decades of Center-Left coalition (Concertación) government that followed the country's return to democracy in 1990? How did the coalition manage to hold on to power for so long—but not longer? And were its policies in fact substantially different from those that preceded them? The authors of this landmark volume address these questions and critically assess the successes and failures of Concertación politics and policies in post-Pinochet Chile.

Kirsten Sehnbruch is director of the Center for New Development Thinking at the Department of Economics, University of Chile. She is author of *The Chilean Labor Market: A Key to Understanding Latin American Labor Markets*. **Peter M. Siavelis** is professor of political science and director of the Latin American and Latino Studies Program at Wake Forest University. His publications include *The President and Congress in Postauthoritarian Chile* and *Pathways to Power: Political Recruitment and Candidate Selection in Latin America* (with Scott Morgenstern).